Springer Series in Synergetics

Editor: Hermann Haken

Synergetics, an interdisciplinary field of research, is concerned with the cooperation of individual parts of a system that produces macroscopic spatial, temporal or functional structures. It deals with deterministic as well as stochastic processes.

Volumes 1–39 are listed on the back inside cover

Guy Jumarie

Relative Information

Theories and Applications

With Forewords by G. J. Klir and H. Haken

Springer-Verlag Berlin Heidelberg New York
London Paris Tokyo Hong Kong

Professor Guy Jumarie

Department of Mathematics and Computer Science,
University of Québec at Montréal, P.O. Box 8888, St.A,
Montréal (Québec), Canada, H3C 3P8

Series Editor:

Prof. Dr. Dr. h.c. Hermann Haken

Institut für Theoretische Physik und Synergetik der Universität Stuttgart,
Pfaffenwaldring 57/IV, D-7000 Stuttgart 80, Fed. Rep. of Germany and
Center for Complex Systems, Florida Atlantic University,
Boca Raton, FL 33431, USA

ISBN 3-540-51905-X Springer-Verlag Berlin Heidelberg New York
ISBN 0-387-51905-X Springer-Verlag New York Berlin Heidelberg

Library of Congress Cataloging-in-Publication Data. Jumarie, Guy. Relative information: theories and applications / Guy Jumarie. p. cm. – (Springer series in synergetics; v. 47) Includes bibliographical references. ISBN 0-387-51905-X (U.S.) 1. Information theory. I. Title. II. Series. Q360.J84 1990 003'.54 – dc20 89-26347

Typesetting: ASCO Trade Typesetting Limited, Hong Kong
2154/3150(3011)-543210 – Printed on acid-free paper

So all my best is dressing old words new,
Spending again what is already spent.

Shakespeare, Sonnet LXXVI

As far as the laws of mathematics refer to reality,
they are not certain, and as far as they are certain,
they do not refer to reality.

Einstein

Foreword

For four decades, information theory has been viewed almost exclusively as a theory based upon the Shannon measure of uncertainty and information, usually referred to as Shannon entropy. Since the publication of Shannon's seminal paper in 1948, the theory has grown extremely rapidly and has been applied with varied success in almost all areas of human endeavor.

At this time, the Shannon information theory is a well established and developed body of knowledge. Among its most significant recent contributions have been the use of the complementary principles of minimum and maximum entropy in dealing with a variety of fundamental systems problems such as predictive systems modelling, pattern recognition, image reconstruction, and the like.

Since its inception in 1948, the Shannon theory has been viewed as a restricted information theory. It has often been argued that the theory is capable of dealing only with syntactic aspects of information, but not with its semantic and pragmatic aspects. This restriction was considered a virtue by some experts and a vice by others. More recently, however, various arguments have been made that the theory can be appropriately modified to account for semantic aspects of information as well. Some of the most convincing arguments in this regard are included in Fred Dretske's *Knowledge & Flow of Information* (The M.I.T. Press, Cambridge, Mass., 1981) and in this book by Guy Jumarie.

This book is a comprehensive presentation of Jumarie's approach to information theory, which he developed during the last decade or so. His principal goal is to develop an information theory that incorporates not only syntactic aspects of information but also its semantic aspects. Contrary to other authors, however, he attempts to achieve this goal by an appropriate modification of the Shannon theory. Jumarie's approach is characterized by introducing observer's viewpoints into the formulation of the theory. He proposes in the book two ways of accomplishing this, one based upon a model of observation with informational invariance (Chap. 4) and one based on a slight modification of the concept of transinformation in the Shannon theory (Chap. 5).

One of the most significant contributions of this book is a careful comparison of discrete and continuous entropies (Chap. 6), which one cannot find in such detail anywhere in the literature. Jumarie argues that the continuous entropy (often called the Boltzmann entropy) is more fundamental than the discrete (or Shannon) entropy. Although this issue will probably remain controversial for some time, his arguments are well developed and convincing.

In the rest of the book, Jumarie develops a unified formalism for information theory that covers both syntax and semantics and integrates both discrete and continuous entropies (Chap. 7), and shows how this formalism can be applied for characterizing the entropy of form and pattern in a way which is quite different from the Kolmogorov entropy (Chap. 8), and for generalizing the classical statistical decision theory (Chap. 9).

In spite of the fact that some topics in the book may be viewed as controversial, the book consists of highly original and thought provoking material and, consequently, it should be of interest to anyone interested in the concept of information.

Jumarie restricts his formulation primarily to information conceptualized in terms of probability theory, even though there are some hints in the book about other possible mathematical frameworks, such as possibility theory or fuzzy set theory. The significance of these new frameworks (in particular fuzzy set theory and the Dempster-Shafer theory of evidence) is that they allow us to distinguish several different types of uncertainty and the associated information. This implies that information must be viewed as a multidimensional entity, as discussed in detail in *Fuzzy Sets, Uncertainty, and Information* (Prentice-Hall, Englewood Cliffs, N.J., 1988), which I coauthored with Tina Folger.

The conception of information as a multidimensional entity opens many new avenues. At this time, however, it captures only syntactic aspects of information. In order to develop a genuine multidimensional information theory, semantic aspects will have to be incorporated in some manner. Jumarie shows us in this book how this can be accomplished for the classical, one-dimensional information theory based upon the Shannon entropy. His key ideas will undoubtedly be important as guiding principles for accomplishing the same within the larger framework of multidimensional information theory. This, perhaps, is the most significant contribution of Jumarie's work.

George J. Klir

Foreword

In modern science we witness an enormous production of new theories and experimental results. In such a situation, unifying ideas become more and more important. One of these ideas is the concept of information that was originally introduced by Shannon to deal with the capacity of communication channels. Because of its close connection with entropy, it soon became an important tool for the discussion of problems of statistical mechanics. More recently, in my book "Information and Self-Organization", I showed that the concept of information plays a fundamental role in the spontaneous formation of spatial, temporal, or functional structures.

The present book by Prof. Guy Jumarie, who has made important contributions to the field of information, will provide the reader with an in-depth presentation of this field. Professor Jumarie carefully develops the theory of information and its various manifestations, taking into account both discrete and continuous random variables. His book shows in an impressive way how the various concepts can be mathematized, interpreted, and related to one another. He also makes important contributions to the problem of subjectivity. In addition, he makes novel proposals on how to define entropy of trajectories, of deterministic functions, and of forms. These chapters lead us to the forefront of research in a field where quite surprising results can surely still be expected.

I am certain that this book will be most useful, both to university faculty members and to students, and not only in the field of classical information theory; all those interested in the phenomena of self-organization and in the mathematics dealing with complex systems, should benefit from this stimulating treatment.

H. Haken

Preface

My first paper (in English) on relative information appeared in 1975, and since this date, I have endeavoured to promote and to develop this idea. The present work follows my 1986 essay, *Subjectivity, Information, Systems: Introduction to a Theory of Relativistic Cybernetics* which itself had followed and largely replaced my 1980 essay in French, *Subjectivité, Information, Systems. Synthèse pour une cybernétique relativiste*. The French publication was on the verge of being philiosphy of science; its English counterpart, however, was technical for the most part but directed towards problems related to cybernetics and general systems; and the present book is frankly technical in the sense of engineering and physics.

My central concern along this trajectory has been always the same: it should be possible to derive a theory of information which explicity takes account of the viewpoint of the observer, and which, furthermore, is consistent with the mathematical theory of communication as initiated by Shannon. In the maze of the possible solutions, I continually came across paths which led me to the same answer: a local model of relative information is quite suitably defined by the so-called Lorentz-Poincaré equations of relativistic physics.

At that time, my unorthodox ideas puzzled and sometimes shocked many scientists, but as time elapsed, it appeared that many new results, derived in more classical ways, were bringing indirect support to this approach. For instance, several generalized informational entropies which have been obtained recently by mathematicians can be thought of as merely special cases of my concept of relative entropy.

As a matter of fact, the thesis which we shall advocate here is that the theory of Shannon contains the key to derive its generalization in the form of the Lorentz-Poincaré equation.

To many mathematicians, information theory is mainly a motivation for mathematical exercises in the form of axioms, solution, uniqueness of solution. It is not so here. Indeed, we would like to address as large a readership as possible and consequently the mathematical prerequisites for understanding the book are small: calculus, elementary probability, the basic elements of the Shannon information theory ... and much critical reflection. In order to facilitate easy reading, each chapter is almost self-contained and could be read separately much like a technical paper. Indeed, it is the relative independence of the various topics that enabled the book to be written in this way.

It is a very great pleasure for me to thank Professor H. Haken who accepted the present monograph in the *Springer Series in Synergetics* and invited me to the Institute of Theoretical Physics at Stuttgart.

Professor G. J. Klir was kind enough to read the manuscript and to make some comments in the form of a foreword, and I am pleased to thank him.

I have had a large number of discussions with Professor G. Battail of the "Ecole Nationale Supérieure des Télécommunications, Paris" and I acknowledge with thanks this indirect contribution.

Other invaluable help since my arrival in Canada in 1971, was provided by the National Research Council of this country which regularly made research grants to me. Many thanks to this institution.

I express my gratitude to Dr. Angela Lahee for her patience in understanding and rectifying my latin English (indeed we are natives of Guadeloupe in the West Indies, and thus French speaking and thinking!).

And last but not least, many thanks to a fine person (Nadia) who has had to suffer from a very strange husband obsessed by the relativity of truth.

G. Jumarie

Contents

1. Relative Information – What For?

This introductory chapter gives a brief description of the main ideas that motivated this book.

1.1 Information Theory, What Is It?

1.1.1 Summary of the Story

In order that a new invention be successful, it is very important that it arrives at a good place at a good time (and with the right price!); this is also true of scientific discoveries.

Indeed, it is generally agreed that *Nyquist* [1.1, 2] was the first author who took an interest in measures of information, and who stated elements for the foundations of a possible theory; but at that time (the 1920s) his papers remained largely unnoticed. He derived the relation between the bandwidth of a channel and the emission speed of the signals; he introduced the notions of speed limit of data processing on the one hand, and of interferences between successive symbols on the other hand, concepts which now are of importance in numerical transmission. Of course these studies deal with communication rather than with information, but at that time there was no important difference recognized between these two topics.

Hartley [1.3] is considered to be the father of information theory. He pointed out that a quantitative measure of information is based upon the number m of distinguishable states of the system α under observation. He derived an expression of this measure in the form

$$H(\alpha) = \ln m \qquad (1.1.1)$$

and by means of a simple example, he obtained the maximum transmission rate of a channel.

In 1948, in his two celebrated papers, *Shannon* [1.4, 5] introduced the concepts of informational source and of communication channel. He took account of the random nature of the phenomenon, and he defined the amount of (potential) information of a discrete random variable X with the probability distribution $\{p(x_i)\}$ by the expression

$$H(X) := -\sum_i p(x_i) \ln p(x_i) , \qquad (1.1.2)$$

and of a continuous random variable with the probability density $p(x)$, by

$$H(X) := -\int_{\mathbb{R}} p(x) \ln p(x) \, dx , \qquad (1.1.3)$$

expressions which are referred to as the entropy of the random variable.

All the many investigations which have been published subsequently are merely a straightforward development of the first results of Hartley and Shannon. We may divide these studies into two main classes: Those of mathematicians who look for the mathematical foundations of the theory and the generalizations of entropy by using a prior set of properties and functional analysis; and more recently, those of physicists and of system engineers who try to modify the theory in order to deal with problems that are not necessarily relevant to communication. In the former approach, one is not interested in the physical significance or practical use of the concept of information; in the latter, one aims to enlarge the efficiency of the theory, as did *Brillouin* [1.6] for instance, who guessed its broad potential application in physics and in the natural sciences in general.

1.1.2 Communication and Information

Many people confuse the "theory of communication" with the "theory of information." The title of Shannon's pioneering paper is "A Mathematical Theory of Communication", and, in effect, it deals exclusively with the consequences of disturbing random noises in data transmission. The main purpose of the communication theory is the manipulation of the signals themselves, irrespective of any meaning they may or may not have.

In contrast, information theory refers to the content and the structure of the message. Assuming that, at the end of a channel, I have a receiver with a sequence of symbols at hand, I shall first use communication theory to recover the exact symbols which have been emitted, and then, by using information theory I shall try to seize the exact content of the message so obtained. In other words, while the theory of communication deals with symbols only, a theory of information should deal with both symbols and their meanings.

In fact, Shannon himself pointed out that his theory does not claim to deal with semantics: the viewpoint is that of the engineer to whom a symbol is a symbol and nothing more (i.e., any meaning it may have is irrelevant), and the task is then to properly transmit it and to recover it.

Scientists generally refer to Shannon theory as "information theory" and this is mainly due to the fact that Shannon introduced a concept of transmission, or transinformation or mutual information $I(X, Y)$ in the form

$$I(X, Y) := H(Y) - H(Y/X) \tag{1.1.4}$$

where $H(Y/X)$ is the so-called conditional entropy of Y given X, and where $I(X, Y)$ measures the amount of information (in the Shannon sense!) that X contains about Y. But this transinformation does not involve the coupling effects which necessarily exist between symbols and meanings, and in this way it could be considered either as a model which deals with syntax only or as a model in which syntax is identical with semantics.

It remains to explicitly introduce the interactions between symbols and meanings in this Shannonian framework.

1.2 Information and Natural Language

1.2.1 Syntax, Semantics, Lexeme

If we consider the terms in the popular sense, we can take for granted that any amount of information may be conveyed by a natural language in the broad sense of this term, which may mean English, Chinese, a picture, or a score of music, for instance. Thus one can expect that a theory of information should apply to natural languages, or at least to some parameters of natural languages.

In as general a theory of information as possible, the corresponding model of natural language should be itself general enough to apply to a broad class of special cases, and, with this prerequisite in mind, we can adopt the following scheme.

Basically, a natural language is defined by a set Ω of symbols (for example letters or words) referred to as a *syntactic space*, and a set Ω' of meanings which is the *semantic space*. Let us write α to denote the generic term for the symbols and a to denote the generic term of the meanings. An observer R who is receiving a message $(\alpha_1 \alpha_2 \alpha_3 \dots)$ simultaneously examines the different possible meanings $a_1, a_2, a_3, \dots$ it may have. In this way, one can claim that R observes the pair (Ω, Ω'), and does not examine one of these spaces only as if it were alone. At the elementary level of observation, the observer R examines a pair (α, a) of a word α taken with a given meaning a and this pair is referred to as a *lexeme* by linguists.

A given symbol α may have several meanings $a_1, a_2, \dots, a_n$, and in the observation process, when R tries to identify α he simultaneously examines which one of the lexemes $(\alpha, a_1), (\alpha, a_2), \dots, (\alpha, a_n)$ is presently involved. At this stage of course, one could consider an approach using the entropy of the pair (α, a) and then write

$$H(\alpha, a) = H(\alpha) + H(a/\alpha)$$

but on doing so, one is implicitly assuming that the dependence of meaning upon symbol is of a random nature, and this may not be true in reality.

As a matter of fact, it is likely that the observation of the pair (Ω, Ω') by R will involve some interferences between Ω and Ω' in such a manner that the result will be (Ω_r, Ω'_r) generally different from (Ω, Ω'). While Γ is an external space with respect to the referential frame of the observer, Ω' can be considered as an internal space defined in advance by the observer himself, so that the coupling effect between the observation of Ω and the observation of Ω' is generally thought of as the result of the *subjectivity* of the observer.

1.2.2 Information, Learning, Dislearning

Assume that we can define the amount of information contained in the syntax by a measure $H(\Omega) \in \mathbb{R}$ and, likewise, let $H(\Omega')$ denote the information involved in the semantic space.

The external uncertainty involved in the natural language (Ω, Ω') can be measured by the quantity $H(\Omega) + H(\Omega')$; it is the maximum amount of uncertainty that one may have about (Ω, Ω') on ignoring the stochastic dependence between Ω and Ω'.

The internal information contained in (Ω, Ω') can be measured by the difference $H(\Omega') - H(\Omega)$ which is always positive for natural languages since one has more meanings than symbols. Clearly, when $H(\Omega) = H(\Omega')$, then on average a symbol has one meaning only, so that in this case we can deal with $H(\Omega)$ or $H(\Omega')$ alone without losing information.

An observer R will not measure the exact values of $H(\Omega)$ and $H(\Omega')$, but rather he will perceive two observed values $H_r(\Omega)$ and $H_r(\Omega')$. A learning observer is one to whom the external uncertainty and the internal information vary in opposite ways in the observation process: that is to say one increases when the other one decreases. In contrast, for a dislearning observer, the external uncertainty and the internal information of the natural language will vary in the same way: simultaneously increasing or decreasing.

At first glance, there are many possible theoretical models to describe this learning process, and the simplest one is probably expressed by the equation [1.7]

$$[H_r(\Omega') - H_r(\Omega)][H_r(\Omega') + H_r(\Omega)] = k ,$$ (1.2.1)

where k is a positive constant, or likewise

$$H_r^2(\Omega') - H_r^2(\Omega) = k .$$ (1.2.2)

All these remarks, and particularly (1.2.2), are directly relevant to straightforward considerations related to natural languages considered as the substratum of information. Here they are derived in a qualitative manner, but our claim is that they should appear in a more formal way in a theory of information which deals explicitly with syntax and semantics.

1.3 Prerequisites for a Theory of Information

In this section, we shall state some requirements which, in our opinion, should be fulfilled in order to convert the communication theory of Shannon into an information theory.

1.3.1 Relativity of Information

A Chinese newspaper offers absolutely no information to the present author for the simple reason that it is meaningless to him. The amount of information contained in the "X-Magazine" is not the same for a businessman and a job seeker, again because this journal does not have the same meaning from the different viewpoints of these two readers. The biological information contained in the DNA is necessarily defined relative to its environment, and, as a special case, if we put this DNA in a glass of sand, it then has no information at all. These examples explicitly demonstrate the meaning of information.

At a first glance, this variation of semantics could be described by a variation of probability distribution in the Shannon framework and to some extent, semantics is already introduced by the conditional entropy $H(\alpha/\alpha_1, \alpha_2, \ldots, \alpha_n)$ of the word α given the n preceding words $\alpha_1, \alpha_2, \ldots, \alpha_n$. But for sufficiently large values of n, we switch from the space of words to the space of sentences, that is to say, loosely speaking, we move from symbols to meanings. There is a discontinuity somewhere, and the latter should appear more explicitly in the formulation than it does at present.

In terms of natural language, we may say that we switch from Ω to Ω'. This suggests a model which would deal simultaneously with both Ω and Ω', for instance by means of weighting coefficients associated with the relative importance of Ω and Ω'.

1.3.2 Negative Information

A student is listening to the teacher, and at a given instant the former partly understands the topic that the latter is explaining. The teacher goes on, and suddenly the student loses touch: he no longer understands anything. In other words, one can claim that the professor has brought negative information to the student.

Brillouin [1.6] discussed the following problem. A telegram is wired and at the end of the message, the sender appends a digit which has the following meaning; $0 :=$ all is wrong, don't use the telegram; $1 :=$ the message is good you can use it. Here again we are dealing with negative information, or equivalently, with variation of semantic space.

These two problems are beyond the scope of the Shannon theory, and it would be wise to generalize the theory in order to properly deal with them. This is because they are exactly the type of problem which is frequently encountered in cybernetics.

1.3.3 Entropy of Form and Pattern

Until now, the concept of entropy as a measure of uncertainty has been defined for random discrete variables and continuous variables, but not for forms, or patterns or trajectories considered as forms. This is rather surprising, because the term information itself comes from the latin verb *informare* which exactly means "to form" or "to shape"! So in its most direct meaning, information should necessarily involve variations of forms!

If we consider a form as being defined by a finite number of features, then the concept of discrete entropy is quite sufficient for our purpose; but in the case of a continuous trajectory, and if we further consider the latter as being an element of an infinite dimensional space, then Shannon theory fails to apply.

We believe that a large part of this difficulty comes from the apparent discrepency which exists between the discrete entropy (1.1.2) and the continuous entropy (1.1.3). Both of these can be considered as being valuable measures of information, and they have proved this by their large number of practical applications; nevertheless, the disturbing feature is that the latter is not the limiting form of the former when the discretizing span tends to zero. In other words, they are actually different in their physical nature! We have two information theories: one for discrete variables and one for continuous variables.

Our claim is that if we can exhibit the differences, we shall better understand the physical meaning of the continuous entropy and then, by using similar arguments, we shall be in a position to tackle the problem of defining the entropy of a continuous form.

1.3.4 Information and Thermodynamics

The relation between information theory and the thermodynamics of closed systems is well known, and the famous equation

$$S = kH , \tag{1.3.1}$$

where S is the thermodynamic entropy and k is the so-called Boltzmann constant, has given rise to a considerable amount of literature.

This being so, we now have at hand a thermodynamics of open systems initiated by *Prigogine* [1.8] and which has been applied to problems of structure, stability and fluctuations. Loosely speaking, the central idea is that the thermodynamic entropy S of the system varies according to

$$dS = dS_i + dS_o , \tag{1.3.2}$$

where S_i is the customary thermodynamic entropy and dS_o is the variation of entropy which describes the interactions between the system and its environment. According to the second law of thermodynamics, one has $dS_i \geq 0$; but dS_o may be both positive, in which case the environment pours entropy into the system, or negative, when it is the system which pours entropy into its environment.

To the best of our knowledge, there is no counterpart of this theory in information theory. Nevertheless, we are entitled to think that it should exist, given the resemblance to the definition of natural languages as outlined above. Such a theory is interesting because it could enable the use of informational entropy in such problems as structure, organization, self-organization, etc.

1.3.5 Information and Subjectivity

Probability and Subjectivity. The term of subjectivity is used in statistics and probability with the essential meaning of prior probability, in contrast to posterior probability. When we say that the probability of getting 4 on tossing a die is $\frac{1}{6}$, we are stating a likelihood based on our knowledge of the geometry of the die. The die may be biased, but if we have no prior reason to believe so, we shall merely assume that it is not; therefore we shall derive the uniform distribution $(\frac{1}{6}, \frac{1}{6}, \ldots, \frac{1}{6})$. In doing so we refer only to the existing internal model of a die as it is stored in our memory; clearly we can use this only to handle fair dice.

If we now do an experiment which consists of tossing the die one thousand times and we can so verify that the probability distribution is effectively the uniform one, then the above prior probability becomes a posterior probability, or similarly, the subjective probability above becomes an objective probability.

To summarize, our subjectivity about the probability distribution which characterizes the die can be thought of as the result of the interaction between this die under observation and our prior internal model of die.

Information and Subjectivity. We have of course the same problem with information. We can meaningfully refer both to prior information and to posterior information, or likewise to subjective information and objective information; the question is to derive a suitable corresponding model.

On a superficial level, one could straightforwardly define subjective entropy by merely using subjective probability in the Shannon framework, but it is likely that on doing so we would have an incomplete approach. Indeed, information refers basically to symbols and meanings, and thus we would seem have one subjective probability for the former and another for the latter; but the trouble is that the subjectivity of the observer causes some interferences between these two probability distributions.

As an illustrative example, consider the following situation. A reporter has at hand a telegram issued by a press agency and he knows that this message is related to social troubles in a given country. The telegram reads as follows: *The long stride of the civil servants has completely undermined the national economy of the country.* The reporter will rectify this and will understand: *The long* strike *of the civil servants....*

An ordinary observer would have the choice between *stride* and *strike* (for instance) in the space of meanings, but the reporter, due to his prior knowledge about the content of the message, has a lexeme restricted to *strike* only. This is this effect of subjectivity on information that we shall explicitly introduce in the theory. As mentioned previously, it is possible to consider an approach via the Shannon framework, by merely using a suitable space of probability functions, but we believe that the theory which would result would be too cumbersome for the applications. We shall instead seek a model with external parameters which could look like weighting coefficients for instance. In short, our purpose is to describe the information resulting from coupling effects between syntax and semantics by a combination of information with probability and information without probability.

1.4 Information and Systems

As a matter of fact, we have already suggested a model to introduce semantics into information theory, and we constructed it in a possible framework for a theory of general systems [1.9]. In the present section we shall outline this approach. It will be useful for two main reasons: first, in order to bring to mind some ideas which will be involved in the following even though they are not explicitly referred to, and second, to suitably define the position of the present book with respect to our preceding one.

1.4.1 A Model of General Systems

The basic element in modelling a general system is the triplet (S, I, R) where S is the system under observation, R is the observer who examines S, and I is the amount of information that R can obtain from S considered as an informational source. Defining S alone is meaningless since S has a significance only with respect to the observer who is considering it, so it is better to talk of (S/R), namely S given R. In the same way, defining I alone is meaningless, and we have to simultaneously consider the source (S/R) which contains this information and the observer R who measures the amount of relative information (I/R). Everything is relative to something.

The system is defined by its inside S and its outside $\bar{S}$, that is to say in the referential frame of S, by its inside (S/S) and its outside $(\bar{S}/S)$. Loosely speaking, $(\bar{S}/S)$ is that part of the universe with which (S/S) exchanges information to govern its own evolution: it is the environment of (S/S). An observer R who tries to get a good understanding of (S/S) will have to observe also $(\bar{S}/S)$ ("If I know your friends I shall understand you better") and as a result, he will define the indirect observation process $[(S/S/R), (\bar{S}/S/R)]$: for instance $\bar{S}$ is observed by R via S.

1.4.2 A Model of Relative Information

A system (S/S) is characterized by its *internal entropy* $H_i(S/S)$ in the Shannon sense, and its *external entropy* $H_o(S/S) := H_i(\bar{S}/S)$; and R will measure only $H_i(S/S/R)$ and $H_o(S/S/R)$ which are generally different from $H_i(S/S)$ and $H_o(S/S)$, respectively. A careful analysis [1.9] shows that $H_o(S/S)$ has properties exactly similar to those of time in physics, so that in analogy with special relativity we shall define

$$H_i(S/S/R) := \varrho[u(S/R)][H_i(S/S) + u(S/R)H_o(S/S)] \tag{1.4.1}$$

$$H_o(S/S/R) := \varrho[u(S/R)]\left[H_o(S/S) + \frac{1}{c^2}u(S/R)H_i(S/S) \right] \tag{1.4.2}$$

with

$$\varrho[u(S/R)] := \left[1 - \frac{1}{c^2}u^2(S/R) \right]^{-1/2}, \tag{1.4.3}$$

where c is a positive constant which can be thought of as related to the measurement units, and $u(S/R)$, with $-1 \leqslant u(S/R) \leqslant +1$, is a parameter which characterizes the efficiency of the observation, or the coupling between the system S and the observer R.

Now consider the observation process $(S/R/R')$ in which the observer R' observes S but via another observer R. Then in a similar way one has the equations

$$H_i(S/R/R') = \varrho[u(R'/R)][H_i(S/R) + u(R'/R)H_o(S/R)] \tag{1.4.4}$$

$$H_o(S/R/R') = \varrho[u(R'/R)]\left[H_o(S/R) + \frac{1}{c^2}u(R'/R)H_i(S/R) \right], \tag{1.4.5}$$

where $u(R'/R)$ characterizes the efficiency of the transfer of information from the observer R to the observer R'. We are thus led to introduce a concept of relative information as follows.

Definition 1.4.1. The amount of information $I_i(S/R/R')$ provided by R to R' about the internal structure of (S/R) is

$$I_i(S/R/R') := H_i(S/R/R') - \varrho[u(R'/R)]H_i(S/R) \tag{1.4.6}$$

$$= \varrho[u(R'/R)]H_o(S/R) \; ; \tag{1.4.7}$$

the external information $I_o(S/R/R')$ provided by R to R' is

$$I_o(S/R/R') := H_o(S/R/R') - \varrho[u(R'/R)]H_o(S/R) \tag{1.4.8}$$

$$= \frac{1}{c^2} u(R'/R) \; ; \tag{1.4.9}$$

and the metric I of this information is

$$I^2(S/R/R') := I_i^2(S/R/R') - c^2 I_o^2(S/R/R') \; . \tag{1.4.10}$$

One can show that for small u one has

$$I_i(S/R/R') = I_o(S/R/R') + o(u)$$

with $o(u) \to 0$ as $u \to 0$, so that Shannon theory can be thought of as identifying syntax with semantics.

1.4.3 A Few Comments

As mentioned above, when we wrote the equations (1.4.4) and (1.4.5) for the first time, we were guided by the observation that $H_o(S/R/R')$ is a parameter quite similar to time in physics.

It is now clear that if we consider the pair $(S, \overline{S})$ as being a natural language in the sense of Sect. 1.2, then we can assume that (1.2.2) is satisfied to yield

$$H_o^2(S/R/R') - H_i^2(S/R/R') = \text{constant} \; .$$

Therefore we once more derive (1.4.4) and (1.4.5). But in doing so, we implicitly assume that R' is a learning observer; and it will be of interest to examine what happens when R' is dislearning, as we shall do later in the book.

A reader who is not interested in general systems might contend that it should be possible to build up an information theory as such, simply by using the characteristics of information without necessarily referring to cybernetics. In addition, from our concern, a straightforward approach to generalized information, if it provides a model similar to the above one, would indirectly support our general system model. And, with this purpose in mind, we shall work outside the framework of cybernetics, and we shall consider only the triplet (natural language, message, observer) in order to examine the type of results we can thereby obtain.

1.5 How We Shall Proceed

1.5.1 Aim of the Book

First of all, in order to define the scope of the book and its relation to the other literature, we shall survey the main concepts of informational entropies which have been proposed, and shall then proceed to a critical review of the Shannon theory, to exhibit both its satisfactory features, and those which require improvements in order to be fruitfully applied to problems that are not directly relevant to technical communication. It is this that is our central motivation. One of the main conclusions of this review will be that, contrary to what is taken for granted by many scientists, the continuous Shannon entropy is much more satisfactory than the discrete one, and involves many interesting properties that the latter does not have but nevertheless should have.

1.5.2 Subjective Information and Relative Information

Following from the remarks in the preceding section, we shall generalize the Shannon theory in two different ways by using two different approaches: the first one proceeds by slightly modifying the definition of transinformation in order to explicitly introduce the semantics of the observer, and the second one via a model of observation with informational invariance.

More explicitly, this first approach considers a subjective transinformation $J(X, Y)$ in the form

$$J(X, Y) := H(Y) - H(YY'/XX') \tag{1.5.1}$$

where Y' can be thought of as the semantics of the symbol Y and likewise X' is the semantics of X. This definition is very simple (but quite relevant!) and direct, and in addition it fully agrees with the classical viewpoint of communication engineering.

In the second approach, we shall assume that the observer R observes the pair $[H(X), H(X')]$ of the entropies of the symbol X and of the meaning X' respectively, but that this observation process does not create nor destroy the total amount of information involved in the vector $[H(X), H(X')]$ considered as a random variable. Basically, we assume that the entropies $H(X)$ and $H(X')$ are continuous Shannon entropies; therefore, we shall straightforwardly obtain conditions for the informational invariance of the observation. This condition will directly imply the concept of relative entropies and of relative information.

1.5.3 Minkowskian Observation of Events

According to the informational invariance of the continuous Shannon entropy, the coupling effect between two random variables X and Y under observation by an external observer is represented by the so-called Lorentz–Poincaré equations which furthermore provide the invariance of the Minkowskian geodesic. We shall assume that the variables which are observed following this Minkowskian process are not $H(X)$ and $H(X')$ themselves, but rather the individual entropies $-\ln p(x_i)$ and h_i

where $p(x_i)$ is the probability $pr(X = x_i)$ and h_i denotes a semantic entropy associated with x_i. As a result, we shall obtain

i) A unified approach which contains most, if not all, the concepts of entropies which have been proposed recently in information theory with probability, for example, in the so-called mixed theory of information.
ii) A new concept of relative probability, which relates probability to possibility and by means of which we shall generalize the statistical decision theory to account for the subjectivity of the decision maker.

1.5.4 A Unified Approach to Discrete Entropy and Continuous Entropy

The above theory is a generalization of the Shannon theory in the sense that the latter is our point of departure, and especially in that the equations of the observation with informational invariance have been derived by using the Shannon entropy as defined for a continuous random variable. As a consequence, it appears necessary that we clarify the differences in physical nature between the discrete entropy and the continuous entropy, at least in order to soundly justify our approach.

Our investigations will lead us to introduce the concept of total entropy (which is a new version of the notion of effective entropy which we proposed previously [1.10]) of a discrete random variable by using a randomization technique on the lattice of definition of the latter. The two main consequences of this model are the following: First, we obtain a unified approach to discrete entropy and continuous entropy and second, by using similar randomization techniques, we can tackle the problem of defining the amount of information involved in a continuous form.

1.5.5 A Word of Caution to the Reader

The book is written in the spirit of physics or engineering mathematics or classical applied mathematics or mathematical physics. We do not want to hide the various intuitions which led us, as physicists, to the theory. Nevertheless, to conform to the modern fashion of mathematicians, and also for the sake of clarity, we have adopted a presentation in the form of axioms and propositions, but the proofs themselves involve only very simple mathematics.

The chapters are written in such a manner that they are mutually independent. This reflects the fact that different rationales yield similar conclusions. As a result, the reader may begin the book with any chapter, and read the chapters in any order.

2. Information Theory – The State of the Art

In order to suitably define the exact role of the present monograph in the relevant literature, it is necessary to review the current state of the art of information theory; this is the purpose of the present chapter.

This task by itself could be the subject of an entire book and so we shall restrict ourselves to a summary only. To this end, we shall follow the story of the theory. Loosely speaking, one can discern three periods in its development. First, the statement of the basic elements of the theory by Shannon and the immediate extensions by his co-workers; second, abstract studies by mathematicians who did not care about communication but were interested rather in functional equations; and third, more recently, investigations on information dealing with both symbols and meanings as stimulated by cybernetics and systems science.

2.1 Introduction

Hartley [2.1] was probably the first author to propose a measure of uncertainty which involves the probability distribution of a finite set of equiprobable random events; but the mathematical theory of information, as known presently, was developed by *Shannon* [2.2, 3], who defined a general framework in which the concept of information could be investigated. He generalized the measure of uncertainty, as suggested by *Hartley*, in the form of an informational entropy similar to the statistical thermodynamic entropy introduced by Boltzmann; he defined the concepts of source, channels, receiver, and derived his fundamental coding theorem.

This pioneering work was mainly the approach of a physicist. Later on, mathematicians undertook the task of giving it sound mathematical foundations. In 1953, *McMillan* [2.4] introduced rigorous mathematical definitions of sources of information and transmission channels, and generalized the theory of Markovian sources to ergodic sources. In 1954, *Feinstein* [2.5] derived the first complete proof of the Shannon coding theorem for channels without memory. In 1956, *Khintchine* [2.6] provided a rigorous mathematical theory for stationary ergodic sources with finite memory.

With the work of *Khintchine*, the foundations of the theory achieved a rigorous final form, and then refinements began to be investigated in two main directions: first, theoretical considerations related to the generalization of the concept of entropy itself, and second, practical applications to diverse areas such as technical communication, theoretical biology, linguistics, music, statistical mechanics, and so on.

Our main purpose in the following is to summarize the state of the art of classical information theory as initiated by Shannon. We shall be concerned mainly with the conceptual foundations of the theory rather than with its mathematical features, so that our discussion, without being completely heuristic, will be rather physical, dropping all the rigorous mathematical proofs which can be easily found elsewhere.

We shall first recap on the basic elements of the Shannon theory, that is to say the concept of informational entropy and of mutual information for both discrete and continuous probabilities. Then we shall survey various extensions of this entropy, and finally we shall outline the problem of defining information without probability.

2.2 Shannon Measure of Uncertainty

2.2.1 The Probabilistic Framework

Basically, the Shannon theory deals with a concept of *uncertainty* defined by means of probability, so that we shall have to refer to "random experiments", an expression which is short for "experiments with random events", and sometimes for "random variables".

Definition 2.2.1. A random experiment α is an experiment which provides the outcomes $A_1, A_2, \ldots, A_m$ with the respective probabilities $p(A_1), p(A_2), \ldots, p(A_m)$ which we abbreviate to $p_1, p_2, \ldots, p_m$, with $p_1 + p_2 + \cdots + p_m = 1$. In the following we shall refer to $\alpha := (p_1, p_2, \ldots, p_m)$ where the symbol := means that the left side is defined by the right side. $\qquad\square$

Given another random experiment $\beta := (q_1, q_2, \ldots, q_m)$; our purpose in the following will be to measure first the amount of uncertainty involved in α and β respectively; and second the amount of knowledge, or information, that one of these experiments brings about the other one.

2.2.2 Shannon Informational Entropy

Assume that we are an experimenter or an observer say R, who intends to make the experiment $\alpha := (p_1, p_2, \ldots, p_m)$ whose possible outcomes have probabilities p_i that are known. Can we guess in advance the outcome which we shall obtain? As a matter of fact, the degree of difficulty of this prediction will vary with the definition of α, and we shall say that it is related to the *uncertainty involved* in α. So the question is then the following: can we measure the amount of uncertainty?

On assuming that such a measure U exists, it necessarily depends upon the various parameters which define α, for example, the probabilities p_i; and we shall emphasize this feature in writting $U(p_1, p_2, \ldots, p_m)$. In the following, for the sake of simplicity, we shall sometimes denote the uncertainty by $H(\alpha)$,

$$U(p_1, p_2, \ldots, p_m) =: H(\alpha) \ . \tag{2.2.1}$$

Now we have to exhibit a set of basic properties that U should satisfy. We have the following axioms.

(A1): U should be a continuous function of its arguments $p_1, p_2, \ldots, p_m$. $\square$

This assumption merely means that small variations of the probabilities should cause only small changes of the uncertainty, which is quite a desirable property.

(A2): When all the probabilities p_i are equal, $p_1 = p_2 = \cdots = p_m = 1/m$, then U should be an increasing function of m. $\square$

Indeed, the larger the number of possible outcomes, the larger the uncertainty in α.

(A3): Assume that a given outcome can be considered as a sequence of two events then the whole uncertainty U should be the weighted combination of the partial uncertainties involved in $(p_1, p_2, \ldots, p_{m-1} + p_m)$ and $(p_{m-1}/(p_{m-1} + p_m), p_m/(p_{m-1} + p_m))$ respectively.
For three events, one should have the relation

$$U(p_1, p_2, p_3) = U(p_1, p_2 + p_3) + (p_2 + p_3)U\left(\frac{p_2}{p_2 + p_3}, \frac{p_3}{p_2 + p_3}\right).$$

$$(2.2.2) \quad \square$$

The practical meaning of relation (2.2.2) is the following.
Assume that $\alpha := (p_1, p_2, p_3)$ has only three possible outcomes A_1, A_2 and A_3; then $H(\alpha)$ measures the amount of prior uncertainty we have about the question as to whether we shall get A_1 or A_2 or A_3; or likewise, it represents the amount of uncertainty involved in the identification process which consists of determining which issue we shall obtain. Assume that we decompose this identification process into two stages. In the first one, we determine whether we have A_1 or, on the other hand, one of A_2 or A_3; and this identification process involves the uncertainty $U(p_1, p_2 + p_3)$. If the outcome is A_1, then the identification is complete. If the outcome is A_2 or A_3, which happens with the probability $(p_2 + p_3)$, then we have to make another experiment to determine which one of A_2 or A_3 we have at hand, and this identification involves the uncertainty $U(p_2/(p_2 + p_3), p_3/(p_2 + p_3))$. Hence we have arrived at equation (2.2.2).
Shannon stated the following result:

Theorem 2.2.1. The function $U(p_1, p_2, \ldots, p_n)$, and the only function which satisfies the axioms A1, A2, A3 above, is

$$U(p_1, p_2, \ldots, p_m) = -k \sum_{i=1}^{m} p_i \ln p_i = H(\alpha) \qquad (2.2.3)$$

where ln denotes the natural logarithm and k is a positive constant which can be thought of as defining the measurement unit. $\square$

Remark About the Proof. The proof (as derived by Shannon) is decomposed into the following steps.

i) Assume that all the probabilities p_i, $1 \leqslant i \leqslant m$ are equal; we then have

$$U\left(\frac{1}{m}, \frac{1}{m}, \ldots, \frac{1}{m}\right) = f(m) \qquad (2.2.4)$$

where f satisfies the condition

$$f(mn) = f(m) + f(n) \ .$$

As a result, one necessarily has

$$f(m) = k \ln m \qquad (2.2.5)$$

ii) Assume now that the probabilities are not the same. We can then write $p_i = m_i / \sum_i m_i$, where the m_i denote integers. Then, by using (2.2.2), we can obtain the relation

$$k \ln \sum m_i = U(p_1, p_2, \ldots, p_m) + k \sum p_i \ln m_i \qquad (2.2.6)$$

and therefore the expression (2.2.3).

Definition 2.2.2. Following Shannon, we shall refer to the measure $U(p_1, p_2, \ldots, p_m) \equiv H(\alpha)$ as the *discrete informational entropy* of the random experiment α. $\square$

In the next section, we shall give a more intuitive derivation of the mathematical expression for $H(\alpha)$.

2.2.3 Entropy of Random Variables

The definition 2.2.2 above generalizes straightforwardly to random variables with the same practical meaning.

Definition 2.2.3. Let $X \in \mathbb{R}$ denote a discrete random variable which takes on the values $x_1, x_2, \ldots, x_n$ with the probabilities $p_1, p_2, \ldots, p_n$; the entropy $H(X)$ of X is then defined by the expression

$$H(X) = -k \sum_{i=1}^{m} p_i \ln p_i \qquad (2.2.7)$$

where k denotes a constant which may be thought of as defining the measurement units. $\square$

2.3 An Intuitive Approach to Entropy

2.3.1 Uniform Random Experiments

A uniform random experiment $\alpha = (A_1, A_2, \ldots, A_m)$ is an experiment whose outcomes all occur with the same probability $1/m$. Let us restrict ourselves to this special case.

i)   A measurement of the amount of uncertainty involved in α should be a function $f(m)$ of m.
ii) Since there is no uncertainty when α has only one possible outcome, one should have $f(1) = 0$.
iii) In addition, the larger m, the larger the uncertainty involved in α, so that $f(m)$ should be an increasing function of m.
iv) Let β be another uniform random experiment $\beta := (B_1, B_2, \ldots, B_n)$ and consider the new random experiment $\alpha\beta := (A_i B_j, 1 \leqslant i \leqslant m, 1 \leqslant j \leqslant n)$ which has mn outcomes occurring with the same probability $1/mn$. Assume that α and β are *independent* from a probabilistic standpoint, that is to say, loosely speaking, that they do not interact with one another.

Given these conditions, one may expect that the uncertainty involved in $\alpha\beta$ is the sum of the uncertainties involved in α and β respectively; in other words, one should have the equation

$$f(mn) = f(m) + f(n) \ . \tag{2.3.1}$$

This is the only prerequisite we can reasonably demand for a measure of uncertainty; moreover, One can show that a function, and in fact the only function, which satisfies the assumptions (i–iv) above is

$$f(n) = k \ln n \ . \tag{2.3.2}$$

2.3.2 Non Uniform Random Experiments

Our task now is to guess the explicit form of $H(\alpha)$ for any $\alpha := (p_1, p_2, \ldots, p_m)$; and, to this end, we shall determine the contribution of each outcome A_i to the total uncertainty.

i)   In the case of a uniform experiment, it is likely that these individual contributions are the same, i.e., one should have

$$H(A_1) = H(A_2) = \cdots = H(A_m) \ ,$$

and, in addition, it seems consistent to assume that

$$H(\alpha) = H(A_1) + H(A_2) + \cdots + H(A_m)$$

so that, by virtue of (2.3.1), one has

$$H(A_i) = \frac{1}{m}(-l \ln m) \ ; \qquad i = 1, 2, \ldots, m \tag{2.3.3}$$

ii) Next, since our purpose is to express $H(\alpha)$ in terms of the probabilities $p_1, p_2, \ldots, p_m$, we shall re-write (2.3.3) and its predecessor in the form

$$H(A_i) = -\frac{1}{m}\left(k \ln \frac{1}{m}\right) \tag{2.3.4}$$

and

$$H(\alpha) = \sum_{i=1}^{n} \frac{1}{m}\left(-k\ln\frac{1}{m}\right) . \tag{2.3.5}$$

iii) This being so, in the ith term of the right-hand side of (2.3.5), $1/m$ may be thought of as being the probability $p(A_i)$ of the event A_i, so that we shall set $1/m = p(A_i)$ to obtain the general expression for $H(\alpha)$ in the form

$$H(\alpha) = -k \sum_{i=1}^{m} p(A_i)\ln p(A_i) . \tag{2.3.6}$$

This derivation of course is not a proof in the sense that we did not mathematically deduce $H(\alpha)$ from a given set of axioms, but nevertheless it provides an intuitive understanding of the physical meaning of this concept.

Important Remark. The constant k in (2.2.3) may be thought of as the base of the logarithm involved in $H(\alpha)$, and so by virtue of the formula

$$\log_a x = \log_a e \times \ln x$$

where $\log_a x$ is the logarithm of x in the base a. So in the following, in order to shorten the notation, we shall put $k = 1$ whenever we do not explicitly need to deal with this parameter.

Nevertheless, when this concept of entropy is utilized in topics which are not directly relevant to technical communication problems, it is not at all clear whether k is merely an integration constant as in the above mathematical derivation, and it is quite likely that it should have a value and a concrete meaning which depends upon the nature of the framework. In any case, the exact characterization of this relation is still an open problem.   □

Note that the entropy $H(\alpha)$ defined by (2.3.6) is the statistical average of the random variable which takes the values $-k\ln p(A_i)$ with the probabilities $p(A_i)$ so that we may consider $-k\ln p(A_i)$ as being the amount of uncertainty involved in the event A_i alone and write

$$H(\alpha) := E\{H(A_i)\}$$

where the symbol $E\{\cdot\}$ represents the mathematical expectation.

Now if we use $H(\alpha)$ instead of the individual $H(A_i)$ it is because, when we repeatedly perform the experiment α, we do not repeatedly obtain the same outcome, but rather all of them, so that only $H(\alpha)$ is really meaningful to us from a practical standpoint.

2.4 Conditional Entropy

2.4.1 Framework of Random Experiments

Consider two random experiments $\alpha := (p_1, p_2, \ldots, p_m)$ and $\beta := (q_1, q_2, \ldots, q_n)$ which are not necessarily statistically independent; in other words, the equation

$p(A_i B_j) = p(A_i)\,p(B_j)$ does not necessarily hold, but rather, one has

$$p(A_i B_j) = p(A_i)p(B_j/A_i) , \qquad \forall i, \forall j \tag{2.4.1}$$

where $p(B_j/A_i)$ denotes the conditional probability of B_j given A_i. This dependence between α and β suggests the following definition.

Definition 2.4.1. The *conditional discrete entropy*, or for short the *conditional entropy* $H(\beta/\alpha)$ of the random experiment β given the random experiment α is defined as

$$H(\beta/\alpha) := \sum_{i=1}^{m} p(A_i)H(\beta/A_i) \tag{2.4.2}$$

where $H(\beta/A_i)$ is given by the expression

$$H(\beta/A_i) := -\sum_j p(B_j/A_i)\ln p(A_i B_j) . \tag{2.4.3}$$

i) For convenience, we define

$$r_{ij} := p(A_i B_j) \tag{2.4.4}$$

$$q_{j/i} := p(B_j/A_i) . \tag{2.4.5}$$

and we bear in mind that

$$\sum_{j=1}^{m} r_{ij} = p_i . \tag{2.4.6}$$

ii) With this notation, and on taking account of (2.4.1), we obtain from (2.4.3)

$$H(\alpha\beta) = -\sum_{ij} r_{ij}\ln p_i - \sum_{ij} p_i q_{j/i}\ln q_{j/i} . \tag{2.4.7}$$

Now, on using property (2.4.6) we find

$$H(\alpha\beta) = -\sum_i p_i\ln p_i + \sum_i p_i \sum_j (-q_{j/i}\ln q_{j/i})$$

or, according to definition 2.4.1,

$$H(\alpha\beta) = H(\alpha) + H(\beta/\alpha) . \tag{2.4.8}$$

$H(\beta)$ is a measure of the entire uncertainty involved in β, irrespective of any external reference; $H(\beta/\alpha)$ measures the uncertainty concerning β given that we previously performed the experiment α. $H(\beta/\alpha)$ is related to the mutual dependence between α and β, and it is the basic element which will allow us to introduce the concept of information in the following.

2.4.2 Application to Random Variables

In Sect. 2.2.3 we defined the entropy of a discrete random variable, and we saw that we can deal with the entropy of a random experiment and the entropy of a discrete random variable in exactly the same way.

Likewise, we can define the conditional entropy of random variables by using similar arguments.

Consider a random variable Y, which takes on the values $y_1, y_2, \ldots, y_n$ with the probabilities $q_1, q_2, \ldots, q_n$. Again consider the random variable X as in Sect. 2.2.3 and define the probability distribution $\{r_{ij}, 1 \leqslant i \leqslant m, 1 \leqslant j \leqslant n\}$ of the pair (X, Y); in other words (X, Y) takes the value (x_i, y_j) with the probability r_{ij} for every (i,j). In this framework, one has $p(Y = y_j/X = x_i) = q_{j/i}$; and all the equations above apply directly. In particular, one has

$$H(X, Y) = H(X) + H(Y/X) \tag{2.4.9}$$

$$= H(Y) + H(X/Y) \qquad \text{with} \tag{2.4.10}$$

$$H(Y/X) := \sum_{i=1}^{m} p(X = x_i) H(Y/x_i) , \tag{2.4.11}$$

$$H(Y/x_i) = - \sum_{j=1}^{n} p(Y = y_j/X = x_i) \ln p(Y = y_j/X = x_i). \tag{2.4.12}$$

2.5 A Few Properties of Discrete Entropy

In this section, we summarize those mathematical properties of $H(\alpha)$, $H(\alpha\beta)$ and $H(\beta/\alpha)$ which we shall need in the following.

i) One has the inequality

$$H(\alpha) \geqslant 0 , \tag{2.5.1}$$

and the equality $H(\alpha) = 0$ holds, if and only if α has only one possible outcome with probability 1, that is to say when α is deterministic.

ii) For a given number m of possible outcomes, the largest possible value of $H(\alpha)$ is $\ln m$, which occurs when all the outcomes have the same probability $(1/m)$.

iii) One has the inequality

$$H(\beta/\alpha) \geqslant 0 \tag{2.5.2}$$

and the equality $H(\beta/\alpha) = 0$ holds if and only if $H(\beta/A_i) = 0$ for every i, that is to say when, for every outcome A_i of α, the result of β is completely determined; in which case one has

$$H(\alpha\beta) = H(\alpha) . \tag{2.5.3}$$

This result follows directly from (2.4.2) where $p(A_i) \geqslant 0, i = 1, 2, \ldots, m$.

iv) When α and β are independent, we then have $\varrho_{ij} = p_i q_j$ and (2.4.8) becomes

$$H(\alpha\beta) = H(\alpha) + H(\beta) . \tag{2.5.4}$$

v) The following *important relation* holds

$$0 \leqslant H(\beta/\alpha) \leqslant H(\beta) . \tag{2.5.5}$$

Remarks About the Proof of (2.5.5). (a) The left-hand inequality is obvious.

b) We note that the function $-x \ln x$ is convex, i.e., it satisfies the following inequality:

$$-\sum_{i=1}^{m} p_i x_i \ln x_i < -\left(\sum_{i=1}^{m} p_i x_i\right) \ln\left(\sum_{i=1}^{m} p_i x_i\right) \tag{2.5.6}$$

provided that $p_1 + p_2 + \cdots + p_m = 1$.

c) Next, in the inequality (2.5.6) we set $p_i = p_i$, $x_i = q_{j/i}$ for a given fixed j, and $i = 1, 2, \ldots, n$. We then have the inequality

$$-\sum_{i=1}^{m} p_i q_{j/i} \ln q_{j/i} < -\left(\sum_{i=1}^{m} p_i q_{j/i}\right) \ln\left(\sum_{i=1}^{m} p_i q_{j/i}\right) \tag{2.5.7}$$

or

$$-\sum_{i=1}^{m} p_i q_{j/i} \ln q_{j/i} < -q_j \ln q_j \ . \tag{2.5.8}$$

d) We now add up all these inequalities for $j = 1, 2, \ldots, m$, and thus obtain the inequality

$$H(\beta/\alpha) < H(\beta) \ .$$

e) The equality $H(\beta/\alpha) = H(\beta)$ holds if and only if α and β are independent.

vi) From a practical viewpoint, the inequality (2.5.5) expresses the fact that performing the experiment α diminishes the initial amount of uncertainty $H(\beta)$ we have about β.

vii) Due to the relation $\alpha\beta = \beta\alpha$, one has the equality

$$H(\alpha) + H(\beta/\alpha) = H(\beta) + H(\alpha/\beta) \ . \tag{2.5.9}$$

viii) The following inequality holds,

$$H(\beta) - H(\alpha) \leqslant H(\beta/\alpha) \leqslant H(\beta) \ . \tag{2.5.10}$$

Indeed, equality (2.5.9) provides the relation

$$H(\beta/\alpha) = H(\alpha/\beta) + [H(\beta) - H(\alpha)] \tag{2.5.11}$$

with $0 \leqslant H(\alpha/\beta) \leqslant H(\beta)$, hence the left side of (2.5.10).

2.6 Prior Characterization of Discrete Entropy

One of the objectives of mathematicians has been to derive the definition of entropy, not in an intuitive way as Shannon did it, although his approach may be considered as being rigorous, but rather as a consequence of some a priori properties that a measure of uncertainty should satisfy. Below we shall list some such characteristics.

2.6.1 Properties of Uncertainty

We shall denote the uncertainty function by $U_m(p_1, p_2, \ldots, p_m)$, with $p_1 + p_2 + \cdots + p_m = 1$, where the subscript m emphasizes the number of the possible outcomes of the considered random experiment α.

Prerequisites. A suitable measure U_m of uncertainty should have the following properties. It should be

(A1): symmetric w.r.t. the p_i's, i.e.

$$U_m(\ldots, p_i, \ldots, p_j, \ldots) = U_m(\ldots, p_j, \ldots, p_i, \ldots) ; \tag{2.6.1}$$

(A2): normalized, i.e.

$$U_2(\tfrac{1}{2}, \tfrac{1}{2}) = 1 ; \tag{2.6.2}$$

to assign the unit of information to the event with probability $\tfrac{1}{2}$.

(A3): expandable for every m, i.e.

$$U_m(p_1, p_2, \ldots, p_m) = U_{m+1}(0, p_1, p_2, \ldots, p_m)$$

$$= U_{m+1}(p_1, p_2, \ldots, p_k, 0, p_{k+1}, \ldots, p_m)$$

$$= U_{m+1}(p_1, p_2, \ldots, p_m, 0) ; \tag{2.6.3}$$

(A4): decisive, i.e.

$$U_2(1, 0) = U_2(0, 1) = 0 ; \tag{2.6.4}$$

(A5): recursive for every $m \geqslant 3$, i.e.

$$U_m(p_1, p_2, \ldots, p_m) = U_{m-1}(p_1 + p_2, p_3, \ldots, p_m)$$

$$+ (p_1 + p_2) U_2\left(\frac{p_1}{p_1 + p_2}, \frac{p_2}{p_1 + p_2}\right) ; \tag{2.6.5}$$

with the convention $0. U_2(0/0, 0/0) = 0$;

(A6): additive for any $m \geqslant 2$ and $n \geqslant 2$, i.e.

$$U_{mn}(p_1 q_1, p_1 q_2, \ldots, p_1 q_n, p_2 q_1, p_2 q_2, \ldots, p_2 q_n, \ldots, p_m q_1, p_m q_2, \ldots, p_m q_n)$$

$$= U_m(p_1, p_2, \ldots, p_m) + U_n(q_1, q_2, \ldots, q_n) ; \tag{2.6.6}$$

(A7): strongly additive for any $m \geqslant 2$ and $n \geqslant 2$, i.e.

$$U_{mn}(p_1 q_{11}, p_1 q_{12}, \ldots, p_1 q_{1n}, p_2 q_{21}, p_2 q_{22}, \ldots, p_2 q_{2n}, \ldots, p_m q_{m1}, p_m q_{m2}, \ldots, p_m q_{mn})$$

$$= U_m(p_1, p_2, \ldots, p_m) + \sum_{j=1}^m p_j U_n(q_{j1}, q_{j2}, \ldots, q_{jn}) ; \tag{2.6.7}$$

(A8): sub-additive, i.e.

$$U_{mn}(p_{11}, p_{12}, \ldots, p_{1n}, p_{21}, p_{22}, \ldots, p_{2n}, \ldots, \ldots, p_{m1}, p_{m2}, \ldots, p_{mn})$$

$$\leqslant U_m\left(\sum_{k=1}^{n} p_{1k}, \sum_{k=1}^{n} p_{2k}, \dots, \sum_{k+1}^{n} p_{mk}\right)$$

$$+ U_n\left(\sum_{j=1}^{m} p_{j1}, \sum_{j=1}^{m} p_{j2}, \dots, \sum_{j=1}^{m} p_{jn}\right) ; \tag{2.6.8}$$

(A9): maximal for $p_1 = p_2 = \cdots = p_n = 1/n$, i.e.

$$U_m(p_1, p_2, \dots, p_m) \leqslant U_m\left(\frac{1}{m}, \frac{1}{m}, \dots, \frac{1}{m}\right) ; \tag{2.6.9}$$

(A10): bounded from above; i.e. there exists K such that

$$U_2(1-p, p) \leqslant K ; \tag{2.6.10}$$

(A11): non-negative, i.e.

$$U_m(p_1, p_2, \dots, p_m) \geqslant 0 ; \tag{2.6.11}$$

(A12): monotonic, i.e. the function $p \to U_2(p, 1-p)$ is non-decreasing on the interval $[0, \frac{1}{2}]$;

(A13): continuous with respect to the p_i's;

(A14): stable; i.e.; for every $p_0 \in {]}0, 1{[}$,

$$\lim U_2(p_0, q) = U_1(p_0) \quad \text{as} \quad q \to 0^+ ; \tag{2.6.12}$$

(A15): small for small probabilities, i.e.

$$\lim U_2(p, 1-p) = 0 \quad \text{as} \quad p \to 0^+ . \tag{2.6.13} \qquad \square$$

2.6.2 Some Consequences of These Properties

It turns out these properties are not independent; for instance, strong additivity implies additivity although the converse is not true: a function which is additive is not necessarily strongly additive.

The Shannon entropy has the properties of symmetry, normality, expandability, decisivity, strong additivity, additivity and recursivity, and it is probably the only one which is so complete.

All the different entropy functions which are presently available in the literature, are obtained by choosing among (A1) to (A15) a minimal number of properties; but the Shannon entropy is the only one which is strongly additive.

2.7 The Concept of Information

2.7.1 Shannon Information

Shannon introduced the concept of information as follows:

Definition 2.7.1. Consider two random experiments α and β; the *transmission, or transinformation* or *mutual information* $I(\beta/\alpha)$ between α and β is defined by the expression

$$I(\beta/\alpha) := H(\beta) - H(\beta/\alpha) \ . \tag{2.7.1} \quad \square$$

Motivation. Our initial uncertainty about β, irrespective of any experiment which can provide us with some inquiries about β is $H(\beta)$. This being so, it may happen that the measurement or the observation of the experiment α, when it precedes β, lowers the number of possible outcomes of β; and, in such a case, our uncertainty about β therefore diminishes. As a matter of fact, our uncertainty about β after performing α is exactly defined by the conditional entropy $H(\beta/\alpha)$. When there is no relation between α and β, then $H(\beta/\alpha) = H(\beta)$; on the other hand, when the outcome of α completely determines the outcome of β, then $H(\beta/\alpha) = 0$. In all cases, one has $0 \leqslant H(\beta/\alpha) \leqslant H(\beta)$. As a result, the difference $H(\beta) - H(\beta/\alpha)$ measures the decrease in uncertainty that the observer has about β after performing the experiment α: this decrease in uncertainty may be considered as an amount of information about β; thence the following definition.

Definition 2.7.2. The transinformation $I(\beta/\alpha)$ expressed by (2.7.1) represents the amount of information contributed by α about β, or likewise the amount of information contained in α about β. $\qquad \square$

Important Remark. Basically, the entropy is a measure of uncertainty, while the information is a difference in uncertainty, that is to say a difference in entropies. This being so, if we consider the expression

$$I(\beta/\beta) = H(\beta) - H(\beta/\beta) \tag{2.7.2}$$

$$= H(\beta) \tag{2.7.3}$$

we are led to consider $H(\beta)$ as being the amount of information contained in β about β itself. It follows that some authors refer to $H(\beta)$ as an uncertainty or an information, and very often as an information only. In our opinion this is regrettable as it is misleading and may lead to incorrect reasoning. Indeed, is the sentence "the amount of information involved in β about β" completely meaningful?

2.7.2 Some Properties of Transinformation

i) One has the inequality

$$I(\beta/\alpha) \geqslant 0 \tag{2.7.4}$$

and the equality holds if and only if $H(\beta/\alpha) = H(\beta)$. $\qquad \square$

In words, the amount of information which is contributed by α about β to the observer R is always positive. There is never a loss of information.

This is one of the characteristics of this theory, and probably the main one, which makes it inapplicable to other areas like biology, linguistics, human sciences, etc. In these areas, the observer reacts to the received information in such a way that there may sometimes be a loss of information, for example, the received information may lead to confusion.

ii) The transinformation is symmetric; clearly one has

$$I(\beta/\alpha) = I(\alpha/\beta) \ . \tag{2.7.5} \quad \square$$

This property is a direct consequence of the equations

$$H(\alpha\beta) = H(\alpha) + H(\beta/\alpha) \tag{2.7.6}$$

$$= H(\beta) + H(\alpha/\beta) \tag{2.7.7}$$

which provide the inequality

$$H(\beta) - H(\beta/\alpha) = H(\alpha) - H(\alpha/\beta) \ . \tag{2.7.8}$$

This symmetry is the reason why one refers to $I(\beta/\alpha)$ as transinformation, or transmission or mutual information.

There is a troublesome element in the symmetry of (2.7.5). Indeed, from a logical viewpoint, $I(\beta/\alpha)$ represents the inference $\alpha \to \beta$, i.e., the procedure of deducing β from α, while $I(\alpha/\beta)$ represents the opposite inference $\beta \to \alpha$. It is not obvious at all that these two processes should involve the same amount of information. It is likely that the observer R will be more efficient with one of these inferences, such that the information which is effectively received by R is larger in one of these processes than in the other.

This asymmetry, which is basically caused by the interaction of the observer with the observable, does not appear in the Shannonian model.

iii) The maximum amount of information involved in α about β is $H(\alpha)$ and this limit is achieved if and only if $H(\alpha/\beta) = 0$, that is to say, when α is completely determined by β. This is a direct consequence of the equation (2.7.8).

iv) β is completely determined by α if and only if $H(\beta/\alpha) = 0$, that is to say, when $I(\beta/\alpha) = H(\beta)$. But then, by virtue of (2.7.5), one has

$$H(\beta) = H(\alpha) - H(\alpha/\beta) \ ; \qquad H(\beta/\alpha) = 0 \ , \tag{2.7.9}$$

in other words, β is completely determined by α when the following conditions are satisfied: $H(\beta) = H(\alpha)$ together with $H(\alpha/\beta) = 0$.

v) The explicit form of the transinformation in terms of probabilities is

$$I(\beta/\alpha) = \sum_{i}^{m} \sum_{j}^{n} p(A_i B_j) \ln \frac{p(A_i B_j)}{p(A_i)p(B_j)} \ , \tag{2.7.10}$$

or, with the definition 2.4.1

$$I(\beta/\alpha) = \sum_{i,j}^{m,n} r_{ij} \ln \frac{p_{ij}}{p_i q_j} \ . \tag{2.7.11}$$

Indeed, first one has

$$H(\beta) = -\sum_{j=1}^{n} q_j \ln q_j = -\sum_{i,j=1}^{m,n} r_{ij} \ln q_j \ .$$

Second,

$$H(\beta/\alpha) = \sum_{i=1}^{m} p_i \sum_{j=1}^{n} -q_{j/i} \ln q_{j/i}$$

$$= -\sum_{i,j} r_{ij} \ln(r_{ij}/p_i) \ ,$$

and on substituting these results into (2.7.1) we have (2.7.11).
   vi) Due to the symmetry of $I(\beta/\alpha)$, one can write

$$I(\beta/\alpha) = H(\alpha) + H(\beta) - H(\alpha\beta) \ . \tag{2.7.12}$$

2.7.3 Transinformation of Random Variables

With the notation of Sect. 2.4.2 the transinformation or transmission, or mutual information between two discrete random variables X and Y is

$$I(Y/X) = H(Y) - H(Y/X) \tag{2.7.13}$$

and all the above results apply without change.   □

2.7.4 Remarks on the Notation

Following Shannon, the notation which is commonly used to represent the trans-information is

$$I(\alpha, \beta) = H(\beta) - H(\beta/\alpha) \ ,$$

and the reader may wonder why we need to change it, and to choose $I(\beta/\alpha)$ instead.
   In our opinion, this notation $I(\alpha, \beta)$ does not make sufficiently clear which of the random experiment brings information about the other. Of course, one could reply to this argument that it does not matter since one has $I(\alpha, \beta) = I(\beta, \alpha)$; but we believe that it is of paramount importance to represent the viewpoint of the observer who considers either α or β as being the information source, and this feature is better emphasized by the notation $I(\alpha/\beta)$ and $I(\beta/\alpha)$ which, furthermore, has a similar meaning to the conditional entropies $H(\alpha/\beta)$ and $H(\beta/\alpha)$.

2.8 Conditional Transinformation

2.8.1 Main Definition

We now deal with three random experiments $\alpha = (p_1, p_2, \ldots, p_m)$, $\beta = (q_1, q_2, \ldots, q_n)$ and $\gamma = (r_1, r_2, \ldots, r_l)$; the possible outcomes of γ are denoted by $C_1, C_2, \ldots, C_l$. We define:

Definition 2.8.1. The conditional transinformation $I_\gamma(\beta/\alpha)$ of the pair (α, β) given γ is defined as

$$I_\gamma(\beta/\alpha) := H(\beta/\gamma) - H(\beta/\alpha\gamma) \ . \tag{2.8.1} \quad \square$$

Clearly, the meaning of this definition is as follows: given that the random experiment γ has been previously performed, the amount of information provided by α about β is measured by $I_\gamma(\beta/\alpha)$. $\quad \square$

2.8.2 Some Properties of Conditional Transinformation

i) The following relation holds,

$$0 \leqslant I_\gamma(\beta/\alpha) \leqslant H(\beta/\gamma) \ . \tag{2.8.2}$$

The equality $I_\gamma(\beta/\alpha) = H(\beta/\gamma)$ holds if and only if $H(\beta/\alpha\gamma) = 0$, that is to say, when the outcome of $\alpha\gamma$ completely determines the outcome of β. In addition, $I_\gamma(\beta/\alpha) = 0$ if and only if $H(\beta/\alpha\gamma) = H(\beta/\gamma)$, in which case, one also has $I(\beta/\alpha\gamma) = I(\beta/\gamma)$: clearly α does not involve more information about β than γ itself supplies about β.

ii) The conditional transinformation is symmetric,

$$I_\gamma(\beta/\alpha) = I_\gamma(\alpha/\beta) \ . \tag{2.8.3}$$

Proof. The definition of the transinformation provides

$$I_\gamma(\beta/\alpha) = H(\beta/\gamma) - H(\beta/\alpha\gamma) \tag{2.8.4}$$

$$I_\gamma(\alpha/\beta) = H(\alpha/\gamma) - H(\alpha/\beta\gamma) \tag{2.8.5}$$

and it then remains to show that the following equality

$$H(\beta/\gamma) + H(\alpha/\beta\gamma) = H(\alpha/\gamma) + H(\beta/\alpha\gamma) \ . \tag{2.8.6}$$

is satisfied.

One has

$$H(\alpha\beta\gamma) = H(\gamma) + H(\alpha/\gamma) + H(\beta/\alpha\gamma) \tag{2.8.7}$$

$$= H(\gamma) + H(\beta/\gamma) + H(\alpha/\beta\gamma) \ ; \tag{2.8.8}$$

so that (2.8.6) is satisfied, and therefore (2.8.3). $\quad \square$

iii) The explicit form of the conditional transinformation is

$$I_\gamma(\beta/\alpha) = \sum_{k=1}^{l} p(C_k) I_{C_k}(\beta/\alpha) \tag{2.8.9}$$

with

$$I_{C_k}(\beta/\alpha) := \sum_{i,j} p(A_i B_j/C_k) \ln \frac{p(A_i B_j/C_k)}{p(A_i/C_k)p(B_j/C_k)} \ . \tag{2.8.10}$$

iv) The following important equation holds:

$$I(\beta/\alpha\gamma) = I(\beta/\alpha) + I_\alpha(\beta/\gamma) \ , \tag{2.8.11}$$

as a consequence of $I(\beta/\alpha\gamma) := H(\beta) - H(\beta/\alpha\gamma)$ and $I(\beta/\alpha) := H(\beta) - H(\beta/\alpha)$.   □

v) One has the following *triangular information formula*;

$$I(\alpha/\beta\gamma) + I(\gamma/\beta) = I(\beta/\alpha\gamma) + I(\gamma/\alpha) \ . \tag{2.8.12}$$

Indeed, one can show that

$$I(\alpha/\beta\gamma) + I(\gamma/\beta) = I(\alpha/\gamma) + I_\gamma(\alpha/\beta) + I(\gamma/\beta) \tag{2.8.13}$$

$$I(\beta/\alpha\gamma) + I(\gamma/\alpha) = I(\beta/\gamma) + I_\gamma(\beta/\alpha) + I(\gamma/\alpha) \tag{2.8.14}$$

and hence the result (2.8.12).   □

2.8.3 Conditional Transinformation of Random Variables

In this case, we shall deal with the variables X and Y as in Sect. 2.6.3 and, in addition, we shall consider a third random variable Z which takes on the discrete values $\{z_1, z_2, \ldots, z_k\}$ with probabilities $\{r_1, r_2, \ldots, r_k\}$; and then we shall define the conditional transinformation

$$I_z(Y/X) := H(Y/Z) - H(Y/Z, X) \ . \tag{2.8.15}$$ □

2.9 Renyi Entropy

In 1960 *Renyi* [2.7] proposed an entropy function different from the Shannon entropy, and which we shall briefly describe.

2.9.1 Definition of Renyi Entropy

Definition 2.9.1. The Renyi entropy of order $c \neq 1$ of the random experiment $\alpha := (p_1, p_2, \ldots, p_m)$, is defined as

$$H_c(\alpha) := \frac{1}{1-c} \ln \sum_{i=1}^m p_i^c \tag{2.9.1}$$

with the convention

$$0^c := 0 \tag{2.9.2}$$

for all real c.

The Renyi entropy is symmetric, normalized, expandable, decisive, additive and nonnegative. When $c \geqslant 0$, it is maximal and bounded, and for $c > 0$, it is small for small probabilities.

But it is not strongly additive, and thus it is not easy to use it to define a concept of transinformation in the form of differences of entropies.

2.9.2 Meaning of the Renyi Entropy

Although the Renyi entropy has been applied to problems of coding [2.8], it does not seem that it could form the basis of a fruitful information theory, for the reason mentioned above.

In fact, from a practical standpoint, it is the meaning of $H_c(\alpha)$ which is not completely clear. At a first glance, in view of (2.9.1), it measures an amount of uncertainty, but if we read this same equation (2.9.1) as

$$H_c(\alpha) - cH_c(\alpha) = \ln \sum_{i=1}^{m} p_i^c \qquad (2.9.3)$$

we then have a difference of uncertainties, that is to say something which looks like an information.

Jumarie [2.9] showed that c can be considered as a gain coefficient which measures the efficiency of the observer R who is considering α; indeed, because of the coupling effects between R and α, the entropy that is observed by R is not $H(\alpha)$ but $H_c(\alpha)$. As a result, when $c > 1$, $H_c(\alpha)$ measures an information, and when $c < 1$, $H_c(\alpha)$ measures a uncertainty.   □

Motivation. This meaning of $H_c(\alpha)$ may be justified as follows.

i) The function $\ln x$ is concave, and thus satisfies the Jensen inequality

$$\ln \left(\sum_{i=1}^{m} p_i x_i \right) \geqslant \sum_{i=1}^{m} p_i \ln x_i \; . \qquad (2.9.4)$$

If we set $x_i = p_i^{c-1}$, $c \neq 1$, then we obtain

$$\ln \left(\sum_{i=1}^{m} p_i^c \right) \geqslant -(1 - c) \sum_{i=1}^{m} p_i \ln p_i \; . \qquad (2.9.5)$$

ii) It follows that

$$H_c(\alpha) > H(\alpha) \; , \qquad 0 < c < 1 \; . \qquad (2.9.6)$$

So if we assume that the presence of R does not bring information about α, we are led to consider $H_c(\alpha)$ as a measure of uncertainty.

iii) Next, one has

$$H_c(\alpha) < H(\alpha) \; , \qquad c > 1 \qquad (2.9.7)$$

so that in this case $H_c(\alpha)$ is a measure of information insofar as we consider $H(\alpha)$ as being the maximum amount of information involved in α.

iv) In addition, one can show that, for given α and β, there is no $c > 1$ such that

$$H_c(\beta) = H(\beta/\alpha) \; . \qquad (2.9.8)$$

We then conclude that the Renyi entropy cannot be considered as a measure of information, and only the case $c < 1$, which corresponds to a measure of uncertainty, is meaningful.

Remark. Another possibility would be to introduce a transinformation in the form

$$I_c(\alpha) = H(\alpha) - H_c(\alpha) \tag{2.9.9}$$

where c would then be a parameter that depends upon the observer state. One could then have either $I_c(\alpha) > 0$ or $I_c(\alpha) < 0$, in which case c would represent a confusing effect.

2.9.3 Some Properties of the Renyi Entropy

In this section, we shall give some mathematical proper- of $H_c(\alpha)$ which will be useful later.

i) A direct calculation yields the relation

$$(1 - c)\frac{d}{dc}H_c(\alpha) - H_c(\alpha) = \frac{\sum_{i=1}^{m} p_i^c \ln p_i}{\sum_{i=1}^{m} p_i^c} \tag{2.9.10}$$

so that, according to (2.9.2), one has

$$\lim(1 - c)\frac{d}{dc}H_c(\alpha) = 0 \quad \text{as} \quad c \to 1 . \tag{2.9.11}$$

ii) Assuming that c is close to the unity, one has the approximation

$$p_i^c = p_i + (c - 1)p_i \ln p_i + o((c - 1)^2) . \tag{2.9.12}$$

We substitute (2.9.12) into the right-hand side of (2.9.10) and take account of (2.9.11) to obtain the relation

$$H_c(\alpha) = H(\alpha) - (c - 1)\left[\sum_{i=1}^{m} p_i(\ln p_i)^2 - H^2(\alpha)\right] + o((c - 1)^2) . \tag{2.9.13}$$

iii) By using the Schwarz' inequality, we can write

$$H(\alpha) = \sum_{i=1}^{m} \sqrt{p_i}(\sqrt{p_i}|\ln p_i|) \leqslant \left(\sum_{i=1}^{m} p_i\right)^{1/2} \sqrt{\sum_{i=1}^{m} p_i(\ln p_i)^2}$$

so that the coefficient of $(c - 1)$ in (2.9.13) is negative. One thus finds again that $H_c(\alpha) > H(\alpha)$ when $c < 1$, and $H_c(\alpha) < H(\alpha)$ for $c > 1$.

2.10 Cross-Entropy or Relative Entropy

2.10.1 The Main Definition

In the framework of mathematical statistics, *Kullback* [2.10], concerned mainly with problems related to prior and posterior probabilities, introduced the concept of *relative entropy*, or *cross-entropy* defined as follows:

Definition 2.10.1. Let $\mathscr{P} := (p_1, p_2, \ldots, p_n)$ and $\mathscr{Q} := (q_1, q_2, \ldots, q_n)$ denote two complete sets of probabilities ($\sum p_i = \sum q_i = 1$). The relative entropy $H(\mathscr{P}//\mathscr{Q})$ of β with respect to α is defined by the expression

$$H(\mathscr{P}//\mathscr{Q}) := \sum_{i=1}^{n} q_i \ln \frac{q_i}{p_i} . \qquad (2.10.1) \quad \square$$

Motivation. The following example provides the heuristics of this definition.

i) Consider a set $E := \{e_1, e_2, \ldots, e_N\}$ of N elements e_i, each characterized by its position in E. If we randomly choose one element of E, the index of this element is a random variable X whose the Shannonian entropy is $H(X) = \ln N$.

ii) Assume now that we have a partition $E_1, E_2, \ldots, E_n$ of E, that is to say, $\sum E_i = E$, $E_i \cap E_j = \varnothing$, $\forall i, j$. We can then define any element of E, by the number Y of the set E_k where it occurs, and by its number (position) Z in E_k. We shall denote by $N_1, N_2, \ldots, N_n$ the numbers of elements in $E_1, E_2, \ldots, E_n$ respectively, and we define $p_i := N_i/N$, $i = 1, 2, \ldots, n$.

iii) Let $E' \subset E$ denote a non-empty subset of E with N' elements, and let N'_k denote the number of elements in $E' \cap E_k$. We then pose the following problem:

An element of E is chosen at random, and we know that it occurs in E'; given this "information", how do we define our new uncertainty about Y? To this end, we shall proceed as follows.

iv) The experiment which consists of determining whether $e_x \in E'$ or $e_x \notin E'$ involves the uncertainty $\ln(N/N')$; and the latter will be decomposed into two components: first the uncertainty about Y, which is $H(\beta//\alpha)$, and second the uncertainty about Z given Y. This last entropy is merely a conditional entropy in the Shannon sense, namely, one has

$$\sum_{i=1}^{n} q_i \ln \frac{N_i}{N'_i} \quad \text{with} \quad q_i := \frac{N'_i}{N'} . \qquad (2.10.2)$$

Clearly, q_i is the probability that the considered element belongs to E_i given that it is an element of E'. We then have the equation

$$\ln \frac{N}{N'} = H(\beta//\alpha) + \sum_{i=1}^{n} q_i \ln \frac{N_i}{N'_i} ; \qquad (2.10.3)$$

and, on noting that $NN'_i/N'N_i = q_i/p_i$ we obtain (2.10.1). $\qquad \square$

2.10.2 A Few Comments

Basically, $\mathscr{P}$ is the *prior probability distribution* of the discrete random variable Y, and $\mathscr{Q}$, is its *posterior probability distribution* given the observation $e_x \in E$.

One can show that $H(\mathscr{P}//\mathscr{Q}) \geqslant 0$. This being so, expanding the expression of $H(\mathscr{P}//\mathscr{Q})$ yields the new form

$$H(\mathscr{P}//\mathscr{Q}) = \sum_{i=1}^{m} q_i \ln p_i - H(\beta) \qquad (2.10.4)$$

which can be thought of as a deviation from $H(\beta)$.

Some authors claim that the relative entropy is one of the most important concepts in information theory, and, to some extent, that it may be considered as the basic notion from where one can derive all the others. See for instance [2.11].

Remark. Sometimes one refers to $H(\mathscr{P}//\mathscr{Q})$ as the *divergence* between $\mathscr{P}$ and $\mathscr{Q}$; but we point out that *Kullback* had already used this term to define the quantity

$$D(\mathscr{P}, \mathscr{Q}) := H(\mathscr{P}//\mathscr{Q}) + H(\mathscr{Q}//\mathscr{P}) \tag{2.10.5}$$

which looks like a distance between two probability distributions.

2.11 Further Measures of Uncertainty

2.11.1 Entropy of Degree c

In the Sect. 2.6, we saw how the Shannon definition of entropy has been generalized in different ways merely by using different prior sets of axioms which characterize measures of uncertainty. In a similar manner, some mathematicians started from prior properties for transinformation and then derived generalized uncertainty functions (see for instance [2.12]). One of these generalizations is the following:

Definition 2.11.1. A measure of uncertainty is the entropy of order defined by *Daroczy* [2.13] as

$$H^c(\alpha) := \frac{\sum\limits_{i=1}^{m} p_i^c - 1}{2^{1-c} - 1} , \qquad c \neq 1 . \tag{2.11.1} \quad \square$$

This is obviously related to the Renyi entropy $H_c(\alpha)$ of (2.9.1) by the relation

$$H_c(\alpha) = \frac{1}{1-c} \ln[(2^{1-c} - 1)H^c(\alpha) + 1] . \tag{2.11.2}$$

But despite this apparent equivalence, the Daroczy entropy, although it is not additive, has some properties that the Renyi entropy does not, mainly it is subadditive, whereas $H_c(\alpha)$ is not, and this characteristic justifies its use in certain problems such as feature selection.

2.11.2 Quadratic Entropy

Definition 2.11.2. The quadratic entropy is defined as

$$H_Q(\alpha) := \sum\limits_{i=1}^{m} p_i(1 - p_i) . \tag{2.11.3} \quad \square$$

It was first used in theoretical physics, by Fermi for example, and more recently it was applied in the framework of risk evaluation for the nearest neighbour classification rule [2.14]. The term "quadratic entropy" was suggested by *Vajda* [2.15], and this entropy has been analyzed by *Ito* [2.16] and *Devijver* [2.17].

2.11.3 R-norm Entropy

This entropy is defined for all $R \neq 1$ by the following formula [2.18]:

$$H_R(\alpha) = \frac{R}{R-1} \left[1 - \left(\sum_{i=1}^{n} p_i^R \right)^{1/R} \right], \tag{2.11.4}$$

and formulas for converting the Renyi and Daroczy entropies into the R-norm entropies are also given in [2.18].

2.11.4 Effective Entropy

In an attempt to define a model of negative information, we [2.19] used a measure of uncertainty defined as follows.

Let X denote a discrete random variable which (theoretically) takes the values $x_1, x_2, \ldots, x_m$ with probabilities $p_1, p_2, \ldots, p_m$. We decompose the practical observation of X into two stages.

First, we assume that $X \in L(x_i)$ with the probability p_i, where $L(x_i)$ denotes the ith interval of the sets $\{L(x_1), L(x_2), \ldots, L(x_m)\}$ of intervals indexed by x_i. The Shannon entropy of this experiment is $H(X)$.

Second, given that X is known to be in the ith interval, we determine its exact position in $L(x_i)$ and we assume that the entropy of this experiment is $U(x_i)$.

We then have the global entropy

$$H_e(X) := H(L, X \in L) = H(L) + H(X/L) \tag{2.11.5}$$

$$= H(X) + \sum_{i=1}^{m} p_i U(x_i) \tag{2.11.6}$$

This entropy is referred to as the *effective* entropy $H_e(X)$ of X.

As such, this derivation is basically a physical approach and it is quite meaningful and realistic from a practical standpoint. In fact, what we have used is merely a randomization of the individual events $X = x_i$, $i = 1, 2, \ldots, m$, to account for an additional uncertainty due to the observer himself, irrespective of the definition of the random experiment.

An Important Special Case. Let h_i denote the length of the interval $L(x_i)$, $i = 1, 2, \ldots, m$, and define

$$U(x_i) = \ln h_i \; ;$$

we then have

$$H_e(X) = H(X) + \sum_{i=1}^{m} p_i \ln h_i \tag{2.11.7}$$

$$= -\sum_{i=1}^{m} p_i \ln \frac{p_i}{h_i} \ .$$

(2.11.8)

This expression (2.11.7) will be referred to in the following as the *total entropy* or *complete entropy*.

Three years after our original work, *Aczel* et al. [2.20] derived exactly the same result. Following the usual procedure of mathematicians, they first stated a set of preliminary axioms which should hold for a measure of uncertainty. In particular, they generalized Shannon's recursive relation (2.2.2) in the form

$$H_m \begin{pmatrix} x_1, x_2, \ldots, x_m \\ p_1, p_2, \ldots, p_m \end{pmatrix} = H_{m-1} \begin{pmatrix} x_1 \cup x_2, x_3, \ldots, x_m \\ p_1 + p_2, p_3, \ldots, p_m \end{pmatrix}$$

$$+ (p_1 + p_2) H_2 \begin{pmatrix} x_1, x_2 \\ \dfrac{p_1}{p_1 + p_2}, \dfrac{p_2}{p_1 + p_2} \end{pmatrix}$$

(2.11.9)

and then they mathematically obtained the expression for the effective entropy as a consequence of this prerequisite.

In view of our method of derivation, it is understandable that this axiom should hold; and the question is to determine whether the physical or the mathematical approach is the best.

Our claim is that the usual Shannonian model, together with a suitable physical framework, is quite sufficient to tackle this kind of problem in a meaningful way.

2.12 Entropies of Continuous Variables

Our main purpose in the present section is to examine the possible extensions of discrete entropies to the case of continuous random experiments or continuous random variables. Such a generalization involves theoretical difficulties of paramount importance, and one may even claim that discrete entropies and continuous entropies are fundamentally different in their nature and, to some extent, in their meanings.

2.12.1 Continuous Shannon Entropy

Using a straightforward formal generalization, Shannon introduced the following definition.

Definition 2.12.1. Let X denote a continuous scalar-valued random variable with the probability density $p(x)$. The entropy $H(X)$ of X is then defined as

$$H(X) = -k \int_{-\infty}^{+\infty} p(x) \ln p(x) \, dx$$

(2.12.1)

where k denotes a positive constant that depends on the measurement units.   □

Here again, $H(X)$ (which is sometimes referred to as Boltzmann entropy) is a measure of the amount of uncertainty involved in X.

Important Remark. It should be noted that the continuous entropy is not the limiting value of the discrete entropy obtained by discretizing the real axis into intervals ε, and then letting the latter tend to zero. Indeed, consider the uniform distribution over the range $[a, b]$, $a < b$; we then have

$$p(x) = \frac{1}{b-a} , \qquad a \leqslant x \leqslant b \tag{2.12.2a}$$

$$= 0 , \qquad x \notin [a, b] \tag{2.12.2b}$$

therefore

$$H(X) = \ln(b - a) . \tag{2.12.3}$$

We now partition the range $[a, b]$ in m equal subintervals to obtain the discrete distribution $(p_1, p_2, \ldots, p_m) = (1/m, 1/m, 1/m)$ whose the entropy is

$$H_m = \ln m .$$

As a result, one has $\lim_{m \to \infty} H_m, m \uparrow \infty$ which is not $\ln(b - a)$. $\qquad \square$

This very simple example illustrates the deep difference of nature between discrete entropy and continuous entropy.

In fact, on a theoretical basis, this is a question relevant to the matter of the absolute continuity of a measure with respect to another one; a continuous probability density is not absolutely continuous with respect to a discrete density, so that we cannot compare a continuous entropy with a discrete one. $\qquad \square$

2.12.2 Some Properties of Continuous Entropy

We shall mention only the two main properties which emphasize the differences between discrete entropy and continuous entropy.

i) While the entropy of a discrete variable is always positive, the entropy of a continuous one may be positive or negative as it is illustrated by the example in (2.12.3).

ii) Assume that we make the change of variable $X = g(Y)$; where g is a differentiable function, then the entropies $H(X)$ and $H(Y)$ are related by the equation:

$$H(Y) = H(X) - \int_{-\infty}^{+\infty} p(g(y))g'(y) \ln |g'(y)| \, dy . \tag{2.12.4}$$

Proof. One can show easily, for instance by making the change of variable $x = g(y)$ in the integral $\int p(x) \, dx = 1$, that the probability density $q(y)$ of Y is $p(g(y))|g'(y)|$.

Next we use this expression for $q(y)$ to calculate the entropy $H(Y)$ of Y and we remark that the result so obtained involves the integral

$$\int_{-\infty}^{+\infty} p(g(y))|g'(y)| \ln p(g(y)) \, dy = H(X) \; . \qquad (2.12.5) \quad \square$$

As a special case, given a constant α, one has

$$H(X + a) = H(X) \qquad (2.12.6)$$

$$H(aX) = H(X) + \ln a \; . \qquad (2.12.7)$$

Comments. These two properties (i) and (ii) can be very troublesome when using definition 2.12.1 as a measure of uncertainty, and some scientists even claim that they are sufficient to disqualify expression (2.12.1) as a basis for an information theory of continuous variables. We believe that we must be very cautious with regard to this point, but should not reject this model out of hand. In fact, on looking more closely, (2.12.1) could turn out to be very interesting.

It turns out that the major drawback of the continuous entropy as expressed by (2.12.1) is that the value $H(X) = -\infty$ does not characterize a deterministic event only, but refers to any discrete probability distribution. If we consider a random variable that is continuous everywhere except at a given point x_0 where one has $\Pr\{X = x_0\} \neq 0$, then $H(X) = -\infty$. In our opinion, the main defect of this measure of uncertainty is not the fact that it may take on the value $-\infty$, but rather that it cannot absolutely characterize a deterministic event.

Other authors state that the property expressed by (2.12.4) is also a serious defect of the continuous Shannonian entropy. However, if we look more closely at this formula, it merely expresses the fact that a change of variable modifies the initial amount of uncertainty involved in X, and this is a real physical property which is easy to observe! Indeed if we make the transformation $Y = aX$ with $a = 0$, there is no uncertainty on Y and one should have $H(Y) = -\infty$; in effect, (2.11.7) yields this result. It would be the invariance of the entropy which would be wrong!

As a matter of fact, the term $\ln|g'(y)|$ in (2.12.4) is related to the amount of uncertainty involved in the pattern, i.e., to the form of the curve defined by the equation $x = g(y)$; and the measure of this uncertainty is an open problem in information theory.

As the last remark, we point out that if we consider the transformation $X \to Y$, that is to say, if we put $y = h(x)$, then one has

$$H(Y) = H(X) + \int_{-\infty}^{+\infty} p(x) \ln|h'(x)| \, dx \; . \qquad (2.12.8) \quad \square$$

2.12.3 Continuous Transinformation

Given the continuous entropy defined by the expression (2.12.1) one may derive continuous transinformation in a similar way to discrete transinformation.

i) Let $Y \in \mathbb{R}$ denote another random variable with the probability density $q(y)$; and let $r(x, y)$ denote the joint probability density of the pair (X, Y). The entropy $H(X, Y)$ of (X, Y) is

$$H(X, Y) = - \int\limits_{-\infty}^{+\infty} r(x, y) \ln r(x, y) \, dx \, dy \ . \tag{2.12.9}$$

ii) Let $q(y/x)$ denote the conditional probability of Y given x, clearly $p(x, y) \, dx \, dy = p(x) q(y/x) \, dx \, dy$, then the conditional entropy $H(Y/X)$ of Y given X is

$$H(Y/X) = \int\limits_{-\infty}^{+\infty} \int\limits_{-\infty}^{+\infty} r(x, y) \ln q(y/x) \, dy \, dx \tag{2.12.10}$$

and one has

$$H(Y/X) \leqslant H(Y) \ . \tag{2.12.11}$$

therefore we can define

Definition 2.12.2. The transinformation or transmission or mutual information $I(Y/X)$ between X and Y is defined by the expression

$$I(Y/X) := H(Y) - H(Y/X) \tag{2.12.12}$$

$$= \int\limits_{-\infty}^{+\infty} \int\limits_{-\infty}^{+\infty} r(x, y) \ln \frac{r(x, y)}{p(x) q(y)} \, dx \, dy \ . \tag{2.12.13} \quad \square$$

The expression (2.12.13) results from the equation

$$q(y) = \int\limits_{-\infty}^{+\infty} r(x, y) \, dx \ . \tag{2.12.14}$$

iii) One has

$$H(Y/X) = H(X/Y) \tag{2.12.15}$$

and therefore

$$H(Y/X) = H(X) + H(Y) - H(X, Y) \ . \tag{2.12.16}$$

2.12.4 Further Extensions

Formally, in analogy with the procedure we used to generalize the Shannon entropy, we can define the continuous relative entropy

$$H(q//p) = \int\limits_{-\infty}^{+\infty} q(x) \ln \frac{q(x)}{p(x)} \, dx \ , \tag{2.12.17}$$

the continuous Renyi entropy

$$H_c(X) = \frac{1}{1 - c} \ln \left(\int\limits_{-\infty}^{+\infty} p^c(x) \, dx \right) , \tag{2.12.18}$$

the continuous structural entropy of degree c

$$H^c(X) := \frac{\int\limits_{-\infty}^{+\infty} p^c(x)\, dx - 1}{2^{1-c} - 1} \; , \qquad c \neq 1 \; , \tag{2.12.19}$$

and the continuous quadratic entropy

$$H_Q(X) := \int\limits_{-\infty}^{+\infty} p(x)[1 - p(x)]\, dx \; . \tag{2.12.20}$$

2.13 Hatori's Derivation of Continuous Entropy

As has been mentioned, Shannon defined $H(X)$ by a formal generalization, without using a set of preliminary axioms which would characterize in advance the concept of uncertainty in the continuous case. But later, *Hatori* [2.21] proposed such an approach which we shall outline in the following.

Preliminary Definitions and Notation. In the following, we shall use the vector notation, and we shall consider the vector $X^t := (X_1, X_2, \ldots, X_n)$, where the superscript t denotes the transpose, with the probability density function $p(x)$. We shall use $\varepsilon_D(x)$ to denote the uniform probability distribution on the measurable set $D \in \mathbb{R}^n$, in the Lebesgue sense. Namely

$$\varepsilon_D(x) = \begin{cases} 1/\int dx, & x \in D \\ 0, & x \notin D \; . \end{cases} \tag{2.13.1a} \tag{2.13.1b}$$

Lastly, we shall denote by $f(x_1, x_2, \ldots, x_k)$ and $g_k(x_{k+1}, x_{k+2}, \ldots, x_n)$ the density of $(X_1, X_2, \ldots, X_k)$ and the conditional density of $(X_{k+1}, X_{k+2}, \ldots, X_n)$.
  This being so, we have the following result.

Theorem 2.13.1. Assume that the following axioms are satisfied;

(H1): The entropy $H(X)$ is a function $U(p)$ of p only;
(H2): If $p(x)$ is a probability density in $\mathbb{R}^n$, if $p(x) \notin \varepsilon_D$ anywhere except on a set with measure zero, and if the domain of $p(x)$ is contained in D, then one has $U(p) < U(\varepsilon_D)$;
(H3): The following relation holds,

$$H(X) = H(X_1, X_2, \ldots, X_k) + H(X_{k+1}, X_{k+2}, \ldots, X_n/X_1, X_2, \ldots, X_k) \; , \tag{2.13.2}$$

or equivalently,

$$U(p) = U(f) + \int\limits_{\mathbb{R}^k} U(g_k) f(x_1, x_2, \ldots, x_k)\, dx_1\, dx_2 \ldots dx_k \; ; \tag{2.13.3}$$

(H4): If $p(x)$ takes on a finite number of values $c_1, c_2, \ldots, c_m$; and if we denote by μ_j the measure

$$\mu_j = \int_{A_j} dx \; ; \qquad A_j = \{x \mid p(x) = c_j\} \; , \qquad j = 1, 2, \ldots, m \; ; \qquad (2.13.4)$$

then $U(p)$ is a function of $c_1, c_2, \ldots, c_m$ and $\mu_1, \mu_2, \ldots, \mu_m$ only; it does not depend upon the dimension n of the space, and we have

$$U(p) = -\lambda \int_{\mathbb{R}^n} p(x) \ln p(x) \, dx \qquad (2.13.5)$$

where λ is a positive constant. □

Proof. Step 1: We first show that when $p(x)$ is a uniform distribution, then one has

$$U(p) = -\lambda \ln p \; . \qquad (2.13.6)$$

i) Let $E(p)$ denote the entropy function of the uniform distribution $\varepsilon_D(x)$ defined by (2.13.1) but for $x \in \mathbb{R}$. Clearly, $E(p)$ is a special case of $U(p)$.

ii) Given the cartesian product $Q := \prod_1^r [0, 1/p]$, one has

$$\varepsilon_{Q(x)} = \begin{cases} p^r, & x \in Q \\ 0, & x \notin Q \end{cases} \qquad \begin{array}{l} (2.13.7a) \\ (2.13.7b) \end{array}$$

so that

$$U(\varepsilon_Q) = E(p^r) \; .$$

iii) Next, (2.13.2) of axiom (H3) yields

$$H(X_1, X_2, \ldots, X_n) = \sum_{i=1}^{n} H(X_i) \; ,$$

therefore we obtain the equation

$$E(p^r) = rE(p) \; , \qquad r > 1 \; . \qquad (2.13.8)$$

iv) In order to show that (2.13.8) is also satisfied for negative r, we proceed as follows. We consider the set $Q' := [0, p] \times [0, 1/p]$ which provides

$$U(\varepsilon_{Q'}) = U(\varepsilon_{[0, p]}) + U(\varepsilon_{[0, 1/p]})$$

and therefore the relation

$$E(1) = E(p) + E(1/p) \; .$$

But according to (2.13.8) one has $E(1) = 0$, and therefore

$$E(p^{-1}) = -E(p) \; . \qquad (2.13.9)$$

v) We now apply (2.13.8) to (p^{-1}), and on taking account of (2.13.9) we obtain

$$E(p^{-r}) = E((p^{-1})^r) = rE(p^{-1}) = -rE(p) \; , \qquad r \geqslant 1$$

so that (2.13.8) is satisfied for both positive and negative r.

vi) One can show, and here we shall take it for granted, that the function $E(p)$ which satisfies (2.13.8) for $r \geqslant 0$ and $r < 0$ is

$$E(p) = -\lambda \ln p , \qquad \lambda \geqslant 0 . \tag{2.13.10}$$

Step 2: (i) We now consider a general density function $p(x)$, $x \in \mathbb{R}^n$. Let $Z := (X, X_{n+1})$ denote the $\mathbb{R}^{n+1}$-vector whose the probability density is uniform on the set

$$S := \{(x_1, \ldots, x_n, x_{n+1}) | 0 \leqslant x_{n+1} \leqslant p(x_1, \ldots, x_n)\} .$$

As a result of the relation

$$\int_Q dx \, dx_{n+1} = \int_{\mathbb{R}^n} p(x) \, dx = 1$$

one has

$$\varepsilon_Q(z) = \begin{cases} 1, & z \in S \\ 0, & z \notin S . \end{cases}$$

It follows that

$$H(X_1, \ldots, X_n, X_{n+1}) = U(\varepsilon_Q) = E(1) = 0 . \tag{2.13.11}$$

ii) Next, the conditional distribution of X_{n+1} given that $X_1 = x_1, \ldots, X_n = x_n$, is the uniform distribution over the interval $[0, p(x_1, \ldots, x_n)]$, so that, by virtue of (2.12.10), one has

$$H(X_{n+1}/X) = \lambda \int_{\mathbb{R}^n} p(x) \ln p(x) \, dx . \tag{2.13.12}$$

This being so, according to (2.13.2) of axiom (H3) and to (2.13.11), one has

$$H(X_1, \ldots, X_m) = -H(X_{n+1}/(X_1, \ldots, X_m))$$

and on taking account of (2.13.12) we straightforwardly obtain (2.13.5).   □

2.14 Information Without Probability

2.14.1 A Functional Approach

A long time ago, some authors (see for instance [2.22]) proposed to use the mutual information $I(X/Y)$ as a measure of the distance $d(X, Y)$,

$$d(X, Y) := H(X) + H(Y) - H(X, Y) , \tag{2.14.1}$$

between two elements X and Y of a system S defined by a family of random variables. It has also been suggested that the quantity

$$d'(X, Y) = 2H(X, Y) - H(X) - H(Y) \tag{2.14.2}$$

could define an informational distance between X and Y.

The basic idea of information without probability is to generalize the distances (2.14.1) or (2.14.2) in such a manner that they apply to a framework which does not necessarily involve probability. *Kampe de Feriet* et al. [2.23] were possibly the first authors to consider such an approach, and we shall now summarize the main features of their model.

i) Let E denote an ordered finite set. We set

$$X^- := \{U \in E: U \leqslant X\} , \qquad X^+ := \{Z \in E: X \leqslant Z\} . \tag{2.14.3}$$

Definition 2.14.1. E is a lower filtering set if and only if for every $X \in E$ and $Y \in E$ there exists $X^- \cap Y^-$. Likewise, E is an upper filtering set if and only if for every $X \in E$ and $Y \in E$ there exist $X^+ \cap Y^+$.   □

Definition 2.14.2. A generalized entropy J is a non-negative real-valued mapping which is decreasing and bounded in E.   □

Definition 2.14.3. For every $X \in E$ and $Y \in E$, we set

$$J_T(X, Y) = \inf J(U) \geqslant 0 , \qquad U \in X^- \cap Y^- \tag{2.14.4}$$

when J and E are lower filtering; and

$$J_R(X, Y) = \sup J(Z) \geqslant 0 , \qquad Z \in X^+ \cap Y^+ \tag{2.14.5}$$

when J and E are upper filtering.

One can then show that the quantity $d(X, Y)$ defined as

$$d(X, Y) := 2J_T(X, Y) - J(X) - J(Y) \tag{2.14.6}$$

$$= J(X) + J(Y) - 2J_R(X, Y) \tag{2.14.7}$$

$$= J_T(X, Y) - J_R(X, Y) \tag{2.14.8}$$

has all the properties required by a metric distance.   □

This is, in essence, the point of departure of a possible information theory without probability. This approach is basically algebraic, but to date, it has not been sufficiently expanded to provide us with a fair assessment of its potential value.

In our opinion, the main advantage of such a theory would be the following. Insofar as one assumes that information is conveyed by *natural languages* involving both syntax and semantics, it may be interesting to derive an information modelling without probability, which could be a valuable framework to represent this semantics. But at present this remains an open problem.

2.14.2 Relative Information

The problem of defining relative information appears when we take account of the meaning of information, for the simple reason that the semantic content of a given message depends upon the observer who receives it.

Haken [2.24] recently outlined an approach which is based upon the concept of attractors. The message is received in different ways by different attractors, and its relative importance is defind by the expression

$$p_j = \sum_k L_{jk} p_k'$$

where p_k' is essentially equivalent to a probability. According to Haken, this concept may serve as a starting point for the development of a dynamical information theory.

2.15 Information and Possibility

2.15.1 A Few Prerequisites

The notion of possibility distributions associated with a set was proposed by *Zadeh* [2.25] in his attempt to develop a theory of possibility within the general framework of the theory of fuzzy sets. He also introduced the concept of possibility measures, which is a special case of the fuzzy measures proposed by *Sugeno* [2.26].

Let X denote a crisp (nonfuzzy) set and let $\mathscr{P}(X)$ denote the (crisp) power set of X. A *fuzzy measure* is then a function

$$m: \mathscr{P}(X) \to [0,1]$$

which has the following properties:

(m1) $m(\varnothing) = 0$

(m2) $A \subseteq B \Rightarrow m(A) \leqslant m(B)$

(m3) $A_1 \subseteq A_2 \subseteq \cdots \Rightarrow m\left(\bigcup_{i=1}^{\infty} A_i\right) = \lim_{i \to \infty} m(A_i)$

(m4) $A_1 \supseteq A_2 \supseteq \cdots \Rightarrow m\left(\bigcap_{i=1}^{\infty} A_i\right) = \lim_{i \to \infty} m(A_i)$.

A possibility measure is a function

$$\pi: \mathscr{P}(X) \to [0,1]$$

which has the following properties

(Π1) $\pi(\varnothing) = 0$

(Π2) $A \subseteq B \Rightarrow \pi(A) \leqslant \pi(B)$

(Π3) $\pi\left(\bigcup_{i \in I} A_i\right) = \sup_{i \in I} \pi(A_i)$.

Any possibility measure can be uniquely determined by a *possibility distribution function*

$$f: X \to [0, 1]$$

by using the definition

$$\pi(A) =: \sup f(x) , \qquad x \in A$$

where $A \subset X$.

2.15.2 A Measure of Uncertainty Without Probability

In this framework, *Higashi* et al. [2.27] defined a measure of uncertainty as follows.

i) For each possibility distribution $g = (\gamma_1, \gamma_2, \dots, \gamma_n)$ and each $l \in [0, 1]$, let $c(g, l)$ denote the function defined as

$$c(g, l) = \{i \in N_n | \gamma_i \geq l\} .$$

This function is called an *l*-cut function and the set $c(g, l)$ is called an *l*-cut of g.

ii) Define $l_g := \max_i \gamma_i$.

iii) Let gl_k, l_{k+1} denote (l_k, l_{k+1})-crisp approximation of g.
U must coincide with the Hartley uncertainty for crisp possibility distributions, hence

$$U(gl_k, l_{k+1}) = \ln |c(g, l_{k+1})|$$

Taking the mean of uncertainties for all (l_k, l_{k+1})-crisp approximations of g with weights representing the gap between the edge value of l_k and l_{k+1}, we obtain

$$U(g) := \frac{1}{l_g} \sum_{j=1}^{r-1} (l_{j+1} - l_j) \ln |c(g, l_{j+1})| \tag{2.15.1}$$

or, in the continuous case,

$$U(g) := \frac{1}{l_g} \int_0^{l_g} \ln |c(g, l)| \, dl . \tag{2.15.2}$$

This definition, which is a direct extension of Hartley's measure of information could be a point of departure to an information theory without probability.

2.16 Conclusions

The conclusion of this short review may be summarized as follows: In its present status, information theory is a subject that has been mainly investigated by mathematicians concerned with its generalization in rigorous formal ways, irrespective of any extension of the model itself in order to enlarge its area of possible applications.

Most of this work endeavours to derive new concepts of uncertainty functions, but despite their generalizing features, from a practical standpoint, these entropies cannot be substituted for the Shannon entropy for the very reason that the latter has nice properties, mainly its strong additivity, that the others do not. In addition, Shannon entropy has provided amazing results of a general nature which considerably reinforce its reputation. Two examples are the following: firstly, one can prove the central limit theorem, which is of fundamental importance in probability theory, by means of this entropy; secondly, Shannon entropy is strongly related to the thermodynamic entropy in physics via the famous Boltzmann equation; and this relation demonstrates a deep similarity which, in our opinion, is not merely fortuitous.

As a matter of fact, the initial purpose of Shannon's theory was to treat technical transmission problems; we recall that the title of the Shannon paper is "A Mathematical Theory of *Communication*", and in fact it has been applied successfully to problems related to this question. But, and this is of importance, whenever it has been used in areas which are not directly relevant to transmission, for instance linguistics and biology, the results obtained were only partial and sometimes quite unsatisfactory.

In our opinion, the main reason for this partial failure is the fact that, basically, the model of language which is considered by Shannon information involves symbols only, irrespective of any meaning they may have, while the languages which appears in other areas deal with both syntax and semantics.

So our claim is the following: the present information theory, based on Shannon entropy, is quite satisfactory if it is considered as a theory of symbols; and the main purpose of any revision of this theory should be the introduction of semantics in order that it may apply to other areas of science that deal with natural languages, that is to say, those involving both syntax and semantics.

3. A Critical Review of Shannon Information Theory

In the preceding chapter, we summarized the basic elements of information theory, and we now proceed to examine and analyze the main characteristics of this theory. The term "critical" in the title of the chapter implies simply that we shall present a review of the main features for and against the theory. To support the theory in its present form, one can mention Shannon results on the capacity of a channel, the Boltzmann equation, and the fact that one can prove the central limit theorem in probability by using the properties of entropy only. Against the present form of the theory we have the apparent discrepancy between discrete entropy and continuous entropy, the absence of a concept of negative information to describe information lost, and the fact that the model does not take explicitly into account syntax and semantics. In the present chapter, we shall review these features and one of our conclusions will be as follows: Contrary to what some scientists are inclined to believe, we maintain that the continuous entropy is soundly defined, and that it merely remains to exhibit the differences in physical nature between discrete entropy and continuous entropy.

3.1 Introduction

Now and then, one can read that the so-called Information Theory is not a complete theory in a final form, and some scientists would even claim that a useful information theory does not exist. We must agree that the concept of information is not easy to define, or to comprehend, as has been pointed out by *Thom* [3.1] and *Jumarie* [3.2].

With the recent explosion of new research interest in systems, cybernetics, organization, self-organization, and so on, information and information theory are very much in fashion, and the latter has been applied to a broad range of topics with variable success and some failures. This recent popularity cannot be considered as an argument against this theory and should rather be thought of as reflecting a great potential importance, the exact significance of which is not yet completely clarified. On the other hand, the fact that the informational entropy can be derived by means of a rigorous axiomatization [3.3, 4] does not entitle us to use it anywhere. Particular care is needed in those areas which are not directly related to technical communication.

The present information theory, as initiated by Shannon, involves two main restrictions of paramount importance which we must keep in mind.

i) The informational entropy is defined by means of probability and it is likely that we shall eventually need a more general concept of information which does not necessarily involve probability.

ii) As pointed out by Shannon himself, his theory does not deal with semantics. A symbol is a symbol, and it is considered as such irrespective of any meaning it may have, and irrespective of any language system (universe of discourse). Here again, it is likely that we shall need an extension of this model to suitably tackle those problems which explicitly involve both syntax and semantics, as in biology and linguistics for instance.

These restrictions do not invalidate the Shannon theory as some authors claim, but rather they invite us to derive generalizations of which this theory should be a special case that is valid under certain conditions.

In the following, we shall review the present information theory from a critical standpoint. By this, we mean that our purpose is not only to examine those questions which at first glance cannot be addressed by the theory, but also to exhibit the properties and results which support the model. These indicate that the model needs to be generalized, but that it cannot be discarded. Indeed, the relation of the informational entropy to the thermodynamic entropy, the fact that we can prove the famous central limit theorem in probability by using the informational entropy, the mathematical properties of the continuous informational entropy, all these results speak in favor of the theory, as we shall show.

3.2 On the Invariance of Measures of Information

In this section, our main purpose is to recall that the amount of uncertainty involved in an informational source depends heavily upon the definition of the latter, that is to say on its the mathematical representation. This is to be expected, since we can consider this definition as being the result of the observation of the source by the observer.

As an example, consider a curve in $\mathbb{R}^2$. One may assume that it contains an absolute amount of uncertainty independent of any coordinate frame, which would be obtained by using its intrinsic equation for instance. This uncertainty could be thought of as being the maximum amount of information available in the curve when considered as an informational source.

Now assume that we define this curve in cartesian coordinates by the equation $y = f(x)$; it is clear that if the measure of uncertainty we have at hand is expressed by means of $f(\cdot)$, then it will depend upon the coordinate axes themselves. For instance, the respective uncertainties involved by the straightlines $y = 2x$ and $y = 0$ would not be the same. Clearly the coordinate frame plays the role of an observer. If we rotate these axes to have the new coordinates (x', y') given by

$$x' = x \cos \theta + y \sin \theta \tag{3.2.1}$$

$$y' = -x \sin \theta + y \cos \theta , \tag{3.2.2}$$

then the equation of the curve becomes

$$x' \sin \theta + y' \cos \theta = f(x' \cos \theta - y' \sin \theta) \qquad (3.2.3)$$

which is obviously different from $y' = f(x')$.

A similar remark applies to scalar valued random variables. Assume that we measure $g(X)$ instead of X; then the map $g(\cdot)$ is an observer exactly like the reference frame above and it may thus affect the amount of information we receive from X.

3.3 On the Modelling of Negative Transinformation

It is by now taken for granted that, in order to fruitfully apply the Shannon theory to topics which are not strictly technical such as biology or human sciences, we need a concept of transinformation which may be positive or negative in order to suitably describe the phenomenon of information loss. But what we want to show in this section is that even in technical problems or in cases which on the surface appear purely technical, we still need negative transinformation. We believe that this missing feature could explain why this theory did not succeed in the design of encoding processes, where it has been superseded by, for example, algebraic models.

3.3.1 Classification of Terms

The present section refers to "negative transinformation" instead of "negative information" mainly to avoid confusion.

Indeed, several scientists consider the entropy $H(\alpha)$ as an amount of information, and strictly speaking this is not wrong. However, it is deeply misleading for the very reason that $H(\alpha)$ is the measure of an amount of information in some special cases only. Basically $H(\alpha)$ defines a degree of uncertainty, and incidentally only this is equivalent to an information! This unfortunate habit originated from the equation

$$I(\alpha/\beta) = H(\alpha) - H(\alpha/\beta) \ ,$$

in which $I(\alpha/\beta)$ is an amount of information, while $H(\alpha)$ and $H(\alpha/\beta)$ measure the respective uncertainties involved in α before and after making the experiment β. Incidentally, when $H(\alpha/\beta) = 0$, that is to say when β does not contain any information about α, then $I(\alpha/\beta) = H(\alpha)$.

Information is no more than a difference of uncertainties, and in the following we shall carefully utilize "uncertainty" and "information" according to their respective meanings, "information" being completely equivalent to "transinformation" in our treatment.

3.3.2 The Problem of Modelling "True" and "False"

In his book, *Brillouin* [3.6] mentions the following problem:

A message M is wired in the form of a telegram. At the end of this telegram a binary digit B is appended, which has the following significance:

0 : everything is wrong, the message should be ignored;
1 : the telegram is correct, you can use it.

How can one describe this situation with the Shannon theory?

At a first glance, one could consider the codeword (M, B) as a whole and ascribe it the value "true" or "false" depending upon the value of B; but in doing so, we would explicitly refer to two spaces of definition: the space of symbols, the syntactic space where the symbol M is defined; and the space of meanings, the semantic space where the meaning of M is given. It is well known that the Shannon theory, in its present form, deals with symbols only, irrespective of any meaning they may have, unless we modify it to enlarge its framework. Indeed, any reference to a semantic space presupposes the explicit introduction of an observer (or likewise a receiver) in the model, and this is outside the scope of the theory.

Assume now that we decompose the observation process into two stages, and in order to simplify matters, assume that there are no transmission errors. In the first stage, we have the message M at hand and we have thus received an amount $I(M/M) = H(M)$ of information. In the second stage, we observe the bit B which is 0, so that the total amount of information that we now have is 0. Clearly, for convenience, we identify the zero state information with the statement "M is false", and in doing so, we explicitly refer to useful information: In other words, there is no information in the message that we can use. If we denote by $I(M/B)$ the amount of information provided by B about M, and if we assume that the additive composition law is valid, then the total amount of information so received about M is $I(M/M) + I(M/B) = 0$, where $I(M/M)$ is the information related to the symbol of M, and $I(M/B)$ is related to the meaning of M. It follows that $I(M/B)$ should be negative. But the conventional information theory for discrete events permits neither negative entropy nor negative information!

The conclusion of this very simple example is clear: we need to enlarge the Shannon theory in order to obtain an information which may be positive or negative. Furthermore it is possible that negative information could appear as a by-product of semantics in information theory, but this is not obvious a priori.

3.3.3 Error-Detecting Codes

In some ways, the above example in Sect. 3.3.2 is reminiscent of the *parity bit* which is appended to the main data, and which is chosen so that the number of 1-bits in the code-word is even (or odd). We shall examine this question for case of *polynomial* or *cyclic redundancy codes*.

Polynomial codes are based upon considering bit strings in the form of polynomials with coefficients defined on the set $\{0, 1\}$. A k-bit message is regarded as the coefficient set of such a polynomial with k terms, ranging from x^{k-1} to x^0. The arithmetic of these polynomials is arithmetic modulo 2. The basic idea of the polynomial code method is the following: First, the sender and the receiver must agree upon a *generator polynomial* $G(x)$, in advance. Assume that a message M with m bits corresponding to the polynomial $M(x)$ is to be sent; one appends a check-sum to the end of the message in such a way that the polynomial represented by the check-summed message is divisible by $G(x)$. When the receiver has the check-summed message at hand, he divides it by $G(x)$. If there is a remainder, then this means that there has been a transmission error.

The algorithm for computing the check-sum is as follows.

i)   Let r denote the degree of $G(x)$. Append r zero bits to the low-order end of the message so that the new message M_a then contains $(m + r)$ bits and corresponds to the polynomial $x^r M(x)$.
ii) Divide, modulo 2, the bit string G corresponding to $G(x)$ into the bit string M_a.
iii) Substract, modulo 2, the remainder (which is always r or fewer bits) from the bit string M_a. The result is the check-summed message to be transmitted.
iv) At the receiving station, the receiver works in the opposite way. He divides G into the received message, and if the remainder is not zero, then a transmission error has occurred.

A Few Comments. The additional bits which are appended to M to yield M_a are somewhat similar to parity bits and in this way, they can be thought of as involving positive or negative information depending on whether or not there is a transmission error.

An alternative point of view is the following: At stage (ii) above, the sender performs the operation

$$M_a = GQ + R$$

so that the signal which is effectively sent is $M_a - R$ and the receiver calculates

$$\frac{M_a - R}{G} = Q$$

to check whether the message involves transmission errors or not. Thus, from an information theoretical standpoint, the problem is then to define the amount of information involved in the operation that consists of making the division $(M_a - R)/Q$. More generally, given a random variable X with entropy $H(X)$, what is the amount of uncertainty involved in $f(X)$? At first sight, this uncertainty should be the combination, in a sense to be defined, of the uncertainty involved in X on the one hand, and of some uncertainty $H(f)$ which characterizes the mapping $f(\cdot)$, on the other hand.

The definition of the entropy of a continuous variable contains a possible measure of $H(f)$ (see Sect. 3.6), but discrete entropy does not, and we believe that this is the very reason why the concept is not of value in the algebraic theory of encoding.

The question is then the following: Would it not be possible to modify the definition of discrete entropy in order that it deals properly with the uncertainty involved in a map, so that we are in a position to estimate how a given transformation affects the uncertainty of a random variable?

We shall meet this problem again in later chapters.

3.4 On the Symmetry of Transinformation

A property of transinformation that is somewhat puzzling is the symmetry $I(\alpha/\beta) = I(\beta/\alpha)$. Indeed, it is not immediately obvious that in an actual observation process, the amount of information provided by α about β should be exactly the same as the amount of information provided by β about α. The present section intends to make this point clearer.

3.4.1 A Diverting Example

The following problem is well known.

Problem. Two cities L and T are located close to one another but on opposite sides of a river. All the people who live in L tell lies, while the inhabitants of T always speak the truth. In addition, for various reasons such as leisure or work, people from L may be encounted in T, and vice versa.

A traveller enters one of these cities, but he does not know which one. So, in order to identify this town, he will put a question to the first pedestrain he meets. We assume firstly, that this pedestrian lives necessarily in L or T, and secondly, that he is not very chatty (he is in a hurry) and as a result, he answers with *yes* and *no* only.

The problem is then: (i) what is the minimum number of questions which the traveller has to put in order to establish the name of the city? and (ii) what question(s) must he ask?

Solution. Only one question should be enough, and for instance, one may ask "Do you live in this city?"   □

3.4.2 Application of Information Theory

Strictly speaking, applying the information theory to the above problem provides the theoretical number of questions required, but it does not provide much help as to how to frame the question itself. Let us consider this problem more closely.

i) Let β denote the experiment whose possible outcomes are L and T; of course one has $H(\beta) = \ln 2$. Let α_j denote the jth question the outcome of which is *yes* or *no*.

ii) The traveller puts n questions $\alpha_1 \alpha_2 \ldots \alpha_n$, and β is completely defined when $H(\beta/\alpha_1 \alpha_2 \ldots \alpha_n) = 0$; in which case, according to (3.2.11) one then has

$$H(\beta) = H(\alpha_1 \alpha_2 \ldots \alpha_n) - H(\alpha_1 \alpha_2 \ldots \alpha_n/\beta) \ . \tag{3.4.1}$$

iii) We then have to optimize the right-hand term of (3.4.1). First one must arrange that

$$H(\alpha_1 \alpha_2 \ldots \alpha_n/\beta) = 0 \ , \tag{3.4.2}$$

in other words the questions $\alpha_1, \alpha_2, \ldots, \alpha_n$ should be such that their answers are completely determined by β. The practical meaning of this condition is that the significance of the questions should be strongly related to β; for instance a question like "are you hungry" would be irrelevant.

iv) Once condition (3.4.2) is satisfied, one has

$$H(\beta) = H(\alpha_1 \alpha_2 \ldots \alpha_n)$$

$$= H(\alpha_1) + H(\alpha_2/\alpha_1) + \cdots + H(\alpha_n/\alpha_1 \alpha_2 \ldots \alpha_{n-1}) \ . \tag{3.4.3}$$

This being so, assume that α_1 is chosen in such a way that it achieves its maximum entropy $H(\alpha_1) = \ln 2$; then one would have

$$H(\beta) = H(\alpha_1) \tag{3.4.4}$$

so that the name of the city would be completely determined (subject to the condition that $H(\alpha_1/\beta) = 0$, of course).

A question which complies with all these constraint is the one mentioned in the solution above.   □

3.4.3 On the Symmetry of Transinformation

One of the most disturbing features in our example is the apparent symmetry that the definition of the transinformation exhibits. Clearly, one has

$$I(\beta/\alpha_1 \alpha_2 \ldots \alpha_n) = I(\alpha_1 \alpha_2 \ldots \alpha_n/\beta) \ ,$$

or in words, the amount of information provided by the question about the name of the city is exactly the same as the amount of information provided by the name of the city about these questions.

From a theoretical standpoint, this symmetry is quite understandable, and it is furthermore necessary to ensure the complete determinacy of the problem. Indeed, solving for β is possible when and only when there is a one-to-one correspondence between β and $\alpha_1 \alpha_2 \ldots \alpha_n$ in such a manner that if we formally write $\beta = f(\alpha_1 \alpha_2 \ldots \alpha_n)$, then the equation $\alpha_1 \alpha_2 \ldots \alpha_n = f^{-1}(\beta)$, where $f^{-1}(\cdot)$ holds for the inverse map, would be quite meaningful. This is the absolute viewpoint independent of the presence of any external receiver.

We argue that when a human receiver enters the observation process the matter is quite different. More explicitly, if the person who defines the questions $\alpha_1 \alpha_2 \ldots \alpha_n$ and the person who decodes the answers to these questions are not the same, then it may happen that

$$I(\beta/\alpha_1 \alpha_2 \ldots \alpha_n) \neq I(\alpha_1 \alpha_2 \ldots \alpha_n/\beta) \ ;$$

as is the case for instance when the receiver is unable to decode the answers, that is to say, to determine the correct name of the city. This merely means that then there is not a one-to-one correspondence between β and $\alpha_1 \alpha_2 \ldots \alpha_n$. Clearly the information $I(\beta/\alpha; R)$ depends upon the observer R.

Qualitatively speaking, the rationale for deducing β from $\alpha_1\alpha_2\ldots\alpha_n$ is not necessarily the inverse of the deduction of $\alpha_1\alpha_2\ldots\alpha_n$ from β, and this property is due mainly to the inference of the observer, which may involve subjective factors.

3.4.4 On a Possible Application of Renyi Entropy

In Chap. 2, (2.9.8), we pointed out that one could consider a possible measure of information in the form of the difference $H(\beta) - H_c(\beta)$ between Shannon entropy and Renyi entropy. In such a case c is a parameter which characterizes the state of the observer, for instance the subjectivity of the latter.

Consider the experiments α and β defined in Sect. 2.4, and assume that (β/A_i), that is to say β given A_i is observed with the parameter c. One could then define a transinformation of order c by the expression

$$I_c(\beta/\alpha) := H(\beta) - \sum_{i=1}^{m} p(A_i)H_c(\beta/A_i) \tag{3.4.5}$$

and we would thus have $I_c(\beta/\alpha) > 0$ or $I_c(\beta/\alpha) < 0$ depending upon whether c is larger or smaller than the unity.

In order to obtain a possible practical meaning for c, assume that α is a variable experiment, depending for instance upon an external parameter e, and define

$$c := 1 - \frac{dH(\beta/\alpha; e)}{dH(\alpha; e)} \ . \tag{3.4.6}$$

One then has $I_c(\beta/\alpha) \geqslant 0$ when

$$\frac{dH(\beta/\alpha; e)}{dH(\alpha; e)} \leqslant 0 \tag{3.4.7}$$

and $I_c(\beta/\alpha) \leqslant 0$ when

$$\frac{dH(\beta/\alpha; e)}{dH(\alpha; e)} > 0 \ . \tag{3.4.8}$$

These conditions are quite meaningful from a practical viewpoint: (3.4.7) defines a learning process while (3.4.8) describes confusing effects.

3.5 Entropy and the Central Limit Theorem

One of the most important theorems of probability theory is the so-called "central limit theorem" which states general conditions for the convergence to the normal law. This theorem of course was first established in the framework of the probability theory, but it can also be derived by means of the informational entropy, and this fact in our opinion, supports the validity of the Shannon theory, since it reveals the genuine thermodynamical meaning of this theorem. The purpose of the present section is to comment on this point.

3.5.1 The Central Limit Theorem

The central limit theorem is as follows.

Theorem 3.5.1 [3.7]. Let X_1, X_2, ... be mutually independent one-dimensional random variables with probability distributions F_1, F_2, ... Assume that

$$E(X_k) = 0 , \qquad \text{Var}(X_k) = \sigma_k^2 , \qquad (3.5.1)$$

and define

$$s_n^2 := \sigma_1^2 + \sigma_2^2 + \cdots + \sigma_k^2 . \qquad (3.5.2)$$

Assume that for each $t > 0$

$$\frac{1}{s_n^2} \sum_{k=1}^{n} \int_{|y| > ts_n} y^2 F_k\{dy\} \to 0 \qquad (3.5.3)$$

or, amounting to the same, that

$$\frac{1}{s_n^2} \sum_{k=1}^{n} \int_{|y| < ts_n} y^2 F_k\{dy\} \to 1 . \qquad (3.5.4)$$

The distribution of the normalized sum

$$S_n^* := \frac{X_1 + X_2 + \cdots + X_n}{s_n} \qquad (3.5.5)$$

$$:= \frac{S_n}{s_n} \qquad (3.5.6)$$

then tends to the normal distribution $\frac{1}{\sqrt{2\pi}} \exp(-x^2/2)$ with zero expectation and unit variance. □

The Lindeberg condition (3.5.3) guarantees that the individual variances σ_k^2 are small compared to their sum s_n^2 in the sense that for given $\varepsilon > 0$ and all n sufficiently large

$$\frac{\sigma_k}{s_n} < \varepsilon , \qquad k = 1, \dots, n \qquad (3.5.7)$$

or equivalently,

$$\frac{\sigma_n}{s_n} \downarrow 0 \quad \text{as} \quad s_n \uparrow \infty . \qquad (3.5.8)$$

The ratio σ_n/s_n may be considered as a measure for the contribution of the element X_n to the weighted sum S_n/s_n so that (3.5.8) may be thought of as describing the fact that, asymptotically, S_n/s_n is the sum of many individually negligible components.

3.5.2 An Information-Theoretical Approach to the Central Limit Theorem

Linnik [3.8] derived an information-theoretical proof of the central limit theorem which can be summarized as follows.

i) First, one introduces the function

$$\tilde{H}(X) := H(X) - \ln \sigma \qquad (3.5.9)$$

which measures the deviation of $H(X)$ from the entropy of the normal law which is $\ln \sigma \sqrt{2\pi e}$.

ii) The basic result is the following: one can show that

$$\tilde{H}(S_{n+1}) - \tilde{H}(S_n) = \frac{1}{2}\sigma_{n+1}^2 \left(\int_{-\infty}^{+\infty} \left(\frac{p_n'}{p_n}\right)^2 p_n \, dx - 1 \right) + tB\sigma_{n+1}^2 \qquad (3.5.10)$$

where $p_n(x)$ is the probability density of S_n^*, p_n' is its derivative, B is a bounded constant and t is the parameter of the Lindeberg condition.

iii) The coefficient of $\dfrac{\sigma_{n+1}^2}{2}$ in (3.5.10) is never negative, and the closer it is to zero, the closer $p_n(x)$ is to $g(x) := \exp\left(\dfrac{-x^2}{2}\right)\dfrac{1}{\sqrt{2\pi}}$. More explicitly, one has

$$\lim \int_{-\infty}^{+\infty} p_n(x) \ln \frac{p_n(x)}{g(x)} dx = 0 , \qquad n \uparrow \infty . \qquad (3.5.11)$$

Expressed in words, the information-theoretical meaning of the Lindeberg condition is the following: if it holds individually for X_{n+1}, then at the $(n + 1)$th stage, the deviation $H(S_n)$ increases in proportion to σ_{n+1}^2, and the sum is very close to being normal. □

A different statement of the central limit theorem in the information-theoretical framework is the following.

Theorem 3.5.2 [3.2]. Let $X_1, X_2, \ldots$ be mutually independent one-dimensional random variables with the continuous probability density functions $p_1, p_2, \ldots$. Assume

i) $\sup p_i(x) \leqslant M < +\infty$, $\forall i$, $\qquad (3.5.12)$

ii) $E(X_i) = 0$, $\qquad \text{var}(X_i) = \sigma_i^2$, $\qquad (3.5.13)$

iii) $s_n \uparrow \infty$ as $n \uparrow \infty$, where s_n is defined by (3.5.2),

iv) for every given arbitrary small ε, and all n sufficiently large, one has

$$\frac{\sigma_{n+1}}{s_n} < \varepsilon , \qquad (3.5.14)$$

v) for every n sufficiently large, one has

$$H(S_n) \geqslant \ln s_n \ . \tag{3.5.15}$$

The distribution of the normalized sum S_n^* then converges to the normal distribution with zero expectation and unit variance. □

Note Concerning the Proof. Condition (3.5.15) is $H(S_n^*) \geqslant 0$. The sequence $H(S_n^*)$ is then a monotonically increasing sequence whose upper bound is the entropy of the normal law, and it is therefore sufficient to show that this bound is achieved, which can be proven by using Cramer's theorem, for instance.

One can further show that if the Lindeberg condition is satisfied, then condition (3.5.15) holds. □

3.5.3 Relation with Thermodynamics

Let H denote the informational entropy of the internal state of a gas medium. The thermodynamic entropy S_T of this medium is *defined as*

$$S_T := kH$$

where k is the Boltzmann constant. The second law of thermodynamics states that, for a closed system, one necessarily has

$$dS_T \geqslant 0$$

and in the limiting case of equilibrium,

$$dS_T = 0 \ .$$

This statement is supported by the fact that S_T is related to the complexity H of the system, so that it cannot decrease.

The central limit theorem does not contradict this principle and is actually quite meaningful in thermodynamic terms. Indeed, according to the meaning of the informational entropy one necessarily has $H(S_{n+1}) \geqslant H(S_n)$; but the sequence $\{S_n\}$ has to be considered as an open system. In order to have the equivalent of a closed system, we must consider variables that satisfy some mathematical constraints. So if we consider the normalized sums $\{S_n^*\}$ with unit variance, and if we assume that the variance is a measure of the amount of energy involved in S_n^*, we then have a set of variables with constant energy: $\{S_n^*\}$ can be thought of as a closed system in the thermodynamic sense.

3.5.4 Continuous Entropy Versus Discrete Entropy

The proof of the central limit theorem by means of the informational entropy explicitly uses probability density functions, so that at first sight, it would not seem to hold for the discrete entropy, whose mathematical nature is very different. The fact that we do not have the same difficulty in the probabilistic framework is mainly because of the concept of the Lebesgues-Stieljes integral, which provides us with a uniform approach to probability distributions. But unfortunately, we have no counterpart of this for the entropy which explicitly uses probability density rather than cumulative distribution functions.

Nevertheless, the central limit theorem applies to discrete variables. Therefore, given its genuine practical meaning, we are entitled to think that it should be possible to generalize or to modify the definition of the discrete entropy in order that it provides an information-theoretical proof of the central limit theorem for discrete variables.

3.6 On the Entropy of Continuous Variables

Many scientists claim that the continuous entropy, as defined by Shannon, has some weaknesses. For instance, it may be negative and it is not necessarily invariant upon transformation of a variable; it is therefore not a "suitable measure of information". But one can reply to these criticisms as follows: first, the entropy is a measure of uncertainty rather than information, and second, the above properties are necessary to suitably define a good measure of uncertainty. And to some extent, one could even state that continuous entropy is a better measure of uncertainty than discrete entropy. This remark will become clearer in the following.

3.6.1 The Sign of the Continuous Entropy

Whereas the entropy of a discrete random variable is positive or zero, the entropy of a continuous random variable may be positive or negative. The typical illustrative example of this feature is the variable $X \in \mathbb{R}$ whose distribution $p(x) = 1/(b - a)$ is uniform over the interval $[a, b]$. In this case, one has $H(X) = \ln(b - a)$, so that $H(X)$ is negative when $(b - a)$ is sufficiently small.

This feature by itself would not be of major importance if, for instance, in the continuous framework, an entropy equal to $-\infty$ could be considered as characterizing a deterministic variable; but this is not the case. Indeed, it is sufficient that the cumulative distribution function of the variable X be discontinuous in order to have $H(X) = -\infty$.

As a matter fact, we currently have two different theories: one for discrete random variables, and another for continuous variables, and they cannot be combined in a unified approach. Mathematicians say that this is related to the absolute continuity of one measure with respect to another: a continuous measure cannot be absolutely continuous with respect to a discrete measure.

In practice, we shall thus have to deal either with discrete variables or with continuous variables, and never with both simultaneously. In fact, this is not so restrictive as it may at first appear. Indeed, in a large number of practical cases, the probability density $p(x)$ of the system under consideration satisfies strong continuity requirements, for instance it is the solution of the Fokker-Plank-Kolmogorov partial differential equation, so that we are in the required situation to use the continuous entropy.

3.6.2 A Nice Property of Continuous Entropy

Assume that X is a random vector $X^t = (X_1, X_2, \ldots, X_m)$, and let $H(X)$ denote its entropy

$$H(X) = - \int_{\mathbb{R}^m} p(x) \ln p(x) \, dx \ . \tag{3.6.1}$$

Assume further that we make the transformation $Y = f(X)$, $Y \in \mathbb{R}^m$. The entropy $H(Y)$ of Y is then

$$H(Y) = H(X) + \int_{\mathbb{R}^m} p(x) \ln \left| \frac{\partial f}{\partial x} \right| dx \tag{3.6.2}$$

where $|\partial f / \partial x|$ is the Jacobian of the transformation f.

This equation (3.6.2) forms the basis of the argument of those scientists who claim that $H(X)$ is not a suitable measure of uncertainty, and we shall comment on this point in the following.

3.7 Arguments to Support Continuous Entropy

3.7.1 On the Negativeness of Continuous Entropy

Assume that $X \in \mathbb{R}$ is a scalar valued random variable with the standard deviation σ, and let us make the transformation $X^* = X/\sigma$, then, according to (3.6.2) we have

$$H(X^*) = H(X) - \ln \sigma \tag{3.7.1}$$

which may be positive or negative depending upon the probability density $p(x)$ of X. This being so, refer to Sect. 3.5.1 devoted to the central limit theorem, and consider the normalized sum S_n^*. According to the above equation (3.7.1) its entropy is

$$H(S_n^*) = H(S_n) - \ln s_n \tag{3.7.2}$$

which may also be positive or negative. However, one of the consequences of the famous Lindeberg conditions, is to ensure that $H(S_n^*)$ is positive (see condition (3.5.15) of theorem 3.5.2); as a result, it is not at all obvious that a continuous entropy needs to be positive to be a suitable measure of uncertainty! Indeed, irrespective of any information theory, the Lindeberg condition is a sufficient condition for the convergence to the normal law, and in some sense it is also a necessary condition; see for instance [3.9].

3.7.2 On the Non-invariance of Continuous Entropy

Assume that $X \in \mathbb{R}$ and consider the transformation $Y = 0X = 0$; it is clear that there is no uncertainty on Y, so that $H(Y) = -\infty$. If we now apply (3.6.2), $\partial f / \partial x = 0$

and we have

$$H(Y) = H(X) - \infty$$

and there is no inconsistency at all.

Next, assume that $-A \leqslant X \leqslant +A$, $A > 0$, and consider the transformation $Y = gX$ where $g > 1$ denotes a constant. Without making any calculation, it is evident that the domain of Y is larger than the domain of X, so that it is quite right to expect that the entropy of Y will be greater than that of X, i.e. we should have $H(Y) > H(X)$. If we now apply (3.6.2), we obtain the relation

$$H(Y) = H(X) + \ln g \tag{3.7.3}$$

which fulfills our expectation.

In other words, the continuous entropy depends implicitly upon the range of variation of X, whereas the discrete entropy does not.

In fact, what many scientists forget, is that the mapping $f(\cdot)$ itself involves its own amount of information so that when one applies $f(\cdot)$ to X, one may either add information or lose information, and it is exactly this possibility which is reflected by the integral term in (3.6.2).

More explicitly, assume that we have at hand a definition of the conditional entropy $H(f/x)$ of the mapping $f(\cdot)$ given x, that is to say at x, then the entropy $H[f(X)]$ may be thought of as the mutual entropy $H(f, X)$ of the pair (f, X), and (3.2.7) yields straightforwardly

$$H(f, X) = H(X) + \int_{-\infty}^{+\infty} p(x)H(f/x)\,dx \ . \tag{3.7.4}$$

A direct comparison of (3.6.2) with (3.6.6) enables us to make the identification

$$H(f/x) := \ln\left|\frac{\partial f}{\partial x}\right| \ . \tag{3.7.5}$$

Of course, we do not have the same model with discrete variables: if $f(\cdot)$ is one-to-one mapping, the set $(x_1, x_2, \ldots, x_m)$ is transformed into $(y_1, y_2, \ldots, y_m)$ with $p(x_i) = p(y_i)$, $i = 1, \ldots, m$, and one has $H(X) = H(Y)$.

Nevertheless there is a somewhat embarrassing problem in this case: Assume that $f(X) = gX$, where g denotes a positive constant, and assume that g tends to zero, we should then have $H(Y) \to 0$ as $g \downarrow 0$, but we know that this is impossible since $H(Y)$ does not depend upon g! This is obviously due to the fact the continuous entropy involves the distance dx between neighbouring elements, while the continuous entropy does not; hence the need for a unified approach to these two measures of uncertainty.

3.7.3 Channel Capacity in the Presence of Noise

Of course, we cannot forget Shannon's famous theorem on the capacity of channels disturbed by random noise, which explicitly refers to the entropy of the normal distribution. Loosely speaking, this result reads as follows.

Assume that a communication channel is submitted to the input signal X and provides the corresponding output Y with $Y = X + W$, where $X \sim N(\mu, \sigma_x^2)$ and $W \sim N(0, \sigma_x^2)$ are two independent Gaussian variables with the respective statistical means μ and 0, and standard deviations σ_x and σ_w. The amount of information contained in Y about X is then equal to

$$I(X/Y) = H(X) + H(Y) - H(X, Y)$$

$$= H(Y) - H(W)$$

$$= H(Y) - \ln \left[\sigma_w \sqrt{2\pi e} \right] .$$

The capacity C of the channel is defined as the maximum value of $I(X/Y)$. We then have to find the maximum of $H(Y)$ given that the mean of Y is equal to μ, and its variance is $\sigma_x^2 + \sigma_w^2$. We finally obtain the expression

$$C = \ln \frac{\sigma_y}{\sigma_w}$$

$$= \frac{1}{2} \ln \left(1 + \frac{\sigma_x^2}{\sigma_w^2} \right)$$

which sheds light on the importance of the term $\dfrac{\sigma_x^2}{\sigma_w^2}$.

3.8 The Maximum Entropy Principle

Another result which, in our opinion, offers arguments in favour of the Shannon theory is the so-called *Principle of Maximum Entropy* first stated by *Jaynes* [3.10] as a general rule of inference in statistical mechanics. It has been successfully applied to a very broad range of fields such as thermodynamics, statistics, reliability estimation, system simulation, traffic networks, queuing theory, computer system modelling, group behaviour, stock market analysis, general probabilistic problem solving, filtering theory, pattern recognition systems, and so on. Any of the results so obtained could be considered as retrospective support of the validity of this principle, and thus of the meaning and the definition of the concept of informational entropy.

3.8.1 Statement of the Principle

The maximum entropy principle. Let $X \in \mathbb{R}^n$ denote a random variable whose probability distribution $\{q_i\}$ or $q(x)$ is unknown. We further assume that this distribution is subject to some given mathematical constraints. The maximum entropy principle states that, of all the distributions which satisfy the constraints, we should choose that one which provides the largest entropy for X. ☐

A generalization of this principle, which applies when a distribution $\{p_i\}$ or $p(x)$ which estimates $q(x)$ is known in addition to the constraints, is the following.

The minimum cross-entropy principle. Of the various distributions $\{q_i\}$ or $q(x)$ that satisfy the constraints, we should choose the one which minimizes the cross-entropy $H(\mathcal{Q}/\!/\mathcal{P})$ expressed by (2.10.1) or (2.12.17)   □

3.8.2 Some Examples

Example 3.1. The most celebrated example is related to the normal distribution. Indeed, the probability density with a given mean value μ and variance σ^2 which maximizes the entropy is the normal distribution

$$g(x) = \frac{1}{\sigma\sqrt{2\pi}}\exp\left(\frac{-(x-\mu)^2}{2\sigma^2}\right) , \qquad x \in \mathbb{R} .$$

In other words, if the only information available about X is its mean value and its variance, all that can be assumed is that its distribution is normal. This result explains in another manner why the normal distribution is so useful in probability theory and statistics: very often we have no alternative other than to assume that the variable under consideration has this probability distribution.

The central limit theorem may also be viewed in this light. The more we increase the number of terms in the normalized sum, the more information we lose about the corresponding distribution, so that we are forced to assume that the resulting density is the normal distribution. This is not a proof of the central limit theorem, but an information-theoretical argument to justify its validity.

Example 3.2. The maximum entropy corresponding to a non-negative random variable with mean μ is exponentially distributed with parameter $\lambda = 1/\mu$; clearly

$$p(x) = \lambda e^{-\lambda x} .$$

Example 3.3. The Cauchy distribution

$$\frac{1}{\pi}\frac{1}{1+(x-\alpha)^2}$$

is a maximum entropy distribution over all distributions satisfying the condition $E\{\ln(1+X^2)\} = \alpha$.

Example 3.4. Consider a stochastic process $X(t)$, whose transition moments satisfy the following conditions

$$E\{Z/x,t\} = \alpha(x,t)\tau \tag{3.8.1}$$

$$E\{Z^2/x,t\} = \beta(x,t)\tau \tag{3.8.2}$$

$$E\{Z^n/x,t\} = o(\tau^2) , \qquad n \geqslant 3 \tag{3.8.3}$$

with

$$Z := x(t + \tau) - x(t) \tag{3.8.4}$$

where $o(\ )$ is the so-called Landau symbol. One can show that the probability density $p(x, t)$ of such a process is the solution of the Fokker-Plank-Kolmogorov equation

$$\frac{\partial p}{\partial t} = -\frac{\partial}{\partial x}(\alpha p) + \frac{1}{2}\frac{\partial^2}{\partial x^2}(\beta p) \tag{3.8.5}$$

with suitable initial conditions. This process is encountered in a very wide range of phenomena and can be considered as the counterpart of the normal distribution for dynamical systems subject to randomness.

With the maximum entropy principle, the viewpoint is the following. Assume that all we know about the process is summarized in the knowledge of its first- and second-order moments expressed by (3.8.1) and (3.8.2) respectively; then all we can assume is that $p(x, t)$ satisfies (3.8.5). Indeed, the transition probability density $q(z, \tau/x, t)$ is then the normal distribution

$$\frac{\exp[-(z - \alpha\tau)^2/2\beta\tau]}{\sqrt{2\pi\beta\tau}} .$$

Therefore one derives (3.8.5).

This approach may be generalized as follows [3.11]. Assume that the prior information available about the process is a knowledge of its first n transition moments

$$E\{z^j/x, t\} = \alpha_j(x, t) , \qquad j = 1, 2, \ldots, n . \tag{3.8.6}$$

All that we may then assume is that $p(x, t)$ is solution of the equation

$$\frac{\partial p}{\partial t} = \sum_{j=1}^{n} (-1)^j \frac{1}{j!}\frac{\partial^j}{\partial x^j}(\alpha_j p) . \tag{3.8.7}$$

3.9 Arguments to Support the Maximum Entropy Principle

3.9.1 Information-Theoretical Considerations

The maximum entropy principle is quite understandable in the framework of information theory.

If we have no prior information about X, then our uncertainty about the latter should be the largest one $H^*(X)$. Any set $\{C\}$ of mathematical constraints on the distribution of X defines the new conditional entropy $H(X/\{C\})$; so that the trans-information, that is to say the information that we thereby obtain with regard to the maximum uncertainty state $H^*(X)$ is

$$I = H^*(X) - H(X/\{C\}) . \tag{3.9.1}$$

The principle minimizes this information: in words, we look for the minimum amount of information involved in $\{C\}$. It could happen that $\{C\}$ contains more information than this minimum, but we do not know it, and even if we did, we are unable to apprehend this additional information.

3.9.2 Thermodynamic Considerations

It should be noted that this principle is quite consistent with the second principle of thermodynamics. Indeed, according to the latter, the thermodynamic entropy $S = kH$ (where k is the Boltzmann constant) of a closed system in equilibrium achieves its maximum value. If we consider the observer R and the variable X together as making up a thermodynamic system, then its entropy should be a maximum.

3.9.3 Axiomatic Derivation

Recently *Shore* et al. [3.12] "proved" the maximum entropy principle in the sense that they derived it as a consequence of a set of preliminary mathematical axioms which should be satisfied. They do not use the properties of entropy as a measure of information, but rather they examine the consequences of requiring that a method of inference should be self-consistent.

The four axioms of these authors are the following.

i) *Uniqueness.* The result of the observation process should be unique.
ii) *Invariance.* The result should be independent of the choice of the coordinate system. In other words, we expect the same answer when we solve the problem in two different coordinate systems.
iii) *System Independence.* It should not matter whether one accounts for independent information about independent systems separately in terms of different densities or together in terms of their joint density.
iv) *Subset Independence.* It should not matter whether one treats an independent subset of system states in terms of a separate conditional density or in terms of the full system density.

The derivation of the maximum entropy principle proceeds as follows: first the result is rigorously obtained for both continuous and discrete cross-entropies, and then it is established for the discrete Shannon entropy considered as relative entropy with respect to the uniform distribution. Clearly, if we define the prior probability distribution $P = (1/n, \ldots, 1/n)$ in (3.2.13), then the relative entropy is

$$H(Q//P) = \ln n - H(X)$$

and minimizing $H(Q//P)$ is equivalent to maximizing $H(X)$.

3.9.4 A Few Comments

The limits of this theorem are obvious and are contained in the assumption; it tells us nothing about the continuous Shannon entropy which does not satisfy the invariance property (ii) above.

Nevertheless, from a practical point of view, by the results it yields, and by the physical arguments which support it, we have every reason to believe that the maximum entropy principle is fully justified for continuous variables, and the above examples 3.1 and 3.4 are quite convincing in this way. In addition we have shown in Sect. 3.7 that the invariance property is not such an obvious prerequisite as it appears initially.

Strictly speaking, we cannot talk about inconsistency in view of all these features, but nevertheless one thing appears to be clear. If we had at hand a uniform approach to discrete entropy and continuous entropy, such difficulties would not occur and we could then claim to have achieved completeness of the theory. Indeed, should we accept that some informational properties which are contained in continuous entropy are not present in the discrete entropy and vice versa? This should not be so, apart from the fact that a continuous variable necessarily involves an infinite number of informational states while, of course, a discrete variable has only a finite number of such states.

3.10 Information, Syntax, Semantics

3.10.1 On the Absolute Nature of Information

There has been a long debate among scientists, and one that is still continuing, as to whether or not a theory of information should deal with semantics. In the view of those authors who are mainly interested in a theory of communication, a symbol is a symbol, and it has to be considered as such, irrespective of any kind of meaning it may have or may be ascribed, and *Shannon* himself [3.13] shared this viewpoint when he pointed out that his theory does not deal with semantics because this equation is beyond his main purpose which was to analyze the effects of random noises in technical communication processes. Likewise, mathematicians, mainly interested in the theoretical foundation of the theory were not interested in introducing semantics into information theory.

In contrast, scientists concerned with the applications of information theory to areas other than technical communication or transmission, very early arrived at the conclusion that the theory should be generalized to account for both syntax and semantics. In his book, *Brillouin* [3.6] already mentioned this problem as a prerequisite for the general use of information theory in sciences; *Bar Hillel* [3.14] analyzed the question with respect to language; *Thom* [3.1] pointed out that it is of basic importance in a suitable modelling of information; *Ryan* [3.15] introduced the concept of informational-entropy interfaces in an approach to biological organization; *Haken* [3.16] sketched a modelling of relative information; the question is relevant in the application of information theory to social sciences ....

Basically, all information should be regarded as information relative to a given observer, and the latter should appear as a parameter in the definition of this information. One way to achieve this is to introduce semantics in the modelling of information since this semantics is not constant but depends upon the observer who receives the informational content of the message.

In our opinion, the problem is closely related to the very nature of natural languages.

3.10.2 Information and Natural Language

When one tries to apply the information theory as derived by Shannon to problems which are not directly relevant to communication, sooner or later one reaches a point where it is necessary to have a concept of information defined with respect to the observer who considers this information; this gives rise to the question of how one should characterize the observer in this framework.

Our claim is that, in the general case, the observer mainly relies on a pre-existing internal model that he has about the observable under consideration, i.e. a set of expectations. A given set of symbols, say a syntax, may have different significances to different observers depending upon the respective interests, that is to say the respective internal states of these observers. If we discard this feature in modelling information, we are missing an important property of human observers, and so we cannot expect to suitably describe information processes involving human factors. One cannot identify a human observer with a technical apparatus, and it is exactly this kind of misunderstanding which meant that the application of the mathematical framework of statistical mechanics to human systems did not yield significant results.

Although we are using the term of human observer, the above considerations can also apply to other systems. In biology for instance, it is quite likely that the amount of information which is contained in the DNA for instance, is defined only with respect to a given medium.

We believe that one way to explicitly introduce the observer in the definition of information is to suitably describe the support of this information, that is to say *natural languages*. In short, we postulate that information in any information process is necessarily conveyed by a natural language.

On the contrary to formal languages, which involve only rules of grammar, irrespective of any external universe, a natural lanuage deals explicitly with a syntactic space Ω and a semantic one Ω'. There is a correspondence, a mapping (symbols $\leftrightarrow$ meanings) between Ω and Ω', and Ω' may vary from one observer to another.

It is Ω' which dictates that the information contained in a set of symbols is only relative information defined with respect to an observer; we believe that a suitable generalized informaton theory should account for this basic feature in its equations.

3.11 Information and Thermodynamics

3.11.1 Informational and Thermodynamic Entropy

Let S_T denote the thermodynamic entropy of medium M. The differential dS_T is defined as $dS_T = dQ/T$ where dQ is the amount of energy received as heat by the medium in a small reversible transformation, and T is its absolute temperature. In order to make contact with the informational entropy, let $\{p_i\}$ denote the probability distribution of the different micro-states of the medium (in contrast to the macro-states which describe the medium as the whole) and define the corresponding informational entropy H. According to a basic result of statistical thermodynamics, one has the following equation

$$S_T = kH \ , \tag{3.11.1}$$

where $k = 1.38 \times 10^{-23}$ J/K is referred to as the Boltzmann constant.

This relation has been criticized, analyzed, and discussed at length in the literature (see for instance *Brillouin* [3.6]) and our purpose here was simply to state it for completeness.

3.11.2 Thermodynamic Entropy of Open Systems

While statistical thermodynamics provides the relation between information theory and the thermodynamics of closed systems via the Boltzmann equation, we have no such microscopic approach for the thermodynamics of open systems, that is to say, systems which exchange both matter and energy with their surroundings. For an infinitesimal change of thermodynamic entropy S_T along an irreversible path, we have

$$dS_T > \left(\frac{dQ}{T}\right)_{\text{rev}} \tag{3.11.2}$$

where dQ is the infinitesimal heat exchange which is positive if it is received by the system, and negative otherwise; T is the thermodynamic temperature at which dQ is delivered; and $(dQ/T)_{\text{rev}}$ is the flow of entropy due to the interaction between the system and its surroundings. We can rewrite dS_T in the form

$$dS_T = d_e S + d_i S$$

where $d_e S := (dQ/T)_{\text{rev}}$ and $d_i S$ is the part of entropy increase resulting from irreversible processes inside the system.

Since the system is open, it is no longer certain that the Boltzmann equation (3.11.1) is meaningful, and all we can suppose is that

$$d_e S = k_e dH_e \qquad \text{and} \qquad d_i S = k_i dH_i \ ,$$

where k_e and k_i are two constants (which might be equal) and H_e and H_i are two informational entropies which remain to be determined. At first sight, the main difficulty with this microscopic approach would be in defining the mathematical constraints which characterize an open system.

Nevertheless, this problem is of interest, because if we possess an equivalence between the thermodynamics of open systems and information theory, then we would have a point of departure for a possible rigorous approach to general systems.

3.12 Conclusions

We shall summarize this review with the following statement: Any information theory which claims to be a generalized information theory should contain the Shannon theory as a special case.

Authors like *Thom* [3.1] for instance claim that the Shannon theory deals with information in a restricted sense only since it is defined by means of probability, whereas, in fact, randomness should not be necessary in such a theory. We agree with this argument but it is our opinion that it can easily be circumvented. Indeed it is sufficient to consider any deterministic variable as being the statistical mean value of a random variable. This is well illustrated by the example of thermodynamics: The state variables involved in classical thermodynamics are nothing other than the statistical averages of the variables introduced in statistical thermodynamics. In other words we would have two different levels of definition: information at the micro-level, which explicitly involves probability, and information at the macro-level, without probability.

We believe that the two problems of greatest importance are the following:

i) From a mathematical standpoint, how can one use the same model to describe the information defined by discrete random events on the one hand, and continuous random events on the other hand, in order to get a unified approach to various theoretical questions?

ii) From a phenomenological viewpoint, how can one define a concept of relative information in order to deal with topics that are not directly related to communication in the technical sense of the word?

The corresponding theoretical framework should not contradict the information theory as initiated by Shannon, but should complete it.

4. A Theory of Relative Information

Basically, this chapter proposes a new model of linear observation in $\mathbb{R}^2$ and a new theory of relative information in the sense that the informational content of a given message explicitly depends upon the state of the observer. After a short analysis of the phenomena of observation and of aggregation, we introduce the particular case of linear observations with informational invariance and we arrive at the existence of two models: one with Euclidean invariance, and the other one with Minkowskian invariance. Then we consider messages defined by natural languages, and, by using very simple and general arguments, we describe them by a syntactic space and a semantic space, that is to say an entropy of symbol $H(\alpha)$ and an entropy of meaning $H(a)$. The main assumption is that the observer receives the syntax and the semantics of the message via a linear transformation with informational invariance, and one can show that this observation is necessarily Minkowskian. One then has two models: the first one in which it is the entropies $H(\alpha)$ and $H(a)$ that are observed by this process, and the second which involves the observation of the Shannonian transinformations $I(\beta/\alpha)$ and $I(b/a)$. The theory is described and comparisons with standard results are made. One of the consequences of the observation modelling is a new approach to fuzziness.

4.1 Introduction

It has long been recognized that the "Mathematical Theory of Communication" as initiated by *Shannon* [4.1] deals mainly with the measure of occurrences of symbols, and cannot be considered as a theory of information in the general sense of this term for the very reason that it does not refer (and it is not its purpose) to the meanings of these symbols.

Why do we need to account for meanings or semantics in an information theory?

When the author has at hand a Chinese newspaper, the latter contains absolutely no information for him, while this is probably not so for a Chinese person.

The amount of information contained in a given issue of a given newspaper is not the same for the businessman who is mainly interested in the stock exchange market and for the jobless person looking for a position somewhere.

As far as we can talk of the "information content" of DNA, it is clear that this information should be defined in relation to the environment of this DNA. Indeed, if we put a DNA string into a glass of sand, then its biological information content becomes completely meaningless.

The parity bit which is appended at the end of the encoded words in technical transmission systems refers to a very simple meaning space: the word is correct or it is not.

Following *Brillouin* [4.2] and *Ashby* [4.3], it is taken for granted that such problems cannot be suitably dealt with in the Shannonian framework, but as long as we were concerned with technical transmission problems only, this drawback had no consequence. Nevertheless, with the expansion of cybernetics and general system theory, it became clear that a modified or generalized information theory is essential for a fruitful analysis of these new topics.

If we ignore those works which are mainly qualitative and related to foundation and concepts, and restrict ourselves to studies which aim to quantitatively measure meanings or semantics, we can partition the various approaches that have been suggested in two main classes: those which use the basic theory of Shannon, but suitably modified in order to account for this new framework of syntax and semantics, and those which try to derive new information concepts comprising Shannon entropy as special case. In the first class, one can mention *Bongard* [4.4] and *Stratonovitch* [4.5, 6] who propose a measure of the quantity and of the value of information in the presence of erroneous messages; *Haken* [4.7] who suggests an approach to dynamic information theory by using the concept of attractors; and *Jumarie* [4.8–10] who introduces a concept of transinformation in the presence of subjectivity. In the second class, we shall mention *Jumarie* [4.10, 11] who proposes a so-called relativistic information theory, and *Kovanic* [4.12] who derived a "gnostical theory for single data" which, does not explicitly refer to information theory, but is nevertheless related to the latter. The main distinguishing features of these two approaches it that the first uses the Minkowski matrix to define information, and that the second considers observation with defects (i.e. measurement errors).

Our purpose in the following is to expand the theory of Minkowskian observation. Whereas in our preceding studies we derived the corresponding metric as a by-product of our general system theory [4.10] and/or by considerations relevant to information versus uncertainty, here, we shall first build up a general theory of linear observation with invariance of information and then we shall show that it is only the Minkowskian observation which applies to our problem. We shall thereby derive the concept of relative entropy and it will thus be possible to expand the theory. Likewise, we shall derive the new concept of relative transinformation.

4.2 Observation, Aggregation, Invariance

4.2.1 Principle of Aggregation

Let us consider the process in which a human observer R observes a given object S in various circumstances. This object may be observed either from a qualitative standpoint, for instance with respect to its form, or in a quantitative framework, in which case S is characterized by a set of variables, say $\Sigma := (x_1, x_2, \ldots, x_n)$. For instance $\Sigma := $ (age, weight, height, ...). As a matter of fact, R may consider S with respect to a single variable only, say x_i; but it is a fact of experience that when R considers the whole of S to obtain a global assessment, he does not estimate each x_i individually one at a time, but rather he defines some combinations of the x_i's, and it is only by using these combinations that he can grasp the features of S.

As an example, assume that $\Sigma := (x_1, x_2, x_3, \dots, x_5)$. Then, depending upon the values of some observer state parameters which have to be identified, R may partition Σ in the form $\Sigma := (\Sigma_1, \Sigma_2) \equiv [(x_1, x_4), (x_2, x_3, x_5)]$ and consider for instance the combinations

$$y_1 := ax_1 + bx_4 , \qquad y_2 := cx_2 + dx_3 + ex_5 .$$

We shall summarize this property in the form of the following axiom.

Aggregation Principle. Given an object S characterized by a set of variables $\Sigma :=$ $(x_1, x_2, \dots, x_n)$, a human observer R, who is observing S does so by means of an observation process which is decomposed into two stages: First, Σ is partitioned in the form $\Sigma := (\Sigma_1, \Sigma_2, \dots, \Sigma_m)$, where Σ_i denotes the set $\Sigma_i := (x_{i1}, x_{i2}, \dots, x_{in_i})$; and second, R characterizes Σ by using aggregate variables in the form $y_i = f_i(x_{i1}, x_{i2}, \dots, x_{in_i})$.   □

4.2.2 Principle of Invariance

As the result of the preceding aggregation process, the system Σ is reduced to $\Sigma' \equiv (y_1, y_2, \dots, y_n)$.

But even with this smaller object, the observer R does not work by measuring each y_i one at a time, at least in the special case where he refers to the object as the whole. In order to grasp the global characteristics of the object, the observer selects some special properties, he builds up his own criteria, and the observation process of this given object works in such a way that the numerical values of these criteria remain invariant. For instance, if the criterion is expressed in the form of a geometrical distance, then the latter should remain constant.

We shall summarize this property in the form of the following axiom.

Invariance Principle. Assume that the aggregation process defines the object S in the form $\Sigma' := (y_1, y_2, \dots, y_k)$. Then a human observer who is observing S does so as follows: First he partitions Σ' in the form $\Sigma' = (\Sigma_1', \Sigma_2', \dots, \Sigma_r')$ where $\Sigma_j' :=$ $(y_{j1}, y_{j2}, \dots, y_{jn_j})$; second he defines a global feature associated with each Σ_j' in the form of a functional $g_j(y_{j1}, y_{j2}, \dots, y_{jn_j})$; and the observation process works in such a way that these features g_j are invariant.   □

4.2.3 A Few Comments

As a matter of fact, the basic principle is the second one, the invariance principle, and the aggregation principle is of interest at the identification stage only. For instance the psychologist has his own definition $(x_1, x_2, \dots, x_n)$, the patient has his modelling $(y_1, y_2, \ldots, y_k)$ and it is the task of the psychologist to determine the relations between these two sets of variables.

It seems that most human observers work in a three-dimensional space, sometimes in a four-dimensional one, but rarely more. This is true for the observation of colors, the identification of tastes, the visual perception process, and so on. As a result, one may restrict the detailed study to the case of three or four variables, x_i, given that any observation process will work in a hierarchical way in such a manner that each stage of the hierarchy involves three or four variables only.

A problem of some importance is that of determining the nature of the global feature $f_j(\cdot)$ above. Our claim is that it is wise to select the simplest one, that is to say to assume that the transformation is of the form

$$Y' = \underline{A} Y \tag{4.2.1}$$

where Y represents the vector $Y^t = (y_1, y_2, \ldots, y_k)$. $\underline{A}$ denotes a constant matrix and the superscript t denotes the transpose.

4.3 Observation with Informational Invariance

Our purpose in the present section is to derive a general invariance property of observation processes, in as straightforward a way as possible. In such a derivation our assumptions should be simple and relevant to common situations so that they do not provide only results of restricted validity.

Step 1. Assume that an observer (who may be a human observer for now) is observing a physical object in the three-dimensional space. This object is described by the point $X \in \mathbb{R}^3$ which takes on the values $x^t = (x_1, x_2, x_3)$ over the spatial domain D where it is defined. We shall assume that the result of the perception of the whole object by R is in the form of the integral

$$V = \int_D f(x)\, dx \tag{4.3.1}$$

where $f(x)$ is a given function which measure the density of perception associated with the element dx about x. This perception may be an intensity, an information or anything else, but the point of importance is that while the differential dx is intrinsically associated with the geometrical representation of the object only, $f(x)$ on the other hand may depend upon both the object itself and the observer R, in which case it is defined relative to this observer.

Step 2. In the framework of our information theoretic purpose, assume that we may associate a probability density function $p(x)$ with X and that the perception of the observer is defined by the informational entropy

$$H(X) = -\int_D p(x) \ln p(x)\, dx \ . \tag{4.3.2}$$

We point out that the unique property of $p(x)$ which we need for our purpose is

$$\int_D p(x)\, dx = 1 \tag{4.3.3}$$

so that, even when we are not explicitly dealing with probability, it is sufficient to consider that $p(x)$ is a distribution of weighting coefficients for instance.

Step 3. Consider the observation defined by the linear transformation $Y = \underline{A}X$, where $\underline{A}$ is a 3×3 matrix; Y has its own probability density $q(y)$ and therefore its own entropy $H(Y)$ defined by (4.3.2) in which we substitute $q(y)$ for $p(x)$. As a useful result in information theory, the following relation holds

$$H(Y) = H(X) + \ln|\det \underline{A}| \tag{4.3.4}$$

where $\det \underline{A}$ is the determinant of $\underline{A}$; this relation is a consequence of the expression (4.3.2) and of the equation (4.3.3) only.

Step 4. The meaning of (4.3.4) is the following: X involves the amount of uncertainty $H(X)$; the transformation $\underline{A}$ also involves its own amount of uncertainty in the sense that it can add or remove uncertainty (for instance when $\underline{A}$ is the zero matrix there is no uncertainty at all in the value of Y). Equation (4.3.4) merely expresses the uncertainty involved in Y as the additive combination of these two previous uncertainties.

Step 5. A useful class of observations are those in which the linear transformation $\underline{A}$ does not add or remove uncertainty, in other words there is conservation of uncertainty,

$$H(X) = H(Y) \ ,$$

and according to (4.3.4) one then has

$$|\det \underline{A}| = 1 \ .$$

Definition 3.1. We shall refer to a linear observation $Y = \underline{A}X$ with $|\det \underline{A}| = 1$ as a *linear observation with informational invariance.*   □

Comments. One can obviously take for granted that the observation does not create information by itself in the sense that the informational source cannot offer more information to the observer than its absolute informational content. But in contrast, an observer who loses information, that is to say when $|\det \underline{A}| < 1$, is quite realistic. Thus by assuming $|\det \underline{A}| = 1$, we restrict ourselves to the study of observation processes with perfect observers.

The situation may be pictured as follows. When we are examining a crystal, we rotate it, we exposure it to light under various incidence angles, etc., in order to get information about its structure, but in no case do we change this structure itself.

4.4 Euclidean Invariance

4.4.1 Orthogonal Transformation

Let $X^t := (x_1, x_2, \ldots, x_n) \in \mathbb{R}^n$ with the Euclidean norm $\|X\|$ derived from the inner product in the form

$$\|X\|^2 = \sum_{ij} g_{ij} x_i x_j \ , \qquad g_{ij} \in \mathbb{R} \tag{4.4.1}$$

$$= (X, X) \geqslant 0 \ , \tag{4.4.2}$$

where the g_{ij} define a positive definite matrix. We now consider the linear transformation $\underline{Y} = \underline{Q}X$ where $\underline{Q}$ denotes an $n \times n$ matrix with real coefficients, and we assume that it satisfies the invariance condition

$$(\underline{Q}X, \underline{Q}X) = (X, X) \ . \tag{4.4.3}$$

Such a matrix is referred to as an orthogonal matrix. Equation (4.4.3) yields

$$(X\underline{Q}^*, \underline{Q}X) = (X, X) \tag{4.4.4}$$

where $\underline{Q}^*$ is the adjoint of $\underline{Q}$, and therefore the condition

$$\underline{Q}^*\underline{Q} = I \tag{4.4.5}$$

(where I is the unit $n \times n$ matrix), which in turn yields

$$|\det \underline{Q}| = 1 \ . \tag{4.4.6}$$

In other words, the Euclidean invariance is a special case of the general criterion proposed in Sect. 4.3.

As an example, assume that $X \in \mathbb{R}^2$. One then has

$$Y = \underline{Q}(\theta)X \tag{4.4.7}$$

or explicitly

$$y_1 = x_1 \cos \theta + x_2 \sin \theta \tag{4.4.8a}$$

$$y_2 = -x_1 \sin \theta + x_2 \cos \theta \tag{4.4.8b}$$

where $\theta \in \mathbb{R}$ is a parameter that characterizes the observation.

4.4.2 Application to the Observation of Probabilities

Problem. Let (p, q) with $p + q = 1$ denote a complete set of probabilities with the entropy H;

$$H := -p \ln p - q \ln q$$

and assume that p and q are observed via the linear orthogonal transformation above. How does this observation affect H?

Solution. Let (p', q') denote the observed probabilities; since one has $p + q = p' + q' = 1$, we are led to introduce the vector $Y^t = (\sqrt{p}, \sqrt{q})$ with $\|Y\| = 1$ and to assume that this observation obeys the equation

$$\sqrt{p'} = \sqrt{p} \cos \theta + \sqrt{q} \sin \theta \tag{4.4.9a}$$

$$\sqrt{q'} = -\sqrt{p}\sin\theta + \sqrt{q}\cos\theta \tag{4.4.9b}$$

where θ characterizes the observation.

In order to obtain a simple form for the new entropy $H' := H(p',q')$, we shall assume that θ is small enough to yield $\sin\theta \cong \theta$. With this approximation, we can write

$$p' = p + q\theta^2 + 2\sqrt{pq}\,\theta + o(\theta^3) \tag{4.4.10a}$$

$$q' = p\theta^2 + 2\sqrt{pq}\,\theta + q + o(\theta^3)\ , \tag{4.4.10b}$$

therefore the new value H' of the entropy is

$$\begin{aligned}
H' &= -(p + 2\sqrt{pq}\theta)\ln\left[p(1 + 2\sqrt{q/p}\theta)\right] \\
&\quad - (q - 2\sqrt{pq}\theta)\ln[q(1 - 2\sqrt{p/q}\theta)] + o(\theta^3) \\
&= -(p + 2\sqrt{pq}\theta)(\ln p + 2\sqrt{q/p}\theta) \\
&\quad - (q - 2\sqrt{pq}\theta)(\ln q - 2\sqrt{p/q}\theta) + o(\theta^3) \qquad \text{and}
\end{aligned}$$

$$H(p',q') = H(p,q) - 2\theta\sqrt{pq}\ln(p/q) - 4\theta^2 + o(\theta^3) \tag{4.4.11}$$

On the Meaning of This Result. Equation (4.4.11) calls for a few comments.

i) Assume that we have positively no information about (p,q), so that the latter appears as a pair of prior probabilities. According to the maximum entropy principle, all we can do is then to put $p = q = \frac{1}{2}$ and (4.4.1) yields

$$H(p',q') = \ln 2 - 4\theta^2 \tag{4.4.12}$$

and as expected, $H(p',q') < H(p,q)$.

ii) Assume that $\theta > 0$ is small and $p < q$; the observation process then yields an increase of entropy and $H(p',q') > H(p,q)$. On the other hand, if $p > q$, we would then have $H(p',q') < H(p,q)$. This result is somewhat embarrassing since it would seem that we could rename (p,q) by (q,p) to again give $H(p',q') > H(p,q)$. This remark suggests that we should perhaps make an additional assumption about the symmetry of the result of the observation with respect to p and q. For instance, if we require that p' and q' should be such that $H(p',q') = H(q',p')$, then the Euclidean observation would not apply. We shall return to this question in later chapters.

iii) The above comment gives rise to the following question. Which property should be considered as being the basic one in the observation process? Is it the invariance $p + q = 1$ or the symmetry of $H(p,q)$? In the first case probability is more important than information, but in the second case, it is information which supersedes probability.

4.4.3 Application to the Observation of Classes

A class is defined as a set of objects whose characteristic function is denoted by $\Phi_A(x)$, namely: $\Phi_A(x) = 1$, $x \in A \subset \mathbb{R}$, $\Phi_A(x) = 0$, $x \notin A$. Let $\bar{A}$ and $\Phi_{\bar{A}}(x)$ denote the complement of A and its characteristic function.

A New Approach to Fuzziness. The relation

$$\Phi_A(x) + \Phi_{\bar{A}}(x) = 1 \tag{4.4.13}$$

suggest that we formally consider the vector $(\phi_A^{1/2}, \phi_{\bar{A}}^{1/2})$ and the transformation

$$[\Phi_A'(x)]^{1/2} = [\Phi_A(x)]^{1/2} \cos\theta + [\Phi_{\bar{A}}(x)]^{1/2} \sin\theta \tag{4.4.14a}$$

$$[\Phi_{\bar{A}}'(x)]^{1/2} = -[\Phi_A(x)]^{1/2} \sin\theta + [\Phi_{\bar{A}}(x)]^{1/2} \cos\theta . \tag{4.4.14b}$$

These equations can be ascribed the following meaning. An observer R examines a given object x, mainly to determine whether or not x belongs to A. To this end, he estimates simultaneously the memberships of x with respect to A and $\bar{A}$, and the results of these estimates are $\Phi_A'(x)$ and $\Phi_{\bar{A}}'(x)$. □

Assume that $x \in A$; then according to equation (4.4.14a), one has

$$\Phi_A'(x) = \Phi_A(x) \cos^2\theta , \qquad x \in A \tag{4.4.15}$$

and $\cos^2\theta$ can be thought of as being the grade of membership of x with respect to A. It is then sufficient to assume that θ depends explicitly upon x, say $\theta(x)$, to obtain an equivalence between the so-called membership function $\mu_A(x)$ in fuzzy set theory and $\cos^2\theta(x)$; clearly

$$\mu_A(x) \equiv \cos^2\theta(x) . \tag{4.4.16}$$

This identification provides a composition law for membership functions with respect to the observers as follows. Assume that an observer R_1 observes a given object with the parameter $\theta_1(x)$; and that another observer R_2 observes the same object with the parameter $\theta_2(x)$. Then, according to (4.4.14a, b), the pair (R_1, R_2) observes this object with the parameter $(\theta_1 + \theta_2)$ and we have

$$\cos^2(\theta_1 + \theta_2) = \cos^2\theta_1 \cos^2\theta_2 + \sin^2\theta_1 \sin^2\theta_2 - 2\sin\theta_1 \cos\theta_1 \sin\theta_2 \cos\theta_2 .$$

Assume that $0 \leqslant \theta_1, \theta_2 \leqslant \frac{\pi}{2}$, one then has the composition law

$$\mu(x/R_1 R_2) = 1 + 2\mu(x/R_1)\mu(x/R_2) - [\mu(x/R_1) + \mu(x/R_2)]$$
$$-2\{\mu(x/R_1)[1 - \mu(x/R_1)]\mu(x/R_2)[1 - \mu(x/R_2)]\}^{1/2} . \tag{4.4.17}$$

Can we use the same technique to derive composition laws for the membership functions with respect to two different sets A and B? A possible approach is the following.

i) *Membership Function for the Intersection $A \cap B$.* It is sufficient to understand $A \cap B$ as "A and B", or more explicitly as the observation of x with respect to A and B, to conclude that $\mu_{A \cap B}(x)$ should be given by (4.4.17) in which A and B are substituted for R_1 and R_2 respectively.

ii) *Membership Function for the Union $A \cup B$.* One way to derive a model for $\mu_{A \cup B}(x)$ is to start with the equation

$$\Phi_{A \cup B}(x) = \Phi_A(x) + \Phi_B(x) - \Phi_{A \cap B}(x) \tag{4.4.18}$$

and to require that this should also apply to the result Φ' of the observation process, namely one would have the relation

$$\Phi'_{A\cup B}(x) = \Phi'_A(x) + \Phi'_B(x) - \Phi'_{A\cap B}(x) \tag{4.4.19}$$

which can then be calculated in an explicit way.

In addition one has

$$\Phi'_{\overline{A\cup B}}(x) = \Phi'_{\overline{A}\cap \overline{B}}(x) \tag{4.4.20}$$

which also can be calculated explicitly, since the parameters associated with $\bar{A}$ and $\bar{B}$ are $-\theta_1$ and $-\theta_2$ respectively, so that the observation parameter of $\bar{A} \cap \bar{B}$ is $-(\theta_1 + \theta_2)$.

Thus, once $\Phi'_{\overline{A\cup B}}$ is known, it becomes possible to determine its parameter χ by using the equations

$$[\Phi'_{A\cup B}(x)]^{1/2} = [\Phi_{A\cup B}(x)]^{1/2} \cos\chi + [\Phi_{\overline{A\cup B}}(x)]^{1/2} \sin\chi \tag{4.4.21a}$$

$$[\Phi'_{\overline{A\cup B}}(x)]^{1/2} = -[\Phi_{A\cup B}(x)]^{1/2} \sin\chi + [\Phi_{\overline{A\cup B}}(x)]^{1/2} \sin\chi \;. \tag{4.4.21b}$$

4.5 Minkowskian Invariance

4.5.1 Lorentz Transformation

With the Euclidean invariance, the bilinear form (4.4.1) which defines the squared norm is positive or zero. But when this bilinear form may be negative, the matrix Q is not the same. It is replaced by the matrix $\underline{K}$ where

$$(\underline{K}X, \underline{K}X) = (X, X) \geqslant 0 \;. \tag{4.5.1}$$

In this case it is customary to refer to the associated invariant as the Minkowskian metric.

As a basic example let us consider the observation of $X \in \mathbb{R}^2$. The corresponding transformation is

$$y_1 = x_1 \cosh\omega + x_2 \sinh\omega \tag{4.5.2a}$$

$$y_2 = x_1 \sinh\omega + x_2 \cosh\omega \tag{4.5.2b}$$

or in matrix form

$$Y = \underline{K}(\omega)X$$

where $\omega \in \mathbb{R}$ is a parameter that defines the observation. On putting

$$u(\omega) := \frac{\sinh\omega}{\cosh\omega} \;, \tag{4.5.3}$$

$$\varrho(u) := (1 - u^2)^{-1/2} \tag{4.5.4}$$

equations (4.5.2a, b) may be rewritten in the form

$$y_1 = \varrho(u)(x_1 + ux_2) \tag{4.5.5a}$$

$$y_2 = \varrho(u)(ux_1 + x_2) \; , \tag{4.5.5b}$$

which are the so-called Lorentz equations.

4.5.2 Application to the Observation of Probabilities

We consider the probability (p, q) of Sect. (4.2) but we remove the condition $p + q = 1$, and assume that the equations (4.5.2a, b) apply to yield

$$p' = p \cosh \omega + q \sinh \omega \tag{4.5.6a}$$

$$q' = p \sinh \omega + q \cosh \omega \; . \tag{4.5.6b}$$

For small ω one has

$$p' = p + q\omega + o(\omega^2) \; , \qquad q' = p\omega + q + o(\omega^2)$$

and the entropy $H(p', q')$ is

$$H(p', q') = -\frac{p' \ln p' + q' \ln q'}{p' + q'} \tag{4.5.7}$$

$$= (1 - \omega)H(p, q) - \omega(q \ln p + p \ln q - 1) + o(\omega^2) \; . \tag{4.5.8}$$

Strictly speaking (p', q') is no longer a probability distribution, but $H(p', q')$ is symmetrical with respect to p' and q'.

4.5.3 Application to the Observation of Classes

In Sect. 4.4.3, we considered the observation of a set and of its complement by an observer R who constantly has in mind the complementarity of these two classes, that is to say the equation (4.4.13). In other words, R more or less implicitly uses the fact that the observed object belongs to one of these classes but not to both.

Suppose that we do not make this assumption explicitly; then R may still observe the classes according to the Euclidean invariance, but he can also do it following the Minkowskian invariance, in which case one has the observation equation

$$\Phi_A(x) = \Phi_A(x)\cosh \omega + \Phi_{\bar{A}}(x)\sinh \omega \tag{4.5.9a}$$

$$\Phi_{\bar{A}}(x) = \Phi_A(x)\sinh \omega + \Phi_{\bar{A}}(x)\cosh \omega \; . \tag{4.5.9b}$$

Comments. The fact that we have two different models for the observation of classes need not be considered as an inconsistency. Indeed the models should depend upon the assumptions that are made at the level of the observation and one of the purposes of system modelling is exactly to select the most suitable set of such hypotheses.

4.6 Euclidean or Minkowskian Observation?

A problem which now arises is the following: Given that the determinant of the linear observation is unity, we have the choice between the Euclidean matrix $\underline{Q}(\theta)$ and the Lorentz matrix $\underline{K}(\omega)$; and the question is which should we select in order to suitably describe the observation process under consideration? It is clear that we shall need additional assumptions of a physical nature to arrive at the corresponding selection criteria.

4.6.1 Selection of the Observation Mode

First Decision Rule. When the observation process involves the Euclidean invariance $x^2 + y^2 = $ constant, then select the corresponding rotation matrix $\underline{Q}(\theta)$, otherwise assume that the observation matrix is the Minkowskian matrix $\underline{\overline{K}}(\omega)$.   □

This decision rule is clearly the direct qualitative translation of the corresponding mathematical equations, and a careful criticism of the invariance of the Euclidean norm is of order.

Indeed, if the observer is a physical apparatus, then one may usefully assume that $x^2 + y^2 = $ constant, that is to say a length is constant, in which case the observation is merely a measurement. But what happens when this observer is a human? Does he use effectively the condition $x^2 + y^2 = $ constant even when the latter is physically meaningful? For instance, assume that he observes a two-dimensional object whose length and the width are respectively denoted by x and y. One may assume that the observation is such that $xy = $ constant, and therefore

$$\log x + \log y = \text{constant} \tag{4.6.1}$$

and

$$(\log x)'^{1/2} = (\log x)^{1/2} \cos \theta + (\log y)^{1/2} \sin \theta \tag{4.6.2a}$$

$$(\log y)'^{1/2} = -(\log x)^{1/2} \sin \theta + (\log y)^{1/2} \cos \theta \tag{4.6.2b}$$

so that these equations could be considered as describing the corresponding observation process.

But now a new question arises: Can we claim that a human observer works by processing the equations (4.6.1) and (4.6.2a, b)? We do not believe this can be answered in the affirmative. If $\log x$ and $\log y$ can be thought of as being amounts of information, then (4.6.2a, b) may be meaningful, but it is more likely that the observer is sensitive to the signs of the respective variations of x and y. Here, x and y vary in opposite direction: x increases when y decreases, and x decreases when y increases. In contrast, the matrix $K(\omega)$ is such that

$$x^2 = y^2 + \text{constant} ,$$

in other words, x^2 and y^2 vary in the same way. We then obtain the following alternative criterion for selecting the observation matrix.

Second Decision Rule. If the variables x^2 and y^2 vary in opposite directions, that is to say x^2 increases when y^2 decreases, then select the matrix $Q(\theta)$. But if x^2 and y^2 vary in the same direction, then select the matrix $\underline{K}(\omega)$.   □

From a practical standpoint, this second decision rule may appear more satisfactory than the first, in the sense that the criteria which are used are not defined in too precise a manner (e.g. via a mathematical definition), but instead are simple qualitative properties that are easily verified at the stage of the modelling itself.

4.6.2 Application to the [Uncertainty, Information] Pair

Let α denote a random experiment (the sending of a letter of an alphabet in a technical transmission for instance) the informational entropy of which is denoted by $H(\alpha) > 0$. This entropy is a measure of the amount of initial uncertainty which an observer R has about α before any observation of α, and, at this stage, the information $I(\alpha) \geqslant 0$ which R has about α is zero.

Assume now that R undertakes the observation of α, in other words, he makes experiments in order to get information about α, then $H(\alpha)$ diminishes and $I(\alpha)$ increases. If we further consider a linear observation with informational invariance, then after the observation the entropy and information $H'(\alpha)$ and $I'(\alpha)$ are such that

$$H'(\alpha) = H(\alpha)\cos\theta + I(\alpha)\sin\theta \tag{4.6.3a}$$

$$I'(\alpha) = -H(\alpha)\sin\theta + I(\alpha)\cos\theta \ . \tag{4.6.3b}$$

At the beginning of the process, $I(\alpha) = 0$ and (4.6.3b) provides

$$I'(\alpha) = H(\alpha)\sin(-\theta) \ . \tag{4.6.4}$$

In the information theoretic framework, when R performs the experiment β to inquire about α, one has

$$I'(\alpha) = I(\alpha/\beta)$$

$$= H(\alpha) - H(\alpha/\beta) \tag{4.6.5}$$

where $H(\alpha/\beta)$ denotes the conditional entropy of α given β, and on identifying (4.6.4) with (4.6.5) we obtain

$$\sin(-\theta) = 1 - \frac{H(\alpha/\beta)}{H(\alpha)} \tag{4.6.6}$$

and hence the expected consistency of the model.   □

The reader may be wondering why it is necessary to define the observation expressed by (4.6.3a, b), since the standard information theory does the same. The answer is simple: This model (4.6.3) applies to uncertainty that does not involve probability; it is more general and can be utilized even when (4.6.5) does not hold.

4.7 Information Processes and Natural Languages

In this section we shall explain why, in our opinion, a theory of information should refer to natural languages.

4.7.1 On the Absoluteness of Information

Scientists who are interested in, and deal with information may be divided into main two categories: on the one hand engineers and mathematicians who work and think about the question in the wake of Shannon, and, on the other hand, students of general systems and cybernetics who attempt to extend the theory and applications of the Shannonian paradigm. Roughly speaking, the difference between these two schools hinges on the question of whether or not an information theory should account for the meaning of symbols.

To the engineer, a symbol is a symbol, and it has no meaning. The important problem is merely to define the best encoding process which allows a given physical device to correctly identify the letter it receives at the end of channel whatever noise may disturb the transmission.

In cybernetics, the situation is quite different: here we cannot discard the fact that a message necessarily involves a meaning to the observer receiving it! The reason behind this statement is quite obvious: While in technical transmission problems, the physical framework is always the same and to some extent can be considered as absolute, in cybernetics it may happen that a given flow of symbols is handled by various systems of different physical natures so that these symbols can involve different meanings with respect to these different systems.

A typical example of such a situation would be a human observer at the end of a transmission channel. He interprets the received message with respect to some known mode of discourse, or merely with respect to some given language. For instance the message has a meaning to me if it is in English, otherwise it is meaningless. Mathematicians claim that such concerns are relevant to philosophy and not to mathematics, because they involve such phenomena as subjectivity which cannot be formally described. However, we note that this equation can arise even in problems which at first glance are pure technical problems. Indeed, as a very simple illustrative example, consider a computer (software + hardware) which receives a program: the latter may be meaningless or meaningful depending upon whether its listing is consistent with the software of the computer.

So our claim is that we may consider as a basic axiom the statement that the meaning of a message is only a meaning relative to a given observer.   □

4.7.2 The Information Process

We can go on to introduce the concepts of *passive observer* and of *active observer*. In general, technical problems involve passive observers only, namely the physical devices that decode the bit strings, while cybernetics deals with active observers who first read the message and then compare its semantic contents with the information already available in their internal memory. The active observer does not restrict these comparisons to specific instances but is continuously comparing new and existing information. In this way we can speak of an information process. Basically, information is not static, but rather dynamical.

As a result, and this is our second remark, the informational content of a given physical message, that is to say of a given set of symbols, will vary with the observer, and for a given physical observer, it will vary with the internal state of the latter.

4.7.3 Natural Language

We now arrive at the problem of representation of information. Our claim is that all information, whatever its nature, is necessarily conveyed by a language in the broadest sense of the term. This language may be English, Chinese, a set of symbols, a mathematical equation, diagrams, pictures, music, and so on; it is simply the means by which the information is represented.

In order to suitably describe the information process introduced above, we need a suitable description of the language that conveys the information; and due to the diversity of these possible languages, we need a model simple enough to encompass a broad class of situations. We shall refer to this model as *natural language* because it is directly suggested by those languages which are naturally utilized by human beings.

Basically, a natural language involves two spaces of objects Ω and Ω', and the purpose of the language is simply to establish a correspondence between Ω and Ω'. As a concrete example, let us consider English.

Syntactic Space. Ω is the space of letters, but it may also be the space of words depending upon the level of our definition. We shall denote the elements of Ω by the generic term α; thus $\Omega = \{\alpha\}$. It is well known that the relative distribution of the words is structurally organized by some rules which are commonly referred to as the grammar or the syntax of the language. For instance the syntax allows the combination "John is handsome" but prohibits "John handsome is".

Semantic Space. Ω' is the space of meanings that are described by Ω. These meanings can be physical objects, for example the object which is commonly associated with the symbol "table"; but they may also be abstract concepts, like "kindness" for instance. We shall denote the elements of Ω' by the generic term a; thus $\Omega' = \{a\}$. As for the elements of Ω, the relations between the elements of Ω' are governed by some rules that characterize the structure of the latter. These rules do not refer to the language itself, but rather are related to the possible meanings of the different combinations of symbols.

Lexeme. When we say that Ω describes Ω', this is formally equivalent to the statement that there is a correspondence between the elements of Ω and those of Ω'; this is referred to by linguistic scientists as a lexemic correspondence. More precisely a lexeme (α_i, a_j) is a word α_i taken with the meaning a_j. Certain words have no meaning, in which case we shall say that they correspond to the lexeme $(\alpha_i, \emptyset)$; in contrast, other words may correspond to several meanings so that one may have the different lexemes (α_i, a_{j1}), (α_i, a_{j2}) for instance.

4.7.4 Information and Natural Language

Once more, in order to guide our thinking, we shall speak of words and meanings, but this does not restrict the generality of the argument. Instead of words we could equally well have letters or sentences or merely symbols.

From the information theoretic standpoint, the simplest way to describe Ω and Ω' is to assume that α and a are defined by their respective informational entropies $H(\alpha)$ and $H(a)$ in the Shannon sense. To this end, it is sufficient to assume that one may define probability distributions for words and meanings respectively; as indeed is perfectly possible. In the same way, one could define the entropy of the lexeme by the equation

$$H(\alpha, a) = H(\alpha) + H(a/\alpha)$$

and then use the standard information theory. However, we wish here to introduce the interaction between information and observer via the preceding model of observation.

To summarize, we shall assume that a natural language, or equivalently a message, is described by a space Ω of symbols referred to as α, and a space Ω' of meanings referred to as a, with a mapping $\Omega \to \Omega'$ that defines the lexemes of the message. Ω and Ω' are characterized by their respective entropies $H(\alpha)$ and $H(a)$, and any observation of an informational source is equivalent to the observation of the pair $[H(\alpha), H(a)]$.

4.8 Relative Informational Entropy

In this section, we shall derive the concept of relative entropy by assuming that the pair $[H(\alpha), H(a)]$ is observed by means of a linear observation with informational invariance.

4.8.1 Introduction to the Relative Observation

The problem of the relativity of the observation appears in the definition of the entropies $H(\alpha)$ and $H(a)$. Clearly, in the expression

$$H(\alpha) = -\sum p_i \ln p_i \tag{4.8.1}$$

the distribution p_i for letters for instance will depend upon whether we are dealing with history or mathematics. The same remark applies to $H(a)$. As an example, assume that, on receiving a message, we find the word *axes*, for which we have the choice of two differents meanings: (i) cutting tools that consist of a heavy edged head fixed to a handle with the edge parallel to the handle, and (ii) reference lines of a coordinate system. If the message is relevant to mathematics and if the observer is aware of this feature, then the lexeme (axes, (i)) is meaningless. In the dictionary, the two lexemes (axes, (i)) and (axes, (ii)) are both meaningful, but in our particular framework it is only the second one that is relevant.

As a second example, consider the case of a reporter who receives the following text: *the long strive of the workers undermined the economy of the country*; it is likely that he will rectify this by reading "the long strike ...". Here again, the reporter has a prior knowledge of the semantic universe under observation, and this enables him to rectify mistakes.

Clearly, the probability distribution $\{p_i\}$ and thus $H(\alpha)$ should depend upon the observer R (via his subjectivity),

$$H(\alpha, R) = -\sum_i p_i(R)\ln p_i(R) \tag{4.8.2}$$

and likewise, one should have

$$H(a, R) = -\sum_i q_i(R)\ln q_i(R) \tag{4.8.3}$$

As a matter of fact one could claim that it is sufficient to measure $\{p_i(R)\}$ and then to utilize the standard theory of Shannon, and indeed, this is a possible approach. In this model, the basic observed variables would be the probability distributions, and the variations of the entropies would be direct consequences of the variations of these distribution.

Basically, this approach is analytic and it is not at all clear that in actual observation processes, the observer is directly concerned with probability distributions. Our claim is that an observer does not observe or measure the probability distributions that define the events, but rather directly observes the information itself and/or the uncertainty of the message, that is to say the entropies $H(\alpha)$ and $H(a)$.

So we shall assume that the natural language which conveys the message is defined in an absolute way by $H(\alpha)$ and $H(a)$, which therefore appear as *predetermined entropies*, while the entropies $H(\alpha, R)$ and $H(a, R)$ which are relevant to the particular message and observer, are the results of a linear observation with informational invariance. In the following section we shall justify this approach. Notice that $H(\alpha/R)$ and $H(a/R)$ are entropies of the whole language, or of the parts of it that we are dealing with, for example a philosophical language.

4.8.2 Informational Invariance of the Observation

First Remark. A message $[H(\alpha), H(a)]$ is a source of information in the sense that it contains an amount of information which is available to any observer R. The latter may grasp all this information or merely a part of it, depending upon his internal state. We shall refer to total available information as the absolute information contained in the message.

Second Remark. Assume that R observes $[H(\alpha), H(a)]$ by using a linear observation process. His own uncertainty about α can then increase, that is to say can be more than $H(\alpha)$, or it can decrease as a result of the coupling effects between the message and himself. That is, one may have $H(a, R) > H(a)$ or $H(a, R) < H(a)$. But in any case the total amount of absolute information which characterizes the message is invariant and remains available to any other observer. There is no production of information in the message, and likewise no loss.

Third Remark. The problem then is to determine whether Euclidean or Minkowskian invariance is the more suitable model, and to this end it would seem that we need the explicit form of the absolute information available in the source. But fortunately we can circumvent this difficulty by noting the following: In learning processes at least, there is evidence that the better our knowledge about the semantics of a message, the better our knowledge of the corresponding syntax; and conversely the better the knowledge of syntax, then the better the knowledge of semantics. As a result, according to Sect. 4.6, we are led to select the Minkowskian observation.

4.8.3 Relative Entropy

According to (4.5.2a, b) and (4.5.5a, b), the entropies that are effectively measured by the observer R are not $H(\alpha)$ and $H(a)$, but $H_r(\alpha)$ and $H_r(a)$ such that

$$H_r(\alpha) = H(\alpha)\cosh\omega + H(a)\sinh\omega \tag{4.8.4a}$$

$$H_r(a) = H(\alpha)\sinh\omega + H(a)\cosh\omega \tag{4.8.4b}$$

or equivalently

$$H_r(\alpha) = \varrho(u)[H(\alpha) + uH(a)] \tag{4.8.5a}$$

$$H_r(a) = \varrho(u)[uH(\alpha) + H(a)] \tag{4.8.5b}$$

where ω and/or u are real-valued parameters that characterize the observation process.

Definition 4.8.1. We shall refer to $H_r(\alpha)$ and $H_r(a)$ as the relative entropies of α and a given observer R. □

Notation. In the following, in order to emphasize that we consider the result of α via the Minkowskian observation, we shall use the notation α_r. For instance, we shall say that the entropy of α is $H(\alpha)$ while the entropy of α_r is $H_r(\alpha)$. □

4.8.4 Comments and Remarks

i) Basically, the informational entropies $H(\alpha)$ and $H(a)$ are measures of uncertainty, and only secondarily do they represent an amount of information; that is to say, only in some special cases, as a consequence of the concepts of transinformation, transmission or mutual information as defined by Shannon. So it is necessary that we restrict ourselves to this uncertainty interpretation in order to clarify the practical significances of the transformation equations. In addition, we shall assume that we are dealing with the entropy of discrete events, i.e. that $H(\alpha) \geqslant 0$ and $H(a) \geqslant 0$.

ii) This being so, assume firstly that $\omega > 0$, i.e. $u > 0$. Then $H_r(\alpha) > H(\alpha)$ and the uncertainty of the observer R about α increases as a result of the linear observation. This describes the situation in which R has wrong preconceptions about the possible practical meaning of the message content.

Assume now that $\omega < 0$; i.e. $u < 0$, whence one may have $H_r(\alpha) < H(\alpha)$. In other words, when the prior knowledge of the semantics is correct, it diminishes the initial uncertainty about the message.

Clearly one has $H_r(\alpha) = 0$ when

$$\tanh \omega = -\frac{H(\alpha)}{H(a)} \; ; \qquad H(\alpha) \leqslant H(a) \tag{4.8.6}$$

or equivalently

$$\omega = \frac{1}{2} \ln \frac{1 - [H(\alpha)/H(a)]}{1 + [H(\alpha)/H(a)]} \tag{4.8.7}$$

When $H(\alpha) = H(a)$ one then has $H_r(\alpha) \geqslant 0$ for any finite ω, but in contrast, when $H(\alpha) \ll H(a)$ that is to say for a small $H(\alpha)/H(a)$, then $H_r(\alpha) = 0$ for small ω. Note that the term $1 - [H(\alpha)/H(a)]$ looks like the redundancy $1 - (H/H \text{ max})$ which has been used by some authors to measure organization of systems.

In the special case where $H(\alpha) = H(a)$, one has the relation

$$H_r(\alpha) = \sqrt{\frac{1 + u}{1 - u}} H(\alpha) \; ; \qquad H(\alpha) = H(a) \tag{4.8.8}$$

which sheds some light on the role of u.

iii) According to (4.8.4a), when $H(a) = 0$, i.e. when all the symbols have the same meaning, then one has $H_r(\alpha) \geqslant H(\alpha)$: in other words the linear observation leads to an increase in uncertainty.

iv) According to (4.8.4a, b) one has

$$H_r^2(a) - H_r^2(\alpha) = H^2(a) - H^2(\alpha) =: \Delta H^2 \tag{4.8.9}$$

and we now examine the practical significance of this invariance:

i) Despite the existence of synonymous words, it is well known that $H(a) > H(\alpha)$ in most natural languages so that $\Delta H^2 \geqslant 0$.

ii) When $H^2(a) = H^2(\alpha)$, then on average each word has only one meaning, so that the difference $H^2(a) - H^2(\alpha)$ can be thought of as the *linguistic information* contained in the natural language.

iii) Let us rewrite (4.8.9) in the form

$$[H_r(a) - H_r(\alpha)][H_r(a) + H_r(\alpha)] = \text{constant} . \tag{4.8.10}$$

Here again, $H_r(a) - H_r(\alpha)$ can be related to the linguistic uncertainty of the natural language, while $H_r(a) + H_r(\alpha)$ is the total absolute uncertainty involved by the language. When one of these quantities decreases, the other increases, and this is quite consistent with standard results of common observation. Indeed, it is well known that information increases when uncertainty decreases and vice versa. Furthermore $H_r(a) - H_r(\alpha)$ is a meaningful measure of information since it is a difference of entropies.

Redundancy of the Natural Language. In the spirit of the comments just above, one may introduce the term

$$\delta := 1 - \frac{H(\alpha)}{H(a)} \qquad (4.8.11)$$

which may be considered as the redundancy of the language or, quite equivalently, of the message. For a large redundancy, one may easily have $H_r(\alpha) = 0$, whereas this is practically impossible for a small redundancy.

Meaning of the Condition $H_r(\alpha) = 0$. Again for discrete probability, the condition $H(\alpha) = 0$ means that there is no uncertainty about α. When $u > 0$, the equation $H_r(\alpha) = 0$ obviously implies $H(\alpha) = H(a) = 0$; but what happens when $u < 0$? We claim the following:

Whatever the sign of u, the condition $H_r(\alpha) = 0$ represents the fact that, after the Minkowskian observation, the observer no longer has any uncertainty about α. This can be justified as follows. The result of the linear observation is to describe $H_r(\alpha)$ by a new probability distribution $p_r(A_i)$ such that

$$H_r(\alpha) := -\sum_i p_r(A_i) \ln p_r(A_i) \qquad (4.8.12)$$

and hence the statement. $\qquad\qquad\qquad\qquad\qquad\qquad\qquad\qquad\qquad\qquad\qquad\square$

4.9 Conditional Relative Entropy

We need such a concept to generalize the definition of transinformation by means of relative entropy.

4.9.1 Relative Entropy of Product of Messages

We consider two messages (α, a) and (β, b) and their product $(\alpha\beta, ab)$. By the term product we mean that if α provides the outcomes $A_1, A_2, \ldots, A_m$ with the probabilities $p_1, p_2, \ldots, p_m$ and β yields the outcomes $B_1, B_2, \ldots, B_n$ with the probabilities $q_1, q_2, \ldots, q_n$; then the outcomes of $\alpha\beta$ are $A_i B_j$, with the probabilities r_{ij}, $1 \leqslant i \leqslant m$, $1 \leqslant j \leqslant n$. Likewise for a, b and ab.

Given that the entropies $H(\alpha\beta)$ and $H(ab)$ are well defined, the linear observation of Sect. 4.8 applies. Thus there exist $\omega_{\alpha\beta}$ and $u_{\alpha\beta}$ such that

$$H_r(\alpha\beta) = H(\alpha\beta)\cosh\omega_{\alpha\beta} + H(a)\sinh\omega_{\alpha\beta} \qquad (4.9.1)$$

or equivalently

$$H_r(\alpha\beta) = \varrho(u_{\alpha\beta})[H(\alpha\beta) + u_{\alpha\beta}H(ab)] \tag{4.9.2}$$

with similar equations for $H(ab)$.

4.9.2 Composition Law for Cascaded Observers

As mentioned previously, the parameter ω depends upon both the message under consideration and the internal state of the observer, so that generally one will have $\omega_{\alpha\beta} \neq \omega_{\beta\alpha}$.

The following question then arises: can we exhibit a functional relation between these parameters?

Proposition 4.9.1. Let $\omega_{\beta/\alpha}$ and $u_{\beta/\alpha}$ denote the observation parameters associated with β given that α is realized. The following equation then holds:

$$u_{\alpha\beta} = \frac{u_\alpha + u_{\beta/\alpha}}{1 + u_\alpha u_{\beta/\alpha}} \ . \tag{4.9.3} \quad \square$$

Proof. Let us define

$$\omega_{\alpha\beta} = \omega_\alpha + \omega_{\beta/\alpha} \ ; \tag{4.9.4}$$

we then have

$$\cosh \omega_{\alpha\beta} = \cosh \omega_\alpha \cosh \omega_{\beta/\alpha} + \sinh \omega_\alpha \sinh \omega_{\beta/\alpha} \tag{4.9.5}$$

$$\sinh \omega_{\alpha\beta} = \sinh \omega_\alpha \cosh \omega_{\beta/\alpha} + \cosh \omega_\alpha \sinh \omega_{\beta/\alpha} \tag{4.9.6}$$

and taking the quotient directly yields (4.9.3).

Important Remark. $u_{\beta/\alpha}$ has a property quite similar to that of conditional probability, that is to say two cases may occur: either $u_{\alpha\beta}$ and u_α are given, and then one may calculate $u_{\beta/\alpha}$; or we have at hand the values of u_α land $u_{\beta/\alpha}$ and then we may define $u_{\alpha\beta}$. $\qquad\qquad\qquad\qquad\qquad\qquad\qquad\qquad\qquad\qquad\qquad\qquad\quad\square$

In addition, it is in order to point out that (4.9.3) does not require any special new assumption; it is merely a direct consequence of our basic hypothesis that the process involves a linear observation with informational invariance.

The being so, we have the following result:

Proposition 4.9.2. The equality

$$H_r(\alpha\beta) = H_r(\beta\alpha) \tag{4.9.7}$$

holds if and only if the following conditions are satisfied:

$$u_{\alpha/\beta} = u_\alpha \quad \text{and} \tag{4.9.8}$$

$$u_{\beta/\alpha} = u_\beta \ . \tag{4.9.9} \quad \square$$

Proof. This result is a consequence of the equation

$$u_{\beta\alpha} = \frac{u_\beta + u_{\alpha/\beta}}{1 + u_\beta u_{\alpha/\beta}} . \qquad (4.9.10)$$

The meaning of $u_{\alpha\beta}$ is related to the cascaded observation processes in which one first observes α and then β. Likewise $u_{\beta\alpha}$ is associated with the process in which one first observes β and then α.

4.9.3 Relative Entropy Conditional to a Given Experiment

Preliminary Remarks. In the Shannonian theory, the conditional entropy $H(\beta/\alpha)$ is defined by the equation

$$H(\alpha\beta) = H(\alpha) + H(\beta/\alpha) \qquad (4.9.11)$$

which therefore provides the expression

$$H(\beta/\alpha) = \sum_i p(\alpha_i)H(\beta/\alpha_i) . \qquad (4.9.12)$$

Analogously, one could define the conditional relative entropy $H_r(\beta/\alpha)$ by the equation $H_r(\alpha\beta) = H_r(\alpha) + H_r(\beta/\alpha)$. But this is not so easy as it looks, due mainly to the practical significance of the parameter $u_{\beta/\alpha}$ defined by (4.9.4) above. Indeed, in the special case where α_r and β_r are stochastically independent and where $\omega_{\beta/\alpha} = \omega_\beta$, one should have $H_r(\alpha\beta) = H_r(\alpha) + H_r(\beta)$. But now let us expand (4.9.1) by using (4.9.4) and (4.9.11) to obtain

$$H_r(\alpha\beta) = H_r(\alpha)\cosh \omega_{\beta/\alpha} + [H(\beta/\alpha)\cosh \omega_{\beta/\alpha} + H(b/a)\sinh \omega_{\beta/\alpha}]\cosh \omega_\alpha$$
$$+ H(\alpha\beta)\sinh \omega_\alpha \sinh \omega_{\beta/\alpha} + H(a)\cosh \omega_\alpha \sinh \omega_{\beta/\alpha}$$
$$+ H(b/a)\sinh \omega_\alpha \cosh \omega_{\beta/\alpha} ; \qquad (4.9.13)$$

and when α_r and β_r are independent, one has

$$H_r(\alpha\beta) = H_r(\alpha)\cosh \omega_\beta + H_r(\beta)\cosh \omega_\alpha + H(\alpha\beta)\sinh \omega_\alpha \sinh \omega_\beta$$
$$+ H(a)\cosh \omega_\alpha \sinh \omega_\beta + H(b)\sinh \omega_\alpha \cosh \omega_\beta . \qquad (4.9.14)$$

It is clear that $H_r(\alpha\beta) \neq H_r(\alpha) + H_r(\beta)$.

It follows that the equation (4.9.11) does not apply to relative entropies, and we are so led to introduce the definition:

Definition 4.9.1. Let $\omega_{\beta/\alpha}$ and $u_{\beta/\alpha} := \tanh \omega_{\beta/\alpha}$ be given by (4.9.3) and (4.9.4). The relative conditional entropy $H_r(\beta/\alpha)$ is then defined by the expression

$$H_r(\beta/\alpha) := \varrho(u_{\beta/\alpha})[H(\beta/\alpha a) + u_{\beta/\alpha}H(b/\alpha a)] . \qquad (4.9.15) \quad \square$$

Motivation. It is important that when we consider the message β_r given α_r, we explicitly mean β_r given the lexeme (α, a); in other words we consider the syntactic space $H(b/\alpha a)$. It remains to define the corresponding observation parameter, and to this end we naturally refer to (4.9.4). $\square$

4.9.4 Applications to Determinacy

According to Sect. 4.8, β_r is completely defined by α_r if and only if

$$H_r(\beta/\alpha) = 0 \ . \tag{4.9.16}$$

i) Assume that $u_{\beta/\alpha} > 0$; then condition (4.9.16) holds if and only if

$$H(\beta/\alpha a) = H(b/\alpha a) = 0 \ ,$$

in other words, β_r is completely determined by α_r if and only if both the symbol β and its meaning b are completely determined by (α, a). In such a case, the linear observation does not bring syntactic information to the observer but instead confuses him. As a result, the conditions for the complete determinacy of β in the presence of this confusing semantics are more stringent, and, in particular, the meaning itself needs to be identified.

ii) Now assume that $u_{\beta/\alpha} < 0$. One may then have $H_r(\beta/\alpha) = 0$ while $H(\beta/\alpha a) \neq 0$. In such a case, the observer can guess the exact value of the symbol under consideration even when β and b are not completely determined by (α, a). This situation is typified by a secretary who can identify a missing letter in a manuscript.

4.9.5 Comparison of $H(\beta/\alpha)$ with $H_r(\beta/\alpha)$

This comparison will be of interest when we introduce the concept of relative transinformation.

The basic remark is the following: one may have either $H_r(\beta/\alpha) > H(\beta/\alpha)$ or $H_r(\beta/\alpha) < H(\beta/\alpha)$.

For illustrative purpose, assume that $u_{\beta/\alpha} =: v$ is small compared to one. In this case we have

$$H(\beta/\alpha) - H_r(\beta/\alpha) \cong H(\beta/\alpha) - H(\beta/\alpha a) - vH(\beta/\alpha a)$$

and according to the relations

$$H(\beta/\alpha) = H(\alpha\beta) - H(\alpha) \ , H(\beta/\alpha a) = H(\alpha a\beta) - H(\alpha) - H(a/\alpha)$$

we also have

$$H(\beta/\alpha) - H_r(\beta/\alpha) \cong H(\alpha\beta) - H(\alpha a\beta) + H(a/\alpha) - vH(b/\alpha a)$$

$$\cong H(a/\alpha) - H(a/\alpha\beta) - vH(b/\alpha a) \ .$$

So assume that $v < 0$. Given that $H(a/\alpha\beta) < H(a/\alpha)$, one then has $H_r(\beta/\alpha) < H(\beta/\alpha)$. Assume now that $H(a/\alpha) = 0$ and $v > 0$. In this case, since one also has $H(a/\alpha\beta) = 0$, it follows that $H_r(\beta/\alpha) > H(\beta/\alpha)$.

4.10 On the Meaning and the Estimation of the Observation Parameter

In this section, we shall examine the question of how to estimate the value of u, and we shall obtain the practical meaning of this parameter.

4.10.1 Estimation of the Observation Parameter

Problem. Let $X^t := (x_1, x_2)$ denote an unknown vector and assume that it is observed, via Minkowskian observations, by two different observers R and R' who obtain the respective measurements $Y^t := (y_1, y_2)$ and $Y'^t := (y_1', y_2')$. The problem is then to estimate X. ☐

Comments. It is clear that the problem has no solution if we have only one measurement at hand. This being so, the fact that by repeatedly observing the same variable X one gets different values Y, Y', ... is merely a consequence of the fact that the internal state ω of the observers is itself varying.

Solution. (i) Let ω and ω' denote the internal states of the observers R and R' respectively; one then has

$$Y = \underline{K}(\omega)X \tag{4.10.1a}$$

$$Y' = \underline{K}(\omega')X \tag{4.10.1b}$$

and therefore

$$\underline{K}^{-1}(\omega)Y = \underline{K}^{-1}(\omega')Y' \tag{4.10.2}$$

ii) Equation (4.10.2) yields

$$\underline{K}(\omega')\underline{K}^{-1}(\omega)Y = Y' \tag{4.10.3}$$

or equivalently, by using the property that $\underline{K}^{-1}(\omega) = \underline{K}(-\omega)$,

$$\underline{K}(\omega' - \omega)Y = Y' \ . \tag{4.10.4}$$

iii) One can then calculate the value of $\Delta\omega := \omega' - \omega$ as follows. First, one expands (4.10.4) in the form

$$y_1 \cosh \Delta\omega + y_2 \sinh \Delta\omega = y_1' \tag{4.10.5a}$$

$$y_1 \sinh \Delta\omega + y_2 \cosh \Delta\omega = y_2' \tag{4.10.5b}$$

to obtain the equation

$$\tanh \Delta\omega = \frac{y_2 y_1' - y_1 y_2'}{y_2 y_2' - y_1 y_1'} \tag{4.10.6}$$

which uniquely defines $\Delta\omega$.

iv) It now remains to determine the value of ω. To this end, we rewrite (4.10.1a, b) as follows

$$X = K(-\omega)Y \tag{4.10.7}$$

$$= K(-\omega - \Delta\omega)Y' \tag{4.10.8}$$

and we concentrate on the component x_1 for which we have

$$x_1 = y_1 \cosh \omega - y_2 \sinh \omega$$

$$= y_1' \cosh(\omega + \Delta\omega) - y_2' \sinh(\omega + \Delta\omega) \ .$$

On expanding $\cosh(\omega + \Delta\omega)$ and $\sinh(\omega + \Delta\omega)$, we obtain

$$\tanh \omega = \frac{y_1 - y_1' \cosh \Delta\omega + y_2' \sinh \Delta\omega}{y_2 - y_2' \cosh \Delta\omega + y_1' \sinh \Delta\omega} \tag{4.10.9}$$

which defines the value of ω in terms of $\Delta\omega$ which has been calculated in (4.10.6).

v) Given ω, one can recover the value of X from the equation

$$X = K^{-1}(\omega) Y \ .$$

This procedure allows us to determine ω, ω', x_1 and x_2 and to check whether the Minkowskian observation is applicable. Indeed, if the right-hand side of (4.10.6) does not lie between -1 and $+1$, this means that our assumptions are wrong.

4.10.2 Practical Meaning of the Observation Parameter

We shall derive the practical meaning of u as follows.

We refer to the equations (4.5.5a, b) which we write in the differential form

$$dy_1 = \varrho(u)(dx_1 + u dx_2) \tag{4.10.10a}$$

$$dy_2 = \varrho(u)(u dx_1 + dx_2) \tag{4.10.10b}$$

and we define the gradients

$$\nabla x := dx_1/dx_2 \tag{4.10.11}$$

$$\nabla y := dy_1/dy_2 \tag{4.10.12}$$

so that (4.10.10a, b) provides

$$\nabla y = \frac{\nabla x + u}{1 + u\nabla x} \ . \tag{4.10.13}$$

If we assume that $\nabla x = 0$, then (4.10.13) yields $\nabla y = u$ when $\nabla x = 0$, in other words, although x_1 is constant, it is perceived by the observer as if it were varying with the gradient $\nabla y = u$.

Practical Determination of u. From the above remark we can derive a general procedure for estimating the numerical value of $u(R)$ for a given observer R:

i) R observes the given fixed pair (x_1, x_2) and the result of this observation is (y_{11}, y_{21}).

ii) A while later, R once more observes (x_1, x_2) to obtain the new measurement (y_{12}, y_{22}).

iii) An estimate $\hat{u}(R)$ of $u(R)$ is then

$$\hat{u}(R) = \frac{y_{12} - y_{11}}{y_{22} - y_{21}} \ . \tag{4.10.14}$$

Comments. (i) This approach can be improved by using more sophisticated techniques to estimate the derivative dy_1/dy_2.

ii) It may happen that by repeatedly performing the same experiment one obtains different values $\hat{u}(R)$. If these variations are due to experimental errors, then one can use statistical techniques. Otherwise it means that the observer R is himself evolving with time.

4.10.3 On the Value of the Observation Parameter $u(R)$

One can relate the value of u to the observer's prior knowledge of the semantic content of the message. When the observer R has a complete and accurate prior knowledge of the meaning of the message, then $u = -1$. But when R has a completely false preconception of this semantics, then $u = 1$. In the latter case R thinks he knows something about the message, but it is something wrong. When u is close to one, then it has the physical properties of a gain coefficient, and the term $uH(a)$ may be thought of as the fraction of the semantics that is effectively "known" to R in advance.

4.11 Relative Transinformation

While in the Shannonian framework the concept of transinformation may be defined in a unique way, mainly because the concept of information itself is considered as absolute, this is not so when we deal with relative entropies. Here the transinformation will depend upon the type of observation considered. In this way we shall have several models of such relative transinformation.

4.11.1 Derivation of Relative Transinformation

Definition 4.11.1. In the framework (syntax, semantics), and on assuming that the entropies are observed via a Minkowskian observation, the amount of information $T(\beta/\alpha)$ provided by α about β is defined by the expression

$$T(\beta/\alpha) := H(\beta) - H_r(\beta/\alpha) \tag{4.11.1}$$

$$= H(\beta) - \varrho(u_{\beta/\alpha})[H(\beta/\alpha a) + u_{\beta/\alpha}H(b/\alpha a)]. \tag{4.11.2} \quad \square$$

Derivation. This definition is obtained as follows.

i) Assume that the observer is interested simply in identifying the symbol β irrespective of any meaning it may have. His initial uncertainty about β is $H(\beta)$, as in the usual framework.

ii) In order to identify β the observer performs the experiment α and we assume that, at this stage of his observation process, he uses not only the pair (α, a) but also the meaning b that β could have given to (α, a). In this case, the identification process does not involve $H(\beta/\alpha)$, but rather $H_r(\beta/\alpha)$.

iii) We now consider the transinformation as a variation of entropy, and are thus led to the above definition. $\square$

Definition 4.11.2. In order to be consistent with the usual terminology, we shall refer to $T(\beta/\alpha)$ as the *relative transinformation*, the *relative transmission*, or the *relative mutual information* between α and β, although these expressions are not entirely suitable since, as we shall see later, $T(\beta/\alpha)$ is not symmetrical with respect to β and α. $\square$

4.11.2 Some Properties of the Relative Transinformation

i) By introducing $H(\beta/\alpha)$ in (4.11.1) one has

$$T(\beta/\alpha) = I(\beta/\alpha) + H(\beta/\alpha) - H_r(\beta/\alpha) \; ; \tag{4.11.3}$$

and according to the result in Sect. 4.9.5 one may have $T(\beta/\alpha) > I(\beta/\alpha)$ or $T(\beta/\alpha) < I(\beta/\alpha)$. This is quite consistent with the practical significance which has been attributed to u.

ii) The relative transinformation can be negative. Indeed, assume for instance that $H(\beta/\alpha) = 0$. One then has $I(\beta/\alpha) = H(\beta)$ and $H(\beta/\alpha a) = 0$ so that

$$T(\beta/\alpha) = H(\beta) - \varrho(u_{\beta/\alpha})u_{\beta/\alpha}H(b/\alpha a) \; .$$

To obtain negative transinformation, it is then sufficient that $u_{\beta/\alpha} > 0$ be large enough, i.e. that the confusing effect due to the coupling between syntax and semantics be important enough.

This feature is of course one of the basic difference from the Shannonian model in which one has $I(\beta/\alpha) \geqslant 0$.

iii) As a consequence of (4.11.3) one has

$$T(\beta/\alpha) - [H(\beta/\alpha) - H_r(\beta/\alpha)] = T(\alpha/\beta) - [H(\alpha/\beta) - H_r(\alpha/\beta)] \; . \tag{4.11.4}$$

Indeed, the expression for $T(\alpha/\beta)$ is

$$T(\alpha/\beta) = I(\alpha/\beta) + H(\alpha/\beta) - H_r(\alpha/\beta) \tag{4.11.5}$$

and in addition one has

$$I(\beta/\alpha) = I(\alpha/\beta) \tag{4.11.6}$$

so that (4.11.3) and (4.11.5) directly yield (4.11.4).

(iv) **Proposition 4.11.1.** Generally one has

$$T(\beta/\alpha) \neq T(\alpha/\beta) \tag{4.11.7}$$

and the equality $T(\beta/\alpha) = T(\alpha/\beta)$ holds if and only if

$$H(\beta/\alpha) - H_r(\beta/\alpha) = H(\alpha/\beta) - H_r(\alpha/\beta) \; . \tag{4.11.8}$$ $\square$

The proof is direct and is a consequence of (4.11.6). Thus, if we consider the difference $H(\beta) - H_r(\beta)$ as a measure of the effects of coupling between syntax and semantics, then (4.11.8) implies that variations in the conditional entropies due to learning or dislearning are the same for (β/α) and (α/β).

4.11.3 Relative Entropy and Information Balance

Here we shall prove the following result:

Proposition 4.11.2. Assume that the entropies are observed via a Minkowskian process. A necessary and sufficient condition for the result of the experiment (α, a) to provide a complete identification of the result of experiment β is

$$H_r(\beta/\alpha) = 0 \tag{4.11.9}$$

$$H(\alpha/\beta) = 0 \ . \tag{4.11.10} \quad \square$$

Proof. (i) First it is necessary that

$$H_r(\beta/\alpha) = 0 \tag{4.11.11}$$

so that the condition for identification of β is

$$T(\beta/\alpha) \geqslant H(\beta) \ . \tag{4.11.12}$$

ii) This being so, according to (4.11.4) and condition (4.11.11) we rewrite (4.11.12) in the form

$$T(\alpha/\beta) + H(\beta/\alpha) - H(\alpha/\beta) + H_r(\alpha/\beta) \geqslant H(\beta); \tag{4.11.13}$$

and on expanding $T(\alpha/\beta)$ we get

$$H(\alpha) - H(\alpha/\beta) \geqslant H(\beta) - H(\beta/\alpha) \ . \tag{4.11.14}$$

iii) We now consider the optimal α such that $H(\alpha/\beta) = 0$, and finally obtain the condition

$$H(\alpha) \geqslant H(\beta) - H(\beta/\alpha) \ , \tag{4.11.15}$$

whose validity is obvious since it is equivalent to $H(\alpha\beta) \geqslant H(\beta)$. $\quad \square$

Comments. (i) In the standard framework, that is to say in the absence of semantics, the conditions for determinacy are the inequalities (4.11.10) and (4.11.15) along with

$$H(\beta/\alpha) = 0 \tag{4.11.16}$$

and it is clear that the latter is not equivalent to condition (4.11.9).

ii) Assume that there is dislearning, i.e. $u_{\beta/\alpha} > 0$. Condition (4.11.9) then requires that one has simultaneously

$$H(\beta/\alpha a) = 0 \tag{4.11.17}$$

$$H(b/\alpha a) = 0 \ . \tag{4.11.18}$$

In other words, the process is so confusing that it is necessary for both the symbol β and its meaning b to be completely defined by the pair (α, a). In addition, note that condition (4.11.17) is more stringent than condition (4.11.16) in the sense that the latter can be satisfied while the former is not.

iii) Now assume that $u_{\beta/\alpha} < 0$; equation (4.11.9) then yields

$$H(\beta/\alpha a) = -u_{\beta/\alpha}H(b/\alpha a) \ . \tag{4.11.19}$$

Expressed in words, it is sufficient that the uncertainty in β conditional on (α, a) be a given fraction of the conditional uncertainty of the corresponding semantics, for the identification to be possible. In short, β is not completely determined by (α, a), but the uncertainty about it is small enough.

This corresponds to the following practical situation. In the transmission of a given message, a letter is missing, but since the receiver fully comprehends the semantics of this message, his uncertainty about this letter is small enough for him to rectify the mistake.

For instance, assume that the whole message is made up of the words *"the long stri?e of the workers"*. The missing letter can be k or v with the same probability. But if the whole message is *"the long stri?e of the workers undermined the economy of the country"*, then the missing letter is almost certainly k.

4.11.4 Application to the Encoding Problem

Problem. We have a given set of words which constitute a language, and we want to encode them by using the letters of a given alphabet. What is the mean number of letters that are necessary to encode one word?

Definitions and Notation. To take a concrete example, let us assume that we have to encode English words by means of binary digits. We shall apply the framework of Sect. 4.11.3 by making the following identifications

$\alpha :=$ generic symbol which refers to the encoding letters, for instance $\alpha = \{0, 1\}$.

$\boldsymbol{\alpha} := \alpha_1 \alpha_2 \ldots \alpha_n$
= sequence of the n letters which encode a given word

$a :=$ set of control bits associated with the sequence $\alpha_1, \alpha_2, \ldots, \alpha_n$

$\beta :=$ generic term which refers to the words to be encoded.

$b :=$ generic term which refers to the objects of a given universe of discourse.

Solution. (i) In a simplified (pessimistic) approach, we shall assume that the letters $\alpha_1, \alpha_2, \ldots, \alpha_n$ are independent so that one has

$$H(\boldsymbol{\alpha}) = nH(\alpha) \tag{4.11.20}$$

and our task is to determine the smallest possible value of n.

ii) The condition (4.11.15) refers to $H(\beta/\alpha)$ and in order to calculate the latter we shall write

$$H(\alpha a\beta) = H(\alpha) + H(\beta/\alpha) + H(a/\alpha\beta)$$

$$= H(\alpha) + H(a/\alpha) + H(\beta/\alpha a)$$

therefore obtaining

$$H(\beta/\alpha) = H(\beta/\alpha a) + H(a/\alpha) - H(a/\alpha\beta) \ . \qquad (4.11.21)$$

iii) Inserting (4.11.21) into (4.11.15) yields the condition

$$H(\alpha) \geqslant H(\beta) - H(\beta/\alpha a) - H(a/\alpha) + H(a/\alpha\beta)$$

and on taking account of (4.11.11) or (4.11.19) we obtain

$$H(\alpha) \geqslant H(\beta) + u_{\beta/\alpha} H(b/\alpha a) - [H(a/\alpha) - H(a/\alpha\beta)] \ . \qquad (4.11.22)$$

Since a is the set of control bits on the one hand, and $H(a/\alpha\beta) \leqslant H(a/\alpha)$ on the other, one has necessarily (on assuming that there is no transmission error in these bits!)

$$H(a/\alpha) = H(a/\alpha\beta) = 0$$

such that (4.11.22) along with (4.11.20) yield

$$n \geqslant n_0 + u_{\beta/\alpha} \frac{H(b/\alpha a)}{H(\alpha)} \ . \qquad (4.11.23)$$

Here n_0, which is defined as

$$n_0 = \frac{H(\beta)}{H(\alpha)} \ ,$$

is the solution provided by the Shannon theory.

iv) Thus, in the absence of any transmission error, there is a one-to-one correspondence between the set $\{\beta\}$ and the set $\{\alpha a\}$ so that one has

$$H(b/\alpha a) = H(b/\beta) \qquad (4.11.24)$$

and (4.11.22) can be re-written in the form

$$n \geqslant n_0 + u_{\beta/\alpha} \frac{H(b/\beta)}{H(\alpha)} \ . \qquad (4.11.25)$$

v) According to Sect. 4.10.2, one may define $u_{\beta/\alpha}$ by the expression

$$u_{\beta/\alpha} = \frac{dH(\beta/\alpha a; R)}{dH(b/\alpha a; R)} \qquad (4.11.26)$$

where R denotes parameters that relate to the observer.

We can now conclude as follows:

Assume that $H(b/\beta) = 0$. Condition (4.11.25) then yields $n = n_0$. Indeed the equality $H(b/\beta) = 0$ can be considered as describing a language without semantics.

Assume that $u_{\beta/\alpha} > 0$; then $n > n_0$. This case represents incorrect prior "knowledge" of the message content.

Assume that $u_{\beta/\alpha} < 0$; then $n < n_0$. This corresponds to accurate prior knowledge of the message content.

According to (4.11.25), one may also say that the condition $u_{\beta/\alpha} < 0$ defines a learning observer while $u_{\beta/\alpha} > 0$ characterizes a dislearning or easily confused observer.

4.12 Minkowskian Relative Transinformation

In this section, we shall assume that the linear observation applies to the transinformation itself.

4.12.1 Definition of Minkowskian Relative Transinformation

Definition 4.12.1. In the framework (syntax, semantics), and on assuming that the Shannonian transinformations $I(\beta/\alpha)$ and $I(b/a)$ are observed via a Minkowskian observation, the total amount of information $T_1(\beta/\alpha)$ and $T_1(b/a)$ provided by (α, a) about (β, b) are defined by the equations

$$T_1(\beta/\alpha) := I(\beta/\alpha)\cosh \Psi_{\beta/\alpha} + I(b/a)\sinh \Psi_{\beta/\alpha} \tag{4.12.1a}$$

$$T_1(b/a) := I(\beta/\alpha)\sinh \Psi_{\beta/\alpha} + I(b/a)\cosh \Psi_{\beta/\alpha} \tag{4.12.1b}$$

or equivalently

$$T_1(\beta/\alpha) := \varrho(v_{\beta/\alpha})[I(\beta/\alpha) + v_{\beta/\alpha}I(b/a)] \tag{4.12.2a}$$

$$T_1(b/a) := \varrho(v_{\beta/\alpha})[v_{\beta/\alpha}I(\beta/\alpha) + I(b/a)] \tag{4.12.2b}$$

with

$$I(\beta/\alpha) := H(\beta) - H(\beta/\alpha) \tag{4.12.3}$$

and where $\Psi_{\beta/\alpha}$ with $v_{\beta/\alpha} = \tanh \Psi_{\beta/\alpha}$ are the observation parameters.

Derivation. This definition is justified as follows.

i) Assume that the observer is interested in the identification of both the symbol β and its meaning b and that his initial uncertainties about β and b are $H(\beta)$ and $H(b)$.

ii) Next, in order to identify β and b, the observer performs the experiment (α, a) in such a manner that the transinformation so obtained is $I(\beta/\alpha)$ and $I(b/a)$. At this stage we assume that there are no coupling effects between syntax and semantics.

iii) Now it is well known that $I(\beta/\alpha)$ and $I(b/a)$ vary in the same way, that is to say both increase or both decrease. This merely reflects the fact that the better the information about β, the better the information about b, and vice versa. We are then led to apply the Minkowskian observation to $I(\beta/\alpha)$ and $I(b/a)$ and hence the equations (4.12.1a, b).   □

4.12.2 Some Properties of Minkowskian Relative Transinformation

i) It is possible to have $T_{\mathrm{I}}(\beta/\alpha) > I(\beta/\alpha)$ or $T_{\mathrm{I}}(\beta/\alpha) < I(\beta/\alpha)$ depending upon the respective values of v, $I(\beta/\alpha)$ and $I(b/a)$.

As an illustrative example, assume that v is small compared to one. Equation (4.12.1a) then provides

$$T_{\mathrm{I}}(\beta/\alpha) \cong I(\beta/\alpha) + vI(b/a) . \tag{4.12.5}$$

Here the sign of v works in the opposite way to that of u; clearly when $v > 0$ there is an increase of information with respect to $I(\beta/\alpha)$, and when $v < 0$ there is loss of information.

ii) One can have $T_{\mathrm{I}}(\beta/\alpha) < 0$. Indeed, it is sufficient to assume that $I(\beta/\alpha) = 0$, that is to say, α does not bring any information about β and $v < 0$. This is the situation typical of confusing processes.

iii) **Proposition 4.12.1.** In general, one has

$$T_{\mathrm{I}}(\beta/\alpha) \neq T_{\mathrm{I}}(\alpha/\beta) \tag{4.12.6}$$

and the equality $T_{\mathrm{I}}(\beta/\alpha) = T_{\mathrm{I}}(\alpha/\beta)$ holds if and only if

$$\Psi_{\beta/\alpha} = \Psi_{\alpha/\beta} . \tag{4.12.7}$$ □

This is a direct consequence of (4.12.1a) together with the relations $I(\beta/\alpha) = I(\alpha/\beta)$ and $I(b/a) = I(a/b)$.

iv) Assume that $v_{\beta/\alpha} > 0$ and $T_{\mathrm{I}}(\beta/\alpha) = 0$, in other word α_r does not contain any information about β. Then according to (4.12.2a), one has $I(\beta/\alpha) = 0$ and $I(b/a) = 0$; clearly α does not contain information about β, and a does not contain information about b.

Assume now that $v_{\beta/\alpha} < 0$. One may then have $T_{\mathrm{I}}(\beta/\alpha) = 0$ even when $I(\beta/\alpha) \neq 0$. Expressed in words, there is effectively an amount of information disposable in α and a relating to β and b, but the observer is unable to grasp this information.

4.12.3 Identification via Information Balance

Proposition 4.12.2. Assume that the information $I(\beta/\alpha)$ and $I(b/a)$ is observed via a Minkowsian process. A necessary and sufficient condition for the result of the experiment (α, a) to provide a complete identification of the result of the experiment β is that

$$H(\alpha/\beta) = 0 \tag{4.12.8}$$

$$H(\alpha) \geqslant H(\beta)\sqrt{1 - v_{\beta/\alpha}^2} - v_{\beta/\alpha}I(b/a) \ . \qquad\qquad (4.12.9) \quad \square$$

Proof. (i) $H(\beta)$ is the amount of information we need to identify β, in other words, one should have

$$T_1(\beta/\alpha) \geqslant H(\beta) \qquad\qquad (4.12.10)$$

or likewise, by using equation (4.12.2a)

$$I(\beta/\alpha) \geqslant H(\beta)\sqrt{1 - v_{\beta/\alpha}^2} - v_{\beta/\alpha}I(b/a) \ . \qquad\qquad (4.12.11)$$

ii) On taking account of the relation $I(\beta/\alpha) = I(\alpha/\beta)$ we rewrite condition (4.12.11) in the form

$$H(\alpha) - H(\alpha/\beta) \geqslant H(b)\sqrt{1 - v_{\beta/\alpha}^2} - v_{\beta/\alpha}I(b/a) \qquad\qquad (4.12.12)$$

iii) Now we consider the optimal α such that all the information it contains is related to β; this requires that $H(\alpha/\beta) = 0$ and hence condition (4.12.9). $\quad\square$

Comments. Here again, we shall compare this result with the balance conditions of the standard theory. These we shall write in the form of the equality (4.12.8) together with

$$H(\alpha) > H(\beta) \ . \qquad\qquad (4.12.13)$$

It is clear that the condition (4.12.9) is much less restrictive than (4.12.13) when $v_{\beta/\alpha} > 0$. For the limiting case, when

$$v_{\beta/\alpha} = \frac{H(\beta)}{I(b/a)}\left[1 + \frac{H^2(\beta)}{I^2(b/a)}\right]^{-1/2} \ ,$$

the determinacy condition is

$$H(\alpha) \geqslant 0 \ .$$

This reflects the fact that the symbol β is known in advance to the observer so that no experiment α is necessary.

In contrast, for a negative and small $v_{\beta/\alpha}$, one has

$$H(\alpha) \geqslant H(\beta) - v_{\beta/\alpha}I(b/a)$$

which is more pessimistic than (4.12.13) in the general case where $I(b/a) > 0$. When $I(b/a) = 0$, one finds the usual condition $H(\alpha) \geqslant H(\beta)$; in other words, when the semantics is confusing, it is better not to use it.

4.13 Effect of Scaling Factor in an Observation with Informational Invariance

Assume that the entropies $H(\alpha)$ and $H(a)$ of Sect. 4.8.3 do not have the same measurement unit, and let $c > 0$ denote a scaling factor such that $H(\alpha)$ and $cH(a)$

have the same measurement unit. According to (4.8.5a, b) one then has the observation equations

$$H_r(\alpha) = \varrho(u)[H(\alpha) + ucH(a)] \qquad (4.13.1a)$$

$$cH_r(a) = \varrho(u)[uH(\alpha) + cH(a)] \qquad (4.13.1b)$$

with $-1 \leqslant u \leqslant +1$. We rewrite (4.13.1b) in the form

$$H_r(a) = \varrho(u)\left[\frac{u}{c}H(\alpha) + H(a)\right]$$

and define

$$v := uc , \qquad -c \leqslant v \leqslant +c \qquad (4.13.2)$$

to finally obtain the observation equations

$$H_r(\alpha) = \varrho\left(\frac{v}{c}\right)[H(\alpha) + vH(a)] \qquad (4.13.3a)$$

$$H_r(a) = \varrho\left(\frac{v}{c}\right)\left[\frac{v}{c^2}H(\alpha) + H(a)\right] \qquad (4.13.3b)$$

which are familiar to the reader.

Assume that c is sufficiently large and v sufficiently small that we can drop the terms in v/c^2 and write

$$H_r(\alpha) \cong H(\alpha) + vH(a) \qquad (4.13.4a)$$

$$H_r(a) \cong H(a) \qquad (4.13.4b)$$

These equations emphasize the asymmetry that appears between $H(\alpha)$ and $H(a)$.

4.14 Comparison with Renyi Entropy

4.14.1 Renyi Entropy and Relative Entropy

For small u, one can write (4.8.5a) in the form

$$H_r(\alpha) = H(\alpha) + uH(a) + o(u^2) , \qquad (4.14.1)$$

and if we identify $H_r(\alpha)$ in this expression with $H_c(\alpha)$ in (2.9.13), we obtain the relation

$$uH(a) \equiv -(c - 1)\left[\sum_{i=1}^{m} p_i(\ln p_i)^2 - H^2(\alpha)\right]. \qquad (4.14.2)$$

Since both $H(a)$ and the quantity in square brackets are positive by virtue of the Schwarz inequality (we assume that the semantic variable is a discrete one), we can decompose this identity and set

$$H(a) \equiv \sum_{i=1}^{m} p_i (\ln p_i)^2 - H^2(\alpha) , \tag{4.14.3}$$

$$c \equiv 1 - u . \tag{4.14.4}$$

Equation (4.14.4) is quite consistent with (3.4.6) which suggests a practical meaning for c.

4.14.2 Transinformation of Order c and Relative Transinformation

We apply (2.9.13) to the entropy $H_c(\beta/A_i)$, $i = 1, 2, \ldots, m$, and substitute the result into the expression (3.4.5) for $I_c(\beta/\alpha)$ to obtain

$$I_c(\beta/\alpha) = I(\beta/\alpha) + (c - 1) \sum_{i=1}^{m} \sum_{j=1}^{n} [r_{ij}(\ln q_{j/i})^2 - p_i H^2(\beta/A_i)] + o[(c - 1)^2] . \tag{4.14.5}$$

This being so, for small $u_{\beta/\alpha}$, (4.11.3) yields

$$T(\beta/\alpha) = I(\beta/\alpha) + H(\beta/\alpha) - H(\beta/\alpha a) - u_{\beta/\alpha} H(b/\alpha a) + o(u_{\beta/\alpha}^2) . \tag{4.14.6}$$

If we assume that the quantity $H(\beta/\alpha) - H(\beta/\alpha a)$ is small, then on equating (4.14.5) and (4.14.6) we obtain the identity

$$u_{\beta/\alpha} H(b/\alpha a) \equiv -(c - 1) \sum_{i=1}^{m} \sum_{j=1}^{n} [r_{ij}(\ln q_{j/i})^2 - p_i H^2(\beta/A_i)] \tag{4.14.7}$$

which we shall decompose in the form

$$H(b/\alpha a) \equiv \sum_{i=1}^{m} \sum_{j=1}^{n} [r_{ij}(\ln q_{j/i})^2 - p_i H^2(\beta/A_i)] \tag{4.14.8}$$

$$c \equiv 1 - u_{\beta/\alpha} . \tag{4.14.9}$$

From a formal standpoint, for small u and small $|1 - c|$, there is some equivalence between the relative entropy $H_r(\alpha)$ and the Renyi entropy $H_c(\alpha)$. But there is a basic difference of a physical nature and this is expressed by (4.14.3). In the relative model, $H(a)$ is an external parameter which does not depend upon the probability distribution $\{p_i\}$, while for the Renyi entropy, $H(a)$ would be defined by $\{p_i\}$.

5. A Theory of Subjective Information

In the present chapter, we shall modify Shannon theory in order to account for symbols and meanings. The approach is based upon two main ideas: first, we describe the space of symbols and the space of meanings by means of two probability distributions; and second, we slightly modify the Shannonian concept of transinformation to introduce some references to semantics in the information transmission from sender to receiver.

More explicitly, this new transinformation is defined as

$$J(\beta/\alpha) := H(\beta) - H(\beta b/\alpha a)$$

where α and β denote the symbols, a and b represent the meanings of α and β respectively, while the transinformation $I(\beta/\alpha)$ as defined by Shannon is

$$I(\beta/\alpha) := H(\beta) - H(\beta/\alpha) \ .$$

This subjective transinformation may be positive or negative; in the latter case it describes loss of information. We shall apply this model to the capacity of a channel, and we shall see that the results obtained are quite consistent with those derived by Shannon. The relation to fuzziness is exhibited, potential applications are outlined, and we shall consider a problem posed by Brillouin.

5.1 Introduction

One of the main drawbacks (and perhaps the only one!) of the information theory as initiated by Shannon, is that it does not provide the concept of *negative information*, which appears to be necessary in some applications such as biology and human sciences for instance, but also in computer sciences, to mention a technical area. Indeed, it is now taken for granted that these systems involve phenomena of information loss which are of basic importance in their dynamics, and a suitable theory should carefully describe this feature.

In Sect. 3.3.2 we touched upon a very simple problem originally stated by Brillouin [5.1] and in which the bit which is used to encode "true" and "false" can be considered as involving negative information.

To some extent, one can assume that the concept of negative information is closely related to the notion of *meanings* or of *semantics*, and that the mathematical formulation of the former necessarily requires the modelling of the latter; this is obviously not the case with the present information theory, which deals with syntax only.

In an approach to the introduction of semantics in information theory, *Jumarie* [5.2–7] proposed a model referred to as *relativistic information*, in the sense that the amount of information contained in the message depends explicitly upon the observer via some parameters which characterize the latter. By using very simple arguments related to subjectivity and natural languages, equations were obtained similar to those of special relativity in physics. It was shown that this model is completely equivalent to the Shannon one in the absence of subjectivity, that is to say when there is no semantics, as far as one can assume that subjectivity is caused by semantics.

One may argue that this relativistic information is defined by means of some parameters that are difficult to measure and to estimate, so that they are rather relevant to fuzziness and fuzzy sets. Although this question has been carefully examined in [5.8], which describes the real meaning of the model in technical situations, this task of deriving an approach to negative information will be considered again here, but now we remain within the classical Shannon framework.

To this end, we shall characterize an informational variable by means of two entropies: an entropy associated with the symbol of this variable, i.e. the usual entropy, and a conditional entropy which describes its semantics. By noting that, in practice, when someone identifies a given symbol, he simultaneously examines its possible meaning, we shall derive a concept of *subjective transinformation*. This is a generalization of the Shannon transinformation and may have negative values.

5.2 Subjective Entropy

5.2.1 Definition of Subjective Entropy

Consider the random experiment α which provides the outcomes $A_1, A_2, \ldots, A_m$ with the respective probabilities $p_1, p_2, \ldots, p_m$; $p_1 + p_2 + \cdots + p_m = 1$. Following Shannon, we measure the uncertainty associated with α, by the entropy

$$H(\alpha) := -k \sum_{i=1}^{m} p_i \ln p_i$$

where k is an integration constant which may be thought of as depending upon the measurement units, and where for convenience the natural logarithm is used. (On associating k with $\ln p_i$ we change the basis of this logarithm according to the formula $\log_a x = \log_a b \cdot \log_b x$). In the following we shall put $k = 1$ whenever this does not affect the generality of the results obtained.

To give a concrete example we assume that $\{A_1, A_2, \ldots, A_m\}$ is the set of the elements of an alphabet, or simply a set of symbols. We assume that each outcome A_i may have the meanings $A'_{ij}, j = 1, 2, \ldots, m'$ with the conditional probability $p'_{j/i}$, so that we consider the A'_{ij} as being the results of a new random event referred to as α'. Since we now account also for the meaning α' of α, we increase the initial uncertainty we may have about α, that is to say the uncertainty without meaning, such that it changes from the value $H(\alpha)$ to the value $H(\alpha\alpha')$:

$$H(\alpha\alpha') = H(\alpha) + H(\alpha'/\alpha) \tag{5.2.1}$$

$$=: H_s(\alpha) \;, \tag{5.2.2}$$

where $H(\alpha'/\alpha)$ denotes the conditional entropy of α' given α: $H(\alpha'/\alpha) = \sum_i p(A_i) H(\alpha'/A_i)$.

In many cases, the semantics is not defined in an absolute way, but rather depends upon the observer; a given symbol may have different meanings to different observers and, to some extent, one may take for granted that α' depends upon the subjectivity of the observer.

Definition 5.2.1. The entropy $H_s(\alpha)$ defined by (5.2.2) is referred to as the *subjective entropy* of α; $H(\alpha)$ is its *syntactic entropy*, and $H(\alpha'/\alpha)$ is its *semantic entropy*.   □

5.2.2 A Few Remarks

i) The term subjective entropy was first coined by *Jumarie* [5.4], see also [5.5] and it has been utilized later by other authors, for instance in the framework of fuzzy set theory [5.9]. But the general sense of this term remains the same: it refers to an entropy that depends upon the observer who considers the symbol.

ii) From a practical standpoint, α' has a meaning only with respect to α, and this feature is emphasized by the notation $H(\alpha'/\alpha)$.

iii) We point out that this approach introduces semantics in the standard framework of the Shannon theory, by merely assuming that the space of meanings is defined by conditional probability distributions. For instance, if α represents the letters of an alphabet, then α' could be associated with the meaning of the observed letter with respect to the word which contains it.

iv) In this framework (syntax α, semantics α'), there is no uncertainty about α if and only if $H_s(\alpha) = 0$, that is to say, if $H(\alpha) = 0$ and $H(\alpha'/\alpha) = 0$ simultaneously.

v) It is important to remark that this subjective entropy can be used to measure the total amount of uncertainty due to randomness on the one hand, and to fuzziness on the other hand [5.10, 11], in so far as we may assume that the fuzzy feature of a variable is mainly caused by ambiguity in its meaning. It is then sufficient to randomize the semantic space of this variable and therefore we shall be able to apply the definition 5.2.1.

vi) In order to simplify the notation, in the following we shall put $\alpha := \{A_i, p_i, p'_{j/i}\}$, $1 \leqslant i \leqslant m$, $1 \leqslant j \leqslant m'$.

vii) The subscript s in $H_s(\alpha)$ refers to "subjective".

5.3 Conditional Subjective Entropy

5.3.1 Definition of Conditional Subjective Entropy

Consider two random experiments $\alpha := \{A_i, p_i, p'_{j/i}\}$, $1 \leqslant i \leqslant m$, $1 \leqslant j \leqslant m'$ and $\beta := \{B_i, q_i, q'_{j/i}\}$, $1 \leqslant i \leqslant n$, $1 \leqslant j \leqslant n'$. The new experiment $\alpha\beta := \{A_i B_j, \varrho_{ij}, \varrho'_{ks/ij}\}$ is obviously well defined and, according to the definition 5.2.1, its subjective entropy is

$$H_s(\alpha\beta) = H(\alpha\beta) + H(\alpha'\beta'/\alpha\beta) \ .$$

In analogy with the equation $H(\alpha\beta) = H(\alpha) + H(\beta/\alpha)$, we shall introduce the following definition:

Definition 5.3.1. The *conditional subjective entropy* $H_s(\beta/\alpha)$ of β given α is defined by the equation

$$H_s(\alpha\beta) =: H_s(\alpha) + H_s(\beta/\alpha) \tag{5.3.1}$$

which yields

$$H_s(\beta/\alpha) = H(\beta/\alpha) + H(\alpha'\beta'/\alpha\beta) - H(\alpha'/\alpha) \tag{5.3.2}$$

$$= H(\beta\beta'/\alpha\alpha') \ . \tag{5.3.3} \quad \square$$

Comments. (i) Equation (5.3.1) is the direct generalization of the definition of $H(\beta/\alpha)$ while (5.3.3) is a consequence of the relations

$$H(\alpha\alpha'\beta\beta') = H(\alpha) + H(\beta/\alpha) + H(\alpha'\beta'/\alpha\beta)$$

$$= H(\alpha) + H(\alpha'/\alpha) + H(\beta\beta'/\alpha\alpha') \ .$$

ii) We remark that it is possible to have $H_s(\beta/\alpha) \geqslant H(\beta/\alpha)$ or $H_s(\beta/\alpha) \leqslant H(\beta/\alpha)$ depending upon the respective values of the different entropies involved. Indeed, let us write

$$H(\alpha\alpha'\beta\beta') = H(\alpha) + H(\alpha'/\alpha) + H_s(\beta/\alpha)$$

$$= H(\alpha) + H(\beta/\alpha) + H(\alpha'/\alpha\beta) + H(\beta'/\alpha\alpha'\beta)$$

to obtain

$$H_s(\beta/\alpha) - H(\beta/\alpha) = H(\alpha'/\alpha\beta) - H(\alpha'/\alpha) + H(\beta'/\alpha\alpha'\beta) \ .$$

This being so, assume that $H(\alpha'/\alpha) = 0$; the relation $0 \leqslant H(\alpha'/\alpha\beta) \leqslant H(\alpha'/\alpha)$ then implies $H(\alpha'/\alpha\beta) = 0$, and one has $H_s(\beta/\alpha) > H(\beta/\alpha)$ as a result of $H(\beta'/\alpha\alpha'\beta) \geqslant 0$. Assume now that $H(\beta'/\alpha\alpha'\beta) = 0$ and $H(\alpha'/\alpha\beta) = 0$, while $H(\alpha'/\alpha) \geqslant 0$; we then obtain $H_s(\beta/\alpha) \leqslant H(\beta/\alpha)$.

5.3.2 Application to Determinacy

The main property of the conditional entropy $H(\beta/\alpha)$ is that, in the absence of semantics, the outcome of α defines completely the outcome of β if and only if $H(\beta/\alpha) = 0$. According to remark (iv) of Sect. 5.2.2 in the presence of semantics, a necessary and sufficient condition for the outcome of β to be completely determined by the outcome of $\alpha\alpha'$ is that $H_s(\beta/\alpha) = 0$, i.e.

$$H(\beta\beta'/\alpha\alpha') = 0 \ . \tag{5.3.4}$$

We then have the following result.

Proposition 5.3.1. In the presence of semantics, the outcome of the random experiment $\alpha\alpha'$ provides the complete identification of the outcome of the random experiment β, if and only if the following conditions are simultaneously satisfied,

$$H(\beta/\alpha\alpha') = 0 \tag{5.3.5}$$

and

$$H(\beta'/\alpha\alpha'\beta) = 0 \ . \tag{5.3.6} \quad \square$$

This result is a direct consequence of condition (5.3.4) written in the form

$$H(\beta/\alpha\alpha') + H(\beta'/\alpha\alpha'\beta) = 0 \ . \tag{5.3.7}$$

By using various inequalities on entropies, the necessary and sufficient conditions (5.3.5) and (5.3.6) yield several *sufficient conditions* for determinacy. Consider the inequalities

$$H(\beta/\alpha\alpha') \leqslant H(\beta/\alpha) \tag{5.3.8}$$

$$\leqslant H(\beta/\alpha') \tag{5.3.9}$$

and

$$H(\beta'/\alpha\alpha'\beta) \leqslant H(\beta'/\alpha\alpha') \leqslant H(\beta'/\alpha') \tag{5.3.10}$$

$$\leqslant H(\beta'/\alpha\beta) \leqslant H(\beta'/\alpha) \tag{5.3.11}$$

$$\leqslant H(\beta'/\alpha'\beta) \leqslant H(\beta'/\beta) \ . \tag{5.3.12}$$

If, for instance, we choose the inequalities (5.3.8) and (5.3.10), we then have the sufficient conditions

$$H(\beta/\alpha) = 0 \tag{5.3.13}$$

$$H(\beta'/\alpha\alpha') = 0 \ . \tag{5.3.14}$$

In doing so, we are obviously losing information in the sense that (α, α', β) involves more information than (α, α') about β', but it is likely that the equation that we shall obtain in this way will be easier to apply in practice.

5.3.3 A Basic Inequality

Proposition 5.3.2. The following inequality holds

$$0 \leqslant H_s(\beta/\alpha) \leqslant H_s(\beta) \ . \tag{5.3.15} \quad \square$$

Proof. (i) The left-hand inequality is obvious.
ii) Explicitly, the right-hand inequality is

$$H(\beta\beta'/\alpha\alpha') \leqslant H(\beta) + H(\beta'/\beta) \ . \tag{5.3.16}$$

But the equations

$$H(\alpha\alpha'\beta\beta') = H(\alpha) + H(\alpha'/\alpha) + H(\beta\beta'/\alpha\alpha') \tag{5.3.17}$$

$$= H(\alpha) + H(\beta/\alpha) + H(\alpha'\beta'/\alpha\beta) \tag{5.3.18}$$

yield

$$H(\beta\beta'/\alpha\alpha') = H(\beta/\alpha) + H(\alpha'\beta'/\alpha\beta) - H(\alpha'/\alpha) \tag{5.3.19}$$

in such a manner that the inequality (5.3.16) can be rewritten

$$H(\beta/\alpha) + H(\alpha'\beta'/\alpha\beta) \leqslant H(\beta) + H(\beta'/\beta) + H(\alpha'/\alpha) \ .$$

But one has $H(\beta/\alpha) \leqslant H(\beta)$, so that it remains to prove the inequality

$$H(\alpha'\beta'/\alpha\beta) \leqslant H(\alpha'/\alpha) + H(\beta'/\beta) \ . \tag{5.3.20}$$

iii) To this end, we shall write

$$H(\alpha'\beta'/\alpha\beta) = H(\alpha'/\alpha\beta) + H(\beta'/\alpha\alpha'\beta)$$

with

$$H(\alpha'/\alpha\beta) \leqslant H(\alpha'/\alpha)$$

and

$$H(\beta'/\alpha\alpha'\beta) \leqslant H(\beta'/\beta) \ ;$$

and, as a result, (5.3.20) is satisfied.   □

5.4 Subjective Transinformation

5.4.1 Introduction

Shannon defined the concept of *transinformation* or *transmission* or *mutual information* $I(\alpha, \beta)$ between α and β by the expression

$$I(\alpha, \beta) := H(\beta) - H(\beta/\alpha) =: I(\beta/\alpha) \ . \tag{5.4.1}$$

This definition is mainly based upon the double inequality

$$0 \leqslant H(\beta/\alpha) \leqslant H(\beta) \tag{5.4.2}$$

which allows us to consider (5.4.1) as the decrease in uncertainty $H(\beta)$ about β that results from the experiment α. This decrease in uncertainty is considered equivalent to a gain of information. In other words, $I(\beta/\alpha)$ is the amount of information provided by α about β.

Although this definition has been shown powerful in a wide variety of applications, it nevertheless has at least two properties which considerably restrict its general use. First, it is always positive or zero, $I(\beta/\alpha) \geqslant 0$, and consequently it cannot describe the phenomenon of information loss. Second, it is symmetrical,

$$I(\beta/\alpha) = I(\alpha/\beta)$$

and this feature presupposes some one-to-one correspondence between α and β, which does not necessarily hold in practice. We refer the reader to the Chap. 2 where we commented at length on this point.

As defined, the mutual information $I(\beta/\alpha)$ is always positive or zero, but this is the result of an averaging effect, and it should be borne in mind that $I(\beta/\alpha)$ itself is an averaging of mutual information! Indeed, if we consider the events A_i and B_j, their mutual information (without averaging) is $\ln[p(A_i/B_j)/p(A_i)]$, and this quantity is negative whenever $p(A_i/B_j) < p(A_i)$, that is to say when A_i and B_j are inconsistent.

In the following, we shall propose a slight modification of the Shannon definition, which will allow us to circumvent these difficulties.

5.4.2 Subjective Transinformation

Definition 5.4.1. In the presence of syntax and semantics, the total amount of information $J(\beta/\alpha)$ provided by α about β is defined by the expression

$$J(\beta/\alpha) := H(\beta) - H_s(\beta/\alpha) \tag{5.4.3}$$

$$:= H(\beta) - H(\beta\beta'/\alpha\alpha') \ . \tag{5.4.4} \quad \square$$

Motivation. Assume that we are interested only in the determination of the symbol β, irrespective of any meaning it may have; it is then only $H(\beta)$ that is relevant to us, and the initial amount of uncertainty we have about β is $H(\beta)$: it is our *prior uncertainty*.

In order to determine β, we perform the experiment $\alpha\alpha'$ and, according to Shannon, our posterior uncertainty is $H(\beta/\alpha\alpha')$. The mutual information is therefore

$$I(\beta/\alpha) = H(\beta) - H(\beta/\alpha\alpha') \ .$$

However, in practice, in order to determine β, we often utilize not only α and α', but also the meaning β' which β could have. In this framework, it might seem that we could measure the amount of information so obtained by the expression

$$I(\beta/\alpha\alpha'\beta') = H(\beta) - H(\beta/\alpha\alpha'\beta') \ ,$$

but on doing so, we would not suitably describe the corresponding observation process. Indeed, what actually happens is as follows: We observe the outcome of $\alpha\alpha'$ while β' is not directly observed but rather is used in our logical reasoning to deduce β from $\alpha\alpha'$. In other words, β' is at the level of β, and we are thus led to consider the conditional entropy $H(\beta\beta'/\alpha\alpha')$ and hence the definition (5.4.4) suggested above. In short, we want to determine β, but we actually identify $\beta\beta'$.

Definition 5.4.2. In order to conform to the usual terminology, we shall refer to $J(\beta/\alpha)$ as the *subjective transinformation*, the *subjective transmission*, or the *subjective mutual information* of β given α although these expressions are not quite appropriate since, as we shall see later, $J(\beta/\alpha)$ is not symmetrical.

5.4.3 A Few Properties of Subjective Transinformation

Result 5.4.1. The following equality holds

$$J(\beta/\alpha) = I(\beta/\alpha) + H(\alpha'/\alpha) - H(\alpha'\beta'/\alpha\beta) \ . \tag{5.4.5}$$

Indeed (5.4.4) can be rewritten in the form

$$J(\beta/\alpha) = H(\beta) - H(\beta/\alpha) + H(\beta/\alpha) - H(\beta\beta'/\alpha\alpha')$$

$$= I(\beta/\alpha) + H(\beta/\alpha) - H(\beta\beta'/\alpha\alpha') \ . \tag{5.4.6}$$

This being so, one has

$$H(\alpha\alpha'\beta\beta') = H(\alpha) + H(\beta/\alpha) + H(\alpha'\beta'/\alpha\beta)$$

$$= H(\alpha\alpha') + H(\beta\beta'/\alpha\alpha') \ ,$$

therefore

$$H(\beta\beta'/\alpha\alpha') - H(\beta/\alpha) = H(\alpha'\beta'/\alpha\beta) + H(\alpha) - H(\alpha\alpha')$$

$$= H(\alpha'\beta'/\alpha\beta) - H(\alpha'/\alpha)$$

and substituting into (5.4.6) this yields (5.4.5). $\qquad\qquad \square$

Result 5.4.2. As a consequence, one has the equality

$$J(\beta/\alpha) - H(\alpha'/\alpha) = J(\alpha/\beta) - H(\beta'/\beta) \ . \tag{5.4.7}$$

Indeed, by using (5.4.5), we have that

$$J(\alpha/\beta) = I(\alpha/\beta) + H(\beta'/\beta) - H(\alpha'\beta'/\alpha\beta) \tag{5.4.8}$$

and therefore the result, on the one hand by virtue of (5.4.5), and on the other due to the symmetry of $I(\beta/\alpha)$.

This relation emphasizes the fact that $J(\beta/\alpha)$ is not symmetrical with respect to α and β. $\qquad\qquad \square$

Result 5.4.3. One may have $J(\beta/\alpha) \geqslant I(\beta/\alpha)$ or $J(\beta/\alpha) \leqslant I(\beta/\alpha)$.

If we expand (5.4.5) in the form

$$J(\beta/\alpha) = I(\beta/\alpha) + H(\alpha'/\alpha) - H(\alpha'/\alpha\beta) - H(\beta'/\alpha\alpha'\beta) \ , \tag{5.4.9}$$

one can see easily that $J(\beta/\alpha) \leqslant I(\beta/\alpha)$ when, for instance, $H(\alpha'/\alpha) = 0$ and $H(\beta'/\alpha\alpha'\beta) > 0$; while $J(\beta/\alpha) \geqslant I(\beta/\alpha)$ provided that $H(\alpha'/\alpha) > 0$ and $H(\beta'/\alpha\alpha'\beta) = 0$. $\qquad\square$

Result 5.4.4. The subjective transinformation may be negative.

This occurs, for instance, when one has simultaneously

$$I(\beta/\alpha) = 0 \ , \qquad H(\alpha'/\alpha) = 0 \ , \qquad H(\beta'/\alpha\alpha'\beta) > 0 \ .$$

This case corresponds to the following situation: the symbol β is completely defined by the symbol α; the meaning α' of α is also well defined by the knowledge of α (for instance there is no error on α); but nevertheless when the observer takes account of the semantics β' of β, he has difficulty in determining β.

Result 5.4.5. According to (5.4.7), the subjective transinformation is only symmetrical, i.e. $J(\beta/\alpha) = J(\alpha/\beta)$, when

$$H(\alpha'/\alpha) = H(\beta'/\beta) \ . \tag{5.4.10}$$

What is the practical meaning of condition (5.4.10)? For a given B_j, $H(\beta'/B_j)$ represents our uncertainty about the meaning of B_j; it relates to the richness, or the degree of freedom of the semantics of β considered as a language; and condition (5.4.10) merely expresses that, on the average, the two languages α and β have the same amount of freedom with respect to their respective semantics. $\qquad\square$

Result 5.4.6. The following equation holds:

$$J(\beta/\alpha) = I(\beta/\alpha) + I_\alpha(\alpha'/\beta) - H(\beta'/\alpha\alpha'\beta) \tag{5.4.11}$$

where $I_\alpha(\alpha'/\beta)$ denotes the *conditional transinformation*, defined as

$$I_\alpha(\alpha'/\beta) := H(\alpha'/\alpha) - H(\alpha'/\alpha\beta) \ . \tag{5.4.12}$$

Indeed, (5.4.11) is merely the equivalent of (5.4.9). This being so, the symmetry of the conditional transinformation provides the relation

$$J(\beta/\alpha) = I(\beta/\alpha) + I_\alpha(\beta/\alpha') - H(\beta'/\alpha\alpha'\beta) \tag{5.4.13}$$

$$= I(\beta/\alpha\alpha') - H(\beta'/\alpha\alpha'\beta) \ , \tag{5.4.14}$$

which elucidates the practical meaning of $J(\beta/\alpha)$: First there is a gain of information, i.e. the positive information that is contributed by α and α', and second, there is a loss of information caused by the conditional event $(\beta'/\alpha\alpha'\beta)$. $\qquad\square$

Result 5.4.7. The symmetry of $I(\beta/\alpha)$ and $I_\alpha(\beta/\alpha')$ yields

$$J(\beta/\alpha) = I(\beta/\alpha) + I_\alpha(\alpha'/\beta) - H(\beta'/\alpha\alpha'\beta) \tag{5.4.15}$$

$$= I(\alpha/\beta) + I_\alpha(\beta/\alpha') - H(\beta'/\alpha\alpha'\beta) \ . \tag{5.4.16} \quad\square$$

5.4.4 Application to Independent Random Experiments

In the usual framework, that is to say without semantics, two random experiments α and β are independent if and only if $H(\alpha\beta) = H(\alpha) + H(\beta)$ or, as amounts to the same, $I(\beta/\alpha) = I(\alpha/\beta) = 0$, and this relation of independence is obviously symmetrical: α does not involve information about β, and conversely, β does not contain information about α. One may generalize this property to the subjective transinformation, but it is clear that in this case we shall no longer have symmetry.

Definition 5.4.3. In the framework (symbols, meanings), we shall say that the experiment β has no effects on the experiment α when $J(\beta/\alpha) = 0$.   □

We note that this does not imply that α has no effect on β as can be seen from (5.4.7). In fact, α and β are only mutually independent if the condition (5.4.10) is satisfied.

5.5 Conditional Subjective Transinformation

5.5.1 Definition

The counterpart of conditional transinformation can be introduced as follows.

Definition 5.5.1. In the framework (syntax, semantics), the *conditional subjective transinformation* $J_\gamma(\beta/\alpha)$ is defined by the expression

$$J_\gamma(\beta/\alpha) := H(\beta/\gamma\gamma') - H(\beta\beta'/\alpha\alpha'\gamma\gamma') \ . \tag{5.5.1} \ \square$$

The meaning of this definition is as follows: Given an outcome of the random experiment $\gamma\gamma'$, $J_\gamma(\beta/\alpha)$ is a measure of the amount of information provided by $\alpha\alpha'$ about β in a process where one uses $\alpha\alpha'$ and β' to determine β.   □

5.5.2 A Few Properties of Subjective Conditional Transinformation

Result 5.5.1. The following equality holds:

$$J_\gamma(\beta/\alpha) = I_{\gamma\gamma'}(\beta/\alpha) + H(\alpha'/\alpha\gamma\gamma') - H(\alpha'\beta'/\alpha\beta\gamma\gamma') \ . \tag{5.5.2}$$

By adding and substracting $H(\beta/\alpha\gamma\gamma')$ on the right-hand side of (5.5.1) one obtains

$$J_\gamma(\beta/\alpha) = I_{\gamma\gamma'}(\beta/\alpha) + H(\beta/\alpha\gamma\gamma') - H(\beta\beta'/\alpha\alpha'\gamma\gamma') \ . \tag{5.5.3}$$

This yields

$$H(\alpha\alpha'\beta\beta'/\gamma\gamma') = H(\alpha/\gamma\gamma') + H(\beta/\alpha\gamma\gamma') + H(\alpha'\beta'/\alpha\beta\gamma\gamma')$$

$$= H(\alpha\alpha'/\gamma\gamma') + H(\beta\beta'/\alpha\alpha'\gamma\gamma') \ ,$$

therefore

$$H(\beta\beta'/\alpha\alpha'\gamma\gamma') - H(\beta/\alpha\gamma\gamma') = H(\alpha'\beta'/\alpha\beta\gamma\gamma') + H(\alpha/\gamma\gamma') - H(\alpha\alpha'/\gamma\gamma')$$
$$= H(\alpha'\beta'/\alpha\beta\gamma\gamma') - H(\alpha'/\alpha\gamma\gamma') ,$$

and substituting this expression into (5.5.3) yields the result.   □

Result 5.5.2. The following equality holds:

$$J_\gamma(\beta/\alpha) - H(\alpha'/\alpha\gamma\gamma') = J_\gamma(\alpha/\beta) - H(\beta'/\beta\gamma\gamma') .$$ (5.5.4)

Using (5.5.2), it is sufficient to write

$$J_\gamma(\alpha/\beta) = I_{\gamma\gamma'}(\alpha/\beta) + H(\beta'/\beta\gamma\gamma') - H(\alpha'\beta'/\alpha\beta\gamma\gamma')$$

and to remark that

$$I_{\gamma\gamma'}(\alpha/\beta) = I_{\gamma\gamma'}(\beta/\alpha) .$$ □

Result 5.5.3. The following equality holds:

$$J(\beta/\alpha\gamma) = J(\beta/\alpha) + I_{\alpha\alpha'}(\beta\beta'/\gamma\gamma') .$$ (5.5.5)

According to the definition (5.4.4), we can write

$$J(\beta/\alpha\gamma) = H(\beta) - H(\beta\beta'/\alpha\alpha'\gamma\gamma')$$
$$= H(\beta) - H(\beta\beta'/\alpha\alpha') + H(\beta\beta'/\alpha\alpha') - H(\beta\beta'/\alpha\alpha'\gamma\gamma')$$

thence the result.   □

Result 5.5.4. The so-called *equation of triangular information* is

$$I(\alpha/\beta\gamma) + I(\gamma/\beta) = I(\beta/\alpha\gamma) + I(\gamma/\alpha) .$$ (5.5.6)

In the framework (syntax, semantics) it becomes

$$J(\alpha/\beta\gamma) + J(\gamma/\beta) - H(\beta'/\beta) = J(\beta/\alpha\gamma) + J(\gamma/\alpha) - H(\alpha'/\alpha) .$$ (5.5.7)

Proof. By using (5.5.5) we can write the following two relations,

$$J(\gamma/\beta) + J(\alpha/\beta\gamma) = J(\alpha/\gamma) + I_{\gamma\gamma'}(\alpha\alpha'/\beta\beta') + J(\gamma/\beta)$$
$$J(\gamma/\alpha) + J(\beta/\alpha\gamma) = J(\beta/\gamma) + I_{\gamma\gamma'}(\beta\beta'/\alpha\alpha') + J(\gamma/\alpha) ;$$

and their difference yields

$$J(\gamma/\beta) + J(\alpha/\beta\gamma) - J(\gamma/\alpha) - J(\beta/\alpha\gamma) = J(\alpha/\gamma) - J(\gamma/\alpha) + J(\gamma/\beta) - J(\beta/\gamma) .$$

Therefore, by virtue of (5.4.7),

$$J(\gamma/\beta) + J(\alpha/\beta\gamma) - J(\gamma/\alpha) - J(\beta/\alpha\gamma) = H(\gamma'/\gamma) - H(\alpha'/\alpha) + H(\beta'/\beta) - H(\gamma'/\gamma)$$

$$= H(\beta'/\beta) - H(\alpha'/\alpha)$$

which is exactly (5.5.7).   □

Remark. It is worth noting that, in the presence of semantics, (5.5.7) is similar to (5.5.6) in the absence of semantics, but only if the equilibrium condition (5.4.10) is satisfied.

Equation (5.5.7) exhibits various relations between the subjective transinformations depending upon the degree of independence of α, β and γ. For instance, if $J(\gamma/\beta) = 0$, that is to say if γ has no effect on β, then a simple calculation yields

$$J(\gamma/\alpha) \leqslant J(\alpha/\beta\gamma) - J(\alpha/\beta)$$

or, by virtue of (5.5.5),

$$J(\gamma/\alpha) \leqslant I_{\beta\beta'}(\alpha\alpha'/\gamma\gamma') \ .$$

5.6 Information Balance

In the present section, our purpose is to determine the conditions under which the outcome of the random experiment $\alpha\alpha'$ provides a complete determination of the outcome of β in the framework (syntax, semantics). We shall say that α is optimal with respect to β when all the information contained in α is information related to β.

5.6.1 Optimum Conditions for Information Balance

Proposition 5.6.1. In the framework (syntax, semantics), necessary and sufficient optimal conditions for the outcome of $\alpha\alpha'$ to provide a complete determination of the result of β are the following:

$$H(\beta\beta'/\alpha\alpha') = 0 \ , \tag{5.6.1}$$

$$H(\alpha/\beta) = 0 \ , \tag{5.6.2}$$

$$H(\alpha) + H(\alpha'/\alpha) \geqslant H(\beta) + H(\alpha'\beta'/\alpha\beta) \ . \tag{5.6.3}$$ □

Proof. (i) $H(\beta)$ is the minimum amount of information which should be provided by $\alpha\alpha'$ to allow us to identify β by using β'; in other words, one should have

$$J(\beta/\alpha) = H(\beta) \ .$$

Therefore, by virtue of (5.4.4), we obtain the condition (5.6.1).

ii) Equations (5.4.5) and (5.4.7) then yield

$$J(\beta/\alpha) = J(\alpha/\beta) + H(\alpha'/\alpha) - H(\beta'/\beta)$$

$$= I(\alpha/\beta) + H(\alpha'/\alpha) - H(\alpha'\beta'/\alpha\beta) \ . \tag{5.6.4}$$

This expression measures the amount of information contained in α about β, and obviously one should have

$$I(\alpha/\beta) + H(\alpha'/\alpha) - H(\alpha'\beta'/\alpha\beta) \geqslant H(\beta) \ . \tag{5.6.5}$$

iii) We now consider the optimal experiment α, i.e. the α such that $I(\alpha/\beta)$ achieves its maximum value $H(\alpha)$. This is obtained when condition (5.6.2) is satisfied, and in such a case, (5.6.5) becomes condition (5.6.3).

iv) This being the case, condition (5.6.1) is a sufficient condition. Indeed, we can rewrite it in the form

$$H(\beta/\alpha\alpha') + H(\beta'/\alpha\alpha'\beta) = 0 \ , \tag{5.6.6}$$

so that one necessarily has

$$H(\beta/\alpha\alpha') = 0 \tag{5.6.7}$$

$$H(\beta'/\alpha\alpha'\beta) = 0 \ . \tag{5.6.8}$$

As a result, β should be completely determined by $\alpha\alpha'$.

Condition (5.6.2) is necessary only to ensure that all the information contained in α is related to β; in this way, α can be considered as a minimum experiment.

Condition (5.6.3) is necessary but is not sufficient, in the sense that it may be satisfied even if the information contained in $\alpha\alpha'$ is not related to β. In addition, it is automatically satisfied provided that conditions (5.6.1) and (5.6.2) hold. Indeed, the equation

$$H(\alpha\alpha'\beta\beta') = H(\alpha) + H(\alpha'/\alpha) + H(\beta\beta'/\alpha\alpha')$$

$$= H(\beta) + H(\alpha/\beta) + H(\alpha'\beta'/\alpha\beta)$$

then yields

$$H(\alpha'\beta'/\alpha\beta) = H(\alpha) + H(\alpha'/\alpha) - H(\beta) \ ,$$

so that (5.6.3) is reduced to the equality.

We can thus derive counterparts of all the various conditions that hold in the absence of semantics. In this case, the equations are

$$H(\beta/\alpha) = 0 \tag{5.6.9}$$

$$H(\alpha/\beta) = 0 \tag{5.6.10}$$

$$H(\alpha) = H(\beta) \ , \tag{5.6.11}$$

and of course (5.6.9) together with (5.6.10) provides (5.6.11). In fact here, (5.6.9) is necessary and sufficient condition; (5.6.10) ensures the maximum efficiency of the process, and (5.6.11) is a necessary but not a sufficient condition.

5.6.2 Non-optimum Conditions for Information Balance

One may expand condition (5.6.3) in two different ways:
 i) First one has

$$H(\alpha'\beta'/\alpha\beta) = H(\beta'/\alpha\beta) + H(\alpha'/\alpha\beta\beta') \ ,$$

and substituting into condition (5.6.3) yields

$$H(\alpha) + I_\alpha(\alpha'/\beta\beta') \geqslant H(\beta) + H(\beta'/\alpha\beta) \qquad (5.6.12)$$

with

$$I_\alpha(\alpha'/\beta\beta') := H(\alpha'/\alpha) - H(\alpha'/\alpha\beta\beta')$$

 ii) Second, one can also write

$$H(\alpha'\beta'/\alpha\beta) = H(\alpha'/\alpha\beta) + H(\beta'/\alpha\alpha'\beta)$$

so that, by virtue of (5.6.7), (5.6.3) becomes

$$H(\alpha) + I_\alpha(\alpha'/\beta) \geqslant H(\beta) \qquad (5.6.13)$$

with

$$I_\alpha(\alpha'/\beta) := H(\alpha'/\alpha) - H(\alpha'/\alpha\beta) \ .$$

Condition (5.6.3) alone is equivalent to conditions (5.6.12) and (5.6.13) together.
 We then obtain the following result:

Proposition 5.6.2. In the framework (syntax, semantics), sufficient conditions for the outcome of $\alpha\alpha'$ to provide a complete determination of the outcome of β are: conditions (5.6.1), (5.6.2) and

$$H(\alpha) \geqslant H(\beta) \ . \qquad (5.6.14) \quad \square$$

Proof. It is sufficient to prove that conditions (5.6.11) and (5.6.12) are then satisfied. This is obvious for (5.6.12). Regarding (5.6.11), it is sufficient to show that

$$I_\alpha(\alpha'/\beta\beta') \geqslant H(\beta'/\alpha\beta)$$

But one has

$$I_\alpha(\alpha'/\beta\beta') = I_\alpha(\beta\beta'/\alpha')$$

$$= H(\beta\beta'/\alpha) - H(\beta\beta'/\alpha\alpha')$$

and according to (5.6.1),

$$I_\alpha(\alpha'/\beta\beta') = H(\beta\beta'/\alpha)$$

$$= H(\beta/\alpha) + H(\beta'/\alpha\beta) \ ,$$

hence the inequality (5.6.14). $\qquad\qquad\qquad \square$

5.7 Explicit Expression of Subjective Transinformation

5.7.1 Discrete Probability

We first consider the case in which the random experiments α, α', β and β' are discrete. Let $p_1, p_2, \ldots, p_m$ denote the probability distribution of α, or in a shortened form $\alpha \sim \{p_i\}$. In a similar manner we define

$$\alpha \sim \{p_i\} \; ; \qquad \alpha' \sim \{p_j'\} \; ; \qquad \beta \sim \{q_k\} \; , \qquad \beta' \sim \{q_l\} \tag{5.7.1}$$

$$\alpha\alpha' \sim \{\pi_{ij}\} \; ; \qquad \alpha\alpha'\beta' \sim \{\pi_{ijl}'\} \tag{5.7.2}$$

$$\alpha\alpha'\beta \sim \{r_{ijk}'\} \; ; \qquad \alpha\alpha'\beta\beta' \sim \{r_{ijkl}\} \; . \tag{5.7.3}$$

In this notation, the indices are associated with the experiments according to their respective order. For instance, in r_{ijk}', i corresponds to α, j to α' and k to β. The conditional probabilities are then defined by

$$r_{ijk}' = \pi_{ij} q_{k/ij} \; ; \qquad \varrho_{ijkl} = \pi_{ij} \pi_{kl/ij}' \; . \tag{5.7.4}$$

With this notation, we have the following result.

Proposition 5.7.1. The explicit expression for the subjective transinformation $J(\beta/\alpha)$ is

$$J(\beta/\alpha) = \sum_{ijkl} r_{ijkl} \ln \frac{r_{ijkl}}{\pi_{ij} q_k} \; . \tag{5.7.5}$$

Proof. We write $J(\beta/\alpha)$ from (5.4.4) in the form

$$J(\beta/\alpha) = H(\beta) - H(\beta/\alpha\alpha') + H(\beta/\alpha\alpha') - H(\beta\beta'/\alpha\alpha')$$

$$= I(\beta/\alpha\alpha') + H(\beta/\alpha\alpha') - H(\beta\beta'/\alpha\alpha') \; . \tag{5.7.6}$$

i)   As a classical result one has

$$I(\beta/\alpha\alpha') = \sum_{ijk} r_{ijk}' \ln \frac{r_{ijk}'}{\pi_{ij} q_k} \; . \tag{5.7.7}$$

ii)   A straightforward calculation yields

$$H(\beta/\alpha\alpha') = -\sum_{ijk} \pi_{ij} q_{k/ij} \ln q_{k/ij}$$

$$= -\sum_{ijk} r_{ijk}' \ln q_{k/ij}$$

$$= -\sum_{ijkl} r_{ijkl} \ln q_{k/ij}$$

$$= -\sum_{ijkl} r_{ijkl} \ln \frac{r_{ijk}'}{\pi_{ij}} \; . \tag{5.7.8}$$

iii) In addition one has

$$H(\beta\beta'/\alpha\alpha') = -\sum_{ijkl} r_{ijkl} \ln \frac{r_{ijkl}}{\pi_{ij}} \ . \tag{5.7.9}$$

iv) On combining (5.7.7), (5.7.8) and (5.7.9) we obtain

$$J(\beta/\alpha) = \sum_{ijk} r'_{ijk} \ln \frac{r'_{ijk}}{\pi_{ij}q_k} + \sum_{ijkl} r_{ijkl} \left(\ln \frac{r_{ijkl}}{r_{ijk}} - \ln \frac{r'_{ijk}}{\pi_{ij}} \right)$$

$$= \sum_{ijkl} r_{ijkl} \left(\ln \frac{r'_{ijk}}{\pi_{ij}q_k} + \ln \frac{r_{ijkl}}{r_{ijk}} - \ln \frac{r'_{ijk}}{\pi_{ij}} \right) \tag{5.7.10}$$

which is equal to the right-hand side of (5.7.5). □

Comments. It is interesting to compare the expression (5.7.5) for $J(\beta/\alpha)$ with that for $I(\beta/\alpha\alpha'\beta')$, namely

$$I(\beta/\alpha\alpha'\beta') = \sum_{ijkl} r_{ijkl} \ln \frac{r_{ijkl}}{\pi'_{ijl}q_k} \ . \tag{5.7.11}$$

The only difference between these two expressions is that one of them involves π'_{ijl} while the other one contains π_{ij}, and it is exactly this difference that causes $I(\beta/\alpha\alpha'\beta')$ to be always positive while $J(\beta/\alpha)$ may be positive or negative.

5.7.2 Continuous Probability

If instead of using random experiments, we consider two pairs of continuous random variables (X, X') and (Y, Y'), then the total information $J(Y/X)$ provided by X about Y is expressed by (5.7.5). In this way, the expression (5.7.5) for $J(\beta/\alpha)$ has its direct counterpart $J(Y/X)$ with continuous probability.

Indeed, let $r(x, x', y, y')$, $\pi(x, x')$ and $q(y)$ denote the probability density functions of (X, X', Y, Y'), (X, X') and Y respectively. One then has

$$J(Y/X) = \int \int \int \int r(x, x', y, y') \ln \frac{r(x, x', y, y')}{\pi(x, x')q(y)} \, dx \, dx' \, dy \, dy' \tag{5.7.12}$$

As in the discrete case, one may compare $J(Y/X)$ with $I(Y/XX'Y')$ which is given by

$$I(Y/XX'Y') = \int \int \int \int r(x, x', y, y') \ln \frac{r(x, x', y, y')}{\pi(x, x', y')q(y)} \, dx \, dx' \, dy \, dy' \tag{5.7.13}$$

5.8 The General Coding Problem

5.8.1 Preliminary Remarks

In the definition of the total entropy $H_s(\beta)$, we have considered β as a symbol, and β' as a meaning. But this framework, which is convenient for deriving the main concepts, should not be used too restrictively: although β itself should refer to the symbols of the message under consideration, in contrast, β' may be anything, provided that it is directly related to the meaning of this symbol.

As an example, let us assume that each result B_j may either have a meaning or may have no meaning in the given semantic universe where it is observed. Thus we may define the probabilities

$$q'_j := \mathrm{pr}\{B_j \text{ has a meaning}\}$$

$$1 - q'_j := \mathrm{pr}\{B_j \text{ has no meaning}\}$$

and therefore the subjective entropy

$$H_s(\beta) = H(\beta) - \sum_{j=1}^{n} q_j[q'_j \ln q'_j + (1 - q'_j)\ln(1 - q'_j)] \ .$$

In some cases, it will be possible to associate β' with the error term of a transmission process, since it is exactly this type of phenomenon that creates the semantic variations of β.

More generally, the identification of the elements $(\alpha, \alpha', \beta, \beta')$ will not be fixed in a definitive manner, but on the contrary will vary with the type of problem considered.

In this respect, there are two main problems in coding theory. The first of these is general and at the level of the symbols. It arises when we translate one alphabet into another, and directly refers to the feasibility conditions of the coding process. The second problem occurs at the level of carrying out the coding, and relates to the determination of transmission errors.

5.8.2 The General Coding Problem

Definition of the Model. β is the generic term which represents the symbols B_1, B_2, ... , B_n that we have to encode, and β' is a random event whose possible outcomes, $B'_1, B'_2, \ldots, B'_n$, are related to the meanings of the B_j's.

α represents the symbols $A_1, A_2, \ldots, A_m$ that are used to encode the symbols of β. For illustration we shall assume that each A_i is a sequence of binary digits, say $A_i = \varepsilon_i^1 \varepsilon_i^2 \ldots \varepsilon_i^{n_i}$. In order to *check the meaning β'* of β, at the end of each symbol α, one appends a symbol $\alpha' = \{A'_1, A'_2, \ldots, A'_n\}$ (which itself can be a sequence of binary digits) in such a manner that the result is as if we were encoding the symbols of (β, β') by those of (α, α'). For instance, α' may be thought of as parity bits.

The observation process in which one identifies (β, β') by means of (α, α') involves the amount of information $I(\beta\beta'/\alpha\alpha')$; the identification of β alone by means of (α, α') involves $I(\beta/\alpha\alpha')$ and these two identification problems, as well as their solutions, are well known in information theory.

In what follows, we shall rather consider the model in which the observer identifies β, by using (α, α') on the one hand, and possible deduction from β' on the other hand.

We have the following result:

Proposition 5.8.1. Assume that (β, β') is encoded by (α, α') via the separation principle, that is to say β is encoded by α and β' is encoded by α', in such a manner that the conditions (5.6.1) and (5.6.2) are satisfied, together with the equality

$$H(\alpha) = H(\beta) \; ; \tag{5.8.1}$$

then α' should be such that

$$H(\alpha'/\alpha) = H(\beta'/\beta) \; . \tag{5.8.2} \quad \square$$

Proof. First we write

$$H(\alpha\alpha'\beta\beta') = H(\alpha\alpha') + H(\beta\beta'/\alpha\alpha')$$

$$= H(\beta\beta') + H(\alpha/\beta\beta') + H(\alpha'/\alpha\beta\beta') \; . \tag{5.8.3}$$

Then, according to condition (5.6.2), one has

$$H(\alpha/\beta\beta') \leqslant H(\alpha/\beta)$$

$$\leqslant 0$$

so that, on using (5.6.1), (5.8.3) and (5.8.4) this yields

$$H(\alpha'/\alpha\beta\beta') = H(\alpha\alpha') - H(\beta\beta')$$

$$= H(\alpha) + H(\alpha'/\alpha) - H(\beta) - H(\beta'/\beta) \; ; \tag{5.8.4}$$

and, on assuming that the condition (5.8.1) is satisfied, one has

$$H(\alpha'/\alpha) - H(\alpha'/\alpha\beta\beta') = H(\beta'/\beta) \; ,$$

that is to say

$$I_\alpha(\alpha'/\beta\beta') = H(\beta'/\beta) \; .$$

This equation is none other than the information balance condition with regard to α' and β'. It achieves its maximum efficiency when $H(\alpha'/\alpha\beta\beta') = 0$, and hence the result. $\qquad\square$

A Few Comments. We draw attention to the symmetry of the equations (5.8.1) and (5.8.2). The former expresses that α and β should involve the same amount of uncertainty, while the latter means that the semantics α' and β' necessarily have the same degree of uncertainty with respect to α and β respectively. Qualitatively speaking, (α, α') is the image of (β, β').

Let us write the condition (5.6.3) in the form

$$H(\alpha) \geqslant H(\beta) + H(\alpha'\beta'/\alpha\beta) - I_\alpha(\alpha'/\beta) \; . \tag{5.8.5}$$

It is then clear that if $I_\alpha(\alpha'/\beta) \geqslant H(\alpha'\beta'/\alpha\beta)$, (5.8.5) can be satisfied while (5.6.10) is not; and if $I_\alpha(\alpha'\beta) \leqslant H(\alpha'\beta'/\alpha\beta)$, the efficiency of the coding with semantics is lower than that of the coding without semantics. In this sense, we can talk of negative information.

5.8.3 On the Problem of Error Correcting Codes Revisited

Transmission of binary digits involves four main elements: (i) the useful signal sent by the source; (ii) the useful signal which arrives at the receiver; (iii) an error term which affects the validity of the useful signal as received; and (iv) control bits which allow the receiver to check whether there are transmission errors, and possibly to rectify them. The entire problem is then to suitably associate these elements to those of the quadruple $(\alpha, \alpha', \beta, \beta')$.

A first idea would be to make the following identification. $\beta :=$ message to be transmitted, $\beta' :=$ set of control symbols, $\alpha :=$ received encoded message, $\alpha' :=$ syndrome which measures the knowledge of α and the knowledge of the encoding process provided about the transmission errors. But, in such a case, one obviously has $H(\alpha'/\alpha) = H(\beta'/\beta) = 0$, $J(\beta/\alpha) = I(\beta/\alpha)$ and the classical theory is sufficient.

We shall consider instead the model in which it is the emitted message itself which contains semantic information. This is the well-known situation in which a written text for example is received with mistakes that can nonetheless be rectified by using its semantics. When the semantics is ambiguous and the error probability is low, then it is possible that it becomes misleading.

In order to describe this model, we shall make the following identification.

$\beta :=$ the useful signal emitted by the source; in this case a message composed of k binary digits.

$\alpha :=$ the useful signal, as received. This received message may have k bits, or, if some bits have been lost in the transmission process, it will have fewer.

$\alpha' :=$ the r control bits which are appended to α

$\beta' :=$ set of outcomes of a random experiment to determine the possible meanings of β, or which allow the receiver to determine the degree of the possible meaning of β in a quantitative approach.

According to the remarks of Sect. 5.8.1, and in order to remain with the technical problem of error-correcting codes, we shall consider β' as being an additional error E, *which alters the initial semantics of* β. We then have

$$\beta =: M = \text{message emitted}$$

$$\alpha =: M + E = \text{message emitted} + \text{error terms}$$
$$= \text{message transmitted}$$

$$\alpha' =: C = \text{control bits transmitted}$$

$$\beta' =: E = \text{error term},$$

and, in addition, we shall assume that E is independent of M.   □

With this identification, the coding condition (5.8.2) is

$$H[C/(M + E)] = H(E/M)$$

In the special case of error burst, one has

$$H(E/M) = \ln k + \ln s \tag{5.8.6}$$

where $\ln k$ is the entropy of the beginning of the burst and s is its length. But one necessarily has

$$H[C/(M + E)] \leqslant \ln r$$

and as a result, the maximum length of error burst that can be rectified using C is r, but it will be impossible to locate the beginning of the burst. An additional source of information is then necessary.

The first idea, and the most direct one, consists of choosing r such that

$$\ln r = \ln k + \ln s \ ,$$

but in doing so, we obviously increase the size of the word (α, α') to be transmitted.

Another method consists in making the identification

$$\alpha' := f_\alpha(C)$$

where $f_\alpha(\cdot)$ is a map which depends upon α, such that the entropy of its possible outcomes is

$$H[f_\alpha(C)/\alpha] = \ln k + \ln s \ . \tag{5.8.7}$$

This is exactly what we are doing in algebraic codes when we divide modulo 2 the bit string corresponding to the polynomial $G(x)$ into the received bit string (Sect. 3.3).

The problem is then to define the amount of information provided by the map $f_\alpha(\cdot)$ and we shall examine this question later.

In the meantime, assume that we can define the entropy $H(f_\alpha(\cdot)/\alpha)$ of the map $f_\alpha(\cdot)$ in such a manner that

$$H[f_\alpha(C)/\alpha] = H(C/\alpha) + H(f_\alpha(\cdot)/\alpha) \tag{5.8.8}$$

with $H(f_\alpha/\alpha) > 0$. Then, according to (5.8.7), r would be given by the equation

$$\ln r = \ln k + \ln s - H(f_\alpha(\cdot)/\alpha) \ .$$

In other words one could drastically diminish the value of r by suitably selecting $f_\alpha(\cdot)$.

5.9 Capacity of a Channel

Our purpose in this section is to examine the kind of results that can be obtained by applying the concept of subjective transinformation to the transmission problem, and more especially to the determination of the capacity of a channel.

5.9.1 The General Model

Problem 5.9.1. In the framework (syntax, semantics), assume that a message is defined by means of a language (β, β'), and then it is transmitted after encoding by another language (α, α'). We shall assume that the semantics β' is independent of (α, α'). What is the maximum amount of subjective transinformation $J_m(\beta/\alpha)$ that one may thereby obtain? This maximum value is referred to as the *capacity of the transmission*. □

Solution. The maximum subjective transinformation $J_m(\beta/\alpha)$ is

$$J_m(\beta/\alpha) = \max_{\alpha, \alpha'} \left[H(\alpha) + H(\alpha'/\alpha) \right] - H(\beta'/\beta) \ . \tag{5.9.1}$$ □

Proof. According to the assumption that β' and (α, α') are independent, one has

$$H(\beta'/\alpha\alpha'\beta) = H(\beta'/\beta)$$

so that (5.4.15) yields

$$J(\beta/\alpha) = I(\alpha/\beta) + I_\alpha(\alpha'/\beta) - H(\beta'/\beta) \ . \tag{5.9.2}$$

In order to maximize $J(\beta/\alpha)$, we shall have to maximize $I(\alpha/\beta)$ and $I_\alpha(\alpha'/\beta)$, that is to say, to satisfy the conditions

$$I(\alpha/\beta) = H(\alpha)$$

and

$$I_\alpha(\alpha'/\beta) = H(\alpha'/\alpha) \ .$$

In addition, we shall have to choose α and α' so as to maximize $H(\alpha) + H(\alpha'/\alpha)$; see for instance (5.8.4). □

We point out that $J_m(\beta/\alpha)$ involves the difference $H(\alpha'/\alpha) - H(\beta'/\beta)$ which is merely the relative importance of the semantic universes of α' and β' respectively. Qualitatively speaking, if the language α' is richer than β', there is a gain of transinformation with respect to $H(\alpha)$, the latter being the transinformation in the presence of syntax only. On the other hand, if α' is poorer than β', then there is loss of information. This result is exactly as one would expect.

5.9.2 Channel with Noise

Problem 5.9.2. A signal X, with the variance σ_x^2, is emitted at the input of the channel, and at the output end, one receives a signal Y,

$$Y := X + V$$

where V denotes a gaussian white noise independent of X, with zero statistical mean, and whose variance is denoted by σ_v^2. What is the maximum amount of transinformation $J_m(X/Y)$ that one can obtain?

This value is referred to as the *capacity of the channel*. □

Solution. The corresponding capacity is

$$J_m(X/Y) = \frac{1}{2}\ln\left(1 + \frac{\sigma_y^2}{\sigma_x^2}\right) .$$ (5.9.3) □

Proof. In order to apply the model (syntax, semantics), we shall set

$$\alpha \equiv \alpha' ; \quad \alpha := Y ; \quad \beta := X ; \quad \beta' := V$$

Clearly, we identify β' with an error which is equivalent to a meaning in the linguistic sense of this term, since one of the effects of error is to change meaning. We also assume that α has no semantics, that is to say $\alpha \equiv \alpha'$. Under these conditions, (5.9.1) yields

$$J_m(X/Y) = \max_Y \left[H(Y) - H(V)\right]$$ (5.9.4)

with

$$H(V) = \ln \sigma_v \sqrt{2\pi e} .$$ (5.9.5)

It is well known that, for a given mean and variance, the entropy is maximum when the corresponding probability density is a normal distribution. In other words, since the variance of Y is $(\sigma_x^2 + \sigma_v^2)$, the maximum value of $H(Y)$ is $\ln[(\sigma_x^2 + \sigma_v^2)^{1/2}(2\pi e)^{1/2}]$ and therefore the result (5.9.3).   □

Notice that, here again, β' has been given the meaning of an error term, exactly as in Sect. 5.8 concerning error-detecting codes. This is strong support for this type of identification!

5.9.3 Channel with Noise and Filtering

Problem 5.9.3. Again we consider the channel with additive gaussian white noise, but we assume that at the receiving station, Y is filtered in order to restore X as nearly as possible. What is the maximum amount of subjective transinformation which one can thereby obtain?

Solution. (i) We make the following identification

$$\alpha := Y ; \quad \alpha' := Y' ; \quad \beta := X ; \quad \beta' := V$$

where Y' is a variable characterizing the accuracy of the filter or the uncertainty associated with its output. In a first general approach, we shall write the conditional entropy $H(Y'/Y)$ in the form

$$H(Y'/Y) = \int_{-\infty}^{+\infty} p(y)\ln g(y)\,dy$$ (5.9.6)

where $p(y)$ is the probability density of Y and $\ln g(y)$ is the density of the conditional entropy of the filter.

Indeed one has

$$H(Y'/Y) = \int\limits_{-\infty}^{+\infty} p(y)H(Y'/y)\,dy \ ,$$

and we merely define

$$H(Y'/y) =: \ln g(y) \ ,$$

where $g(y)$ may have the practical meaning of a gain for instance.

In the special case where the filtering is simply a nonlinear transformation $Z = f(Y)$, one has the equation

$$H(Z) = H(Y) + \int\limits_{-\infty}^{+\infty} p(y)\ln\left|\frac{\partial f}{\partial y}\right|dy$$

$$=: H(Y) + U_g(p) \tag{5.9.7}$$

and therefore $g(y) \equiv \left|\dfrac{\partial f}{\partial y}\right|$, which is the Jacobian of the transformation.

ii) First Case. Assume that $y \in \mathbb{R}$, and $g(y) > 1$. One then has $U_g(p) > 0$, and a simple calculation yields

$$J_m(X/Y) = \frac{1}{2}\ln\left(1 + \frac{\sigma_v^2}{\sigma_x^2}\right) + U_g(p^*) \tag{5.9.8}$$

with

$$U_g(p^*) = [2\pi(\sigma_x^2 + \sigma_v^2)]^{-1/2} \int\limits_{-\infty}^{+\infty} g(y)\exp\left(-\frac{y^2}{\sigma_x^2 + \sigma_v^2}\right)dy \ ; \tag{5.9.9}$$

in other words, the capacity of the channel has been increased by using the nonlinear transformation.

Second Case. Assume that $y \in \mathbb{R}$ and $0 < g(y) < 1$. $U_f(p) = -|U_g(p)|$ is then negative and the capacity of the channel is

$$J_m(X/Y) = \max_p\ [H(Y) - |U_g(p)|] - H(V) \ ; \tag{5.9.10}$$

in other words it diminishes. The maximum is no longer achieved when p is a normal distribution, and a classical calculation with Lagrange multipliers on the augmented transinformation

$$-\int\limits_{-\infty}^{+\infty} p(y)\ln\left[\frac{p(y)}{g(y)}\right]dy + \lambda_0\left[\int\limits_{-\infty}^{+\infty} p(y)\,dy - 1\right] + \lambda_1\int\limits_{-\infty}^{+\infty} yp(y)\,dy$$

$$+ \lambda_2\left[\int\limits_{-\infty}^{+\infty} y^2p(y)\,dy - \sigma_y^2\right]$$

yields

$$p^*(y) = g(y)e^{-(u_0 + u_1 y + u_2 y^2)}$$

where u_0, u_1 and u_2 are constants that are defined by the first-order and second-order moments of Y. We thus obtain the normal distribution multiplied by the gain of the filter.

As a matter of fact, strictly speaking, there is no new result. All we have shown is that the concept of subjective transinformation yields results that are quite consistent with those already known. Nevertheless, the difference here is that this approach leads us to a physical interpretation which can suggest topics for further research. For instance, a possible question is: How can one characterize the semantics that could be associated with a given mathematical operator?

In addition, we note that some proofs are simpler here than in the standard framework.

5.10 Transinformation in the Presence of Fuzziness

5.10.1 On the Entropy of a Fuzzy Set

Basically, a set is fuzzy mainly because there is ambiguity in the meaning of some of its elements with respect to a given semantic space. In other words, in order to completely define a fuzzy set, we need a space of values and a space of meanings, so that we work entirely in the framework (syntax, semantics) of the preceding informational model. The main problem can be stated as follows: Do we need probability distributions to describe the semantic space?

Zadeh [5.12] proposed the following definition for the entropy of a fuzzy event:

Definition 5.10.1. Let $X \in \mathbb{R}$ denote a continuous random variable with the probability density $p(x)$. Let A denote a fuzzy set defined by its membership function $\{\mathbb{R} \to [0,1], x \to \mu_A(x)\}$. The entropy $H_z(\mu_A)$ of the fuzzy event $X \in A$ is then defined by the expression

$$H_z(\mu_A) := - \int_{-\infty}^{+\infty} \mu_A(x) p(x) \ln p(x)\, dx \ . \qquad (5.10.1) \quad \square$$

As defined, this entropy would measure the combined uncertainty resulting from the simultaneous effects of randomness and fuzziness. As a special case, it should yield random entropy in the absence of fuzziness. So let us assume that there is no fuzziness. $\mu_A(x)$ is then the characteristic function $\phi_A(x)$ of A, that is to say, $\phi_A(x) = 1$, $x \in A$ and $\phi_A(x) = 0$, $x \notin A$. Equation (5.10.1) yields

$$H_z(\phi_A) = - \int_A p(x) \ln p(x)\, dx \ . \qquad (5.10.2)$$

But in information theory, it is well known that the entropy of the random event $X \in A$ is

$$H\{X \in A\} = \frac{-\int_A p(x)\ln p(x)\,dx}{\int_A p(x)\,dx} \tag{5.10.3}$$

which is the entropy of incomplete probability. Thus there is an evident inconsistency between (5.10.2) and (5.10.3). One may of course circumvent this difficulty by introducing the new definition

$$H_z'(\mu_A) = \frac{-\int_{-\infty}^{+\infty} \mu_A(x)p(x)\ln p(x)\,dx}{\int_A \mu_A(x)p(x)\,dx} \tag{5.10.4}$$

where A denotes the set $A = \{X|\mu_A(x) > 0\}$, but this would be rather formal and artificial.

In analogy to the Fermi entropy

$$-\sum_i [p_i \ln p_i + (1 - p_i)\ln(1 - p_i)]$$

the fuzzy entropy proposed by *De Luca* and *Termini* [5.13] is defined as follows.

Definition 5.10.2. The entropy $H_L(\mu_A)$ of the continuous fuzzy set defined by the membership function $\mu_A(x)$ is

$$H_L(\mu_A) := -\int_{-\infty}^{+\infty} [\mu_A \ln \mu_A + (1 - \mu_A)\ln(1 - \mu_A)]\,dx \ . \tag{5.10.5} \quad \square$$

This entropy of course refers to the uncertainty caused by fuzziness only. Given the formal derivation of this definition by its authors, one could equally well take the expression $-\int \mu_A \ln \mu_A$, but they justify the simultaneous use of μ_A and $(1 - \mu_A)$ by the need to have the maximum value of the density of uncertainty at $x = \frac{1}{2}$. This prerequisite, although likely from a practical viewpoint, is theoretically speaking not necessary at all.

In our opinion, the major argument in support of this definition is that it allows us to consider a membership function as a probability distribution so that we are entitled to combine random entropy and fuzzy entropy, since they then have the same physical dimensions.

For instance, it is then sufficient to put,

$$\mu_A(x) = \mathrm{pr}\{x \in A\}$$

$$1 - \mu_A(x) = \mathrm{pr}\{x \notin A\}$$

so that, in the stochastic sense, the entropy of the random experiment to determine whether $x \in A$ or $x \notin A$ is

$$-\mu_A(x)\ln \mu_A(x) - [1 - \mu_A(x)]\ln[1 - \mu_A(x)] \ . \tag{5.10.6}$$

It is clear that the entropy functions $H_z(\mu_A)$, $H'_z(\mu_A)$ and $H_L(\mu_A)$ can be readily applied to discrete variables. For instance one has

$$H_z(\mu_A) = -\sum_i \mu_A(x_i) \ln \mu_A(x_i) \tag{5.10.7}$$

$$H'_z(\mu_A) = -\frac{\left[\sum_i \mu_A(x_i) \ln \mu_A(x_i)\right]}{\sum_j p(x_j)}, \qquad \mu(x_j) > 0 \tag{5.10.8}$$

$$H_L(\mu_A) = -\sum_i \mu_A(x_i) \ln \mu_A(x_i) + [1 - \mu_A(x_i)] \ln[1 - \mu_A(x_i)] . \tag{5.10.9}$$

Equation (5.10.9) is the definition proposed by *De Luca* and *Termini* [5.13].

In the special case of a continuous membership function, *Jumarie* [5.14] suggested the following definition.

Definition 5.10.3. The entropy $H_J(\mu_A)$ of a fuzzy set described by the differentiable membership function $\mu_A(x)$ is defined by the expression

$$H_J(\mu_A) = -\int_{-\infty}^{+\infty} |\mu'_A(x)| \ln |\mu'_A(x)| \, dx \tag{5.10.10}$$

where $\mu'_A(x) := d\mu_A(x)/dx$.   □

The intention behind this definition is to consider $-\ln |\mu'_A(x)|$ as the density of uncertainty due to fuzziness. Thus $|\mu'_A(x)|$ would be the counterpart of a probability density.   □

5.10.2 Application of Subjective Transinformation

Our purpose in this section is to quantitatively estimate the effects of fuzziness in the phenomenon of information loss.

Description of the Model. We assume that β is encoded by α; and that β', which is independent of α, is the error on β, as caused by fuzziness. In addition, we set $\alpha \equiv \alpha'$, that is to say, α has no semantics.

With these assumptions, (5.4.6) yields,

$$J(\beta/\alpha) = I(\beta/\alpha) + H(\beta/\alpha) - H(\beta\beta'/\alpha)$$

$$= I(\beta/\alpha) - H(\beta'/\beta) . \tag{5.10.11}$$

If we assume that $H(\beta'/B_i)$ is the entropy of the fuzzy event $X \in E_i$ where E_i is a fuzzy set with the membership function $\mu_i(x_j)$, then we can make the definition $H(\beta'/B_i) := H_L(\mu_i)$ whose meaning is quite consistent with our information theoretic modelling. More explicitly one has

$$J(\beta/\alpha) = I(\beta/\alpha) - \sum_j p(B_j) H_L(\mu_j) \tag{5.10.12}$$

or with the notation of Sect. 5.3.1

$$J(\beta/\alpha) = \sum_{ij} r_{ij} \left[\ln \frac{r_{ij}}{p_i q_j} - H_L(\mu_j) \right] . \tag{5.10.13}$$

A Few Remarks. (i) It is clear that if the effect of the fuzziness is extreme, one may have $J(\beta/\alpha) = 0$, as might be expected.

ii) Let us set $\alpha \equiv \beta$ in (5.10.8). We then obtain

$$J(\beta/\beta) = I(\beta/\beta) - \sum_j q_j H_L(\mu_j)$$

$$= H(\beta) - \sum_j q_j H_L(\mu_j) . \tag{5.10.14}$$

Expressed in words, the initial amount $H(\beta)$ of information available in β is diminished by $\sum_j q_j H_L(\mu_j)$ due to the fuzziness.

5.10.3 The Brillouin Problem

Although the Brillouin problem that we mentioned in Sect. 1.3 is not strictly relevant to fuzzy sets, the equation (5.10.7) can provide a solution, at least a partial solution. Indeed, in this specific case, we are not interested in $H(\beta)$, but rather in $J(\beta/\beta)$, i.e.

$$J(\beta/\beta) = H(\beta) - H(\beta\beta'/\beta) . \tag{5.10.15}$$

Assume that $H(\beta'/\beta)$ depends upon an external parameter u, say $H(\beta'/\beta, u)$ in such a manner that

$$H(\beta'/\beta, 1) = 0 ; \qquad H(\beta'/\beta, 0) = H(\beta) ;$$

then the function $J_u(\beta/\beta)$ indexed by u will have the values

$$J_0(\beta/\beta) = 0 ; \qquad J_1(\beta/\beta) = H(\beta) .$$

When $u = 1$, we have no uncertainty about the practical value of the amount $H(\beta)$ of information, while when $u = 1$, this uncertainty is very large and is equal to $H(\beta)$ itself.

More generally, one may assume that $H(\beta'/\beta, u)$ varies continuously with u. This can desribe the effects of a semantic universe that depends upon a control parameter.

5.11 On the Use of Renyi Entropy

In Sect. 3.4.4, we introduced a transinformation $I_c(\beta/\alpha)$ of order c and our purpose here is to examine whether it can be identified with subjective transinformation, at least in some special cases.

5.11.1 Renyi Entropy and Subjective Entropy

Assume that c in $H_c(\alpha)$ is close to unity, and let us identify $H_c(\alpha)$ with $H_s(\alpha)$. Equations (2.9.13) and (5.2.1) then yield the equality

$$H(\alpha'/\alpha) \equiv -(c-1)\left[\sum_{i=1}^{m} p(\ln p)^2 - H^2(\alpha)\right] + o((c-1)^2) , \tag{5.11.1}$$

which can be understood as follows. If we assume that the subjectivity of the observer is mainly due to the presence of the semantics (α'/α), then c can be considered as a parameter that accounts for this subjectivity in the definition and the measure of uncertainty.

In other words $H_c(\alpha)$ could be thought of as another possible approach to the definition of entropy in the presence of subjectivity.

5.11.2 Transinformation of Order c and Shannon Transinformation

Equations (2.9.13) and (3.4.5) yield

$$I_c(\beta/\alpha) = I(\beta/\alpha) + (c-1)\sum_{i=1}^{m}\sum_{j=1}^{n}[r_{ij}(\ln q_{j/i})^2 - p_i H^2(\beta/A_i)] + o((c-1)^2) \tag{5.11.2}$$

where $r_{ij} := p_i q_{j/i}$.

Using the Schwarz inequality, one can write

$$\sum_i p_i H(\beta/A_i) = \sum_i \sum_j \sqrt{p_i q_{j/i}}(\sqrt{p_i q_{j/i}}|\ln q_{j/i}|)$$

$$\leqslant \left(\sum_i \sum_j r_{ij}\right)^{1/2}\left(\sum_i \sum_j r_{ij}(\ln q_{j/i})^2\right)^{1/2}$$

such that the coefficient of $(c-1)$ in (5.11.2) is positive.

As a result one has $I_c(\beta/\alpha) \geqslant I(\beta/\alpha)$ when $c > 1$, and $I_c(\beta/\alpha) \leqslant I(\beta/\alpha)$ when $c < 1$.

These conclusions are just as expected and suggest that $I_c(\beta/\alpha)$ could play a role similar to that of $J(\beta/\alpha)$, at least in some special cases.

6. A Unified Approach to Discrete and Continuous Entropy

In the third chapter we reviewed the main properties of discrete and of continuous entropy, and after a careful analysis, we concluded that, to a large extent, the latter is a more suitable measure of uncertainty than the former.

As a matter of fact, even for a discrete random variable, a complete measure of uncertainty should take account of the uncertainty due to the spans of the lattice where the variable is defined.

Starting from this remark, we propose a slight modification of the axiomatic derivation of the discrete entropy and we thereby obtain the new concept of *total entropy* which exhibits properties quite similar to those of continuous entropy.

The method applies to Shannon entropy and Renyi entropy, and some consequences are examined. The total entropy can be considered as a special case of the *effective entropy* which we introduced previously to account for defects in observation, and we shall show that there is a complete equivalence between this effective entropy and the so-called *inset entropy* which was later defined by *Aczel* and *Daroczy* [6.1].

This unified approach will be helpful to tackle the problem of defining the amount of uncertainty involved in forms and patterns.

6.1 Introduction

In the third chapter we carefully reviewed the definition and some consequences of the continuous entropy and we arrived at the conclusion that the latter has nice properties that the discrete entropy has not, therefore the need arises for a uniform approach to these two concepts. Let us summarize our main arguments.

i) The discrete entropy has been derived as the consequence of a set of preliminary axioms (see for instance [6.2]). *Shannon* [6.3, 4] defined the continuous entropy formally by substituting the integral for the summation in the expression of the discrete entropy. Later *Hatori* [6.5] proved this result by using several axioms and mainly the property $H(X, Y) = H(X) + H(Y/X)$.

ii) The value of the continuous entropy is affected by a continuous transformation of variables, and this feature merely reflects the fact that the transformation itself involves its own amount of information. We thus have a first approach to the problem of defining the amount of information contained in a form (see for instance [6.6] for some comments on this question).

iii) One can use the continuous entropy to prove the so-called central limit theorem [6.7]. This result is of importance because it exhibits a similarity between the informational entropy and the thermodynamic entropy on the one hand, and it sheds light on the analogy between the central limit theorem and the second principle of thermodynamics on the other hand. We reconsidered this proof from a theoretical standpoint and showed that the basic condition for the convergence to the normal law is $H(S_n) > s_n$ (see Sect. 3.5 for the notation). We were then able to generalize this central limit theorem.

We do not have similar results with the discrete entropy.

iv) The maximum entropy principle first stated by *Jaynes* [6.8, 9] has been "proven" by *Shore* and *Johnson* [6.10], but for discrete probability distributions only; we have no similar proof for the continuous entropy. But in view of the number of theoretical and practical results which were obtained by applying the principle to continuous entropy, there is no doubt that the theorem should hold in this case also.

Physicists like to point out that the continuous entropy is very questionable because, from a practical viewpoint, we have to account for the accuracy of the measurement device. But one can reply by saying that the continuous entropy can be considered as being a potential uncertainty in the sense that it is the limiting value of the uncertainty that we may have on assuming that the observation errors tend to zero.

6.2 Intuitive Derivation of "Total Entropy"

6.2.1 Preliminary Definitions and Notation

Let $X \in \mathbb{R}$ denote a discrete random variable which takes on the values $x_1, x_2, \ldots,$ x_m with the respective probabilities $p_1, p_2, \ldots, p_m$; we shall denote its *total uncertainty* by $H_e(X)$ (the subscript e stands for *effective*).

When X is upper bounded and lower bounded, and takes a finite number m of values, then we shall define the bounds

$$a := \min_i x_i \; ; \qquad b := \max_i x_i \; ; \qquad i = 1, 2, \ldots, m \qquad (6.2.1)$$

and the mean length of interval

$$h := \frac{b - a}{m - 1} \; . \qquad (6.2.2)$$

When X may have an infinite number of values, then h is taken in the form

$$h := \lim \frac{x_{m+1} - x_1}{m} \quad \text{as} \quad m \uparrow \infty \; . \qquad (6.2.3)$$

Again for a finite set of possible values, we shall define the family of intervals $\{L_i\}$ along with their respective lengths as

$$L_1 := \left[x_1 - \frac{x_2 - x_1}{2}, \frac{x_1 + x_2}{2} \right]$$

$$:= [\xi_1, \xi_2] \; ; \qquad h_1 := \xi_1 - \xi_2 \qquad (6.2.4)$$

$$L_i := \left[\frac{x_i + x_{i-1}}{2}, \frac{x_i + x_{i+1}}{2} \right]$$

$$:= [\xi_i, \xi_{i+1}] ; \qquad h_i := \xi_{i+1} - \xi_i \tag{6.2.5}$$

$$L_m := \left[\frac{x_{m-1} + x_m}{2}, x_m + \frac{x_m - x_{m-1}}{2} \right]$$

$$:= [\xi_m, \xi_{m+1}] ; \qquad h_m := \xi_{m+1} - \xi_m . \tag{6.2.6}$$

When the lattice is not finite, one will define the set $\{L_i\}$ as the limit of the above finite set when $m \uparrow \infty$.

In words, we associated with each x_i an interval L_i such that

$$L_i \cap L_j = \emptyset \qquad i \neq j ,$$

$$[x_1, x_m] \subset \bigcup_{i=1}^{m} L_i .$$

In the special case where $x_{i+1} - x_i = h = $ constant for every i, then x_i is the middle point of L_i, and the length of the latter is exactly h.

These intervals will play a role similar to that of the intervals $L(x_i)$ in Sect. 2.11.4 related to effective entropy.

6.2.2 Physical Derivation of $H_e(X)$

The intuitive derivation of the explicit form of $H_e(X)$ is decomposed as follows.

Step 1. We refer to the remark of Sect. 3.6.2 which points out that the total uncertainty involved in X results from the uncertainty of random nature associated with the probability distribution $\{p_i\}$, and from an additional uncertainty due to the interval $[a, b]$ on which X is defined, i.e. given the assumption that X is bounded. The simplest way to obtain a model for this uncertainty is to assume that the additive law of entropies applies, and to write

$$H_e(X) := H(X) + g(b - a) \tag{6.2.7}$$

where $g(b - a)$ is a function which defines the amount of uncertainty involved in the interval $[a, b]$.

Again, according to the remark of Sect. 3.6.2, $g(b - a)$ should be an increasing function of $(b - a)$ and one such that

$$\lim g(b - a) \neq 0 \quad \text{as} \quad b - a \downarrow 0 \tag{6.2.8}$$

since otherwise we would have $H_e(X) \cong H(X)$ for small $(b - a)$.

Step 2. A second model can be guessed in the form

$$H_e(X) = H(X) + \tilde{g}(h) \tag{6.2.9}$$

where $\tilde{g}(h)$ has characteristics similar to those of $g(b-a)$ above. Indeed according to (6.2.2), which defines h in term of $(b-a)$, the right-hand terms of (6.2.7) and (6.2.9) have the same mathematical properties.

Note that the expression (6.2.9) can be re-written as

$$H_e(X) = -k\sum_i p_i \ln p_i + \sum_i p_i \tilde{g}(h) \tag{6.2.10}$$

$$= -k\sum p_i \ln \frac{p_i}{e^{\tilde{g}(h)/k}} . \tag{6.2.11}$$

Step 3. We can continue this procedure of generalization. Indeed we may assume that the second uncertainty related to the observation process is directly dependent upon the intervals L_i themselves so that a direct extension of (6.2.10) allows us to write

$$H_e(X) = -k\sum_{i=1}^{m} p_i \ln p_i + \sum_{i=1}^{m} p_i g_i(h_i) \tag{6.2.12}$$

where again $g_i(h_i)$ is an increasing function of h_i for every i.

Step 4. As a special case, assume that the uncertainty function $g_i(h_i)$ is taken in the form of the *Hartley* entropy [6.11], that is to say

$$g_i(h_i) = k\ln h_i . \tag{6.2.13}$$

Equation (6.2.12) then yields

$$H_e(X) = -k\sum_{i=1}^{m} p_i \ln \frac{p_i}{h_i} . \tag{6.2.14}$$

We point out that all this development is very straightforward and simple (it may even look naive), without mathematics, and refers to prerequisites which are known to anyone who is slightly acquainted with the definition and practical meaning of Shannon entropy.

In the following section, we shall derive the expression (6.2.11) in a more rigorous manner, as the consequence of a preliminary set of axioms considered as desiderata for a complete measure of uncertainty.

6.3 Mathematical Derivation of Total Entropy

6.3.1 The Main Axioms

We now state the main axioms which should be satisfied by the total entropy $H_e(X)$.

(C1) $H_e(X)$ is a function $\chi[(p_1,h_1),(p_2,h_2),\ldots,(p_m,h_m)]$, whose value should not be modified by any permutation of the set $\{(p_1,h_1),(p_2,h_2),\ldots,(p_m,h_m)\}$.

(C2) $\chi(\cdot)$ is continuous with respect to p_i and h_i for every i, except possibly at $h_i = 0$.

(C3) $\chi(\cdot)$ is an increasing function of h_i for every i.

(C4) Let $\Phi(p_1, p_2, \ldots, p_m)$ denote the Shannon entropy $H(X)$ of X, then the following equation is satisfied:

$$\chi[(p_1, 1), (p_2, 1), \ldots, (p_m, 1)] = \Phi(p_1, p_2, \ldots, p_m) \ . \tag{6.3.1}$$

(C5) Let $\{(q_1, h_1'), (q_2, h_2'), \ldots, (q_n, h_n')\}$ denote the parameters of another discrete random variable Y; one then has the equality

$$\chi[(p_1 q_1, h_1 h_1'), \ldots, (p_i q_j, h_i h_j'), \ldots, (p_m q_n, h_m h_n')]$$

$$= \chi[(p_1, h_1), \ldots, (p_m, h_m)] + \chi[(q_1, h_1'), \ldots, (q_n, h_n')] \ . \tag{6.3.2}$$

Comments. Axioms (C1) and (C2) are standard in information theory and they are continuity requirements only. Axiom (C3) represents our basic remark in Sect. 3.6.2. Axiom (C4) can be thought of as a normalization condition which explains the way in which we want to extend the concept of entropy. Axiom (C5) describes the multiplicative effects of the lengths of the intervals L_i on the value of the total uncertainty.

6.3.2 Derivation of Total Entropy

We have the following result.

Proposition 6.3.1. A measure of the total uncertainty $H_e(X)$ which satisfies the axioms (C1) to (C2) above is given by the expression

$$H_e(X) = H(X) + K \sum_{i=1}^{m} p_i \ln h_i \ . \tag{6.3.3}$$

Proof. (i) Let us seek a solution in the form

$$\chi(\cdot) = f(p_1, \ldots, p_m) + \sum_{i=1}^{m} g_i(p_i, h_i) \tag{6.3.4}$$

with the additional condition

$$g_i(p_i, 1) = 0 \ , \qquad i = 1, 2, \ldots, m \ . \tag{6.3.5}$$

ii) Assume that the function $g_i(p, h)$ can be expressed in the separable form

$$g_i(p, h) = a_i(p) b_i(h) \ . \tag{6.3.6}$$

Equations (6.3.4) and (6.3.6) then yield

$$\sum_{i,j} a_{ij}(p_i q_j) b_{ij}(h_i h_j') = \sum_i a_i(p_i) b_i(h_i) + \sum_j a_j(q_j) b_j(h_j') \ . \tag{6.3.7}$$

We re-write (6.3.7) in the form

$$\sum_{i,j} a_{ij}(p_i q_j) b_{ij}(h_i h_j') = \sum_{i,j} q_j a_i(p_i) b_i(h_i) + \sum_{i,j} p_i a_j(q_j) b_j(h_j') \ ,$$

and thus obtain the equality

$$a_{ij}(p_i q_j)b_{ij}(h_i h_j') = q_j a_i(p_i)b_i(h_i) + p_i a_j(q_j)b_j(h_j') . \qquad (6.3.8)$$

iii) Let us now look for a solution such that

$$a_{ij}(p_i q_j) = q_j a_i(p_i) = p_i a_j(q_j) .$$

This condition is fulfilled when

$$a_i(p_i) = p_i ; \qquad a_j(q_j) = q_j$$

and on substituting into (6.3.8) we obtain

$$b_{ij}(h_i h_j') = b_i(h_i) + b_j(h_j') .$$

A solution to this equation is

$$b_j(h_j') = K \ln h_j'$$

where K denotes a constant.

iv) According to axiom (C3), K is positive. This completes the proof.

On the Uniqueness of the Solution. Do we need to verify that the solution so obtained is unique? Our claim is that we do not.

Indeed, we stated a set of desiderata for a measure of total uncertainty; we got a mathematical expression which satisfies this prerequisite; and we are quite entitled to use it for future studies even though it may not be a unique solution. We have exactly the same situation in classical information theory where several types of entropies are consistent with the same set of mathematical axioms! But it does not matter. Indeed, it is not as if we were modelling the dynamics of a physical system by a partial differential equation for instance. If we had two solutions to this equation, which one of them would be the right one, for example to implement an automatic control device?

6.3.3 On the Expression of the Total Entropy

The expression (6.3.3) can be re-written in the more compact form

$$H_e(X) = -k \sum_{i=0}^{m} p_i \ln \frac{p_i}{h_i K/k} , \qquad K > 0 \qquad (6.3.9)$$

and in the special case where $K = k$, which *might* amount to saying that the two uncertainties are defined with the same measurement units, one has

$$H_e(X) = -k \sum_{i=1}^{m} p_i \ln \frac{p_i}{h_i} , \qquad K = k \qquad (6.3.10)$$

Definition 6.3.1. The entropy $H_e(X)$ defined by Equation (6.3.10) will be referred to as the *total Shannon entropy* or for short the *total entropy* of the discrete random variable X.

Equation (6.3.10) is exactly the expression (6.2.14) which we obtained previously by using intuitive arguments only.

6.4 Alternative Set of Axioms for the Total Entropy

6.4.1 Generalization of Shannon Recurrence Equation

In the set of axioms (C1) to (C5) above, there is Axiom (C4) which explicitly refers to the Shannon entropy, and this is quite understandable since $H_e(X)$ was considered as an extension of $H(X)$, in such a manner that it should contain the latter as the special case where $h_1 = h_2 = \cdots = h_m = 1$. But one can refine these axioms such that they no longer refer to $H(X)$. An alternative set of desiderata reads as follows:

(D1), (D2), (D3) similar to (C1), (C2) and (C3) respectively.
(D4) The following equation is satisfied, that is

$$\chi[(p_1, h_1), \ldots, (p_m, h_m)] = \chi[(p_1 + p_2, 1), (p_3, h_3), \ldots, (p_m, h_m)]$$
$$+ (p_1 + p_2)\chi\left[\left(\frac{p_1}{p_1 + p_2}, h_1\right), \left(\frac{p_2}{p_1 + p_2}, h_2\right)\right]. \tag{6.4.1}$$

Equation (6.4.1), which is none other than a modified version of the axiom first stated by Shannon himself, has the following meaning: We decompose the observation of X into stages:

i)   In the first stage, we determine whether the state of X has the value $(x_1 \cup x_2)$ or is one of the set $(x_3, x_4, \ldots, x_m)$.
ii) If the value is x_i, $i = 3, 4, \ldots, m$, then the uncertainties due to the intervals h_3, $h_4, \ldots, h_m$ are relevant, while the uncertainty caused by h_1 and h_2 are not involved. The corresponding entropy is the first term of the right-hand side of (6.4.1).
ii) Otherwise, if the value of X is $x_1 \cup x_2$, then we make a second experiment to locate x, and we have to account for the uncertainty due to h_1 and h_2. The corresponding entropy is the second term of the right-hand side of (6.4.1)

It is a simple matter to verify that $H_e(X)$ satisfies this set of axioms.

6.4.2 A Model via Uniform Interval of Definition

Until now, we have used axioms which explicitly involve the individual effects of each interval L_i via its length h_i, and we thereby obtained a suitable theoretical framework for the equation (6.2.14) of our intuitive derivation. But we can also define a concept of total entropy by using the average length h given by (6.2.2); and to this end the following set of axioms is relevant.

(E1) $H_e(X)$ is a function $\eta(p_1, p_2, \ldots, p_m; h)$ whose value should not be modified by any permutation of the set $\{p_1, p_2, \ldots p_m\}$.

(E2) $\eta(\cdot)$ is continuous with respect to p_i for every i, and with respect to h except possibly at $h = 0$.

(E3) $\eta(\cdot)$ is an increasing function of h.

(E4) The following equation holds,

$$\eta(p_1, p_2, \ldots, p_m; 1) = \Phi(p_1, p_2, \ldots, p_m) \ . \tag{6.4.2}$$

(E5) Let $\{(q, q, , \ldots, q); h'\}$ denote the parameters of a second discrete random variable Y. One then has the equality

$$\eta(p_1 q_1, \ldots, p_i q_j, \ldots, p_m q_n; hh') = \eta(p_1, p_2, \ldots, p_m; h)$$

$$+ \eta(q_1, q_2, \ldots, q_n; h') \ . \tag{6.4.3}$$

One can easily show that a function which satisfies these axioms is

$$H_e(X) := -k \sum_{i=1}^{m} p_i \ln \frac{p_i}{h} \ . \tag{6.4.4}$$

6.5 Total Entropy with Respect to a Measure

The following generalization is straightforward.

Proposition 6.4.1. Let $\mu(L)$ denote a measure in the mathematical sense of the term, which satisfies the normalizing condition

$$\mu(L_i) = 1 \quad \text{iff} \quad h_i = 1 \ . \tag{6.5.1}$$

Then a measure of uncertainty which satisfies all the axioms (C1) to (C5) above but in which $\mu(L_i)$ is substituted for h_i everywhere, is given by the expression

$$H_e(X/\mu) := -k \sum_{i=1}^{m} p_i \ln \frac{p_i}{[\mu(L_i)]^{K/k}} \ , \qquad K > 0 \ . \tag{6.5.2}$$

The proof follows exactly like the proof of proposition 6.3.1.

$H_e(X/\!/\mu)$ can be thought of as the *total Shannon entropy of x with respect to the measure μ.*

6.6 Total Renyi Entropy

In the present section, we shall use the same randomization technique to derive a generalization of the Renyi entropy.

6.6.1 Preliminary Remarks About Renyi Entropy

For a discrete random variable $X \in \mathbb{R}$ which takes on the values $x_1, x_2, \ldots, x_m$ with the respective probabilities $p_1, p_2, \ldots, p_m$ *Renyi* [6.12, 13] obtained a measure $H_e(X)$

of uncertainty in the form

$$H_c(X) = \frac{k}{1-c} \ln\left(\sum_{i=1}^{m} p_i^c\right)$$ (6.6.1)

where k is a positive constant and c is a real-valued scalar parameter.

For a continuous variable $X \in \mathbb{R}$, it is customary to define $H_c(X)$ by the expression

$$H_c(X) := \frac{1}{1-c} \ln \int_{\mathbb{R}} p^c(x)\, dx \ .$$ (6.6.2)

But, contrary to the case of the continuous Shannon entropy, there exists no theoretical derivation of the continuous Renyi entropy via a preliminary set of axioms.

And here we have exactly the same pitfall! The expression (6.6.2) cannot be considered as the limiting form of (6.6.1) when the discretizing span tends to zero. This remark is the basic reason why we generalize the definition of the discrete Renyi entropy in order to account for the range of variation of the variable.

6.6.2 Axioms for Total Renyi Entropy

Notation. We refer to the mean interval length h defined by (6.2.2) and we denote the total Renyi entropy by $H_c^e(X)$.

Statement of the Main Axioms. A list of desiderata for $H_c^e(x)$ is as follows:

(F1) $H_c^e(X)$ is a function $\theta(p_1, p_2, \ldots, p_m; h)$ whose value should not be modified by any permutation of the set $\{p_1, p_2, \ldots p_m\}$.
(F2) $\theta(\cdot)$ is continuous with respect to $p_1, p_2, \ldots, p_m$ and h except possibly at $h = 0$.
(F3) $\theta(\cdot)$ in an increasing function of h.
(F4) The following relation is satisfied:

$$\theta(p_1, p_2, \ldots, p_m; 1) = H_c^e(X)$$ (6.6.3)

(F5) Let $\{q_1, q_2, \ldots, q_m; h'\}$ denote the parameters of another discrete random variable; then one has

$$\theta(p_1 q_1, \ldots, p_i q_j, \ldots, p_m q_n; hh') = \theta(p_1, p_2, \ldots, p_m; h)$$
$$+ \theta(q_1, q_2, \ldots, q_n; h') \ .$$ (6.6.4)

6.6.3 Total Renyi Entropy

Proposition 6.6.1. A measure $H_c^e(X)$ which satisfies the axioms (F1) to (F5) above is

$$H_c^e(X) = H_c(X) + K \ln h$$ (6.6.5)

where K denotes a positive constant.

The proof of this result is quite similar to the proof of proposition (6.3.1) and is left to the reader.

One can rewrite $H_c^e(X)$ in the form

$$H_c^e(X) = \frac{k}{1-c} \ln\left(\sum_{i=1}^{m} p_i^c / h^{(K/k)(c-1)} \right) \tag{6.6.6}$$

where k is the constant which defines the (usual) Renyi entropy. In the special case where $K = k$, one has

$$H_c^e(X) = \frac{k}{1-c} \ln\left[\sum_{i=1}^{m} \left(\frac{p_i}{h}\right)^c h \right], \qquad K = k . \tag{6.6.7}$$

Definition 6.6.1. We shall refer to $H_c^e(X)$ as defined by the expression (6.6.8) as the *total Renyi entropy* of the variable X.

6.6.4 Total Renyi Entropy with Respect to a Measure

Proposition 6.6.2. Let $v(h)$ denote a positive increasing $\mathbb{R} \to \mathbb{R}$ function which satisfies the following conditions

$$v(0) = 0 , \tag{6.6.8}$$

$$v(1) = 1 . \tag{6.6.9}$$

A measure of uncertainty which satisfies all the axioms (F1) to (F5) but in which $v(h)$ is substituted for h everywhere, is then given by the expressions

$$H_c^e(X//v) = H_c(X) + K \ln v(h) \tag{6.6.10}$$

$$= H_c(X) + K \sum_{i=1}^{m} p_i \ln v(h) \tag{6.6.11}$$

$$= \frac{k}{1-c} \ln\left(\sum_{i=1}^{m} p_i^c / [v(h)]^{(K/k)(c-1)} \right) . \tag{6.6.12}$$

In the special case where $K = k$, one has

$$H_c^e(X//v) = \frac{k}{1-c} \ln\left\{ \sum_{i=1}^{m} \left[\frac{p_i}{v(h)}\right]^c v(h) \right\} , \qquad K = k . \tag{6.6.13}$$

6.7 On the Practical Meaning of Total Entropy

6.7.1 General Remarks

i) On referring to the expression (6.3.3), we are directly led to consider $H_e(X)$ as being the entropy $H(\alpha, \alpha')$ of two random events α and α' defined as follows: The first event α is related to the uncertainty associated with the determination of the interval L_i which contains X, that is to say the entropy $H(X)$. The second event α' is associated with the uncertainty in the determination of the value of X inside this interval; it is clearly the entropy $\ln h_i$.

It follows that all the results that have been derived in information theory using $H(X)$ have their counterparts with $H_e(X)$.

ii) We now refer to the equation (6.3.10), which we consider as the mathematical expectation of $-\ln(p_i/h_i)$. We then conclude that while the discrete entropy $H(X)$ defines the amount of uncertainty involved in the event $(X = x_i)$ as being equal to $-\ln p_i$, in the total entropy this uncertainty is $-\ln(p_i/h_i)$.

iii) The point of importance is that the total entropy distinguishes between the uncertainty involved in a random experiment and the uncertainty involved in a random variable, while the Shannon entropy does not.

Indeed, let α denote a random experiment which provides the possible outcomes $A_1, A_2, \ldots, A_m$ with the respective probabilities $p_1, p_2, \ldots, p_m$; its uncertainty is defined by $U(p_1, p_2, \ldots, p_m)$ [see (2.2.3)] as a consequence of the axioms which assume that this uncertainty should depend upon the probability distribution only.

This being so, when the random event is a random variable which takes on the values $x_1, x_2, \ldots, x_m$ with the respective probabilities $p_1, p_2, \ldots, p_m$, it is customary to assume that the uncertainty involved in X is again defined by $U(p_1, p_2, \ldots, p_m)$.

Our claim is that in doing this, we lose information about the practical nature of X because the set $\{x_i\}$ is ordered while the set $\{A_i\}$ is not; and in most cases $\{A_i\}$ cannot be meaningfully ordered!

iv) Given a practical problem, which quantity, $H(X)$ or $H_e(X)$, is more suitable? If the set $\{x_1, x_2, \ldots, x_m\}$ is well defined (without ambiguity) and the corresponding uncertainty is due to the probability distribution only, then $H(X)$ is sufficient. But if the x_i's themselves are defined with some inaccuracy, then $H_e(X)$ is more suitable.

6.7.2 Total Entropy and Relative Entropy

For small values of the observation parameter u, (4.8.5a) yields the relative entropy $H_r(X)$ in the form

$$H_r(X) = H(X) + uH(X') + o(u^2) \tag{6.7.1}$$

where $H(X')$ is the semantic entropy associated with the syntactic entropy $H(X)$. A comparison with (6.3.10) suggests the identification

$$uH(X') \equiv \sum_{i=1}^{m} p_i \ln h_i \ ,$$

but this formal identity is physically meaningless since it does not apply when $u = 0$.

Clearly total entropy cannot be identified with relative entropy since they are two measures of uncertainty which apply at different levels of observation. In analogy to the Shannon entropy, the total entropy can be considered as a measure of the absolute amount of information contained in the *random variable* X (not the probability distribution!) while the relative entropy accounts for the interactions with the observer.

In fact, the Minkowskian theory of observation applies to the total entropy itself to yield (with the notation of Sect. 4.8)

$$[H_e(X)]_r = \varrho(u)[H_e(X) + uH_e(X')] \tag{6.7.2a}$$

$$[H_e(X')]_r = \varrho(u)[H_e(X') + uH_e(X)] \tag{6.7.2b}$$

6.7.3 Total Entropy and Subjective Entropy

For a random variable X, the subjective entropy defined by (5.2.1) is

$$H_s(X) = H(X) + H(X'/X) \tag{6.7.3}$$

where X' is the semantic variable associated with X, and comparison with (6.3.10) then yields the meaningful identification

$$H(X'/X) \equiv \sum_{i=1}^{m} p_i \ln h_i \ . \tag{6.7.4}$$

More explicitly, if we write

$$H(X'/X) = \sum_{i=1}^{m} p_i H(X'/x_i) \tag{6.7.5}$$

then (6.7.4) yields

$$H(X'/x_i) \equiv \ln h_i \ .$$

The total entropy thus appears as a special case of the subjective entropy.

6.8 Further Results on the Total Entropy

6.8.1 Some Mathematical Properties of the Total Entropy

i) *Sign of $H_e(X)$*. While $H(X)$ is always positive or zero, one may have $H_e(X) \geqslant 0$ or $H_e(X) \leqslant 0$ depending upon the value of $\{h_i\}$.

ii) *Translation*. The following relation holds:

$$H_e(X + b) = H_e(X) \tag{6.8.1}$$

where $X \in \mathbb{R}$ and $b \in \mathbb{R}$ denotes a constant.

iii) *Scaling Factor*. Let $X \in \mathbb{R}$ and $b \in \mathbb{R}$, then one has

$$H_e(bX) = H_e(X) + \ln|b| \ . \tag{6.8.2}$$

The proof is direct. First the probability distributions of X and bX are the same, and second one has

$$\max(bX) - \min(bX) = |b|(\max X - \min X) \ .$$

iv) *Transformation of Variables.* First we refer to the notation of Sect. 6.2.1, and we define

$$\nabla f(x_i) := f\left(\frac{x_i + x_{i+1}}{2}\right) - f\left(\frac{x_i + x_{i-1}}{2}\right)$$

$$=: f(\xi_{i+1}) - f(\xi_i) \tag{6.8.3}$$

This being so, let us consider the total entropy

$$H_e(Y) := -\sum_{i=1}^{m} q_i \ln\left(\frac{q_i}{h_i'}\right) \tag{6.8.4}$$

and assume that we make the transformation $Y = f(X)$. X and Y have the same probability distribution, $(p_1, p_2, \ldots, p_m) \equiv (q_1, q_2, \ldots q_m)$; moreover, one has

$$h_i' = \left(\frac{\nabla_i f}{h_i}\right) h_i$$

so that on substituting into (6.8.4), we directly obtain the sought-after relation

$$H_e(Y) = H_e(X) + k \sum_{i=1}^{m} p_i \ln\left[\frac{\nabla f(x_i)}{h_i}\right]^{K/k} \tag{6.8.5}$$

$$= H_e(X) + k \sum_{i=1}^{m} p_i \ln\left[\frac{\Delta f(\xi_i)}{h_i}\right]^{K/k}. \tag{6.8.6}$$

In dealing with the entropy of patterns and forms (Chap. 8), this relation will be of paramount importance as it will allow us to suitably define the entropy of a discrete map.

v) *Change of Logarithm.* For the sake of simplicity, the entropy and the total entropy have been defined by means of the natural logarithm, but it is obvious that we can use any logarithm. For instance, if we use the entropy

$$_2H(X) = -\sum_i p_i \log_2 p_i \tag{6.8.7}$$

as is customary in technical communication, we shall then have the total entropy

$$_2H_e(X) = {}_2H(X) + \log_2 h . \tag{6.8.8}$$

vi) *Total Entropy of a Deterministic Event.* Assume that X takes one value only, then $H(X) = 0$, $h = 0$ so that one has

$$H_e(X) = -\infty \tag{6.8.9}$$

which is the total entropy of the deterministic event.

Conversely, if the condition (6.8.9) is satisfied, then X is necessarily a deterministic variable. Indeed we then have

$$H(X) + \ln h = -\infty$$

and since one has $H(X) \geqslant 0$ for discrete random variables, it follows that $\ln h = -\infty$, thence the result.

vii) *Total Entropy and Kullback Entropy.* Superficially, the Kullback entropy $H(\mathcal{Q}//\mathcal{P})$ [see (2.10.4)] is similar to the total entropy $H_e(X//\mu)$ with respect to a measure defined by the expression (6.5.2), but this is a formal resemblance only, and there are deep differences between these two expressions:

a) Indeed, depending upon the magnitudes of the $\mu(h_i)$'s, one may have $H_e(Y//\mu) > 0$ or $H_e(Y//\mu) < 0$, while it is well known that $H(\mathcal{Q}//\mathcal{P}) \geqslant 0$. This remark suggests that these two quantities cannot be related to the same physical concept.

b) Now let us assume *formally* that $p_i \equiv \mu(h_i)$. One then has $H_e(Y//\mu) \equiv -H(\mathcal{Q}//\mathcal{P})$. In other words, if the first of these measures a uncertainty, the second is related to something else, for instance it could be the negentropy introduced by *Brillouin* [6.14].

c) From a theoretical standpoint, the unique difference between (2.10.4) and (6.5.2) is due to the fact that $\mu(h_i)$ is not necessarily a probability distribution.

d) From a practical standpoint, this difference may be illustrated as follows:

First, by expanding (6.5.2) in which we assume that $K = k$, we obtain the expression

$$H_e(Y//\mu) = H(Y) + k \sum_{j=1}^{n} p_j \ln \mu(L_j) \tag{6.8.10}$$

which is effectively an entropy in the Shannon sense, insofar as we can consider $\ln \mu(L_j)$ as a conditional entropy given $Y = y_j$.

Next, one has

$$H(\mathcal{Q}//\mathcal{P}) = -k \sum_{j=1}^{n} q_j \ln p_j - \left(-k \sum_{j=1}^{n} q_j \ln q_j \right) \tag{6.8.11}$$

and this expression should be considered rather as a transinformation, and therefore its positive sign.

6.8.2 On the Entropy of Pattern

Again we refer to the discrete random variables X and Y, and we assume that they are independent. Consider two occurrences (X_1, Y_1) and (X_2, Y_2) of (X, Y) and let A and B denote the points which they define in the (x, y) coordinates. We thus obtain a straight line segment AB, and our purpose is to measure its uncertainty $U(AB)$.

The most direct approach is to choose the measure $U_1(AB)$ defined by the equation

$$U_1(AB) = H(A) + H(B)$$
$$= H(X, Y) + H(X, Y)$$
$$= 2[H(X) + H(Y)] \tag{6.8.12}$$

but in doing so, we lack the information on the size of AB, and this is mainly due to the fact that $H(X, Y)$ does not depend upon the values (x_1, y_1) and (x_2, y_2)

themselves. The numerical value of (6.8.12) does not enable us to say how long AB is. As such $U_1(AB)$ is an incomplete measure of the uncertainty involved in the pattern AB; and this is not surprizing at all since we do not have at hand the exact values of the x_i's and y_j's.

A method to take into account the size of AB is to introduce the lengths $L_x := |x_2 - x_1|$ and $L_y := |y_2 - y_1|$ and to select the measure

$$U_2(AB) = 2H(X, Y) + K \ln L_x L_y \qquad (6.8.13)$$

where K is a positive constant.

If we define $h := L_x/2$ and $h' := L_y/2$, and if we choose $K = 2$, we then have

$$U_2(AB) = 2H_e(X, Y) + 2 \ln 2^2 . \qquad (6.8.14)$$

In other words, the total entropy offers a better measure of the uncertainty of a pattern than the Shannon entropy.

6.9 Transinformation and Total Entropy

We use the term transinformation in the Shannon sense: Clearly the transinformation $I(Y/X)$ is the amount of information contained in X about Y. It is clear that a theory of information can be founded entirely on the total entropy. This is for the genuine reason that the latter provides a concept of total conditional entropy. We examine this question in the present section.

6.9.1 Total Entropy of a Random Vector

For the sake of simplicity, we derived the total Shannon entropy and the total Renyi entropy for a scalar-valued random variable only, but it is clear that these definitions can be extended to random vectors.

Let (X, Y) denote a pair of random variables which take on the values (x_i, y_j), $1 \leqslant i \leqslant m$, $1 \leqslant j \leqslant n$, with the respective probabilities r_{ij}. Following the intuitive derivation of Sect. 6.2, we shall define their total Shannon entropy $H_e(X, Y)$ in the form

$$H_e(X, Y) = -\sum_{i,j} r_{ij} \ln r_{ij} + \sum_{i,j} r_{ij} g_{ij}(h_i, h_j') \qquad (6.9.1)$$

where h_i and h_j' are the respective ranges of values of X and Y, and where $g_{ij}(h_i, h_j')$ is an increasing function of h_i and h_j' which satisfies the additional conditions

$$\lim g_{ij}(h_i, \cdot) \neq 0 \quad \text{as} \quad h_i \downarrow 0 , \qquad (6.9.2)$$

$$\lim g_{ij}(\cdot, h_j') \neq 0 \quad \text{as} \quad h_j' \downarrow 0 . \qquad (6.9.3)$$

In terms of desirable mathematical properties, the axioms which we have to assume are exactly the counterparts of the statements (C1) to (C5) in Sect. 6.3. Briefly,

i) $H_e(X, Y)$ is a function $\chi[(r_{11}, h_1 h'_1), (r_{12}, h_1 h'_2), \ldots, (r_{mn}, h_m h'_n)]$ whose value is not modified by any permutation of the set $\{(r_{ij}, h_i h'_j)\}$; (ii) $\chi(\cdot)$ is continuous with respect to r_{ij}, h_i and h'_j for every i and j except possibly at $h_i = 0$ and/or at $h'_j = 0$; (iii) $\chi(\cdot)$ provides the Shannon entropy when $h_i = h'_j = 1$ for every i and j; (iv) $\chi(\cdot)$ satisfies the additive law.

We can straightforwardly state:

Corollary 6.9.1. The direct generalization of proposition 6.3.1 provides the total Shannon entropy of the pair (X, Y) in the form

$$H_e(X, Y) = H(X, Y) + K \sum_{i=1}^{m} \sum_{j=1}^{n} r_{ij} \ln(h_i h'_j) \tag{6.9.4}$$

$$= -k \sum_{i=1}^{m} \sum_{j=1}^{n} r_{ij} \ln \frac{r_{ij}}{(h_i h'_j)^{K/k}} \ . \tag{6.9.5}$$

As a matter of fact, one could have stated this result as the main one and then deduce the total entropy $H_e(X)$ of X, but we chose the presentation above for pedagogical reasons.

In the same way one has

Corollary 6.9.2. The generalization of proposition (6.6.1) provides the total Renyi entropy of the pair (X, Y) in the form

$$H_c^e(X, Y) = H_c(X, Y) + K \sum_{i=1}^{m} \sum_{j=1}^{n} r_{ij} \ln(hh') \tag{6.9.6}$$

$$= \frac{k}{1-c} \ln \left[\sum_{i=1}^{m} \sum_{j=1}^{n} r_{ij}^c / (hh')^{(K/k)(c-1)} \right], \tag{6.9.7}$$

or in the special case where $K = k$

$$H_c^e(X, Y) = \frac{k}{1-c} \ln \left[\sum_{i=1}^{m} \sum_{j=1}^{n} \left(\frac{r_{ij}}{hh'} \right)^c hh' \right]; \quad K = k \ . \tag{6.9.8}$$

6.9.2 Conditional Total Entropy

Corollary 6.9.3. Let the conditional total entropy $H_e(Y/X)$ be defined by the equation

$$H_e(X, Y) = H_e(X) + H_e(Y/X) \ . \tag{6.9.9}$$

One then has

$$H_e(Y/X) = \sum_{i=1}^{m} p_i H_e(Y/x_i) \ . \tag{6.9.10}$$

The proof is direct: Equation (6.9.4) yields

$$H_e(X, Y) = H(X) + \sum_i p_i H(Y/x_i) + K \sum_{i,j} r_{ij}(\ln h_i + \ln h'_j) \ ,$$

and on denoting the conditional probability distribution of Y by $q_{j/i}$, one has

$$H_e(X, Y) = H_e(X) - \sum_{i,j} p_i q_{j/1} \ln q_{j/i} + K \sum_{i,j} r_{ij} \ln h'_j \qquad (6.9.11)$$

$$= H_e(X) + \sum_i p_i \left(-\sum_j q_{j/i} \ln q_{j/i} + K \sum_j q_{j/i} \ln h'_j \right) \ , \qquad (6.9.12)$$

which is (6.9.10).

6.9.3 On the Definition of Transinformation

Basically, the transinformation defined by the expression (2.12.12) represents a variation in the entropy. In words, it represents the decrease of the amount of uncertainty one has about Y, and is thus equivalent to the amount of information which is contributed by X about Y; therefore the term transinformation.

It is easy to see that one has the relation

$$I(Y/X) = H_e(Y) - H_e(Y/X) \ , \qquad (6.9.13)$$

which is quite consistent with the definition of transinformation for continuous variables. Indeed, in this case, the limiting form of the total entropy is the continuous entropy (we shall prove this result later) and we then have the transinformation as defined by Shannon.

This relation (6.9.13) might explain why the discrete entropy has been adequate in many problems related to discrete variables.

An Alternative to Transinformation. We may also consider the expression

$$I_e(Y/X) := H(Y) - H_e(Y/X) \ . \qquad (6.9.14)$$

This again measures the change in the uncertainty between initial definition of the observable and subsequent observation, but now involves a change of attitude in the rationale of the observer. Indeed, $H(Y)$ does not take account of the uncertainty due to the interval lengths h_i whereas $H_e(Y//X)$ does. Despite its apparent inconsistency, this situation is quite meaningful in practice and occurs, for instance, when the absolute uncertainty of Y is defined by $H(Y)$ while the observation of (Y/X) involves ambiguity described by means of $H_e(Y/X)$.

We have exactly the equivalent of the subjective transinformation $J(Y/X)$ defined by (5.4.3), and in a like manner $I_e(Y/X)$ may be positive or negative.

6.9.4 Total Kullback Entropy

We can use the above remarks to derive a concept of total Kullback entropy, and to this end we shall proceed as follows.

i) First we shall consider $H(\mathcal{Q}//\mathcal{P})$ [see (2.10.1) for the notation] as the mathematical expectation of the transinformation about each outcome of the experiment, namely

$$H(\mathcal{Q}//\mathcal{P}) := E\{(\text{prior uncertainty}) - (\text{posterior uncertainty})\}$$

$$= \sum_{i=1}^{m} q_i[-\ln p_i - (-\ln q_i)] \ .$$

ii) Now assume that we are considering random variables and that we deal with total entropy; we shall then write

$$H_e(\mathcal{Q}//\mathcal{P}) := E\{(\text{total prior uncertainty}) - (\text{total posterior uncertainty})\}$$

$$= \sum_{i=1}^{m} q_i\left[-\ln\frac{p_i}{h_i} - \left(-\ln\frac{q_i}{h_i'}\right)\right] ,$$

$$H_e(\mathcal{Q}//\mathcal{P}) = H(\mathcal{Q}//\mathcal{P}) + \sum_{i=1}^{m} q_i \ln\frac{h_i}{h_i'} \ . \tag{6.9.15}$$

We shall refer to the $H_e(\mathcal{Q}//\mathcal{P})$ so defined as the *total Kullback entropy* or the *total cross-entropy* of $\mathcal{Q}$ with respect to $\mathcal{P}$.

6.10 Relation Between Total Entropy and Continuous Entropy

Our main motivation in introducing this new concept of total entropy was to derive a unified approach to discrete entropy and continuous entropy, and we now examine this question.

6.10.1 Total Shannon Entropy and Continuous Entropy

We have the following result.

Proposition 6.10.1. Let $X \in \mathbb{R}$ denote a random variable with the continuous probability density $p(x)$ and assume that its entropy $H(X)$ exists and is bounded. Let h denote a given discretization span, and let $\tilde{p}_1, \tilde{p}_2, \ldots, \tilde{p}_m$ denote the discrete probability distribution derived from $p(x)$ by using the h-discretization. Then the total entropy $H_e(\tilde{X}_h)$ so obtained satisfies the relation

$$\lim H_e(\tilde{X}_h) = H(X) \quad \text{as} \quad h \downarrow 0 \ . \tag{6.10.1}$$

Proof. (i) Let us first assume that X is lower and upper bounded, namely $a \leqslant X \leqslant b$, $|a|, |b| \leqslant M < M < \infty$, and let us consider the lattice $\xi_1, \xi_2, \ldots, \xi_m$ defined by

$$\xi_0 = a; \quad \xi_m = b; \quad \xi_{i+1} - \xi_i = h \ .$$

ii) Now consider the discrete probability distribution $\tilde{p}_1, \tilde{p}_2, \ldots, \tilde{p}_m$ defined by the equation

$$\tilde{p}_i := \int_{\xi_{i-1}}^{\xi_i} p(x)\,dx \qquad (6.10.2)$$

and whose total entropy is

$$H_e(\tilde{X}_h) := -k \sum_{i=1}^{m} \tilde{p}_i \ln \frac{\tilde{p}_i}{h} \ . \qquad (6.10.3)$$

iii) By virtue of the continuity assumption regarding $p(x)$, the first mean value theorem for integrals applied to (6.10.2) yields

$$\tilde{p}_i = hp(x_i) \ , \qquad \xi_{i-1} < x_i < \xi_i$$

so that we may rewrite $H_e(\tilde{X}_h)$ in the form

$$H_e(\tilde{X}_h) = - \sum_{i=1}^{m} hp(x_i) \ln p(x_i) \qquad (6.10.4)$$

the limit of which is $H(X)$ when h tends to zero. Clearly, for a given small positive ε there exists $\eta > 0$ such that $h < \eta$ implies $|H(X) - H_e(\tilde{X}_h)| \leqslant \varepsilon$.

iv) Next, assume that X is not bounded; then, following a well-known technique of elementary analysis, we shall introduce two limits a and b such that

$$|H_T(X) - H(X)| \leqslant \frac{\varepsilon}{2}$$

where $H_T(X)$ [read truncated $H(X)$] is defined by the expression

$$H_T(X) := -k \int_a^b p(x) \ln p(x)\,dx \ .$$

With this, we restrict ourselves to the interval $[a, b]$ and apply the discretization scheme (i) to (iii) above. If we select h in such a manner that

$$|H_e(\tilde{X}_h) - H_T(X)| \leqslant \frac{\varepsilon}{2} \ ,$$

then we shall have

$$|H(X) - H_e(\tilde{X}_h)| \leqslant \varepsilon$$

and thus the result.

6.10.2 Total Renyi Entropy and Continuous Renyi Entropy

Similarly to proposition 6.10.1, we state:

Proposition 6.10.2. Let $X \in \mathbb{R}$ denote a random variable with the continuous probability density $p(x)$, and assume that its Renyi entropy $H_e(X)$ exists and is bounded. Let h denote a given discretization span, and let $\tilde{p}_1, \tilde{p}_2, \ldots, \tilde{p}_m$ denote the discrete probability distribution derived from $p(x)$ by using the h-discretization. Then the total Renyi entropy $H_c^e(\tilde{X}_h)$ so obtained is such that

$$\lim H_c^e(\tilde{X}_h) = H_c(X) \quad \text{as} \quad h \downarrow 0 . \tag{6.10.5}$$

Proof. The proof proceeds exactly like that of proposition 6.10.1. Equation (6.6.8) provides

$$H_c^e(\tilde{X}_h) = \frac{1}{1-c} \ln \left[\sum_{i=1}^{m} p(x_i)h \right] \tag{6.10.6}$$

and thus the result.

6.10.3 Application to an Extension Principle

An interesting consequence of this result is that, in some cases, it will be possible to extend the validity of properties that apply to discrete entropy such that they also hold for continuous entropy. This is achieved by letting the discretization span tend to zero.

Indeed, consider the simplest form of $H_e(X)$ which is

$$H_e(X) = H(X) + \ln h$$

and assume that $H(X)$ has a mathematical property P. Assume further that P is not affected by the presence of h, so that $H_e(X)$ also has the characteristic P.

This being so, for any given continuous probability density $p(x)$, we shall define its corresponding estimate by the discrete distribution $\tilde{p}_h(x_i)$ such that

$$\left| \int_{-\infty}^{+\infty} p(x)\,dx - h \sum_{-\infty}^{+\infty} \tilde{p}_h(x_i) \right| \leqslant \varepsilon ; \qquad \varepsilon > 0$$

where ε defines the accuracy of the approximation. The property P is satisfied by the distribution $\tilde{p}_h(x_i)$ and, as a result, we can conclude that it is also satisfied by $p(x)$ to within an accuracy of ε.

An Example. As mentioned in the introduction to the present chapter, *Shore* and *Johnson* [6.10] have proved the maximum entropy principle, but for discrete probability distributions only. In fact they first proved it for the Kullback entropy and then showed that the result also applies to the Shannon entropy by considering the latter as a Kullback entropy with respect to the uniform distribution.

By using the logical inference technique outlined above, one arrives at the conclusion that this theorem also holds for continuous probability density to within an arbitrary accuracy ε.

6.11 Total Entropy and Mixed Theory of Information

In this section we shall examine the relations between the above concept of total entropy and the "inset entropy" introduced recently in the framework of the so-called mixed theory of information, and in which the uncertainty involved in a discrete variable depends both on the probability distribution and on the value of this variable.

6.11.1 Background to Effective Entropy and Inset Entropy

In 1975 we introduced the concept of *effective entropy* [6.15] as follows. We considered the discrete random variable X of Sect. 6.2 along with the set of intervals $\{L_i\}$ and decomposed its observation into two stages.

i) First we determined which interval L_i contains X; the entropy of this experiment is $H(X)$;

ii) we then determined the exact value of X in this interval. The conditional entropy of this second experiment is $H(X/x_i)$.

We were thus led to consider the effective entropy

$$H_e(X) := H(L, X)$$

$$= H(L) + H(X/L)$$

$$= H(L) + \sum_{i=1}^{m} p_i \tilde{H}_i , \tag{6.11.1}$$

and in this form (6.11.1) is none other than the total entropy $H(X//\mu)$ with respect to a measure.

The question which then arises is the following: Given that the total entropy can be derived using the Shannonian framework alone, is it necessary to state new axioms to obtain it? The answer is not "yes" or "no" but rather "it depends upon whether one considers the matter from a physical or a mathematical viewpoint.

Indeed, in an applied (physical) approach, (6.11.1) is quite sufficient, subject to the condition that we assume the decomposition of the observation process. Nevertheless, this decomposition requires a randomization with respect to the measures of the intervals L_i, and it is this randomization which is fully described by our axioms in Sect. 6.3.1.

We shall summarize the difference between the two approaches as follows: when we wrote (6.11.1), we implicitly assumed that the uncertainty $H(X/x_i)$ was expressed by means of probability, while the axioms (C1) to (C5) define the same entropy $H(X/x_i)$ without referring to the probabilistic framework.

By using a preliminary set of axioms and in particular the recursion equation (2.11.7), *Aczel* and *Daroczy* [6.16] obtained the inset entropy

$$H_m(X, \mathscr{P}) = H(X) - \sum_{i=1}^{m} p_i g(x_i) + g\left(\bigcup_{i=1}^{m} x_i\right) \tag{6.11.2}$$

where $\mathscr{P}$ represents the set $\{p_1, p_2, \ldots, p_m\}$ and where $g(\cdot)$ denotes a $\mathbb{R} \to \mathbb{R}$ map.

6.11.2 Inset Entropy is an Effective Entropy

We shall show this equivalence as follows:

i) As a result of (6.11.2), $g(x_i)$ necessarily has the physical dimensions of an entropy so that we can make the identification

$$g(x_i) := H(Y/x_i) \tag{6.11.3}$$

where Y denotes another discrete random variable.

We can therefore write

$$g\left(\bigcup_{i=1}^{m} x_i\right) =: H\left(Y \middle/ \bigcup_{i=1}^{m} x_i\right) \tag{6.11.4}$$

and inserting (6.11.3) and (6.11.4) into (6.11.2) yields

$$H_m(X, \mathscr{P}) = H(X) + \sum_{i=1}^{m} p_i\left[H\left(Y \middle/ \bigcup_{i=1}^{m} x_j\right) - H(Y/x_i)\right] . \tag{6.11.5}$$

ii) If $q(y_j/\cdot)$ denotes the conditional probability distribution of Y given $(\cdot)$, one has

$$q\left(y_j \middle/ \bigcup_{i=1}^{m} x_i\right) = q(y_j) \tag{6.11.6}$$

and thus the equality

$$H\left(Y \middle/ \bigcup_{i=1}^{m} x_i\right) = H(Y) .$$

As a result, one can rewrite (6.11.5) in the form

$$H_m(X, \mathscr{P}) = H(X) + \sum_{i=1}^{m} p_i[H(Y) - H(Y/x_i)] . \tag{6.11.7}$$

iii) On comparing this expression with (6.11.1) we obtain the identification

$$\tilde{H}_i := H(Y) - H(Y/x_i) .$$

Conclusion. In the formulation of the inset entropy, H_i appears to be the amount of transinformation $I(Y/x_i)$ which is contained in x_i about Y.

In our physical approach to effective entropy we identified H_i with a conditional entropy; in other words, we defined the new variable Z such that

$$H(Z/x_i) := H(Y) - H(Y/x_i) . \tag{6.11.8}$$

The inset entropy deals with the pair (X, Y) while the effective entropy refers to (X, Z). There is thus a complete equivalence between these two entropies.

In view of this result, our claim is that the Shannonian framework is quite sufficient and that we do not need any new axioms to meaningfully define the effective entropy.

7. A Unified Approach to Informational Entropies via Minkowskian Observation

By using very simple axioms related to information, the phenomenon of interaction between the observer and the observable can be described by means of the so-called Lorentz-Poincaré equations. This result applies to any class of observables provided that the relevant axioms are physically meaningful. One then assumes that the observable is the Hartley's uncertainty ($-\ln p_i$), and one assumes that the informational entropy of the experiment is the mathematical expectation of the Hartley entropy so as to derive a broad class of relative entropies which furthermore provide a unified approach to results that have been given previously in the literature.

The theory is first stated for discrete variables, and then continuous entropies are derived as the limiting forms of the discrete entropies obtained by using a concept of total discrete entropy which explicitly takes account of the discrete feature of the variable.

7.1 Introduction

As we pointed out in the second chapter, many measures of uncertainty have been proposed which more or less generalize Shannon entropy.

Mathematicians state a long list of desiderata for such a measure, then they choose some of these requirements, and finally they derive the expression for the entropy, let us call it the mathematical entropy, which satisfies these conditions. Practitioners start from qualitative considerations mainly related to syntax and semantics, and then they suggest definitions of entropy, let us call them physical entropies, which are consistent with these preliminary ideas.

As mentioned in Chap. 2, there exist some formal relations between the different mathematical entropies, and in the same way the physical entropies are not quite independent in the sense that some can be considered as special cases of others.

In the present chapter, we shall show that, if we assume that the uncertainty is observed at the level of the event itself (rather than at the level of the experiment that is to say the set of all the possible events), then the model of observation with informational invariance provides a unified approach to most of these measures of uncertainty. But before doing so, we shall once more consider the basic principles of the Minkowskian observation mode, and state its axioms in a more formal manner than in Chap. 4.

7.2 Axioms of the Minkowskian Observation

Let $X \in \mathbb{R}$ and $X' \in \mathbb{R}$ denote two continuous random variables with the probability density $p(x, x')$.

7.2.1 Definition of the Observation Process

We shall define the dynamics of the observation process as follows. We assume that R is observing an object, or else a physical observable which is described by the pair (x, x'). He simultaneously observes x and x', and his first purpose of course is to determine their exact values, but unfortunately, he cannot observe them separately, i.e. one at a time. We shall assume that he uses x to identify x', and conversely he refers to x' to define x via coupling effects between x and x'.

As a result, one may expect that there exist two functions $\Phi(\cdot)$ and $\Psi(\cdot)$ such that one has

$$x_r = \Phi_R(x, x') \tag{7.2.1}$$

$$x'_r = \Psi_R(x, x') \tag{7.2.2}$$

where the subscript R emphasizes that they depend explicitly upon the observer R.

From a dynamic standpoint, in assuming that the variables vary with the discrete time n, one would have

$$x_r(n + 1) = \Phi[x(n), x'(n)] \tag{7.2.3}$$

$$x'_r(n + 1) = \Psi[x(n), x'(n)] \tag{7.2.4}$$

the steady state of which are equations (7.2.1) and (7.2.2).

7.2.2 Statement of the Axioms

The salient features of the observation process are summarized by the following axioms.

(A1) The main purpose of the observer R is to define the exact values of x and x', but the observation results in two observed values x_r and x'_r which are linear combinations of x and x'; that is to say

$$x_r = g_{11}x + g_{12}x' \tag{7.2.5}$$

$$x'_r = g_{21}x + g_{21}x' \ . \tag{7.2.6}$$

(A2) The observation process occurs in such a way that it neither creates nor destroys information in the informational source (X, X').

(A3) In the special case where $x \equiv x'$, that is to say when R observes one variable only, then the equations of the observation reduce to

$$x_r = Gx \tag{7.2.7}$$

where G denotes a constant gain.

(A4) The amount of uncertainty involved in the pair (X, X') to the observer R is defined by the Shannon entropy.

7.2.3 A Few Comments

i) The first assumption (A1) can be considered either as the framework of modelling or as a linearization hypothesis related to a local coupling equivalent to a small deformation in geometry.

Assumption (A2) states that there is conservation of information: the information contained in X alone or in X' alone may be varying to R; indeed it will likely vary, but nonetheless, the total amount of information contained in the pair (X, X') will be constant.

Axiom (A3) requires some explanation. In the case where we observe one variable z alone, one of the simplest hypotheses (and possibly the simplest one) is to assume that the result z_r of the corresponding observation is in the form

$$z_r = Gz$$

where G denotes a gain coefficient which is independent of z and characterizes the observer R himself. In such a case, we are quite entitled to expect that when X is identical to X', the above model expressed by (7.2.5) and (7.2.6) should reduce to the gain model (7.2.7). We further note that this is not equivalent to assuming that one has merely $X \equiv X$ and $X' = 0$ and that we are thus observing the pair $(X, 0)$ with possible coupling between X and 0. On the contrary, formally making $X \equiv X'$ is equivalent to observing the pair (X, X) which is obviously different from $(X, 0)$!

ii) At this point, the following remark is in order: A common, and probably the most useful model of observation is defined by the equation

$$x_{\text{obs}} = x + \varepsilon \tag{7.2.8}$$

where ε is generally considered as an error term, and on the surface, this equation (7.2.8) could be a valuable basic model as well. But in fact, there is neither inconsistency nor arbitrariness in our approach. Indeed (7.2.8) presupposes implicitly that we are observing the pair (x, ε), so that in the framework of the assumptions (A1)–(A4) above, suitable equations would be

$$x_r = g_{11} x + g_{12} \varepsilon \tag{7.2.9}$$

$$\varepsilon_r = g_{21} x + g_{22} \varepsilon \tag{7.2.10}$$

and then (7.2.8) appears as a special case of the general equation (7.2.9).

iii) From practical standpoint, and on referring to the coupling effects defined by the observation model, the equation $z_r = Gz$ would express an interaction of z with itself, and at first glance, this is rather difficult to accept. Indeed, how can one understand such interaction process?

One way to make this axiom more rigorous on a formal basis is to assume that the two spaces Ω and Ω' are close to each other in the sense of a given distance, and to set

$$X' = X + \lambda \tilde{X}', \qquad \lambda \in \mathbb{R}, \qquad \tilde{X}' \in \mathbb{R} \tag{7.2.11}$$

where λ denotes a small real-valued parameter, which is further assumed not to be affected by the observation itself. Equations (7.2.5) and (7.2.6) then yield

$$x_r = (g_{11} + g_{12})x + \lambda g_{12}\tilde{x}' \tag{7.2.12}$$

$$x_r + \lambda \tilde{x}'_r = (g_{21} + g_{22})x + \lambda g_{22}\tilde{x}' \tag{7.2.13}$$

and we then require that these two equations reduce to the same equation as λ tends to zero, that is to say, the following condition must hold:

$$g_{21} + g_{22} = g_{11} + g_{12} \ . \tag{7.2.14}$$

This presentation, which is somewhat akin to a perturbation theory, may seem to offer more satisfactory support of axiom (A3).

iv) Axiom (A4) emphasizes the informational framework of the approach. With these axioms, it is very easy to obtain the equations

$$x_r = \varrho(u)(x + ux') \tag{7.2.15}$$

$$x'_r = \varrho(u)(ux + x') \tag{7.2.16}$$

where $\varrho(u)$ is defined by (4.5.4).

7.3 Properties of the Minkowskian Observation

7.3.1 Learning Process

On differentiating the Minkowskian invariance equation

$$x^2 - x'^2 = \text{constant} \tag{7.3.1}$$

we have

$$\frac{dx}{dx'} = \frac{x'}{x} \ . \tag{7.3.2}$$

Assume that the framework is such that x and x' are positive (for instance they are two discrete probabilities or two discrete entropies); one then has $dx/dx' > 0$.

This being so, let us consider dx and dx' as being two error terms. According to the assumption above, they have the same sign and, as a result, we can say that the observer is a learning one in the sense that his knowledge increases on both x and x' simultaneously.

In this way, the Euclidean invariance

$$x^2 + x'^2 = \text{constant} \tag{7.3.3}$$

which yields

$$\frac{dx}{dx'} = -\frac{x'}{x} \tag{7.3.4}$$

characterizes a dislearning process.

7.3.2 Practical Determination of u

In the special case where x is identical to x', the equations (7.2.11) and (7.2.12) yield

$$x_r = \varrho(u)(1 + u)x \ . \tag{7.3.5}$$

This equation provides a practical method to determine the value of u on assuming that it is constant from one experiment to another.

Indeed, let G denote the gain which is effectively measured in an experiment that consists of observing one variable only, namely $z_r = Gz$, one then has

$$\varrho(u)(1 + u) = G \tag{7.3.6}$$

and therefore

$$u = \frac{G^2 - 1}{G^2 + 1} \ . \tag{7.3.7}$$

iv) The reader will have probably noticed that the equations (7.2.11) and (7.2.12) of the observation are written with the lower cases (x, x') instead of the upper case (X, X'). Why is this? In fact, X is the name of the variable (it could equally well be *Michael*!), so that an equation expressed in terms of X and X' would be meaningless. In addition this notation emphasizes that the observation applies to the data itself rather than to its corresponding class.

The result of the present section completes those of Sect. 4.10.2 related to the practical meaning of u.

7.3.3 Cascaded Observation of Variables

We now consider the simultaneous observation process which is equivalent to the independent observation of the two pairs (x, x') and (y, y') one at a time, and we state:

Proposition 7.3.1. Assume that the pairs (x, x') and (y, y') are serially observed independently of one another via Minkowskian matrices defined by means of the constant coefficients (ω_1, u) and (ω_2, v), respectively. Then the observation of the resulting pair $((x, x'), (y, y'))$ is equivalent to the observation of a single pair (z, z') but with the matrix involving the parameters $(\omega_1 + \omega_2)$ or the parameter w such that

$$w = \frac{u + v}{1 + uv} \ . \tag{7.3.8}$$

Proof. (i) Let X, X', Y, Y' denote the random variables associated with x, x', y and y', respectively, and let us assume that (X, X') and (Y, Y') are stochastically independent. From an informational standpoint one has the relation

$$H(X, X', Y, Y') = H(X, X') + H(Y, Y') \tag{7.3.9}$$

and since the observation process does not affect $H(X, X')$ or $H(Y, Y')$, it will not affect $H(X, X', Y, Y')$ either.

ii) Now let us consider the equivalent vector (x, x', y, y') as being the object under observation. According to axiom (A1) and to the serial assumption above, the corresponding matrix equation is

$$\begin{bmatrix} x_r \\ x'_r \\ y_r \\ y'_r \end{bmatrix} = \begin{bmatrix} g_{11} & g_{12} & 0 & 0 \\ g_{21} & g_{22} & 0 & 0 \\ 0 & 0 & g_{33} & g_{34} \\ 0 & 0 & g_{43} & g_{44} \end{bmatrix} \begin{bmatrix} x \\ x' \\ y \\ y' \end{bmatrix} \qquad (7.3.10)$$

where the zero elements are due to exactly this independence. Moreover, g_{11}, g_{12}, g_{21} and g_{22} are defined by (4.5.2a, b) in terms of ω_1 while g_{33}, g_{34}, g_{43} and g_{44} are similar coefficients but with ω_2.

iii) The amount of information involved in the linear transformation (7.3.7) is defined by the logarithm of its determinant which is

$$\left| \begin{pmatrix} g_{11} & g_{12} \\ g_{21} & g_{22} \end{pmatrix} \begin{pmatrix} g_{33} & g_{34} \\ g_{43} & g_{44} \end{pmatrix} \right| = \begin{vmatrix} \cosh(\omega_1 + \omega_2) & \sinh(\omega_1 + \omega_2) \\ \sinh(\omega_1 + \omega_2) & \cosh(\omega_1 + \omega_2) \end{vmatrix} \qquad (7.3.11)$$

and the interpretation of this result provides the statement of the proposition 7.3.1.

iv) We can now lift the assumption of stochastic independence regarding the pairs (X, X') and (Y, Y'). In this case one has

$$H(X, X', Y, Y') = H(X, X') + H(Y, Y'/X, X') \ ,$$

but according to the assumption of serial observation, the equation (7.3.11) applies again, and by virtue of the fact that (ω_1, u) and (ω_2, v) are supposed to be constant, the conclusion follows.

This result can be generalized as follows to observations that exhibit some mutual dependence.

Proposition 7.3.2. Assume that the pair (x, x') is observed via a Minkowskian matrix involving the constant coefficients (ω_1, u_1) and then the pair (y, y') is observed with a Minkowskian observation defined by means of the conditional coefficients $(\omega_{2/1}, v_{2/1})$. The observation of the resulting pair $[(x, x'), (y, y')]$ is then equivalent to the observation of one pair (z, z') but with a matrix involving the parameter $(\omega_1 + \omega_{2/1})$ or the parameter w_{12} such that

$$w_{12} = \frac{u_1 + v_{2/1}}{1 + u_1 v_{2/1}} \ . \qquad (7.3.12)$$

Important Remark. It is clear that for an observation with mutual dependence the value w of the resulting observation coefficient will depend explicitly upon whether it is x or y that is observed first. On assuming that y is observed first, the observation coefficient becomes

$$w_{21} = \frac{u_2 + v_{1/2}}{1 + u_2 v_{1/2}} \qquad (7.3.13)$$

and it is obvious that in general

$$w_{21} \neq w_{12} .$$

On the Practical Meaning of This Result. Assume that we first observe x and then y and then add the results; we thereby obtain

$$x_r + y_r = \varrho(u)x + \varrho(v)y + \varrho(u)ux' + \varrho(v)vy' \qquad (7.3.14)$$

provided the observations are independent. Likewise, if we multiply the observed values, we shall have

$$x_r y_r = \varrho(u)\varrho(v)(x + ux')(y + vy') \qquad (7.3.15)$$

and in neither case do we have to use the observation coefficient defined by (7.3.5). In other words, propositions (7.3.1) and (7.3.2) do not apply to these cases.

In order to gain more insight into these statements, we shall proceed as follows.

i) Assume that we first observe the pair (x, x') with the parameter u_1 to obtain $((x_r)_1, (x'_r)_1)$; and then we observe this last pair with the coefficient $u_{2/1}$ to obtain $((x_r)_2, (x'_r)_2)$. According to (7.2.11) and (7.2.12) one can write

$$(x_r)_2 = \varrho(\tilde{w})(x + \tilde{w}x') \qquad (7.3.16)$$

$$(x'_r)_2 = \varrho(\tilde{w})(\tilde{w}x + x') \qquad \text{with} \qquad (7.3.17)$$

$$\tilde{w} = \frac{u_1 + u_{2/1}}{1 + u_1 u_{2/1}} .$$

As a result, one can say that the pair (x, x') is observed with the coefficient $\tilde{w}$.

ii) We shall extend this point of view by stating that the pair $\{[x, (x_r)_1], [x', (x'_r)_1]\}$ is observed with the coefficient $\tilde{w}$ to provide the pair $[(x_r)_2, (x'_r)_2]$.

iii) Assume now that we substitute the pair (y, y') for $[(x_r)_1, (x'_r)_1]$ above; if one has $y \equiv (x_r)_1$ and $y' \equiv (x'_r)_1$, then the statement (ii) above holds.

If $y \neq (x_r)_1$ and $y' \neq (x'_r)_1$, then strictly speaking (ii) is meaningless, but according to the determinant equation (7.3.8) everything follows as if (y, y') were the image of (x, x') via the Minkowskian observation with coefficient u_1. Thus we shall once more say that $[(x, y), (x', y')]$ is observed with the coefficient w.

From a practical standpoint, if $f(x)$ involves u and $g(y)$ refers to v, then $h(x, y)$ will refer to w.

7.4 Minkowskian Observation in $\mathbb{R}^3$

7.4.1 Derivation of the Equations

The Minkowskian model can be extended to $\mathbb{R}^3$ to deal with the observation of the triplet (X, X', X''). To this end, one may start from the general equations of the linear transformation, that is to say that $\mathbb{R}^3$-counterpart of the linear system (7.2.1) and

(7.2.2) and study its invariance properties independently of the preceding results for $\mathbb{R}^2$.

Another approach is to consider the observation of (x, x', x'') as a combination of the observations of the pairs (x, x'), (x, x'') and (x', x''). So if $K(\omega_1)$, $K(\omega_2)$ and $K(\omega_3)$ denote the matrices associated with these transformations, then the matrix $K(\omega_1, \omega_2, \omega_3)$ that defines the observation of (x, x', x'') is

$$K(\omega_1, \omega_2, \omega_3) = K(\omega_1) \, K(\omega_2) \, K(\omega_3) \ . \tag{7.4.1}$$

One has

$$K(\omega_1) = \begin{pmatrix} \cosh \omega_1 & \sinh \omega_1 & 0 \\ \sinh \omega_1 & \cosh \omega_1 & 0 \\ 0 & 0 & 1 \end{pmatrix} \tag{7.4.2}$$

$$K(\omega_2) = \begin{pmatrix} \cosh \omega_2 & 0 & \sinh \omega_2 \\ 0 & 1 & 0 \\ \sinh \omega_2 & 0 & \cosh \omega_2 \end{pmatrix} \tag{7.4.3}$$

$$K(\omega_3) = \begin{pmatrix} 1 & 0 & 0 \\ 0 & \cosh \omega_3 & \sinh \omega_3 \\ 0 & \sinh \omega_3 & \cosh \omega_3 \end{pmatrix}, \tag{7.4.4}$$

and therefore

$$K(\omega_1, \omega_2, \omega_3) = \begin{pmatrix} \cosh \omega_1 \cosh \omega_2 & \cosh \omega_1 \sinh \omega_2 \sinh \omega_3 + \mathrm{sihn}\, \omega_1 \cosh \omega_3 \\ \sinh \omega_1 \cosh \omega_2 & \sinh \omega_1 \sinh \omega_2 \sinh \omega_3 + \cosh \omega_1 \cosh \omega_3 \\ \sinh \omega_2 & \cosh \omega_2 \sinh \omega_3 \end{pmatrix}$$

$$\begin{pmatrix} \cosh \omega_1 \sinh \omega_2 \cosh \omega_3 + \sinh \omega_1 \sinh \omega_3 \\ \sinh \omega_1 \sinh \omega_2 \cosh \omega_3 + \cosh \omega_1 \sinh \omega_3 \\ \cosh \omega_2 \cosh \omega_3 \end{pmatrix} \cdot \tag{7.4.5}$$

If x_r denotes the observed vector (x_r, x'_r, x''_r) associated with $x := (x, x', x'')$, then one has the observation equation

$$x_r = K(\omega_1, \omega_2, \omega_3)x \ . \tag{7.4.6}$$

7.4.2 A Few Comments

i) In this derivation, we have assumed that each $\mathbb{R}^2$-observation is Minkowskian, that is to say is associated with a learning process; but it may happen that one or more of these observations are dislearning processes, in which case we shall be dealing with the Euclidean invariance defined by the rotation matrix $Q(\theta)$, see

(4.4.8a, b). For instance, if it is the observation of the pair (x, x') that involves $Q(\theta)$, then x_r is given by the equation

$$x_r = Q(\theta)K(\omega_2)K(\omega_2)K(\omega_3)x \ . \tag{7.4.7}$$

ii) This model could be used as the basic principle of a theory of multi-dimensional information.

As an illustrative example, consider the sentence S: *John eats five eggs for breakfast*. We can consider it with respect to both its syntax and its semantics, in other words we observe its syntactic entropy $H(\alpha)$ and its semantic entropy $H(a)$ (Sect. 4.7) which are assumed to be defined by means of probability distributions.

One may also consider the sentence in the framework of possibility theory (Sect. 2.15). Loosely speaking, while the probability is the frequency distribution defined by the observation of John over a long period of time, the possibility would be the frequency distribution associated with all the population of the city (for instance) on a given morning. In this case, we are dealing with an uncertainty $U(S)$ of a non-random nature.

It follows that the sentence is described by the three entropies $H(\alpha)$, $H(a)$ and $U(S)$ which are observed simultaneously, so that the above result applies.

7.5 The Statistical Expectation Approach to Entropy

7.5.1 Preliminary Remarks

As mentioned in Sect. 7.1, in the wake of Shannon, most people who were interested in generalizing the concept of entropy (and it is mainly mathematicians who follow this trend!) did so by first stating a set of prior axioms which a measure of uncertainty is likely to satisfy; they then derived a solution, and finally, as a delightful mathematical exercise, they showed that the measure so obtained is unique.

But, in the present case, we claim that it is quite useless to worry about the uniqueness of a solution. Indeed the present situation is quite different from the modelling of a physical system by means of a partial differential equation, for instance. In the latter case, it is of paramount importance to verify that the dynamic model so obtained has only one output because otherwise it would be quite meaningless. But in our informational problem, we have a set of prior desiderata for entropy, we get a corresponding possible mathematical expression, and we are quite entitled to use this whether it is unique or not.

To some extent, this approach can be considered as a global one. Indeed we define the entropy as a functional $U(p_1, p_2, \ldots, p_m)$ of the probability distribution, and in doing so we implicitly assume, from the experimental standpoint, that the observer directly observes the experiment as the whole, that is to say the set of all the possible outcomes, without considering each event, i.e. each outcome, individually.

In contrast, in the analytical approach, one considers the individual contribution of each possible event to the uncertainty involved in the entire experiment.

7.5.2 Entropy and Statistical Expectation

In this section we consider the following derivation.

Definition 7.5.1. In a statistical expectation approach to the concept of entropy, we shall define the uncertainty involved in a random experiment α which provides the outcomes $A_1, A_2, \ldots, A_m$ with the respective probabilities $p_1, p_2, \ldots, p_m$ as the mathematical expectation of the individual uncertainties contributed by each result A_i. $\qquad\square$

All problem then amounts to measuring the uncertainty associated with each outcome.

Example 5.1. If we consider the uncertainty involved in A_i as being its Hartley entropy $(-\ln p_i)$ we then obtain the Shannon entropy.

As a matter of fact, this remark is well known to practitioners in information theory, but here we shall use it systematically to generate various models of measures of uncertainty.

Example 5.2. Let us now consider the Renyi entropy of order c defined by (2.9.1). If we take it as a mathematical expectation, then we are led to assume that the uncertainty associated with the ith event is

$$H_c(A_i) := \frac{1}{1-c} \frac{1}{p_i} \ln \left(\sum_{i=1}^{m} p_i^c \right). \tag{7.5.1}$$

The reader might wonder why this individual contribution should depend upon the other $p_j's, j \neq i$. One way to understand this feature is to assume that there is some mutual interaction between the different events A_i.

This being so, we note that the argument of the logarithm in (2.9.1) is a mathematical expectation, say

$$H_c(\alpha) = \frac{1}{1-c} \ln E\{p^{c-1}\}$$

so that we have actually found another possible general approach to uncertainty which could be formulated in the form

$$H_f(\alpha) = f(E\{g(p)\})$$

where $g(\cdot)$ is a function to be suitably defined. When $f(\cdot)$ is the identity, one then has the definition 7.5.1.

Example 5.3. Assume that the uncertainty involved in the ith event A_i is not necessarily of a random nature, but rather is caused by fuzziness, or even that it is the result of both fuzziness and randomness, then definition 7.5.1 applies and is quite meaningful in practical terms.

7.6 Relative Entropy and Subjective Entropy

In this section, we shall show that there is a complete consistency between relative entropy and subjective entropy, and that the latter can be considered as a special case of the former.

7.6.1 Comparison of H_r with H_s

For small u, (4.8.5a) yields

$$H_r(\alpha) = H(\alpha) + uH(a) + o(u^2) \tag{7.6.1}$$

so that, on identifying this with expression (5.2.1) for $H_s(\alpha)$ we have the equivalence

$$H(\alpha/\alpha') \equiv uH(a) + o(u^2) \ . \tag{7.6.2}$$

But α' is the semantic space associated with α, so that we have exactly $H(a) \equiv H(\alpha')$, and (7.6.2) therefore yields

$$u \equiv H(\alpha'/\alpha)H(\alpha') \ . \tag{7.6.3}$$

This identification is quite meaningful and consistent with the relation we found between relative entropy and Renyi entropy (Sect. 4.13), but we point out that it holds only for positive u.

7.6.2 Comparison of $T(\beta/\alpha)$ with $J(\beta/\alpha)$

On the one hand, for small $u_{\beta/\alpha}$, the relative transinformation $T(\beta/\alpha)$ is [see (4.11.2)]

$$T(\beta/\alpha) = H(\alpha) - H(\beta/\alpha a) - u_{\beta/\alpha}H(b/\alpha a) + o(u_{\beta\alpha}) \ , \tag{7.6.4}$$

on the other hand, (5.4.4) yields

$$J(\beta/\alpha) = H(\beta) - H(\beta/\alpha a) - H(b/\alpha a\beta) \ , \tag{7.6.5}$$

so that the identification $T(\beta/\alpha) \equiv J(\beta/\alpha)$ provides

$$u_{\beta/\alpha} = \frac{H(b/\alpha a\beta)}{H(b/\alpha a)} \ . \tag{7.6.6}$$

Equation (7.6.6) could be considered as a measure of $u_{\beta/\alpha}$, but for small values only. In other words, when the subjective effects are small, the classical theory, suitably modified by means of (7.6.5), is quite sufficient, while for subjective effects of large magnitude, the Minkowskian observation model would be more appropriate. We have an analogous situation in mechanics where the additive composition law is sufficient for small velocities, whereas large velocities require the relativistic law.

7.7 Weighted Relative Entropy

7.7.1 Background on Weighted Entropy

At approximately the same time *Zadeh* [7.7] and *Belis* and *Giuasu* [7.8] introduced the so-called *weighted entropy* concept for discrete random variables in the form

$$H_w(X) := - \sum_{i=1}^{m} \mu_1(X)p_i \ln p_i \qquad (7.7.1)$$

where μ_i, $\mu_i \geqslant 0$, $i = 1, \ldots, m$ denote a set of positive coefficients associated with the utility of the different events. *Zadeh* defined this entropy in the framework of the fuzzy set theory in which case μ_i is known as a membership function, while Belis and Guiasu claimed that $H_w(X)$ is more suitable in cybernetics. These coefficients μ_i' may have several possible meanings from a practical standpoint. Thus it is not easy to derive composition laws for this entropy.

Let Y denote a second discrete random variable with the weighted entropy

$$H_w(Y) = - \sum_{j=1}^{n} v_j(Y)q_j \ln q_j \ . \qquad (7.7.2)$$

The weighted entropy of the pair (X, Y) can then be written in the form

$$H_w(X, Y) = - \sum_{i=1}^{m} \sum_{j=1}^{n} \gamma_{ij}(X, Y)r_{ij} \ln r_{ij} \qquad (7.7.3)$$

where $\{r_{ij}\}$ is the probability distribution of the pair (X, Y). But then what is the relation, if any, between $\gamma_{ij}(X, Y)$, $\mu_i(X)$ and $v_j(Y)$?

One usually defines

$$\gamma_{ij}(X, Y) := \max[\mu_i(X), v_j(Y)] \qquad (7.7.4)$$

but other alternatives are available as well, for example, one could take

$$\gamma_{ij}(X, Y) := \lambda \mu_i(X) + (1 - \lambda)v_j(Y) \qquad (7.7.5)$$

where λ, $0 \leqslant \lambda \leqslant 1$, would be determined by further experiments.

The Minkowskian observation provides a new approach to this question as follows.

7.7.2 Weighted Relative Entropy

Assume that the observer R is not sensitive to the amount of uncertainty involved in the entire experiment, say X, but only perceives the uncertainty related to each individual event x_i, that is to say $(-\ln p_i)$. Assume that this observation process is performed in a linguistic framework, in such a way that x_i can be considered as a symbol with the entropy $(-\ln p_i)$ while its meaning has the entropy H_i'. This semantic entropy should be considered in the broad sense of the term and may, for instance, merely be related to fuzziness.

According to (7.2.12), the relative uncertainty $(-\ln p_i)_r$, which is measured by the observer is

$$(-\ln p_i)_r = \varrho(u_i)(-\ln p_i + u_i H'_i) \ . \tag{7.7.6}$$

We now consider the weighted relative entropy as being the statistical average of $(-\ln p_i)_r$, namely

$$H_{wr}(X) = E\{(-\ln p)_r\} \ , \tag{7.7.7}$$

to obtain the following definition:

Definition 7.7.1. Let X denote a discrete random variable which takes the values $x_1, x_2, \ldots, x_m$ with the respective probabilities $p_1, p_2, \ldots, p_m$. Assume that a semantic entropy is associated with each x_i, and assume further that an external observer R observes the pair $(-\ln p_i, H'_i)$ via the Minkowskian observation process involving the parameter u_i. Then the amount of uncertainty which R observes in X is given by the *weighted relative entropy* defined as

$$H_{wr}(X) := - \sum_{i=1}^{m} \varrho(u_i) p_i \ln p_i + \sum_{i=1}^{m} \varrho(u_i) u_i p_i H'_i \ . \tag{7.7.8} \quad \square$$

Comments. (i) One may ask whether $H'_i, i = 1, \ldots, m$ should be considered equivalent to the entropy of a discrete or a continuous variable. There is no definitive answer, and it is essentially a matter of the relevant practical framework. If x_i is a word and H'_i is the entropy of its meaning, then H'_i is the entropy of a discrete event; but if for instance x_i is a nominal value, and H'_i is the uncertainty associated with an error of observation, then H'_i is the entropy of a continuous variable.

As is evident, the situation in which the symbols and the meanings are discrete is of special interest since then $H'_i \geqslant 0$. Indeed, assume that $u_i \geqslant 0$ for every i, then $H_{wr}(X) \geqslant 0$, and one has $H_{wr}(X) = 0$ if and only if X is deterministic. Next, if we assume that in this framework of discrete events, the entropy of the ith event cannot be negative for any i, then the above meaning of the condition $H_{wr}(X) = 0$ applies again.

ii) By the same token, the weighted relative entropy associated with the semantics of X, say the semantic weighted relative entropy of X, is H'_{wr} such that

$$H'_{wr}(X) = E\{H'_r\} \tag{7.7.9}$$

$$= E\{\varrho(u)(-u \ln p + H')\} \tag{7.7.10}$$

$$= \sum_{i=1}^{m} \varrho(u_i) p_i H'_i - \sum_{i=1}^{m} \varrho(u_i) u_i p_i \ln p_i \ . \tag{7.7.11}$$

iii) Assume that the semantics are discrete (together with X of course) and that $H'_i = 0$ for every i. Equation (7.7.11) then yields

$$H'_{wr}(X) = - \sum_{i=1}^{m} \varrho(u_i) u_i p_i \ln p_i \ ; \tag{7.7.12}$$

in other words, the observer believes that each symbol x_i has several possible meanings while in fact they do not; clearly the meaning of x_i is x_i itself.

In this case the weighted relative entropy of X is

$$H_{\mathrm{wr}}(X) = -\sum_{i=1}^{m} \varrho(u_i)p_i \ln p_i \tag{7.7.13}$$

which is exactly the weighted entropy $H_{\mathrm{w}}(X)$ given by (7.7.1).

iv) Assume now that u_i is positive and small for every i so that one has $\varrho(u_i) \cong 1$. Equation (7.7.11) then yields

$$H_{\mathrm{wr}}(X) \cong H(X) + \sum_{i=1}^{m} p_i u_i H_i' \tag{7.7.14}$$

which is exactly the effective entropy defined by (2.11.6).

Re-definition of Notation. We define the constant a_i by the equation

$$H_i' =: -a_i \ln p_i \tag{7.7.15}$$

and then re-write $H_{\mathrm{wr}}(X)$ in the more compact form

$$H_{\mathrm{wr}}(X) = -\sum_{i=1}^{m} \varrho(u_i)(1 + a_i u_i)p_i \ln p_i \ .$$

$$=: \sum_{i=1}^{m} \mu_i p_i \ln p_i \tag{7.7.16}$$

which invites a few remarks:

i) If H_i' is a discrete Shannon entropy, then one has $a_i \geqslant 0$. In constrast, if it is a continuous entropy, then one may have either $a_i \geqslant 0$ or $a_i < 0$, and this is the relevant case, for instance, when $H' = \ln h_i$ is the entropy of a uniform distribution.

ii) Next, can we draw any conclusions regarding the magnitude of a_i with respect to unity? The answer is positively no: one may have either $|a_i| \geqslant 1$ or $|a_i| < 1$. For instance, if p_i is close to unity, $p_i = 1 - \varepsilon_i$, and if the corresponding x_i has several possible semantic meanings, then a_i will be every large.

iii) As a result, the coefficients $(1 + a_i u_i)$ in (7.7.16) may be positive, negative or zero. Indeed, the zero case occurs when $a_i u_i = -1$ which is practically quite meaningful. For example, when the semantic entropies themselves are discrete, one should have $u_i < 0$; in other words the observation process should yield a decrease of uncertainty, as is quite possible, when the observer has a prior knowledge of the observable. This property is the basic difference between $H_{\mathrm{wr}}(X)$ and the weighted entropy $H_{\mathrm{w}}(X)$ expressed by (7.7.1).

7.7.3 Weighted Relative Entropy of a Vector

Let (X, Y) denote a pair of random variables which take the values (x_i, y_j), $1 \leqslant i \leqslant m$, $1 \leqslant j \leqslant n$ with the probabilities r_{ij}. Let w_{ij} denote the observation coefficients associated with the process "x_i observed first and then y_j". Then the weighted relative entropy $H_{wr}(X, Y)$ of the pair (X, Y) is

$$H_{wr}(X, Y) = -\sum_{i=1}^{m} \sum_{j=1}^{n} \varrho(w_{ij}) r_{ij} \ln r_{ij} + \sum_{i=1}^{m} \sum_{j=1}^{n} \varrho(w_{ij}) w_{ij} r_{ij} H'_{ij} \qquad (7.7.17)$$

where H'_{ij} is the semantic entropy related to (x_i, y_j) and w_{ij} is defined as

$$w_{ij} = \frac{u_i + v_{j/i}}{1 + u_i v_{j/i}} . \qquad (7.7.18)$$

In the same way, the process "Y observed first and then X" has the entropy

$$H_{wr}(Y, X) = -\sum_{i=1}^{m} \sum_{j=1}^{n} \varrho(w_{ji}) r_{ij} \ln r_{ij} + \sum_{i=1}^{m} \sum_{j=1}^{n} \varrho(w_{ji}) w_{ji} r_{ij} H'_{ij} \qquad (7.7.19)$$

with

$$w_{ji} = \frac{v_j + u_{i/j}}{1 + v_j u_{i/j}} .$$

Generally one will have

$$H_{wr}(X, Y) \neq H_{wr}(Y, X) \qquad (7.7.20)$$

and the equality will only hold if the coefficients u_i and v_j of x_i and y_j satisfy the conditions

$$u_{i/j} = u_j , \qquad (7.7.21)$$

$$v_{j/i} = v_j , \qquad (7.7.22)$$

for every i and j. $\qquad\qquad\qquad\qquad\qquad\qquad\qquad\qquad\qquad\qquad\qquad\quad$ □

Again defining a_{ij} by the equation

$$H'_{ij} = -a_{ij} \ln r_{ij} , \qquad (7.7.23)$$

one has the equivalent expression

$$H(X, Y) = -\sum_{i=1}^{m} \sum_{j=1}^{m} \varrho(w_{ij})(1 + a_{ij} w_{ij}) r_{ij} \ln r_{ij} . \qquad (7.7.24)$$

7.7.4 Total Weighted Relative Entropy

At first glance it would seem that the concept of weighted relative entropy could apply straightforwardly to the total entropy $H_e(X)$ as defined by (2.11.8), but in fact the matter is not that simple, and a word of caution is in order.

The question reduces to defining exactly which one of the informational variables is effectively observed via the Minkowskian matrix. Indeed, on referring to the expression (2.11.8) for $H_e(X)$, one could directly assume that it is the information $-\ln(p_i/h_i)$ that is observed, but can we be sure that this viewpoint is meaningful in practice.

To shed more light on this question, let us return to the expression for $H_e(X)$ and expand this in the form

$$H_e(X) = - \sum_{i=1}^{m} p_i \ln p_i + \sum_{i=1}^{m} p_i \ln h_i .$$ (7.7.25)

According to the practical meaning of $H_e(X)$ one may assume that both $(-\ln p_i)$ and $\ln h_i$, $i = 1, 2, \ldots, m$, are observed via a Minkowskian process, in which case one will have the observed $(-\ln p_i)_r$ which we recall for convenience,

$$(-\ln p_i)_r = \varrho(u_i)(-\ln p_i + u_i H_i')$$ (7.7.26)

$$= -\varrho(u_i)(1 + a_i u_i) \ln p_i$$ (7.7.27)

and the observed $(\ln h_i)_r$,

$$(\ln h_i)_r = \varrho(u_i')(\ln h_i + u_i' H_i'')$$ (7.7.28)

$$= \varrho(u_i')(1 + a_i' u_i') \ln h_i ,$$ (7.7.29)

where u_i', H_i'' and a_i' are the parameters related to $\ln h_i$; namely

$$H_i'' = a_i' \ln h_i .$$ (7.7.30)

As a result, a general expression for the total weighted entropy would be

$$\text{Total weighted entropy} := \sum_{i=1}^{m} p_i[(-\ln p_i)_r + (\ln h_i)_r]$$

$$= - \sum_{i=1}^{m} \varrho(u_i)(1 + a_i u_i) p_i \ln \frac{p_i}{h^{\eta_i}}$$ (7.7.31)

with

$$\eta_i := \frac{\varrho(v_i)(1 + a_i' u_i')}{\varrho(u_i)(1 + a_i u_i)} .$$ (7.7.32)

Nevertheless, due to the particular meaning of the interval length h_i in relation to uncertainty, we shall consider instead a special case of (7.7.31) as follows.

Proposition 7.7.1. Assume that the individual uncertainties $(-\ln p_i)$ and $\ln h_i$ are each observed via independent Minkowskian matrices. Assume further that for each i the uncertainty of the ith event is an increasing function of h_i regardless of the values of the observation parameters. The resulting uncertainty about X is then the *total weighted relative entropy* $H_{\text{ewr}}(X)$ defined as

$$H_{\text{ewr}}(X) := - \sum_{i=1}^{m} \varrho(u_i)(1 + a_i u_i) p_i \ln \frac{p_i}{h_i} .$$ (7.7.33) $\square$

Proof. (i) The second assumption merely states that the larger h_i, the larger the uncertainty concerning x_i in the corresponding interval, regardless of the observation state of the observer. This hypothesis is quite understandable: one cannot decrease the ith local uncertainty by increasing h_i.

ii) Next, according to (7.7.31) the ith individual uncertainty is $-\ln(p_i/h_i^{\eta_i})$; and by virtue of (i) one should have $\eta_i > 0$ for every i.

iii) This being the case, we have seen that the term $(1 + a_i u_i)$ can be positive or negative, and likewise for $(1 + a_i' u_i')$, so that the second condition will be satisfied provided that

$$\text{sgn}(1 + a_i u_i) = \text{sgn}(1 + a_i' u_i') \ . \tag{7.7.34}$$

iv) Next, from a physical standpoint, we have the following alternatives: either the pairs (a_i, u_i) and (a_i', u_i') are unrelated to each other, or they are the same. The first case, of course, may contradict condition (7.7.34), and thus one requires $a_i = a_i'$ and $u_i = u_i'$.   □

Remark. We point out that this increase with h_i is exactly the basic assumption which allowed us to derive the concept of total entropy. This requirement is supported by the following argument. Consider a discrete random variable X which takes values in the range $-\infty < x_1 < \cdots < x_m < +\infty$; if we make the transformation $Y = kX$, then the uncertainty about Y should decrease as k tends to zero, since then all the kx_i tend to be confined in the neighborhood of zero.

In the derivation of the total entropy, we assume that it is this entire total entropy which increases with h_i whereas here we make the same assumption, but now for the entropies of the events since the weighting coefficients can be either positive or negative.

7.7.5 Observation and Subjectivity

This model of weighted entropy can be considered as a model of observation involving subjectivity. Indeed, subjectivity can be defined as the result of some interaction between the measurements and the prior definition of the observable, so that if we consider the semantic entropy H_i' as being related to this prior definition, (7.7.6) is nothing other than a coupling between the prior and posterior definition.

7.8 Weighted Transinformation

7.8.1 Some Preliminary Remarks

As has been mentioned several times, a measure of uncertainty is valuable if and only if it both meaningfully describes our real world and can also provide a manageable measure of information. This latter criterion is of paramount importance.

In the classical Shannonian framework, there are two main ways to define the information $I(X, Y)$ provided by X about Y.

One may use the identity

$$I(X, Y) = H(X) + H(Y) - H(X, Y) \tag{7.8.1}$$

whose practical meaning is as follows: $H(X) + H(Y)$ measures the amount of uncertainty that would be involved in X and Y if they were stochastically independent, and $H(X, Y)$ is the actual amount of uncertainty contained in the pair (X, Y). As a result their difference reflects the dependence of X upon Y in the framework of a theory of uncertainty; we shall say that it defines the amount of information contained in one of these variables with respect to the other.

Another approach, which is more straightforward and meaningful from a practical point of view, is to introduce the conditional entropy $H(Y/X)$ of Y given X by the expression

$$H(Y/X) := \sum_{i=1}^{m} p_i H(Y/x_i) , \tag{7.8.2}$$

and then to define

$$I(X, Y) := H(Y) - H(Y/X) . \tag{7.8.3}$$

This definition is motivated by the relation

$$H(Y/X) \leqslant H(Y) , \tag{7.8.4}$$

which shows that $H(Y) - H(Y/X)$ represents a decrease of uncertainty and thus defines an amount of information.

The problem is to decide which approach best enables us to define a concept of transinformation in the presence of Minkowskian observation. Equation (7.8.1) is evidently not meaningful enough since $H_{wr}(X, Y) \neq H_{rw}(X, Y)$, and thus we prefer to use a generalization of (7.8.3).

7.8.2 Weighted Relative Conditional Entropy

We return to the random vector (X, Y) of Sect. 7.7.3, and we denote by $q_{j/i}$ the probability

$$q_{j/i} := P_r\{Y = y_j/X = x_i\} . \tag{7.8.5}$$

Similarly, let $v_{j/i}$ and $b_{j/i}$ [see (7.7.15) for the definition of $b_{j/i}$] denote the observation coefficients of y_j given that $X = x_i$. We then make the definition:

Definition 7.8.1. The weighted relative conditional entropy $H_{wr}(Y/x_i)$ of Y given the outcome $X = x_i$ is defined as

$$H_{wr}(Y/x_i) := - \sum_{j=1}^{m} \varrho(v_{j/i})(1 + b_{j/i} v_{j/i}) q_{j/i} \ln q_{j/i} \tag{7.8.6}$$

and the weighted relative conditional entropy $H_{wr}(Y/X)$ is

$$H_{wr}(Y/X) := \sum_{i=1}^{n} p_i H_{wr}(Y/x_i) \tag{7.8.7}$$

$$= -\sum_{i=1}^{m} \sum_{j=1}^{n} \varrho(v_{j/i})(1 + b_{j/i}v_{j/i})r_{ij}\ln q_{j/i} . \tag{7.8.8} \quad \square$$

In a more detailed form, one has

$$H_{wr}(Y/x_i) := -\sum_{j=1}^{n} \varrho(v_{j/i})q_{j/i}\ln q_{j/i} + \sum_{j=1}^{n} \varrho(v_{j/i})v_{j/i}q_{j/i}K'_{j/i} \tag{7.8.9}$$

and

$$H_{wr}(Y/X) := -\sum_{i=1}^{m} \sum_{j=1}^{n} \varrho(v_{j/i})r_{ij}\ln q_{j/i} + \sum_{i=1}^{m} \sum_{j=1}^{n} \varrho(v_{j/i})v_{j/i}r_{ij}K'_{j/i} \tag{7.8.10}$$

where $K'_{j/i}$ is the semantic entropy associated with the event $(y_j/X = x_i)$.

Comments. (i) Assume that

$$v_{j/i} = v_i \quad \text{and} \quad K'_{j/i} = K_i$$

for every i and j, then $b_{j/i} = b_i$ and one has

$$H_{wr}(Y/X) := \sum_{i=1}^{m} \varrho(v_i)(1 + b_iv_i)p_iH(Y/x_i) . \tag{7.8.11}$$

ii) The reader will have understood that definition 7.8.1 is a straightforward generalization of $H(Y/X)$ as given by expression (7.8.2). It is furthermore quite meaningful from a practical standpoint.

The basic assumption is that it is the individual amount of information ($-\ln q_{j/i}$) which is observed via a Minkowskian matrix given x_i; and this is quite consistent with practical observations. Indeed, in the process (Y/x_i) the observer tries to identify the value of Y and he is not directly concerned with x_i which, strictly speaking, is meaningless to him.

7.8.3 Weighted Transinformation

A word of caution is called for before we tackle the definition of weighted transinformation. In the definition of $I(X, Y)$ as given by (7.8.3), $H(Y)$ is basically a measure of the prior uncertainty that the observer R has about Y, while $H(Y/X)$ is the posterior uncertainty given the observation of X. Well obviously, in Shannon framework, there is no problem of subjectivity of observation so that $H(Y)$ and $H(Y/X)$ are defined absolutely and irrespective of the observer.

The matter is different when we introduce subjectivity into the observation process. Indeed, we may assume that the observer's prior uncertainty about Y is again defined by $H(Y)$, in which case we implicitly assume that Y is merely a symbol, without semantics, whose uncertainty is due to its probability distribution alone. But one may also assume that the observer has some prior belief (i.e. knowledge or misknowledge) about Y, so that the corresponding prior uncertainty is not $H(Y)$ but $H_{wr}(Y)$. Given that the first situation may be considered as a special case of the second one, we shall examine only the latter.

Definition 7.8.2. Let $X \in \mathbb{R}$ and $Y \in \mathbb{R}$ denote two random variables which take the values $\{x_1, x_2, \ldots, x_m\}$ and $\{y_1, y_2, \ldots, y_n\}$ with the respective probabilities $\{p_1, p_2, \ldots, p_m\}$ and $\{q_1, q_2, \ldots, q_n\}$. Let v_j and b_j, $j = 1, \ldots, m$ denote the observation coefficients of the individual information $(-\ln q_j)$. Let $\{q_{j/i}\}$ denote the conditional probability distribution of Y given that $X = x_i$, and assume that the observation of the information $(-\ln q_{j/i})$ is of Minkowskian nature with the coefficients $v_{j/i}$ and $b_{j/i}$. The amount $I_{wr}(Y/X)$ of information provided by X about Y is then defined by the expression

$$I_{wr}(Y/X) = H_{wr}(Y) - H_{wr}(Y/X) . \qquad (7.8.12) \quad \square$$

Proposition 7.8.1. The information $I_{wr}(Y/X)$ has the following explicit form

$$I_{wr}(Y/X) = \sum_{i=1}^{m} \sum_{j=1}^{n} r_{ij} \ln \frac{r_{ij}^{\eta_{ij}}}{p_i^{\eta_{ij}} q_j^{v_j}} , \qquad (7.8.13)$$

where the coefficients v_j and η_{ij} are such that

$$H_{wr}(Y) = - \sum_{j=1}^{n} v_j q_j \ln q_j \qquad (7.8.14)$$

$$H_{wr}(X, Y) = - \sum_{i=1}^{m} \sum_{j=1}^{n} \eta_{ij} r_{ij} \ln q_{j/i} , \qquad (7.8.15)$$

namely

$$v_j = \varrho(v_j)(1 + b_j v_j) \qquad (7.8.16)$$

$$\eta_{ij} = \varrho(v_{j/i})(1 + b_{j/i} v_{j/i}) . \qquad (7.8.17) \quad \square$$

The proof can be derived by calculating the term on the right-hand side of (7.8.2).

7.8.4 Relation to Renyi Entropy

We point out that this expression is a straightforward generalization of the transinformation $I(Y/X)$ which corresponds to $\eta_{ij} = v_j = 1$ for every i and j.
This being so, assume that

$$\eta_{ij} = \eta \qquad \text{and} \qquad v_j = v$$

then

$$I_{wr}(Y/X) = \sum_{i=1}^{n} \sum_{j=1}^{m} r_{ij} \ln \frac{r_{ij}^{\eta}}{p_i^{\eta} q^{v}}$$

and these exponents η and ν look like the exponent c in the definition of the Renyi entropy (2.9.1).

So the question which then arises is the following: can we make the straight-forward identification

$$c(u) = \mu^\delta$$
$$= \varrho^\delta(u)(1 + au)^\delta \tag{7.8.18}$$

(where δ is a suitable exponent to be defined) in (2.9.1), to obtain a practical meaning for this entropy? Note that this conjecture is far from meaningless!

Indeed, with the notation of (2.9.1), let us consider the entropy

$$H_{c(u)}(X) = \frac{1}{1 - c(u)} \ln \sum p_i^{c(u)} \tag{7.8.19}$$

where $c(u)$ is defined by expression (7.8.18).

i) One has

$$\lim c(u) = 1 \qquad \text{as} \qquad u \to 0 \tag{7.8.20}$$

so that

$$\lim H_{c(u)}(X) = H(X) \qquad \text{as} \qquad u \to 0 \tag{7.8.21}$$

where $H(X)$ denotes the Shannon entropy – a result which is quite consistent with the practical meaning of u.

ii) Next we bear in mind in following inequalities

$$H_c(X) > H(X) , \qquad 0 < c < 1 \tag{7.8.22}$$

$$H_c(X) < H(X) , \qquad c > 1 \tag{7.8.23}$$

obeyed by $H_c(X)$ and $H(X)$ for different values of c.

iii) By virtue of the practical significance of u as exhibited by the Minkowskian observation equations (7.2.11) and (7.2.12) applied to entropy, the case $u > 0$ describes an increase of uncertainty, while $u < 0$ reflects a decrease of uncertainty. Thus, to be consistent with the inequalities (7.8.2) and (7.8.3) we should have

$$c(u) < 1 , \qquad u > 0 \tag{7.8.24}$$

$$c(u) > 1 , \qquad u < 0 . \tag{7.8.25}$$

iv) This being the case, in order to simplify, assume that $a = 1$ to yield

$$c(u) = \left(\frac{1 + u}{1 - u}\right)^\delta ;$$

then according to the conditions (7.8.24) and (7.8.25) above, we are led to put $\delta = -1$, and therefore to the equality

$$c(u) = \frac{1-u}{1+u} \qquad (7.8.26)$$

which completes the identification. $\qquad\qquad\qquad\qquad\qquad\qquad\square$

Note that there is no inconsistency with the preliminary identification suggested by (3.4.6), but rather that we can now refine the latter in the form

$$c := \frac{1 - \dfrac{dH(\beta/\alpha; e)}{dH(\alpha; e)}}{1 + \dfrac{dH(\beta/\alpha; e)}{dH(\alpha; e)}} \ . \qquad (7.8.27)$$

7.9 Weighted Cross-Entropy, Weighted Relative Entropy

7.9.1 Background on Kullback Entropy

Kullback [7.9] introduced the divergence or cross-entropy $H(\mathscr{P}//\mathscr{Q})$ defined by equation (2.10.1) to measure the distance between the probability distributions $\mathscr{P} := (p_1, p_2, \dots, p_m)$ and $\mathscr{Q} := (q_1, q_2, \dots, q_m)$.

He arrived at this definition by way of heuristic arguments and mathematicians later showed that the definition can be derived as the consequence of axioms related to recursivity, continuity and symmetry. In the following, we shall obtain this entropy by using physical arguments only. In particular, we shall show that it can be considered as an application of the Minkowskian observation process; and as has been emphasized several times, one of the advantages of such a practical approach is that it exhibits the genuine meaning of the various parameters that appear in the model.

We bear in mind that in his pioneering work Kullback considered $\mathscr{P}$ as a prior probability distribution while $\mathscr{Q}$ was a posterior distribution, and so he used $H(\mathscr{P}//\mathscr{Q})$ as a cost function in statistical estimation.

7.9.2 Weighted Kullback Entropy

In order to derive this cross-entropy by using relative observation, we proceed as follows.

i) We first remark that the Kullback entropy is a transinformation in the sense that it does not measure a uncertainty, but rather an amount of information; in effect one has

$$H(\mathscr{P}//\mathscr{Q}) = E_{\mathscr{Q}}\{\mathscr{J}_i\} \qquad (7.9.1)$$

where $\mathscr{J}_i$ denotes the charge of entropy, that is to say the information

$$\mathscr{J}_i := (-\ln p_i) - (-\ln q_i) \qquad (7.9.2)$$

provided by the posterior probability q_i about the prior one p_i.

ii) Assume that this information $\mathscr{I}_i$ is observed via the Minkowskian equations (7.2.11) and (7.2.12). One then has the measure

$$\left(\ln \frac{q_i}{p_i}\right)_r = \varrho(u_i)\ln \frac{q_i}{p_i} + \varrho(u_i)u_i\mathscr{I}_i' \tag{7.9.3}$$

where $\mathscr{I}_i'$ denotes the semantic information associated with $\ln(p_i/q_i)$.

iii) We now take the mathematical expectation of this expression with respect to the distribution $\mathscr{Q}$ to obtain

$$H_w(\mathscr{P}//\mathscr{Q}) = \sum_{i=1}^{m} \varrho(u_i)q_i\ln \frac{q_i}{p_i} + \sum_{i=1}^{m} \varrho(u_i)u_iq_i\mathscr{I}_i' . \tag{7.9.4}$$

Definition 7.9.1. The entropy $H_w(\mathscr{P}//\mathscr{Q})$ defined by (7.9.4) in which $\varrho(u)$ is given by (4.5.4) with the condition $-1 < u < +1$ will be referred to as to the *weighted Kullback entropy between $\mathscr{P}$ and $\mathscr{Q}$.*   □

Again, if we set

$$\mathscr{I}_i' =: c_i\ln \frac{q_i}{p_i} , \tag{7.9.5}$$

one has

$$H_w(\mathscr{P}//\mathscr{Q}) = \sum_{i=1}^{m} \varrho(u_i)(1 + c_iu_i)q_i\ln \frac{q_i}{p_i} . \tag{7.9.6}$$

7.10 Weighted Relative Divergence

We come back to the components $\ln q_i - \ln p_i$ of the transinformation in Kullback entropy, and we assume that the observer does not consider them as a whole, but rather observes $(-\ln q_i)$ and $(-\ln p_i)$ separately, following the Minkowskian model.
We then have the individual observed information

$$(-\ln p_i)_r = \varrho(u_i)(-\ln p_i + u_iH_i') \tag{7.10.1}$$

and

$$(-\ln q_j)_r = \varrho(v_j)(-\ln q_j + v_jK_j') \tag{7.10.2}$$

where H_i' and K_j' denote the corresponding semantic entropies.
Thus, in analogy to the Kullback entropy, we may consider the cross-entropy

$$H_{rw}(\mathscr{P}//\mathscr{Q}) := \sum_{i=1}^{m} q_i[(\ln q_i)_r - (\ln p_i)_r] \tag{7.10.3}$$

the explicit form of which is

$$H_{rw}(\mathscr{P}//\mathscr{Q}) = \sum_{i=1}^{m} \varrho(v_i)q_i \ln q_i - \sum_{i=1}^{m} \varrho(u_i)q_i \ln p_i + \sum_{i=1}^{m} q_i[\varrho(u_i)u_iH_i' - \varrho(v_i)v_iK_i'] \ .$$

$$(7.10.4)$$

Definition 7.10.1. We shall refer to $H_{rw}(\mathscr{P}//\mathscr{Q})$ defined by (7.10.4) as the *weighted relative divergence between $\mathscr{P}$ and $\mathscr{Q}$*.   □

As before, if we define a_i and b_j by the equations

$$H_i' =: -a_i \ln p_i \qquad (7.10.5)$$

$$K_j' =: -b_j \ln q_j \qquad (7.10.6)$$

we can then re-write $H_{rw}(\mathscr{P}//\mathscr{Q})$ in the form

$$H_{rw}(\mathscr{P}//\mathscr{Q}) = \sum_{i=1}^{m} \varrho(v_i)(1 + b_iv_i)q_i \ln q_i - \sum_{i=1}^{m} \varrho(u_i)(1 + a_iu_i)q_i \ln p_i \ . \qquad (7.10.7)$$

For the special case in which

$$\varrho(u_i) = A = \text{constant for all } i$$

$$\varrho(v_j) = B = \text{constant for all } j$$

equation (7.10.4) yields

$$H_{rw}(\mathscr{P}//\mathscr{Q}) = B \sum_{i=1}^{m} q_i \ln q_i - A \sum_{i=1}^{m} q_i \ln p_i + \sum_{i=1}^{m} q_i C_i \qquad (7.10.8)$$

where C_i is defined as

$$C_i := Au_iH_i' - Bv_iK_i' \ . \qquad (7.10.9)$$

This simplified expression for $H_{rw}(\mathscr{P}//\mathscr{Q})$ is exactly the divergence introduced by *Kannapan* [7.10] to measure the closeness of two probability distributions.

Comment. In view of (7.10.7), it is clear that the divergence $H_{rw}(\mathscr{P}//\mathscr{Q})$ can be considered as a generalization of the weighted Kullback entropy $H_w(\mathscr{P}//\mathscr{Q})$. More explicitly, if one has $u_i = v_i$ and $a_i = b_i$ for every i, then $H_w(\mathscr{P}//\mathscr{Q}) = H_w(\mathscr{P}//\mathscr{Q})$.

By using the coefficients μ_i and v_j defined by (7.7.16) and (7.8.16) respectively, (7.10.7) can be re-written in the form

$$H_{rw}(\mathscr{P}//\mathscr{Q}) = \sum_{i=1}^{m} q_i \ln \frac{q_i^{v_i}}{p_i^{\mu_i}} \qquad (7.10.10)$$

which sheds light upon the meaning of this generalization.

7.11 Application to Continuous Distributions

In this section, we shall generalize the various definitions above to continuous probability distributions. These derivations will be neither formal nor particularly mathematical; instead they will be made in a very simple way by using the concepts of total entropies.

7.11.1 The General Principle of the Derivations

In order to obtain the expression for the continuous entropy, we shall refer to the corresponding *total weighted entropy* in which we shall make the discretizing span h tends to zero, and in this way we shall readily obtain our result. As an illustrative example we consider the following statements.

Proposition 7.11.1. Let $p(x)$, $x \in \mathbb{R}$, denote a continuous probability distribution; and let $\ldots x_i, x_{i+1}, \ldots$ be a lattice with the span h, i.e. $x_{j+1} - x_j =: h$ for every j. Define the discrete probability distribution $\tilde{p}_i$ of the discrete variable $\tilde{X}$ as

$$\tilde{p}_i = \int_{x_i}^{x_{i+1}} p(x)\, dx \ . \tag{7.11.1}$$

The total entropy $H_e(\tilde{X})$ defined by $\{\tilde{p}_i\}$ and h then converges to the continuous entropy defined by $p(x)$ as h tends to zero.   □

The proof is straightforward if one takes the integral above in the Riemann sense, and it is left to the reader. Broadly speaking, one has

$$\tilde{p}_i = p(\tilde{x}_i)h$$

so that the corresponding total entropy is

$$\tilde{H}_e = -\sum_i p(\tilde{x}_i) \ln p(\tilde{x}_i)h \tag{7.11.2}$$

the limiting value of which is the continuous entropy when h tends to zero.

This scheme will allow us to derive all the continuous counterparts of the various entropies introduced above. In order to emphasize that they are not new definitions but rather direct deductions, we shall state the results in the form of propositions.

7.11.2 Continuous Weighted Relative Entropy

Proposition 7.11.2. Let $X \in \mathbb{R}$ denote a random variable with the probability distribution $p(x)$, and let $(\tilde{X}, \{\tilde{p}_i\})$ denote the associated discrete variable as defined in proposition 7.11.1. Then the limiting value of $H_{ewr}(\tilde{X})$ when h tends to zero exists and is given by

$$\lim_{h \to 0} H_{ewr}(\tilde{X}) = - \int_{-\infty}^{+\infty} \varrho[u(x)][1 + a(x)u(x)]p(x) \ln p(x)\, dx \tag{7.11.3}$$

$$=: H_{wr}(X) \ . \tag{7.11.4}$$

It is referred to as the weighted relative entropy of X.   □

On expanding expression (7.11.3) we have in addition

$$H_{\mathrm{wr}}(X) = - \int\limits_{-\infty}^{+\infty} \varrho[u(x)]p(x)\ln p(x)\,dx - \int\limits_{-\infty}^{+\infty} \varrho[u(x)]a(x)u(x)p(x)\ln p(x)\,dx$$

$$(7.11.5)$$

and we are thus led to make the identification

$$H'(x) =: -a(x)\ln p(x)\ , \tag{7.11.6}$$

which provides the expression

$$H_{\mathrm{wr}}(X) = - \int\limits_{-\infty}^{+\infty} \varrho[u(x)]p(x)\ln p(x)\,dx + \int\limits_{-\infty}^{+\infty} \varrho[u(x)]u(x)p(x)H'(x)\,dx\ .$$

$$(7.11.7)$$

The term $H'(x)$ defined by (7.11.6) is the semantic entropy associated with the observed value x.

According to the notation of (7.8.15–18) one can write

$$H_{\mathrm{rw}}(Y) = - \int\limits_{-\infty}^{+\infty} v(y)q(y)\ln q(y)\,dy \tag{7.11.8}$$

$$v(y) := \varrho[v(y)][1 + b(y)v(y)] \tag{7.11.9}$$

$$H_{\mathrm{rw}}(X, Y) = - \int\limits_{-\infty}^{+\infty} \int\limits_{-\infty}^{+\infty} \eta(x, y)r(x, y)\ln q(y/x)\,dy\,dx \tag{7.11.10}$$

$$\eta(x, y) := \varrho[v(y/x)][1 + b(y/x)v(y/x)] \tag{7.11.11}$$

therefore the continuous transinformation is

$$I_{\mathrm{wr}}(Y/X) = \int\limits_{-\infty}^{+\infty} \int\limits_{-\infty}^{+\infty} r(x, y)\ln \frac{r(x, y)^{\eta(x, y)}}{p(x)^{\eta(x, y)}q(y)^{v(y)}}\,dx\,dy\ . \tag{7.11.12}$$

7.11.3 Continuous Weighted Kullback Entropy

Strictly speaking, we do not have a concept of total Kullback entropy so that it would appear impossible to rigorously define continuous Kullback entropy; but this initial impression is false.

Indeed, let us expand the expression (7.9.7) for $H_{\mathrm{w}}(\mathscr{P}//\mathscr{Q})$ to obtain

$$H_{\mathrm{w}}(\mathscr{P}//\mathscr{Q}) = - \sum_{i=1}^{m} \varrho(u_i)(1 + c_iu_i)q_i\ln p_i - \left(-\sum_{i=1}^{m} \varrho(u_i)(1 + c_iu_i)q_i\ln q_i \right)$$

$$(7.11.13)$$

which looks like the difference of two weighted entropies.

Assume that the framework of the observation is such that the observer is interested in the total individual entropies $-\ln(p_i/h_i)$ and $-\ln(q_i/h_i)$ rather than $-\ln p_i$ and $-\ln q_i$. We then have to consider the difference

$$H_{ew}(\mathscr{P}//\mathscr{Q}) = \left[-\sum_{i=1}^{m} \varrho(u_i)(1 + c_i u_i)q_i \ln\frac{p_i}{h_i} \right] - \left[-\sum_{i=1}^{m} \varrho(u_i)(1 + c_i u_i)q_i \ln\frac{q_i}{h_i} \right] .$$

(7.11.14)

and of course, one has the equality

$$H_{ew}(\mathscr{P}//\mathscr{Q}) = H_w(\mathscr{P}//\mathscr{Q}) .$$

(7.11.15)

This leads us to the following result.

Proposition 7.11.3. Let $p(x)$ and $q(x)$ denote two probability density functions defined on the interval $[a,b] \subset \mathbb{R}$; and let $\mathscr{P} := \{\tilde{p}_i\}$ and $\mathscr{Q} := \{\tilde{q}_i\}$ denote the associated discrete distributions with the same h, as defined in proposition 7.11.1. Then the limiting value of $H_{ew}(\mathscr{P}//\mathscr{Q})$, see (7.11.14), exists and is given by

$$\lim_{h \to 0} H_{ew}(\mathscr{P}//\mathscr{Q}) = \int_{-\infty}^{+\infty} \varrho[u(x)][1 + c(x)u(x)]q(x) \ln\frac{q(x)}{p(x)} dx$$

(7.11.16)

$$=: H_w(\mathscr{P}//\mathscr{Q}) .$$

(7.11.17)

It is referred to as the weighted Kullback entropy of the distributions $\mathscr{P}$ and $\mathscr{Q}$. □

If we put

$$\mathscr{I}'(x) := c(x)\ln\frac{q(x)}{p(x)} ,$$

(7.11.18)

which is the density of semantic information corresponding to $\ln[q(x)/p(x)]$, one also has

$$H_w(\mathscr{P}//\mathscr{Q}) = \int_{-\infty}^{+\infty} \varrho[u(x)]q(x) \ln\frac{q(x)}{p(x)} dx + \int_{-\infty}^{+\infty} \varrho[u(x)]u(x)\mathscr{I}'(x) dx .$$

(7.11.19)

7.11.4 Continuous Weighted Relative Divergence

On referring to the definition of $H_{rw}(\mathscr{P}//\mathscr{Q})$, see (7.10.7), and using arguments similar to those in Sect. 7.11.3, we shall now write the total weighted relative divergence $H_{erw}(\mathscr{P}//\mathscr{Q})$, which is the counterpart of $H_{rw}(\mathscr{P}//\mathscr{Q})$, as

$$H_{erw}(\mathscr{P}//\mathscr{Q}) := \sum_{i=1}^{m} \varrho(v_i)(1 + b_i v_i)q_i \ln\frac{q_i}{h_i} - \sum_{i=1}^{m} \varrho(u_i)(1 + a_i u_i)q_i \ln\frac{p_i}{h_i}$$

(7.11.20)

and we can state straightforwardly:

Proposition 7.11.4. Consider the framework of proposition 7.11.3. The limiting value of $H_{erw}(\mathscr{P}//\mathscr{Q})$, see (7.11.20), exists and is given by

$$\lim_{h \to 0} H_{\mathrm{erw}}(\mathscr{P}//\mathscr{Q}) = \int_{-\infty}^{+\infty} \varrho[v(x)][1 + b(x)v(x)]q(x)\ln q(x)\,dx$$

$$- \int_{-\infty}^{+\infty} \varrho[u(x)][1 + a(x)u(x)]q(x)\ln p(x)\,dx \qquad (7.11.21)$$

$$=: H_{\mathrm{rw}}(\mathscr{P}//\mathscr{Q}) \;. \qquad (7.11.22)$$

It is referred to as the weighted relative divergence of the distributions $\mathscr{P}$ and $\mathscr{Q}$. $\square$

If we now expand expression (7.11.21) and return to the semantic entropies H' and K', we have the equivalent form

$$H_{\mathrm{rw}}(\mathscr{P}//\mathscr{Q}) = \int_{-\infty}^{+\infty} \varrho[v(x)]q(x)\ln q(x)\,dx - \int_{-\infty}^{+\infty} \varrho[u(x)]q(x)\ln p(x)\,dx$$

$$+ \int_{-\infty}^{+\infty} \{\varrho[u(x)]u(x)H'(x) - \varrho[v(x)]v(x)K'(x)\}\,dx \;. \qquad (7.11.23)$$

7.12 Transformation of Variables in Weighted Relative Entropy

It is well known that if two random variables $X \in \mathbb{R}$ and $Y \in \mathbb{R}$ are related by $Y = f(X)$, then their Shannon entropies are such that

$$H(Y) = H(X) + \int_{-\infty}^{+\infty} p(x)\ln|f'(x)|\,dx \qquad (7.12.1)$$

where $f'(x)$ is the derivative of $f(x)$. Our purpose in the following is to examine whether a similar relation holds for the weighted relative entropy.

To this end we proceed as follows:

i) Let us assume that $f'(x) \geqslant 0$ and let us make the transformation $y = f(x)$ in the integral

$$H_{\mathrm{wr}}(Y) = -\int_{-\infty}^{+\infty} v(y)q(y)\ln q(y)\,dy \;; \qquad (7.12.2)$$

we then obtain the expression

$$H_{\mathrm{wr}}(Y) = -\int_{-\infty}^{+\infty} v[f(x)]q[f(x)]\ln q[f(x)]f'(x)\,dx \qquad (7.12.3)$$

which we re-write as

$$H_{\mathrm{wr}}(Y) = -\int_{-\infty}^{+\infty} v(f)q(f)f'(x)\ln[q(f)f'(x)]\,dx$$

$$+ \int_{-\infty}^{+\infty} v(f)q(f)f'(x)\ln f'(x)\,dx \;. \qquad (7.12.4)$$

ii) We now remark that the probability density $p(x)$ of X is

$$p(x) = q(f)f'(x) \tag{7.12.5}$$

so that we re-write (7.12.4) in the form

$$H_{wr}(Y) = - \int_{-\infty}^{+\infty} v(f)p(x)\ln p(x)\,dx + \int_{-\infty}^{+\infty} v(f)p(x)\ln f'(x)\,dx \ . \tag{7.12.6}$$

iii) If we *assume* that the weighting function $\mu(x)$ of X in the expression

$$H_{wr}(X) = - \int_{-\infty}^{+\infty} \mu(x)p(x)\ln p(x)\,dx \tag{7.12.7}$$

is such that

$$\mu(x) = v[f(x)] \ , \tag{7.12.8}$$

then we can re-write (7.12.6) as

$$H_{wr}(Y) = H_{wr}(X) + \int_{-\infty}^{+\infty} \mu(x)p(x)\ln f'(x)\,dx \ .$$

iv) Now, for an arbitrary $f(x)$, by separately considering the intervals where $f'(x) \geqslant 0$ and those where $f'(x) < 0$ one finally obtains

$$H_{wr}(Y) = H_{wr}(X) + \int_{-\infty}^{+\infty} \mu(x)p(x)\ln|f'(x)|\,dx \tag{7.12.9}$$

provided that (7.12.8) is satisfied.   □

Application. An interesting consequence of this property is the following. On assuming once more that (7.12.8) is satisfied, which is quite realistic, the weighted relative entropy is invariant provided that $|f'(x)| = 1$ or det $|\partial f/\partial x| = 1$ in the case of several variables. As a result, the Minkowskian model of observation applies provided we consider the weighted relative entropy instead of the Shannon entropy. Thus its area of application has been extended.

7.13 Conclusions

In this chapter, we have used three very natural and straightforward principles to tackle the general problem of defining the amount of uncertainty involved in a random variable. The resulting framework is very simple in theoretical terms, in contrast to the mathematical approach, which moreover hides much of the physical meaning. Let us recall these three principles.

i)   The basic measure of uncertainty is Hartley's entropy.
ii) The uncertainty involved in a random experiment is the mathematical expectation of the uncertainty contained in each individual event.

iii) The uncertainty that is effectively perceived by an external observer is the result of a Minkowskian observation process which describes interactions between syntax and semantics.

These principles do not rely on any sophisticated prerequisites, and they are quite consistent with the practical meaning of the term uncertainty.

Thus, in a uniform approach, we have derived a broad class of entropies which had been previously proposed by various scientists. In particular, we again obtained the concept of *effective entropy* which was introduced earlier [7.6].

The main advantage of this approach is that it is very close to physics and clearly exhibits the practical meanings of the various parameters involved.

8. Entropy of Form and Pattern

In the previous chapters we have considered the classical information theory as initiated by Shannon, and have modified this in various ways, mainly in order to account for the relative effects of the observer via the meaning of the observable under consideration. In all these studies, we restricted ourselves to the entropy of scalar-valued random variables and of random vectors. In the present chapter we shall examine ways in which we can generalize the results to measure the amount of uncertainty involved in patterns and forms.

In Webster's dictionary, we find the following definitions. A form is "the shape and structure of something as distinguished from its material", and a pattern is "a form or model proposed for imitation". In other words, whenever we refer to a form with the purpose of duplication or of identification, the term of pattern would be more suitable than that of form. From the viewpoint of information theory, this slight semantic difference has no importance and we shall thus use the expressions "entropy of form" and "entropy of pattern" with exactly the same meaning.

Basically, a form is an infinite-dimensional vector, and it is likely that the uncertainty it involves will depend upon the type of representation we choose to define it. As a result, we shall have not one but several possible expressions for measuring the amount of uncertainty of a form. We shall examine this question in the present chapter.

8.1 Introduction

8.1.1 Entropy of Form and Fractal Dimension

To the best of the author's knowledge, the first approach proposed as a measure of the amount of uncertainty involved in a curve is the model described by *Kolmogorov* [8.1] who proceeds as outlined below.

Assume that the curve is defined in a finite domain of $\mathbb{R}^2$ and let ε denote a positive real number. We cover the corresponding graph by means of circles with radius ε in such a manner that they do not intersect. Let $N(\varepsilon)$ denote the smallest number of such circles that is necessary to cover the graph or portion of graph. The ε-entropy of the graph is then defines as being $\ln N(\varepsilon)$ where the natural logarithm is chosen for convenience only. Let us remark in passing that this definition is somewhat related to the concept of "dimension" or "fractal dimension" D as introduced by *Mandelbrot* [8.2] and which is defined by the relation

$$\ln N(\varepsilon) = -D \ln \varepsilon + \sigma(\varepsilon) \tag{8.1}$$

for small ε.

More recently, *Mendes France* and coworkers [8.3] defined the entropy of a plane curve in terms of its number of intersection points with a random straight line, and he used the Gibbs distribution, which maximizes this entropy, to define the temperature of the curve.

With the advent of artificial intelligence and more generally of cybernetics (for instance, organization and self-organization problems) this question is beginning to attract the interest of scientists. Indeed, insofar as the concept of information is of importance in a general systems theory, it is likely that the problem of defining the amount of uncertainty involved in a form should be quite relevant. Don't forget that symbols, in the sense of communication theory, are nothing other than a special case of forms and patterns!

8.1.2 Entropy and Pattern Representation

In attempting to define the entropy of a form one encounters two main difficulties:

i) The problem of *pattern representation*. How do we represent a practical form, defined initially by drawings and curves, in a formal structure that can be mathematically processed?

ii) The problem of *inference generation*. How do we use the formal structures above to generate useful information regarding the form under observation?

These problems are exactly the same as those encountered in knowledge engineering, and this is not a mere coincidence!

The first problem refers of course to the well-known dichotomy "discrete modelling versus continuous modelling". We now have good evidence that the human optical system grasps the crucial features of a visual pattern by using a scanning process. Thus it would seem that a discrete representation scheme is quite relevant and quite meaningful. Nevertheless, we believe that this remark should not disqualify the continuous representation, since the latter actually exists in our real universe. For instance, we could consider the amount of uncertainty involved in a continuous pattern as a sort of information potential, that is to say, the maximum amount of information which is available in the pattern, but which is not necessarily registered by the observer because we may suppose that the scanning process loses some information.

This being so, it is likely that, for a given pattern, different optical cortices will select different features of the pattern as the key items for identifying the object, and in this way one can ask how does this information vary with the observer? There is evidence that the angles are the principal features which the brain uses to store and recognize patterns. Can we claim then that we need consider only the information contained in these angles?

These remarks suggest that we should not expect to obtain only one definition for the entropy of a pattern, but probably several definitions depending upon how the pattern itself is defined, or how it is observed by the experimenter who deals with the information. We note that we have already encountered a similar problem with a mere discrete random variable X. Indeed, assume that $-\infty < a \leqslant X \leqslant b < +\infty$. If we think of X as a random experiment with m possible outcomes, then $H(X)$

is the Shannon entropy; but if we consider X as a scalar real-valued random variable (as it is!) then we have to consider the additional uncertainty contributed by the interval $[a, b]$ and we then obtain the total entropy $H_e(X)$ of X.

8.1.3 Randomized Definition or Geometrical Approach?

From a theoretical standpoint, one may question the definition of Shannon entropy in the sense that it requires the existence of a probability distribution. But in practical applications, it is well known that it is sufficient to have a set of weighting coefficients (or relative frequencies) to circumvent this difficulty and to meaningfully use this entropy. As a result, the problem of whether or not information should be defined by means of probability, has not been of paramount interest in communication engineering.

We cannot claim that the same will be true in an approach to the entropy of pattern, and here we have to consider the various measures of uncertainty which may be obtained using randomization techniques as well as geometrical models which do not refer to probability.

The main content of the present chapter is as follows. By using a randomization of time, we shall derive a definition of the entropy of a Markovian process. We shall then examine how we can measure the uncertainty involved in a deterministic form. We shall proceed one step at a time, first generalizing our previous concept of "total entropy" for dealing with random vectors, and then defining total entropy for discrete quantized processes.

8.2 Total Entropy of a Random Vector

In Chap. 6, we defined the concept of "total entropy" mainly in order to derive a unified approach to discrete and continuous entropy. For the sake of simplicity we considered scalar-valued random variables and two-dimensional random vectors; but it is clear that this concept can be generalized to m-dimensional vectors.

8.2.1 Definition of the Total Entropy of an m-Vector

Notation. Let $X^t := (X_1, X_2, \ldots, X_m) \in \mathbb{R}^m$ denote a real-valued random vector whose probability distribution $p(x_1^{i_1}, x_2^{i_2}, \ldots, x_m^{i_m})$ where $x_i^{i_j}$, $j = 1, 2, \ldots, m_i$ is the generic term denoting the values taken on by X_i. Following the technique used in Chap. 6, we shall associate with each discrete random variable X_i the set of intervals $\{J_i^j\}$, $j = 1, \ldots, m_i$ and their respective lengths h_i^j defined as

$$J_i^1 := \left\{ x \,\middle|\, x \in \left[x_i^1 - \frac{x_i^2 - x_i^1}{2}, \frac{x_i^1 + x_i^2}{2} \right) \right\}, \qquad h_i^1 := x_i^2 - x_i^1 \qquad (8.2.1)$$

$$J_i^j := \left\{ x \,\middle|\, x \in \left[\frac{x_i^j + x_i^{j-1}}{2}, \frac{x_i^j + x_i^{j+1}}{2} \right) \right\}, \qquad h_i^j := \frac{x_i^{j+1} - x_i^j}{2}$$

$$j = 1, 2, \ldots, m - 1 \qquad (8.2.2)$$

$$J_i^{m_i} := \left\{ x \mid x \in \left[\frac{x_i^{m_i-1} + x_i^{m_i}}{2}, x_i^{m_i} + \frac{x_i^{m_i} - x_i^{m_i-1}}{2} \right] \right\}, \ldots \quad h_i^{m_i} := x_i^{m_i} - x_i^{m_i-1} .$$

$$(8.2.3)$$

With this notation, we can straightforwardly state the following result.

Proposition 8.2.1. The direct generalization of proposition 6.5.1 provides the total entropy $H_e(X)$ of the discrete random vector X in the form

$$H_e(X) = -k \sum_{i_1 \ldots i_m} p(x_1^{i_1}, x_2^{i_2}, \ldots, x_m^{i_m}) \ln \frac{p(x_1^{i_1}, x_2^{i_2}, \ldots, x_m^{i_m})}{(h_1^{i_1} h_2^{i_2}, \ldots, h_m^{i_m})^{K/k}} \quad (8.2.4)$$

where k, $k > 0$, is the constant which defines the Shannon entropy, and K is positive constant associated with the uncertainty generated by the parameters h_i^j.
In the special case where $K = k$, one has

$$H_e(X) = -k \sum_{i_1 \ldots i_m} p(x_1^{i_1}, x_2^{i_2}, \ldots, x_m^{i_m}) \ln \frac{p(x_1^{i_1}, x_2^{i_2}, \ldots, x_m^{i_m})}{h_1^{i_1} h_2^{i_2}, \ldots, h_m^{i_m}} . \quad (8.2.5) \quad \square$$

8.2.2 Some Properties of the Total Entropy of m-Vectors

In the case of a three-dimensional vector (X, Y, Z) with the respective interval lengths h_i, h_j' and h_k'', one has

$$H_e(X, Y, Z) = -k \sum_{i,j,k} p(x_i, y_j, z_k) \ln \frac{p(x_i, y_j, z_k)}{h_i h_j' h_k''} \quad (8.2.6)$$

$$= H_e(X) + H_e(YZ/X) \quad (8.2.7)$$

$$= H_e(X) + H_e(Y/X) + H_e(Z/X, Y) \quad (8.2.8)$$

with

$$H_e(Y/X) := \sum_i p(x_i) H_e(Y/x_i) \quad (8.2.9)$$

$$H_e(Z/X, Y) := \sum_{i,j} p(x_i, y_j) H_e(Z/x_i, y_j) . \quad (8.2.10)$$

As in the case of one or two variables, $H_e(X, Y, Z)$ expresses that the uncertainty in the triplet (X, Y, Z) is a combination of an uncertainty of a random nature generated by the probability distribution $p(x_i, y_j, z_k)$ on the one hand, and of an uncertainty of a geometrical nature contributed by the lattices themselves, that is to say the interval lengths $h_i h_j'$ and h_k''.

It is clear that we could have directly stated proposition 8.2.1 before the proposition 6.5.1, but we have chosen the present procedure for the sake of simplicity and clarity.

8.3 Total Entropy of a Discrete Quantized Stochastic Process

8.3.1 Preliminary Remarks

As mentioned previously, there is a difference of paramount importance between the amount of uncertainty involved in a qualitative random experiment (for instance one in which the possible outcome is either blue or red), and that in a discrete random variable. The essential difference is that the latter is defined on an ordered set while the former is not. As a result, the uncertainty of a random variable encompasses something more than the uncertainty contained by a qualitative random experiment, namely, it is the range of variation of the random variable. This remark allowed us to clarify the apparent discrepency between discrete entropy and continuous entropy, and to take for granted that, to some extent, the latter is a more complete measure of information than the former.

As a matter of fact, this controversial point of view contradicts the opinion that is most widely held by scientists. They often claim that the discrete entropy is a better measure of uncertainty while the continuous entropy has some drawbacks. For instance *Oswald* [8.4] claims that the fact that we increase the size of a letter in a message cannot modify the amount of information contained in this letter. This is partly correct and partly wrong. Indeed if we consider the letter with respect to its meaning in the alphabet only, then we may agree with this viewpoint; but if we first identify the letter as a drawing in the sense of pattern recognition, then it is not at all clear that this rationale is sufficient.

We now come back to stochastic processes, that is to say to stochastic dynamical systems. In the following, the term 'discrete process' refers to a process $X(t_i)$ whose states change at discrete instants $t_0, t_1, \ldots, t_i, \ldots, t_N$; and such a process is quantized for every t_i when $X(t_i)$ itself is a discrete random variable. As a result, the graph of a realization of $X(t)$ over the time range $[t_0, t_N]$ is a function with discrete steps.

This being the case, assume that

$$-\infty < m \leqslant X(t_i) \leqslant M < +\infty \qquad \text{and} \qquad t_0 \leqslant t_i \leqslant t_N \quad \text{for every } i \ .$$

From the geometrical or pattern recognition standpoint, we are entitled to assume that a measure of the amount of uncertainty in the portion of the *trajectory* over $[t_0, t_N]$ should explicitly depend upon the differences $(M - m)$ and $(t_N - t_0)$. This is readily understandable as far as the effect of $(M - m)$ is concerned, for the very reason that the smaller $(M - m)$, the smaller the corresponding uncertainty. Now, assume that we make the transformation $t' = f(t)$ where $f(t)$ denotes a continuous one-to-one mapping, and assume further that $t_0' = f(t_0)$ and $t_m' = f(t_m)$ are such that $t_0 < t_0' < t_m' < t_m$. From the geometrical standpoint once more, that is to say, on considering the graph of $X(t)$, it is quite right to assume that our uncertainty regarding the transformed trajectory on the range $[t_0', t_m']$ is smaller than our uncertainty about the initial trajectory defined on $[t_0, t_m]$. In the special theoretical case where both $(M - m)$ and $(t_m - t_0)$ are reduced to zero, there is no uncertainty at all.

All these remarks suggest the use of a randomization with respect to the intervals $(t_{i+1} - t_i)$ similar to the randomization with respect to $(x_{i+1} - x_i)$ which allowed us to derive the expression for the total entropy.

8.3.2 Axioms for the Total Uncertainty of a Discrete Trajectory

In analogy to the intervals J_i which we introduced to derive the total entropy, we define the time ranges T_i as follows:

$$T_1 := \left\{ t | t \in \left[t_1 - \frac{t_2 - t_1}{2}, \frac{t_2 + t_1}{2} \right] \right\}, \qquad \tau_1 := t_2 - t_1 \; ; \tag{8.3.1}$$

$$T_i := \left\{ t | t \in \left[\frac{t_i + t_{i-1}}{2}, \frac{t_i + t_{i+1}}{2} \right] \right\}, \qquad \tau_i := \tfrac{1}{2}(t_{i+1} - t_{i-1}) \; ;$$
$$i = 2, 3, \ldots, m - 1 \; ; \tag{8.3.2}$$

$$T_m := \left\{ t | t \in \frac{t_{n-1} + t_n}{2}, t_n + \frac{t_n - t_{n-1}}{2} \right\}, \qquad \tau_m := t_m - t_{m-1} \; . \tag{8.3.3}$$

Preliminary Axioms. We shall assume that the total uncertainty or the *total entropy* $H_{ee}(F)$, of the discrete quantized stochastic trajectory

$$F := \{ X(t) = X(t_i), t_i \leqslant t \leqslant t_{i+1}, i = 1, 2, \ldots, m \}$$

should satisfy the following axioms:

(A1) $H_{ee}(F)$ is a function $\Psi[H_e(X_1, X_2, \ldots, X_m); \tau_1, \tau_2, \ldots, \tau_m]$, $X_i := X(t_i)$, the value of which is not modified by any permutation on the set $\{(X_1, \tau_1), \ldots, (X_m, \tau_m)\}$.

(A2) $\Psi(\cdot)$ is continuous with respect to $H_e(X_1, X_2, \ldots, X_m)$ and $\tau_1, \tau_2, \ldots, \tau_m$.

(A3) $\Psi(\cdot)$ is an increasing function of τ_i for every i.

(A4) The following normalization condition is satisfied:

$$\Psi[H_e(X_1, X_2, \ldots, X_m); 1, 1, \ldots, 1] = H_e(X_1, X_2, \ldots, X_m) \; . \tag{8.3.4}$$

(A5) Let $\{(Y_1, \tau_1'), (Y_2, \tau_2'), \ldots, (Y_n, \tau_n')\}$ denote another discrete quantized trajectory. The following equality then holds:

$$\Psi\{H_e[(X_1, Y_1), \ldots, (X_i, Y_j), \ldots, (X_m, Y_n)]; \tau_1 \tau_1', \ldots, \tau_i \tau_j', \ldots, \tau_m \tau_n'\}$$
$$= \Psi[H_e(X_1, \ldots, X_m); \tau_1, \ldots, \tau_m] + \Psi(H_e(Y_1, \ldots, Y_n); \tau_1', \ldots, \tau_n'] \; . \tag{8.3.5}$$

Comments. Axiom (A1) expresses $H_{ee}(F)$ explicitly in terms of $H_e(X)$, and in this way, we can think of the former as a generalization of the latter. In addition, one assumes that a permutation on the set $\{X_i, \tau_i\}$ does not affect the value of $H_{ee}(F)$, and it is well known that this type of assumption is quite relevant in the definition of the measure of uncertainty. In the same way, the continuity expressed by (A2) is quite in order.

Axiom (A3) reflects the remark in Sect. 8.3.1, regarding the effect of the time range $(t_m - t_0)$ on the value of the uncertainty involved in the trajectory. The normalizing condition (A4) merely defines the way in which H_e is extended to yield H_{ee}. Finally, the multiplicative law (8.3.5) is well known in information theory.

8.3.3 Expression for the Total Entropy of the Trajectory

We then have the following result

Proposition 8.3.1. A measure $H_{ee}(F)$ of the total uncertainty which satisfies the axioms (A1)–(A5) of Sect. 8.3.2 is given by the expression

$$H_{ee}(F) = -k \sum_{i_1 \ldots i_m} p(x_1^{i_1}, x_2^{i_2}, \ldots, x_m^{i_m}) \ln \frac{p(x_1^{i_1}, x_2^{i_2}, \ldots, x_m^{i_m})}{(\prod h_j^{i_j})^{K_1/k}(\prod \tau_i)^{K_2/k}}$$

$$= H_e(X_1, X_2, \ldots, X_m) + K_2 \ln(\tau_1 \tau_2 \cdots \tau_m) \qquad (8.3.6)$$

where k, K_1 and K_2 are positive constants associated with the measurement units of the uncertainties generated by $p(\cdot)$, $\{h_i^{ij}\}$ and $\{\tau_i\}$ respectively.

Notes on the Proof. The proof of this result can be derived exactly like the proof of proposition 6.5.1.

Briefly, one seeks a separable solution in the form

$$H_{ee}(F) = f[H_e(X_1, X_2, \ldots, X_m)] + g(\tau_1, \tau_2, \ldots, \tau_m) . \qquad (8.3.7)$$

According to the condition (8.3.4), one then has

$$f(H_e) = H_e(X_1, X_2, \ldots, X_m) - g(1, 1, \ldots, 1) .$$

Next, by virtue of Axiom (A1), it is wise to determine $g(\cdot)$ in the form

$$g(\tau_1, \tau_2, \ldots, \tau_m) = \sum_{i=1}^{m} g_i(\tau_i) ,$$

and then, on using (8.3.5), one obtains the relation

$$g_{ij}(\tau_i \tau_j') = g_i(\tau_i) + g_j(\tau_j') ,$$

and therefore the solution

$$g_i(\tau) = K \ln \tau . \qquad (8.3.8)$$

Axiom (A3) implies that K is positive.

On the Uniqueness of the Solution. Here again, we don't need to check the uniqueness of the expression derived. Indeed, we presented a list of desiderata for a measure of uncertainty, we obtained a solution, and we are now quite entitled to use it. There might be another solution, but we don't need to worry about it, since from the theoretical standpoint, the above solution is quite satisfactory. We also point out that the rationale of this approach is completely rigorous from the viewpoint of the methodology.

A Useful Special Case. When $k = K_1 = K_2$ we have

$$H_{ee}(F) = H_e(X, X, \ldots, X) + k \ln(\tau_1 \tau_2 \cdots \tau_m) \tag{8.3.9}$$

where $H_e(\cdot)$ is defined by (8.2.5)

8.3.4 Some Properties of the Total Entropy of the Trajectory

i) While the discrete Shannon entropy is always positive (or zero for a deterministic event), this is not so for $H_{ee}(F)$ which may be positive or negative.

ii) Assume that the "trajectory" is merely composed of X_1 and X_2. It is then a simple matter to show that one has the equation

$$H_{ee}(X_1, X_2) = H_{ee}(X_1) + H_{ee}(X_2/X_1) \tag{8.3.10}$$

where the conditional total entropy $H_{ee}(X_2/X_1)$ is defined by the expression

$$H_{ee}(X_2/X_1) := \sum_j p(x_1^j) H(X_2/x_1^j) .$$

iii) The following inequality holds:

$$H_{ee}(X_2/X_1) \leqslant H_{ee}(X_2) \tag{8.3.11}$$

and the corresponding proof is straightforward.

iv) Assume that the discrete trajectory is Markovian; one then has

$$H_{ee}(F) = H_{ee}(X_1) + \sum_{i=1} H_{ee}(X_i/X_{i-1}) . \tag{8.3.12}$$

v) In the special case where all the states X_i are mutually independent or, which amounts to the same, where the process is a discrete white noise, one has

$$H_{ee}(F) = \sum_{i=1}^{m} H_{ee}(X_i) \tag{8.3.13}$$

$$= -\sum_{i,j} p(x_i^j) \ln \frac{p(x_i^j)}{h_i^j \tau_i} \tag{8.3.14}$$

$$= \sum_{i=1}^{m} H_e(X_i) + \sum_{i=1}^{m} \ln \tau_i . \tag{8.3.15}$$

8.3.5 A Generalization

Assume that all the states X_i are mutually independent, and that the amount of random uncertainty involved in x_i^j is *defined* as being $-\ln f[p(x_i^j)]$, [instead of $-\ln p(x_i^j)$], where $f: \mathbb{R} \to \mathbb{R}^+$ denotes a given continuous function. One then has a straightforward generalization of (8.3.15) in the form

$$H_{ee}(F) := -\sum_{i,j} p(x_i^j) \ln \frac{f[p(x_i^j)]}{h_i^j \tau_i} .$$
(8.3.16)

In this model, we merely assume that the elementary uncertainty as perceived by the observer is

$$-\ln p_r(x_i^j) := -\ln f[p(x_i^j)]$$

and we define $H_{ee}(F)$ by the expression

$$H_{ee}(F) := -\sum_{i,j} p(x^j) \ln p_r(x_i^j) + \sum_{i,j} \ln h_i^j \tau_i .$$

This approach is quite consistent with the relative point of view which we have adopted to define and measure uncertainty and information.

8.4 Total Renyi Entropy of Discrete Quantized Stochastic Processes

It may be interesting to examine ways of generalizing the so-called Renyi entropy H_c, sometimes referred to as *entropy of order c*, to measure the uncertainty involved in a stochastic process. Indeed, in technical communication problems (in the engineering sense of this term) it does not seem that this entropy is of any use, but we have shown that the parameter c itself looks like a weighting coefficient defining the efficiency of the observation, so that this measure of uncertainty could be of help when dealing with the subjectivity of the observer.

8.4.1 Total Renyi Entropy of a Vector

Consider the random vector $X^t := (X_1, X_2, \ldots, X_m)$ of Sect. 8.2.1, and define the mean interval length h_i between x_i^j and x_i^{j+1}, or likewise the average value of the differences $x_i^{j+1} - x_i^j$, for every $i = 1, 2, \ldots, m$ [see (6.4.2) and (6.4.3)]. We then have the following result.

Proposition 8.4.1. The direct generalization of proposition 6.8.1 provides the total Renyi entropy $H_s^e(X)$ of the discrete random vector X in the form

$$H_s^e(X) = \frac{k}{1-c} \ln \left[\sum_{i_1, \ldots, i_m} \frac{p^s(x_1^{i_1}, x_2^{i_2}, \ldots, x_m^{i_m})}{(h_1 h_2 \ldots h_m)^{(K/k)(c-1)}} \right]$$
(8.4.1)

$$= H_s^e(X) + K \sum_{i_1, \ldots, i_m} p(x_1^{i_1}, x_2^{i_2}, \ldots, x_m^{i_m}) \ln(h_1 h_2 \ldots h_m)$$
(8.4.2)

where k is the constant appearing in the definition of $H_c(X)$, and K is the constant associated with the measurement unit of the uncertainty generated by the parameters $h_1, h_2, \ldots, h_m$.

In the special case where $K = k = 1$, one has

$$H_c^e(X) = \frac{1}{1-c} \ln \left\{ \sum_{i_1,\ldots,i_m} \left[\frac{p(x_1^{i_1}, x_2^{i_2}, \ldots, x_m^{i_m})}{h_1 h_2 \ldots h_m} \right]^c h_1 h_2 \ldots h_m \right\} . \tag{8.4.3}$$

8.4.2 Derivation of the Total Renyi Entropy

In order to obtain the counterpart $H_c^{ee}(F)$ of $H_{ee}(F)$, we shall assume that the former should have the following properties.

Preliminary Axioms

(B1) $H_c^{ee}(F)$ is a function $\chi[H_c^e(X_1, X_2, \ldots, X_m); \tau_1, \tau_2, \ldots, \tau_m]$, the value of which is not modified by any permutation on the set $\{(X_1, \tau_1), (X_2, \tau_2), \ldots, (X_m, \tau_m)\}$.
(B2) $\chi(H_c^e; \tau_1, \tau_2, \ldots, \tau_m)$ is continuous with respect to H_c^e and $\tau_1, \tau_2, \ldots, \tau_m$.
(B3) $\chi(H_c^e; \tau_1, \tau_2, \ldots, \tau_m)$ is an increasing function of τ_i for every i.
(B4) The following normalization condition is satified:

$$\chi(H_c^e; 1, 1, \ldots, 1) = H_c^e .$$

(B5) Let $\{(Y_1, Y_2, \ldots, Y_n); \tau_1', \tau_2', \ldots, \tau_m'\}$ denote another discrete quantized trajectory; then the following equality holds:

$$\chi\{H_c^e[X_1, Y_1), \ldots, (X_i, Y_j), \ldots, (X_m, Y_n)]; \tau_1\tau_1', \ldots, \tau_i\tau_j', \ldots, \tau_m\tau_n'\}$$

$$= \chi[H_c^e(X_1, X_2, \ldots, X_m); \tau_1, \ldots, \tau_m]$$

$$+ \chi[H_c^e(Y_1, Y_2, \ldots, Y_n); \tau_1', \ldots, \tau_n'] . \tag{8.4.4}$$

We can then make the following statement.

Proposition 8.4.2. A measure $H_c^{ee}(F)$ of the total uncertainty, which satisfies the axioms (B1)–(B5) above is given by the expression

$$H_c^{ee}(F) = \frac{1}{1-c} \ln \left[\sum_{i_1,\ldots,i_m} \frac{p^c(x_1^{i_1}, x_2^{i_2}, \ldots, x_m^{i_m})}{(h_1 h_2 \ldots h_m)^{(K_1/k)(c-1)}(\tau_1\tau_2 \ldots \tau_m)^{(K_2/k)(c-1)}} \right] \tag{8.4.5}$$

$$= H_c^e(X_1, X_2, \ldots, X_m) + \sum_{i=1}^{m} \ln \tau_i \tag{8.4.6}$$

where the positive constant k defines $H(X)$; the constants k, K_1, with $K_1 > 0$, define $H_c^e(X)$, and K_2, with $K_2 > 0$, is associated with the measurement unit of the uncertainty generated by $\tau_1, \tau_2, \ldots, \tau_m$. $\qquad\square$

The proof is left to the reader, and can be driven exactly like the proof of proposition 6.8.1 where we obtained $H_c^e(F)$.

In the special case where $k = K_1 = K_2 = 1$, (8.4.5) takes on the simpler form

$$H_c^{ee}(F) = \frac{1}{1-c} \ln \left\{ \sum_{i_1,\ldots,i_m} \left[\frac{p(x_1^{i_1}, x_2^{i_2}, \ldots, x_m^{i_m})}{\left(\prod_i h_i\right)\left(\prod_i \tau_i\right)} \right]^c \left(\prod_i h_i\right)\left(\prod_i \tau_i\right) \right\} . \tag{8.4.7}$$

A direct consequence of this result is as follows

Corollary 8.4.1. Assume that $k = K_1 = K_2 = 1$, and that the states $X(t_i)$, $i = 1, 2,$ ..., m, are mutually independent; one then has

$$H_c^{ee}(F) = \frac{1}{1-c} \sum_{i=1}^{m} \ln \left\{ \sum_j \left[\frac{p(x_i^j)}{h_i \tau_i} \right]^c h_i \tau_i \right\} \tag{8.4.8}$$

$$= \sum_{i=1}^{m} H_c^e(X_i) + \ln \tau_1 \tau_2 \ldots \tau_m \tag{8.4.9}$$

$$= \sum_{i=1}^{m} H_c^{ee}(X_i) , \tag{8.4.10}$$

where $H_c^{ee}(X_i)$ is defined by the expression

$$H_c^{ee}(X_i) := \frac{1}{1-c} \ln \sum_j \left[\frac{p(x_i^j)}{h_i \tau_i} \right]^c h_i \tau_i . \tag{8.4.11}$$

This result of course is not particularly surprising. Indeed, we straightforwardly applied the definition of $H_c^{ee}(F)$ to derive (8.4.8), and (8.4.10) merely reflects the fact that we could have use the relation

$$H_c^{ee}(X, Y) = H_c^{ee}(X) + H_c^{ee}(Y) ,$$

which holds when X and Y are independent, in order to define $H_c^e(F)$ in this case.

8.5 Entropy of Order c Revisited

8.5.1 Preliminary Remarks

Assume that we are trying to define a measure of uncertainty which should have some given prior properties and which should apply to scalar-valued variables as well as to vector variables. Basically, we have two ways of doing this. On the one hand, one may first define this uncertainty for $X \in \mathbb{R}$, and then extend this definition to the vector $(X, Y) \in \mathbb{R}^2$ by using the specific properties of the measure so obtained. For instance, in the case of the Shannon entropy, one may assume that $H(X)$ and $H(Y/X)$ are defined and then consider that $H(X, Y)$ is given by the equation

$$H(X, Y) := H(X) + H(Y/X) . \tag{8.5.1}$$

Alternatively, one may first define the uncertainty of a vector and then consider a scalar-valued variable as a one-dimensional vector. It is this latter approach which is usually followed. Thus for instance, (8.5.1) does not define $H(X, Y)$ but rather $H(Y/X)$.

For the mostpart, it is exactly this second approach that we adopt here. The derivation of the total Renyi entropy in Sect. 6.8 merely provided us with a rationale to guess our result. We then ignored Chap. 6, and stated a new set of axioms from which we obtained $H_c^{ee}(F)$.

In the present section, we shall examine the type of results that can be derived by generalizing the physical definition of $H_c^e(X)$. There are two reasons for doing this. The first is technical, and stems from the fact that (8.4.10) is a bit troublesome when we try to generalize it in order to measure the uncertainty involved in a continuous trajectory. The second reason is that we are quite entitled to make the generalization since a curve may involve some features which are not necessarily transparent in a vector.

8.5.2 A New Definition of Total Entropy of Order c

The above remarks lead us to the following definition.

Definition 8.5.1. Let $X(t_i)$, $i = 1, 2, \ldots, m$, denote a discrete quantized stochastic process whose states $X(t_i)$ are mutually independent, and let $p(x_i^j)$, $j = 1, 2, \ldots, n_i$ denote the probability distribution of $X(t_i)$. In addition, consider the sequences of intervals $\{h_i^j\}$ and $\{\tau_i\}$ which appear in the expression (8.3.6) for $H_{ee}(F)$. Then the *total entropy of order c of the trajectory F* is defined as

$$H_c^{em}(F) := \frac{1}{1-c} \ln \sum_{i,j} \left[\frac{p(x_i^j)}{h_i^j \tau_i} \right]^c h_i^j \tau_i \; . \tag{8.5.2}$$

Comments. (i) Consider a discrete random vector (X, Y) which takes the values (x_i, y_j) with the probability $p(x_i, y_j)$ and which is defined with the interval lengths h_i and h_j'; one then has

$$H_c^e(X, Y) = \frac{1}{1-c} \ln \sum_{i,j}^m \left[\frac{p(x_i, y_j)}{h_i h_j'} \right]^c h_i h_j' \; . \tag{8.5.3}$$

Formally, (8.5.2) and (8.5.3) are exactly the same, and this analogy pictures how the effect of time is randomized to yield $H_c^{em}(F)$.

ii) Assume that $\tau_i = \tau$ and $h_i^j = h_i$ for every i. Equation (8.5.2) then yields

$$H_c^{em}(F) := \frac{1}{1-c} \ln \sum_i \sum_j \left[\frac{p(x_i^j)}{h\tau} \right]^c h + \ln \tau$$

$$= \frac{1}{1-c} \ln \sum_i \exp\{(1-c)H_e(X_i)\} + \frac{1}{1-c} \ln \tau^{(1-c)}$$

$$= \frac{1}{1-c} \ln \sum_i [\tau \exp(H_e(X_i))]^{1-c} \; . \tag{8.5.4}$$

8.6 Entropy of Continuous White Stochastic Trajectories

8.6.1 Notation and Remarks

By the term "white trajectory", we mean the realization of a stochastic process $X(t) \in \mathbb{R}$ for which $X(t_2)$ is independent of $X(t_1)$ for any t_1 satisfying the condition

$t_1 < t_2$. The term "continuous" merely reflects the fact that the process evolves at each time; it does not refer to stochastic continuity in the mathematical sense of this word.

In Chap. 6, we obtained the Shannon entropy of a continuous random variable as the limiting form of the total entropy of a discrete variable. This was quite simple, because it is very easy to construct a discrete probability distribution $\{\tilde{p}_j\}$ equivalent to the probability density $p(x)$, namely

$$\tilde{p}_i := \int_{\xi_j}^{\xi_{j+1}} p(x)\,dx$$

$$= h_j p(x_j) \; , \tag{8.6.1}$$

where $\{\xi_j\}$ denotes a lattice defined by the spans $h_j := \xi_{j+1} - \xi_j$. We could obviously try the same technique with the continuous time-dependent density $p(x,t)$, by using the total entropy $H_{ee}(F)$. Here, however, it is not so easy to use a discretization scheme with respect to time. More explicitly, if we define $\tilde{p}_{ij}$ by the expression

$$\tilde{p}_{ij} := \int_{\eta_i}^{\eta_{i+1}} \int_{\xi_j}^{\xi_{j+1}} p(x,t)\,dx\,dt \; , \tag{8.6.2}$$

where $\{\eta_i\}$, $\tau_i := \eta_{i+1} - \eta_i$, is the lattice of discretization with respect to time, then one has $\sum_i \tilde{p}_{ij} \neq 1$. This troublesome feature (which is due to the fact that t is not a random variable) induces us to look for new approaches in order to tackle this question.

8.6.2 A List of Desiderata for the Entropy of a White Trajectory

In this section, we summarize the main properties that should be satisfied by a measure of the uncertainty of a stochastic trajectory.

i) Let F denote the trajectory generated by the process $X(t)$ from the initial time 0 to the final time T. The uncertainty $H(F;0,T)$ involved in F should depend continuously on the probability density $p(x,t)$ and the end point T.

ii) More explicitly, $H(F;0,T)$ is the combination of an uncertainty of random nature due to $p(x,\cdot)$ and an uncertainty generated by the time interval T.

iii) For a small $T = \tau$, the entropy $H(F;\tau)$ should reduce to the total entropy $H_{ee}(X;0)$,

$$H(F;0,\tau) = H_{ee}(X;0)$$

$$= H_e(X;0) + K \ln \tau \; , \tag{8.6.3}$$

where $H_e(X;0)$ denotes the total entropy of $X(0)$, and where K is the positive constant associated with the measurement unit of the uncertainty in time.

8.6.3 Towards a Mathematical Expression of the Trajectory Entropy

We now try to guess the expression for $H(F;0,T)$ by using various arguments of a qualitative nature.

First Approach. Assume that $p(x, t) = p(x)$; one may then define

$$H(F; 0, T) := H(X) + K \ln T \qquad (8.6.4)$$

which we re-write in the form

$$H(F; 0, T) = \frac{1}{T} \int_0^T H(X)\,dt + K \ln T \ . \qquad (8.6.5)$$

Thus, in view of (8.6.5), when $p(x, t)$ depends explicitly upon time t, we are led to define

$$H(F; 0, T) := \frac{1}{T} \int_0^T H(X; t)\,dt + K \ln T \ , \qquad (8.6.6)$$

with

$$H(X; t) := -\int_{\mathbb{R}} p(x, t) \ln p(x, t)\,dx \ . \qquad (8.6.7)$$

Second Approach. Let us first bear in mind that for a pair of discrete random variables (X, Y), the total entropy $H_e(X, Y)$ is

$$H_e(X, Y) = -\sum_{i,j}^m p(x_i, y_j) \ln \frac{p(x_i, y_j)}{h_i h_j'}$$

the limit of which is the continuous entropy

$$H(X, Y) = -\int_{\mathbb{R}^2} p(x, y) \ln p(x, y)\,dx\,dy \qquad (8.6.8)$$

as $h_i \downarrow 0$ and $h_j' \downarrow 0$ for every i and j.

The idea then is to apply (8.6.8) to the pair (X, t). To this end, we shall randomize t by introducing the probability density

$$p_T(x, t) := p(x, t)/T \qquad (8.6.9)$$

so that

$$\int_0^T \int_{\mathbb{R}} p_T(x, t)\,dx\,dt = 1 \ . \qquad (8.6.10)$$

One can then meaningfully define

$$H(F; 0, T) := -\int_0^T \int_{\mathbb{R}} p_T(x, t) \ln p_T(x, t)\,dx\,dt \qquad (8.6.11)$$

which is exactly (8.6.6) in which one has set $K = 1$.

Third Approach. Consider $H(X, Y)$ as expressed by (8.6.8). It defines the amount of uncertainty involved in X and Y when they run over $\mathbb{R}^2$; we may emphasize this by writing $H(X \in \mathbb{R}, Y \in \mathbb{R})$. If we now consider the uncertainty involved in (X, Y) when $X \in \mathbb{R}$ and $Y \in [a, b]$, we obtain the expression

$$H(X \in \mathbb{R}, Y \in [a, b]) = \frac{-\int_a^b \int_{\mathbb{R}} p(x, y) \ln p(x, y)\, dx\, dy}{\int_a^b \int_{\mathbb{R}} p(x, y)\, dx\, dy} \tag{8.6.12}$$

in which the coefficient of $-\ln p(x, y)$ is normalized to unity.

By formally applying the same equation to the pair $(X, t \in [0, T])$ one has

$$H(X \in \mathbb{R}, t \in [0, T]) := -\frac{1}{T} \int_0^T \int_{\mathbb{R}} p(x, t) \ln p(x, t)\, dx\, dt\ , \tag{8.6.13}$$

and it is then sufficient to define

$$H(F; 0, T) := H(X \in \mathbb{R}, t \in [0, T]) + K \ln T \tag{8.6.14}$$

to once more obtain Eq. (8.6.5).

Fourth Approach. We apply the discretization procedure by using the lattices $\{\xi_j\}$ and $\{\eta_i\}$ (Sect. 8.6.1) and we assume that the resulting local uncertainty, that is to say the local uncertainty at (x_j, t_i), is measured by $-\ln \tilde{p}_{ij}$, where $\tilde{p}_{ij}$ is defined by (8.6.2).

This being so, one has

$$\sum_{i,j} \frac{\tilde{p}_{ij}}{T} = 1\ ,$$

and on noticing that one can write $p_{ij} = \tau_i h_j p(x_j, t_i)$, the corresponding total temporal entropy is

$$H_{ee} = -\frac{1}{T} \sum_{i,j} h_j \tau_i p(x_j, t_i) \ln \frac{h_j \tau_i p(x_j, t_i)}{h_j \tau_i}\ , \tag{8.6.15}$$

the limiting form of which is $H(X \in \mathbb{R}, t \in [0, T])$ as expressed by (8.6.13). We then apply (8.6.14) to obtain $H(F; 0, T)$.

8.6.4 Entropy of Continuous White Trajectories

From the aforegoing we are led to suggest the following definition.

Definition 8.6.1. Let $X(t) \in \mathbb{R}$ denote a continuous white trajectory, and let $p(x, t)$ denote its probability density. The entropy $H(F; 0, T)$ of the corresponding trajectory F over the time range $[0, T]$ is defined by the expression

$$H(F; 0, T) := -\frac{1}{T} \int_0^T \int_{\mathbb{R}} p(x, t) \ln p(x, t)\, dx\, dt + K \ln T \tag{8.6.16}$$

where the positive constant K is associated with the measurement unit of the uncertainty generated by time. $\square$

8.7 Entropy of Form and Observation Modes

8.7.1 Relative Uncertainty via Observation Modes

One may consider information either from an absolute viewpoint or, in contrast, in a relative framework. For instance, for a communications engineer, a digit is a digit and nothing more. Its information potential is $\ln 2$, and the entire problem is to convey this information with the best possible efficacy. In contrast, in cybernetics, we cannot forget that there is a human observer R who is receiving this information bit, and that various interactions between R and the observable may mean that the information potential of the digit is no longer $\ln 2$ but something like $(a \ln 2 + b)$ where a and b are two parameters which characterize, for instance, the subjectivity of the human receiver.

This subjectivity is itself the result of two different factors: first, an internal built-in model that the observer has previously stored in his active memory; and second, the type of observation used by the observer to analyze the observable.

As a matter of fact, the same problem occurs when one tries to define the entropy of a continuous mapping considered as a form. Irrespective of any concern related to subjectivity, here too we have to take account of the definition of the mode of observation. *Clearly, the entropy of a form depends upon how the latter is defined by the observer.*

8.7.2 Classification of Observation Modes

i) *Vertical White Observation.* To give a concrete example, consider a scalar-valued stochastic process in which R observes each point $(X; t)$ one at a time and as if it were alone, i.e. independently of the other points. R thereby measures the entropy $H(X; t)$ at the instant t. The entropy of the whole trajectory over the time range $(0, T)$ is the aggregate, in a sense that will not be elaborated here, of these entropies $H(X; t)$.

From a geometrical perspective, one can describe this as the intersection of the trajectory F of the point $(t, x(t))$ by a set of straight lines parallel to the X-axis. We then consider the respective entropies of the points so obtained.

For convenience, we shall refer to this process as *X-white observation* or *white observation.*

ii) *Horizontal White Observation.* Here we assume that the observer R intersects the trajectory by straight lines parallel to the t-axis. For a given $x(t) = x$, we then obtain a set E_x of points whose entropy is $H(E_x; x)$, and the resulting entropy of the entire trajectory F is the aggregate of these individual entropies. This process will sometimes be referred to as *t-white observation.*

Note that the difference between X-white observation and t-white observation is similar to the difference between a Riemann integral and a Lebesgues integral.

iii) *Local Markovian Observation.* Let τ denote an infinitely small increment of time, and assume that the observer R considers the trajectory F at the instants 0, τ, 2τ, 3τ, ... , $n\tau$, ... only. In this observation process, the observer defines the trajectory in the form of the sequence $(x(0), x(\tau))$, $(x(\tau), x(2\tau))$, $(x(2\tau), x(3\tau))$, ... ; and he observes each pair $(x(i\tau), x((i + 1)\tau))$ irrespective of the other ones, and as if it were alone. He thus measures the uncertainty $H(x(t), x(t + \tau))$, and the trajectory entropy so obtained is the aggregate of these individual entropies as τ tends to zero.

Note that the observation may be Markovian even when the process is not so.

Geometrically, this is equivalent to intersecting the trajectory by two straight lines parallel to the X-axis. We then examine the resulting portion of trajectory.

iv) *Global Markovian Observation.* Consider again the discretizing scheme of the local Markovian observation, but assume that each point is observed relative to the preceding one. Formally, we then have the finite conditional sequence $x(0)$, $x(\tau)/x(0)$, $x(2\tau)/x(\tau)$, $x(3\tau)/x(2\tau)$, ... ; the observer measures the conditional entropies $H[x(t + \tau)/x(t)]$, and the trajectory entropy is the aggregate of these individual conditional entropies.

The geometrical meaning of this observation process is as follows: We first determine the position of $x(0)$ [since we are observing the trajectory over the time range $(0, T)$], and then we follow the trajectory and examine its deviation from its tangent straight lines.

v) *Radial Observation.* Here we consider the intersection of the trajectory by radial straight lines, i.e., straight lines which pass through the coordinate origin. Exactly as above, we may have white radial observation, Markovian radial observation and global Markovian radial observation. In such a case, polar coordinates are useful in the corresponding mathematical modelling.

vi) *Observation via Selection of Salient Features.* In this mode, the pattern is characterized by a few specific features, for instance angles and radii of curvature, so that it is sufficient to apply the Shannon theory to the resulting finite vector.

The problem of defining the entropy of a stochastic process under white observation is relatively simple. Thus we shall concentrate our attention more especially on Markovian observations, for which we shall be able to expand the theory and obtain results in the form of explicit formulas.

8.7.3 Trajectory Entropy via White Observation

It is obvious that the entropy corresponding to white observation, $H_w(F; 0, T)$, is given by (8.6.16) in which $p(x, t)$ is now the state probability density of the process.

8.8 Trajectory Entropies of Stochastic Processes

8.8.1 Trajectory Shannon Entropy

In order to have a general model for the trajectory entropy of a stochastic process, we shall extend the definition of the entropy of a continuous white trajectory, (8.6.16), as follows.

Definition 8.8.1. Let $(X; t)$ denote a scalar-valued stochastic process with the state probability density $p(x, t)$. Assume that the corresponding trajectory is observed by an observer R. Then from the viewpoint of information theory, this observation is characterized by a weighting function $\mu(t)$ in such a manner that the uncertainty involved in the trajectory F over the time range $(0, T)$ is measured by the expression

$$H(F; 0, T) := -\frac{1}{T} \int_0^T \int_{\mathbb{R}} \mu(t) p(x, t) \ln p(x, t) \, dx \, dt + K \ln T \qquad (8.8.1)$$

where K is a constant associated with the measurement unit of the uncertainty generated by time over the range $(0, T)$.

Important Remark. As defined, $H(F; 0, T)$ is an average uncertainty, but in some applications it may be of interest to use the quantity $TH(F; 0, T)$ which could then be thought of as a total uncertainty.

The rationale for this definition is as follows. In analogy with the well known equation

$$H(X, Y) = H(X) + H(Y/X)$$

$$= H(X) + \mu H(Y) , \qquad 0 < \mu \leqslant 1 ,$$

one assumes that for small positive τ, one may write

$$H[(F; 0, T), x(t + \tau)] = H(F; 0, T) + \mu(t, \tau) H(x(t + \tau)) , \qquad (8.8.2)$$

with the additional condition

$$\mu(t) = \lim \mu(t, \tau) \quad \text{as} \quad \tau \downarrow 0 . \qquad (8.8.3)$$

8.8.2 Renyi Entropy of a Stochastic Trajectory

i) For a white process, the Renyi entropy of the trajectory is defined as

$$H^c(F; 0, T) = \frac{1}{1 - c} \ln \left[\frac{1}{T} \int_0^T \int_{\mathbb{R}} p^c(x, t) \, dx \, dt \right] + K \ln T \qquad (8.8.4)$$

with $c \in \mathbb{R}, c \neq 1$.

Here again, the definition is quite soundly supported by our randomization technique with respect to time.

ii) When the process is not white, we state as a conjecture that one could define the Renyi entropy in the form

$$H^c(F; 0, T) := \frac{1}{1 - c} \ln \left(\frac{1}{T} \int_0^T \int_{\mathbb{R}} \mu(t, c) p^c(x, t) \, dx \, dt \right) + K \cdot \int_0^T \mu(t, c) \, dt \qquad (8.8.5)$$

with

$$\lim \mu(t, c) = \mu(t) \quad \text{as} \quad c \to 0 \ . \tag{8.8.6}$$

8.8.3 A Few Comments

i) The entropy (8.8.1) as defined appears to be the combination of two types of uncertainty emanating from different sources: an uncertainty of random nature due to the probability density $p(x, t)$, and an uncertainty due to the interval range $(0, T)$, which is a direct consequence of the randomization with respect to time. From a practical viewpoint, e.g. in the engineering framework, one may discard the $\ln T$ term in the applications, but from a physical point of view, this term is not meaningless, and some scientists are asking whether time might not generate entropy.

ii) It is apparent that (8.8.3) could give rise to considerable theoretical difficulties, and thus, for the moment, we consider it only formally. In particular it can be thought of as a framework in which one can investigate possible refinements of this definition of $\mu(t)$.

iii) It is apparent that $\mu(t)$ should depend upon the process $(X; t)$. Namely, given $x(t)$ and $y(t)$, one would expect to have $\mu_x(t) \neq \mu_y(t)$, and it is likely that this property will not be of help in deriving the expression for the corresponding transinformation. Nevertheless, we are entitled to suppose that in a first simplified but general model, $\mu(t)$ should be defined by the class of the relevant stochastic processes rather than by the processes themselves, so that $\mu(t)$ should be the same even when $x(t) \neq y(t)$, provided x and y are in the same class.

8.9 Trajectory Entropy of a Stochastic Process Under Local Markovian Observation

8.9.1 Markovian Processes

We consider the scalar-valued stochastic process defined by Itô's stochastic differential equation

$$\dot{x}(t) = a(x, t) + b(x, t)w(t) \ , \qquad x \in \mathbb{R} \tag{8.9.1}$$

where $a(x, t)$ and $b(x, t)$ satisfy the required mathematical conditions for the existence of $x(t)$, and where $w(t)$ is a white Gaussian noise with zero mean and unit variance. We state the following:

Proposition 8.9.1. Assume that the Markovian process defined by (8.9.1) is observed via a local Markovian observation. The time-randomized uncertainty $H(F; 0, T)$ involved in the trajectory F over the time range $(0, T)$ is then defined by the expression

$$H_1(F; 0, T) = -\frac{1}{T} \int_0^T \int_{\mathbb{R}} p(x, t) \ln \frac{p(x, t)}{[2\pi e b^2(x, t)]^{1/2}} \, dx \, dt + \ln T \tag{8.9.2}$$

where $p(x, t)$ is the solution of the Fokker-Plank-Kolmogorov equation

$$p_t(x, t) = -(ap)_x + \frac{1}{2}(b^2 p)_{xx} \tag{8.9.3}$$

in which the subscript denotes the partial derivative.   □

Proof. (i) Let τ denote a small positive increment of time. According to (8.8.1), one has

$$H_1(F; t, t + \tau) \cong -\mu(t) \int_{\mathbb{R}} p(x, t) \, dx + K \ln \tau \tag{8.9.4}$$

for any t in the range $0 < t < T$. We then have to determine the explicit form of $\mu(t)$ and K.

ii) This being so, for a small τ one has the identification

$$H_1(F; t, t + \tau) = H[x(t), x(t + \tau)]$$

$$= H[x(t)] + H[x(t + \tau)/x(t)] \tag{8.9.5}$$

which merely means that the "segment" of trajectory over $(t, t + \tau)$ is completely defined by the points $(t, x(t))$ and $(t + \tau, x(t + \tau))$.

iii) Next we have

$$x(t + \tau) = x(t) + a(x, t)\tau + b(x, t)w(t)\tau + o(\tau^2) \ ,$$

and therefore

$$H[x(t + \tau)/x(t)] = \int_{\mathbb{R}} p(x, t) H[b(x, t)w(t)\tau/x(t)] \, dx + o(\tau^2)$$

$$= H(w) + \int_{\mathbb{R}} p(x, t) \ln |\tau b(x, t)| \, dx + o(\tau^2)$$

$$= \ln \sqrt{2\pi e} + \int_{\mathbb{R}} p(x, t) \ln |\tau b(x, t)| \, dx + o(\tau^2)$$

$$= \int_{\mathbb{R}} p(x, t) \ln [|b(x, t)| \sqrt{2\pi e}] \, dx + \ln \tau + o(\tau^2) \ . \tag{8.9.6}$$

In addition, we bear in mind that

$$H[x(t)] = -\int_{\mathbb{R}} p(x, t) \ln p(x, t) \, dx \ . \tag{8.9.7}$$

iv) We now substitute (8.8.4), (8.9.6) and (8.9.7) into (8.9.5) to obtain the identification

$$-\mu(t)H[x(t)] + K\ln\tau \equiv H[x(t)] + \int_{\mathbb{R}} p(x,t)\ln[|b(x,t)|\sqrt{2\pi e}]\,dx$$

$$+\ln\tau + o(\tau^2)\;. \tag{8.9.8}$$

We then derive the equality $K = 1$, therefore Eq. (8.9.2).

8.9.2 Non-Markovian Processes

Assume now that $(X;t)$ is not a Markovian process, whereas the observation is Markovian. From a practical standpoint, this means that $(X;t)$ will be observed in the form $(Y;t)$ where $(Y;t)$ is a Markovian process which satisfies the *observation equation*

$$\dot{y}(t) = a'(y,t) + b'(y,t)w(t) \tag{8.9.9}$$

and the problem is then to determine the explicit values of $a'(y,t)$ and $b'(y,t)$.

A possible approach to this question is as follows.

i) It is well known that the state moments $m_k(t)$, $k = 1, 2, 3\ldots$, of the process $(X;t)$ are such that

$$\dot{m}_1(t) = \int_{\mathbb{R}} a(x,t)p(x,t)\,dx \tag{8.9.10}$$

$$\dot{m}_k(t) = \int_{\mathbb{R}} \left[kx^{k-1}a(x,t) + \frac{1}{2}k(k-1)x^{k-2}b^2(x,t) \right] p(x,t)\,dx \;,\; k \geqslant 2\;. \tag{8.9.11}$$

We shall make the working assumption that the process $(X;t)$ is completely well defined so that $p(x,t)$ can be considered as given.

ii) This being the case, it is well known that a system described by Itô's stochastic differential equation is completely determined by its moments. This suggests that one may estimate $a(x,t)$ and $b(x,t)$ using a Galerkin procedure in the following way. We define the approximations

$$a'(x,t) := a_0(t) + a_1(t)x + a_2(t)x^2 + \cdots \tag{8.9.12}$$

$$b'^2(x,t) := b_0(t) + b_1(t)x + b_2(t)x^2 + \cdots \tag{8.9.13}$$

and then minimize the square deviation

$$\min\left[\dot{m}_k - \int_{\mathbb{R}} \left(kx^{k-1}a' + \frac{1}{2}k(k-1)x^{k-2}b'^2\right)p(x,t)\,dx \right]^2 \tag{8.9.14}$$

with respect to $a_i(t)$ and $b_j(t)$ for every i and j.

8.9.3 Transformation of Variables

Proposition 8.9.2. Consider the Markovian process of Sect. 8.9.1 and assume that we make the transformation $y = f(x,t)$ where $f: \mathbb{R}^2 \to \mathbb{R}_+$ is continuously differentiable with respect to both x and t. The local entropies H_1 of the X-trajectory F_x and the Y-trajectory F_y over the time range $(0, T)$ are related by the equation

$$H_1(F_y; 0, T) = H_1(F_x; 0, T) + \frac{1}{T} \int_0^T \int_{\mathbb{R}} p(x, t) \ln |f_x(x, t)| \, dx \, dt \qquad (8.9.15)$$

where f_x is the partial derivative of f with respect to x. □

Proof. For the sake of simplicity (in our opinion!) we shall make the transformation in the opposite way. In other words, we shall put $x = g(y, t)$ where g is continuously differentiable with respect to x and t.

i) First, it is well known that the probability density $q(y, t)$ of Y is then defined by the equation

$$q(y, t) = p[g(y, t), t] |g_y(y, t)| . \qquad (8.9.16)$$

ii) The variations ΔX and ΔY in the range $(t, t + \tau)$ are related by the equation

$$\Delta X = g_y(y, t) \Delta Y + g_t(y, t)\tau$$

and therefore the mathematical expectation is

$$E\{\Delta Y / y, t\} = g_y^{-1}[a(g, t) - g_t]\tau . \qquad (8.9.17)$$

iii) In a similar manner one has

$$E\{(\Delta X)^2 / y, t\} = E\{(g_y \Delta Y + g_t \tau)^2 / y, t\}$$
$$= g_y^2(y, t) E\{(\Delta Y)^2\} + o(\tau^2)$$

whereby we obtain the relation

$$E\{(\Delta Y)^2\} = g_y^{-2} b^2(g, t)\tau . \qquad (8.9.18)$$

iv) We then write $H_1(F_y; 0, T)$ in the form

$$H_1(F_y; 0, T) = -\frac{1}{T} \int_0^T \int_{\mathbb{R}} p(g, t)|g_y| \ln \frac{p(g, t)|g_y|}{(2\pi e b^2 g_y^{-2})^{1/2}} \, dy \, dt + \ln T$$

which we decompose as

$$H_1(F_y; 0, T) = -\frac{1}{T} \int_0^T \int_{\mathbb{R}} p(g)|g_y| \ln \frac{p(g, t)|g_y|}{(2\pi e b^2(g, t))^{1/2}} \, dy \, dt + \ln T$$

$$- \frac{1}{T} \int_0^T \int_{\mathbb{R}} p(g)|g_y| \ln |g_y| \, dy \, dt$$

$$= H_1(F_x; 0, T) - \frac{1}{T} \int_0^T \int_{\mathbb{R}} q(y, t) \ln |g_y| \, dy \, dt . \qquad (8.9.19)$$

v) We now make the substitution $Y \to X$, $X \to Y$, $q(y,t) \to p(x,t)$, $g_y(y,t) \to f_x(x,0)$ in (8.9.19) and thereby obtain the result.

8.9.4 A Few Remarks

i) If we discard the term $\ln T$ in (8.9.2), the entropy $H(F;0,T)$ is a weighted entropy similar to the total entropy defined in Chap. 7.

ii) The expression of $H(F;0,T)$ looks like a Kullback relative entropy or cross-entropy, i.e.

$$D(p,q) = \frac{1}{T} \int_0^T \int_{\mathbb{R}} p(x,t) \ln \frac{p(x,t)}{q(x,t)} \, dx \, dt \qquad (8.9.20)$$

but this is a semblance only. Indeed, a Kullback cross-entropy is basically a transinformation, that is to say a difference of uncertainties since both $p(x,t)$ and $q(x,t)$ are probability densities, while $H(F;0,T)$ is precisely a sum of uncertainties.

iii) More generally, if we assume that the local relative uncertainty $H(X;t+\tau/x,t)$ is in the form

$$H(X;t+\tau/x,t) = \ln[h(x,t)] + \ln \tau , \qquad (8.9.21)$$

then one has

$$H_1(F;0,T) = -\frac{1}{T} \int_0^T \int_{\mathbb{R}} p(x,t) \ln \frac{p(x,t)}{h(x,t)} \, dx \, dt + \ln T . \qquad (8.9.22)$$

The significance of this expression (8.9.22) is that it provides straightforward generalizations to account for the cases where $h(x,t)$ is not an uncertainty of random nature, but is due, for instance, to fuzziness.

iv) We have used Itô's stochastic differential equation to describe the system under consideration, but this is not actually necessary. A rigorously equivalent representation consists of using the infinitesimal transition moments

$$E\{\Delta X/x,t\} = a(x,t)\tau \qquad (8.9.23)$$

$$E\{(\Delta X)^2/x,t\} = b^2(x,t)\tau \qquad (8.9.24)$$

$$E\{(\Delta X)^k/x,t\} = o(\tau^2) , \qquad k \geqslant 3 \qquad (8.9.25)$$

where ΔX represents the increment $\Delta X := x(t+\tau) - x(t)$, together with the condition that the process is Markovian.

v) According to the first integral mean value theorem, (8.9.22) yields

$$H(F;0,T) = -\int_{\mathbb{R}} p(x,t_c) \ln \frac{p(x,t_c)}{h(x,t_c)} \, dx + K \ln T .$$

In other words, everything happens as if the uncertainty involved in the entire trajectory were present only in $x(t_c)$. Broadly speaking, this result is a parallel to the fact that the human visual cortex characterizes a form by selecting only certain salient points of the latter.

8.10 Trajectory Entropy of a Stochastic Process Under Global Markovian Observation

8.10.1 Markovian Processes

We consider the stochastic process of Sect. 8.9.1 and we state:

Proposition 8.10.1. Assume that the Markovian process defined by (8.9.1) is observed by way of a global Markovian observation. The time-randomized uncertainty $H(F; 0, T)$ involved in the trajectory F over the time range $(0, T)$ is then defined by the expression

$$H_g(F; 0, T) = H(X; 0) + \frac{1}{T} \int_0^T \int_{\mathbb{R}} p(x, t) \ln \sqrt{2\pi e b^2(x, t)} \, dx \, dt + \tfrac{1}{2} \ln T \ . \quad (8.10.1)$$

Proof. (i) For a small positive increment of time τ, the variation $\Delta H(X; t)$ of the entropy due to the observation is

$$\Delta H(X; t) = H[x(t + \tau), x(t)] - H(X; t)$$

$$= H(X; t + \tau/x, t)$$

$$= H(\Delta X; \tau/x, t) \ . \quad (8.10.2)$$

ii) This being the case, $(\Delta X; \tau/x, t)$ is a normal random variable with the mathematical expectation $\tau \, a(x, t)$ and the variance $\tau b^2(x, t)$; but the entropy of the normal law $N(\mu, \sigma^2)$ is $\ln \sqrt{2\pi e^2}$, so that one has

$$\Delta H(X; t) = \int_{\mathbb{R}} p(x, t) \ln \sqrt{2\pi e b^2(x, t)} \, dx + \tfrac{1}{2} \ln \tau \quad (8.10.3)$$

$$= \int_{\mathbb{R}} p(x, t) \ln [h(x, t)] \, dx + \tfrac{1}{2} \ln \tau \quad (8.10.4)$$

where $h(x, t)$ is defined by (8.9.21) and (8.9.22).

iii) In terms of the contribution of the uncertainty in the trajectory F over the time range $(t + \tau, t)$, and by virtue of the definition of the observation mode, we necessarily have the identification

$$H_g(F; t + \tau, t) \equiv \Delta H(X; t) \ ; \quad (8.10.5)$$

but according to (8.8.1) one also has

$$H_g(F; t + \tau, t) = -\mu(t) \int_{\mathbb{R}} p(x, t) \ln p(x, t) \, dx + K \ln \tau \ . \quad (8.10.6)$$

iv) We now substitute (8.10.3) and (8.10.6) into (8.10.4) to obtain the result (8.10.1).

8.10.2 Non-Markovian Processes

The rationale of Sect. 8.9.2 holds here too.

8.10.3 Transformation of Variables

We have the following result.

Proposition 8.10.2. Assume that we make the transformation $y = f(x, t)$ where $f \colon \mathbb{R} \times \mathbb{R}_+ \to \mathbb{R}$, is continuously differentiable with respect to x and t. The entropies H_g of the X-trajectory F_x and of the Y-trajectory F_y over the time range $(0, T)$ are related by the equation

$$H_g(F_y; 0, T) = H_g(F_x; 0, T) + \int_{\mathbb{R}} p(x, 0) \ln |f_x(x, 0)| \, dx$$

$$+ \frac{1}{T} \int_0^T \int_{\mathbb{R}} p(x, t) \ln |f_x(x, t)| \, dx \, dt. \tag{8.10.7}$$

Proof. (i) The relation between $H(Y; 0)$ and $H(X; 0)$ is well known and is a classical result of Shannon theory.

ii) For the remaining conditional term, the proof is a direct duplication of the proof of Proposition 8.9.2 with exactly the same material, and we leave it to the reader.

8.10.4 A Few Remarks

i) Let us denote by $H_i^i(F; 0, T)$ the integral part of $H_1(F; 0, T)$, by $H_g^i(F; 0, T)$ the integral part of $H_g(F; 0, T)$, and by $H_w^i(F; 0, T)$ the integral part of $H_w(F; 0, T)$, see (8.6.16).

By comparing (8.6.16), (8.9.2) and (8.10.2) we can directly write the relation

$$H_i^i(F; 0, T) = H_w^i(F; 0, T) + H_g^i(F; 0, T) \tag{8.10.8}$$

which shows that the local Markovian observation is the process involving the larger amount of uncertainty. This is quite understandable considering that we are simultaneously estimating the value of $x(t)$ and that of $x(t + \tau)$.

ii) It is quite evident that

$$H_g^i(F; 0, T) \leqslant H_w^i(F; 0, T)$$

which is a direct consequence of the fact that

$$H(X; t + \tau) = H[x(t) + a(x, t)\tau + b(x, t)w(t)\tau + o(\tau^2)]$$

$$\geqslant H[b(x, t)w(t)\tau] \ .$$

iii) It may be of interest to analyze the time dependence of the integrands in the different entropies above. To this end, we shall use the property that if $L(t)$ is defined by the expression

$$L(t) := \int_{\mathbb{R}} p(x,t)l(x,t)\,dx$$

then its time derivative is given by the expression

$$\dot{L}(t) = \int_{\mathbb{R}} (l_t + al_x + \tfrac{1}{2}b^2 l_{xx})p(x,t)\,dx$$

which follows directly from the Fokker-Plank-Kolmogorov equation.

8.11 Trajectory Entropies of Stochastic Vectors

8.11.1 Notation and Preliminary Results

In the present section, we shall extend some of the previous results to stochastic vectors. We shall consider the multivariate process $X^t(t) := (X_1(t), X_2(t), \dots, X_m(t))$, (the superscript t denotes the transpose), with the probability density $p(x,t)$, and we shall define its trajectory entropy $H(F; 0, T)$ on the time interval $(0, T)$.

The Markovian process which we shall consider is defined by the transition conditions [see (8.9.23–25)]:

$$E\{\Delta X_i/x,t)\} = a_i(x,t)\tau \tag{8.11.1}$$

$$E\{\Delta X_i \Delta X_j/x,t\} = b_{ij}(x,t)\tau \tag{8.11.2}$$

where the higher order moments can be neglected since they are $o(\tau^2)$. Furthermore, we shall put

$$|B| := \text{determinant of the matrix } B := (b_{ij}) \tag{8.11.3}$$

$$a^t := \text{the vector } (a_1, a_2, \dots, a_m)^t \ .$$

With these notations, the well known conditional probability density can be written

$$q(\Delta x/x,t) := \sqrt{(2\pi\tau)^m |B|}\,\exp[-\tfrac{1}{2}(\Delta x - a\tau)^t B^{-1}(\Delta x - a\tau)] \ , \tag{8.11.4}$$

and the corresponding conditional entropy is thus

$$H(\Delta X/x(t) = x) = \tfrac{1}{2}\ln[(2\pi e\tau)^m |B|] \ . \tag{8.11.5}$$

8.11.2 Trajectory Entropies in $\mathbb{R}^n$

Definition 8.11.1. The general form of the entropy $H(F; 0, T)$ of the trajectory generated by $(X; t)$ over the time range $(0, T)$ is

$$H(F; 0, T) = -\frac{1}{T}\int_0^T \int_{\mathbb{R}^m} \mu(t)p(x,t)\ln p(x,t)\,dx\,dt + K\ln T \tag{8.11.6}$$

where $\mu(t)$ is a weighting function which characterizes the type of observation and K is a constant defining the measurement unit of the uncertainty generated by time.

From a purely theoretical standpoint, we could have first stated this general definition, and then considered the entropy of a one-dimensional process, i.e. (8.8.1), as a special case. But, for the sake of clarity, we prefer to work in the opposite way.

In a similar manner, one can straightforwardly state

Proposition 8.11.1. Assume that the multivariate Markovian process defined by (8.11.1) and (8.11.2) is observed by means of a local Markovian observation. The time-randomized uncertainty $H_1(F; 0, T)$ involved in the trajectory F over the time range $(0, T)$ if then defined by the expression

$$H_1(F; 0, T) = -\frac{1}{T} \int_0^T \int_{\mathbb{R}^m} p(x, t) \ln \frac{p(x, t)}{[(2\pi e)^m |B(x, t)|]^{1/2}} \, dx \, dt + m \ln T \qquad (8.11.7)$$

where $p(x, t)$ is the solution of the Fokker-Plank-Kolmogorov equation

$$p_t(x, t) = -\sum_{i=1}^m (a_i p)_{x_i} + \tfrac{1}{2} \sum_{i=1}^m \sum_{j=1}^m (b_{ij} p)_{x_i x_j} \, . \qquad \qquad \square$$

Proof. The proof is identical to the proof of proposition 8.9.1, and is based upon (8.11.5).

Another result is the following.

Proposition 8.11.2. Assume that the multivariate Markovian process defined by (8.11.1) and (8.11.2) is observed by means of a global Markovian observation. The time-randomized uncertainty $H_g(F; 0, T)$ involved in the trajectory F over the time range $(0, T)$ is then defined by the expression

$$H_g(F; 0, T) = H(X; 0) + \frac{1}{T} \int_0^T \int_{\mathbb{R}^m} p(x, t) \ln \sqrt{(2\pi e)^m |B(x, t)|} \, dx \, dt + \frac{m}{2} \ln T \, .$$

$$(8.11.8) \quad \square$$

Proof: Similar to the proof of proposition 8.10.1, but now via (8.11.5).

8.12 Transinformation of Stochastic Trajectories

8.12.1 Definition of Transinformation of Trajectories

It is apparent that there are two main ways to define a model of transinformation for stochastic trajectories.

First by using an equation similar to

$$H(X, Y) = H(X) + H(Y/X) \qquad (8.12.1)$$

one can introduce a concept of conditional trajectory entropy, and then use this to define trajectory transinformation via an equation of the type

$$I(Y/X) = H(Y) - H(Y/X) \ . \tag{8.12.2}$$

The second possibility is to seek a suitable generalization of the equation

$$I(Y/X) = H(X) + H(Y) - H(X, Y) \ . \tag{8.12.3}$$

Theoretically, these two approaches should be equivalent, but the first one may be troublesome in that the definition of the conditional weighting function $\mu_x(x, t)$ associated with the conditional trajectory (F_y/F_x) is not sufficiently explicit to provide tractable expressions of transinformation when one uses the general form of trajectory entropy. It follows that a definition via an extension of (8.12.3) is more suitable.

As is evident, we have no such problems with trajectories under local or global Markovian observation so that the generalization of (8.12.2) remains quite relevant in these cases.

8.12.2 Transinformation Measures of Stochastic Trajectories

Notation. Equation (8.10.4) defines the quantity $h(x, t)$ involved in the Markovian entropies $H(F_x; 0, T)$ of the trajectory generated by $x(t)$. Likewise, we shall define

$$h'(y, t) := \sqrt{2\pi e b'^2(y, t)} \tag{8.12.4}$$

to denote the corresponding term for $y(t)$, i.e. the term involved in the trajectory entropy $H(F_y; 0, T)$. Furthermore, let

$$l(x, y, t) := \sqrt{(2\pi e)^2 |B(x, y, t)|} \tag{8.12.5}$$

denote the corresponding term in the entropy $H(F_{xy}; 0, T)$ of the trajectory F_{xy} generated by the vector $(X, Y; t)$.

We can then introduce the following definition:

Definition 8.12.1. The mutual information or transinformation contained in F_x about F_y or in F_y about F_x over the time range $(0, T)$ is defined by the trajectory transinformation

$$I(F_y/F_x; 0, T) := H(F_x; 0, T) + H(F_y; 0, T) - H(F_{xy}; 0, T) \ . \tag{8.12.6}$$

One has the following result:

Proposition 8.12.1. Let $c(x, y, t)$ denote the function defined by the expression

$$c(x, y, t) := \frac{E\{\Delta X \Delta Y\}}{\sqrt{E\{(\Delta X)^2\} E\{(\Delta Y)^2\}}} \ . \tag{8.12.7}$$

The trajectory transinformation obtained by local Markovian observation is then

$$I_1(F_y/F_x; 0, T) = \frac{1}{T} \int_0^T I(Y/X; t)\, dt$$

$$- \frac{1}{T} \int_0^T \int_{\mathbb{R}^2} r(x, y, t) \ln \sqrt{1 - c^2(x, y, t)}\, dx\, dy\, dt \;, \qquad (8.12.8)$$

and the trajectory transinformation under global Markovian observation is

$$I_g(F_y/F_x; 0, T) = I(Y/X; 0) - \frac{1}{T} \int_0^T \int_{\mathbb{R}^2} r(x, y, t) \ln \sqrt{1 - c^2(x, y, t)}\, dx\, dy\, dt \;.$$

$$(8.12.9) \quad \square$$

Proof. (i) On expanding the right-hand side of (8.12.6) by means of the explicit form of the trajectory entropy $H_1(F; 0, T)$, we obtain the transinformation

$$I_1(F_y/F_x; 0, T) = \frac{1}{T} \int_0^T \int_{\mathbb{R}^2} r(x, y, t) \ln \frac{\dfrac{r(x, y, t)}{p(x, t)q(y, t)}}{\dfrac{l(x, y, t)}{h(x, t)h'(y, t)}}\, dx\, dy\, dt$$

$$= \frac{1}{T} \int_0^T I(Y/X; t)\, dt - \frac{1}{T} \int_0^T \int_{\mathbb{R}^2} r(x, y, t) \ln \frac{l(x, y, t)}{h(x, t)h'(y, t)}\, dx\, dy\, dt \;.$$

$$(8.12.10)$$

ii) Next, the definitions of h^2, h'^2 and l^2 yield

$$h^2(x, t) = 2\pi e \frac{E\{\Delta X^2\}}{\tau}$$

$$h'^2(y, t) = 2\pi e \frac{E\{\Delta Y^2\}}{\tau}$$

$$l^2(x, y, t) = (2\pi e)^2 \frac{E\{\Delta X^2\} E\{\Delta Y^2\} - E^2(\Delta X \Delta Y)}{\tau^2}$$

and on substituting into (8.12.10), we obtain the result (8.12.8).

iii) The proof for $I_g(F_y/F_x; 0, T)$ proceeds in exactly the same way.

Comments. As defined, $I(F_y/F_x; 0, T)$ appears to be a mean value of the transinformation with respect to time, and in some problems it may be more useful to consider the total quantity $TI(F_y/F_x; 0, T)$.

8.12.3 Application to the Derivation of Conditional Trajectory Entropies

According to the expressions (8.12.8) and (8.12.9), the local and global Markovian transinformations are both positive, so that following the original Shannon point of view, we are entitled to consider these transinformations as decrements of entropy. Therefore the two concepts of conditional trajectory entropies defined as follows.

Definition 8.12.2. The conditional trajectory entropy $H_1(F_y/F_x; 0, T)$ under local Markovian observation, of the trajectory F_y given the trajectory F_x is defined as

$$H_1(F_y/F_x; 0, T) := H_1(F_y; 0, T) - I_1(F_y/F_x; 0, T) \tag{8.12.11}$$

and likewise, the conditional trajectory entropy $H_g(F_y/F_x; 0, T)$ under global Markovian observation is

$$H_g(F_y/F_x; 0, T) := H_g(F_y; 0, T) - I_g(F_y/F_x; 0, T) . \tag{8.12.12}$$

Proposition 8.12.2. The explicit forms of the conditional trajectory entropies under local and global Markovian observation are, respectively,

$$H_1(F_y/F_x; 0, T) = \frac{1}{T} \int_0^T H(Y/X; t)\, dt$$

$$+ \frac{1}{T} \int_0^T \int_{\mathbb{R}^2} r(x, y, t) \ln \sqrt{2\pi e b'^2(y, t)[1 - c^2(x, y, t)]}\, dx\, dy\, dt . \tag{8.12.13}$$

and

$$H_g(F_y/F_x; 0, T) = H(Y/X; 0)$$

$$+ \frac{1}{T} \int_0^T \int_{\mathbb{R}^2} r(x, y, t) \ln \sqrt{2\pi e b'^2(y, t)[1 - c^2(x, y, t)]}\, dx\, dy\, dt . \tag{8.12.14}$$

Proof. The proof is direct: it is sufficient to calculate the right-hand side of (8.12.11) by means of the expressions (8.9.2) and (8.12.8), and to calculate the right-hand side of (8.12.12) using (8.10.1) and (8.12.9).

8.13 On the Entropy of Deterministic Pattern

8.13.1 Background on Some Results

It is well known that if $f: \mathbb{R}^n \to \mathbb{R}^n$, $y = f(x)$ is a continuously differentiable mapping, then one has

$$H(Y) = H(X) + \int_{\mathbb{R}^n} p(x) \ln|f'(x)|\, dx \tag{8.13.1}$$

where $f'(x)$ is the Jacobian or the functional determinant of $f(x)$.

We have suggested [8.5] that this relation should be considered equivalent to the equation

$$H(Y) \equiv H(X, f)$$

$$= H(X) + H(f/X) ,$$ (8.13.2)

whereby we defined the *conditional entropy of* $f(\cdot)$ *given* X by the expression

$$H[f(\cdot)/X] := \int_{\mathbb{R}^n} p(x) \ln|f'(x)| \, dx$$ (8.13.3)

or equivalently

$$H[f(\cdot)/X = x] = \ln|f'(x)| .$$ (8.13.4)

8.13.2 On the Entropy of Deterministic Pattern

The problem of defining the entropy of a deterministic form gives rise to many questions of importance which we shall now briefly review.

i) First of all, it is this author's opinion that the main purpose and the unique interest of a measure of uncertainty is to provide some concept of transinformation. A definition of entropy is of little use by itself if it does not generate a relevant theory of transfer of information. An example of such an information-theoretic problem of practical interest is the following.

Assume that we are dealing with the scalar-valued mapping $f(x)$, but that unfortunately we cannot directly observe $f(x)$: the unique measurement we have at hand is the quantity $g[f(x)]$ where g is a continuously differentiable mapping. How can one estimate the amount of information obtained about $f(x)$, or likewise, the amount of information contained in $g(f)$ about f? We believe that the definition of entropy should aim to provide a satisfactory answer to this question.

ii) Another question of importance can be stated as follows: must we assume that the entropy of a deterministic mapping is necessarily the continuation, i.e. the extension in some sense, of the entropy of random variables, or can we consider the former to be a new theory that can be developed independently of the Shannon theory?

For instance, one could try to build up this theory by using the equation (8.13.3), or alternatively, one could consider another approach which consists of suitably adapting the various results obtained previously for stochastic processes. The right way is not obvious: on the one hand it is likely that all these aspects should exhibit common features, but on other hand, it may be dangerous to deal with deterministic phenomena using the mathematical apparatus of stochastic systems.

8.13.3 Dependence of the Entropy upon the Observation Mode

The entropy of a deterministic mapping will depend upon the way in which this mapping is defined in the observation process used by the observer. Indeed a given graph or curve may be defined in various manners and, as a consequence, we may expect to obtain different values for the uncertainty involved in this same curve. Some examples are outlined below.

i) If we intersect the curve by straight lines parallel to the y-axis, we then observe the graph in the form $y = f(x)$ and thus have to define the entropy of the mapping $f(\cdot)$.

ii) If we intersect the curve by straight lines parallel to the x-axis, the graph is then observed in the form $x = f^{-1}(y)$ and we have to define the entropy of the mapping $f^{-1}(\cdot)$.

iii) If we intersect the curve by radial straight lines that pass through the coordinate origin, then the graph is observed in the form $\varrho = g(\theta)$ where ϱ and θ are the polar coordinates, and we have to define the entropy of the mapping $g(\cdot)$.

iv) Assume now that we are observing the curve irrespective of any (x, y) reference frame, that is to say by moving our eyes along the trajectory. The graph is then defined by its intrinsic equation $s = l(\theta)$ where s is the arc length and θ is the angle from the x-axis to the tangent of the curve at the considered point; the entropy of the curve is then defined by the mapping $l(\cdot)$.

Many authors would claim that a suitable measure of the uncertainty involved in a continuous random variable should be independent of the coordinate frame, but it is this author's opinion that this is not correct, or is at best only partially correct. Indeed, the absolute uncertainty associated with the variable, i.e. the information potential of the latter, is likely to be independent of the system of coordinates, but the uncertainty detected by an observer via a particular reference frame necessarily depends upon the chosen frame.

This fundamental remark also applies to the entropy of a deterministic mapping so that we should not be too surprised that a given geometrical pattern may have several different values of the entropy for the same intrinsic uncertainty.

8.14 Entropy of a Differentiable Mapping

In this section, we shall refine the approach suggested by the equation (8.13.3).

8.14.1 Entropy with Respect to a Family of Distributions

Definition 8.14.1. Let $f(x)$, $\mathbb{R} \to \mathbb{R}$, denote a continuously differentiable mapping, and let P be a class of admissible (cumulative) distribution functions. Then the entropy $H[f(\cdot)/P]$ or for short $H(f/P)$ of $f(\cdot)$ conditional on P is defined as

$$H[f(\cdot)/P] = \max_{P} \int_{\mathbb{R}} \ln|f'(x)|\, dP(x) , \qquad P(x) \in P \qquad (8.14.1)$$

where the integral is Stieltjes integral.

When the admissible distribution functions are derived from probability densities $p(x)$, we merely have

$$H[f(\cdot)/P] = \max_{p} \int_{\mathbb{R}} \ln|f'(x)|p(x)\, dx , \qquad \text{for admissible } p . \qquad (8.14.2)$$

Derivation. (i) We first recall the inequality

$$H(X/Y) \leqslant H(X) \ .$$

It is well known that the equality holds if and only if X and Y are mutually independent, so that we can write the equality

$$H(X) = \max_{r} H(X/Y) \ , \qquad \text{for admissible } r(x, y)$$

where $r(x, y)$ is the probability density of the pair (X, Y). If we decompose $r(x, y)$ in the form

$$r(x, y) = p(x)q(y/x)$$

where $q(y/x)$ is the conditional density of Y, we can also write

$$H(X) = \max_{q} H(X/Y) \ , \qquad \text{for admissible } q(y/x)$$

and this maximum is achieved when $q(y/x) = q(y)$ independent of x.

ii) By using the same rationale, we refer to (8.13.2) and write

$$H[f(\cdot)/X] \leqslant H[f(\cdot)]$$

and thence the equation (8.14.1).

Important Comment. The fact that $H(f/P)$ depends upon a class P of admissible distribution functions merely reflects the dependence of the uncertainty involved in $f(\cdot)$ on the way in which $f(\cdot)$ is observed. And this is perfectly correct.

Indeed, it has been shown experimentally that in human vision of forms and patterns, the cortex works by using a scanning procedure which varies from one observer to another. In the context of modelling, this scanning defines a weighting function which can be thought of as equivalent to a probability density function. In this way, $H(f/P)$ is a relative entropy defined relative to a given observer.   □

8.14.2 Maximum Entropy of a Differentiable Mapping

We have the following result.

Proposition 8.14.1. According to definition 8.14.1, the maximum value of the entropy of a continuously differentiable mapping $f(x)$, $\mathbb{R} \to \mathbb{R}$, is

$$H[f(\cdot)] = \ln \left[\max_{x} |f'(x)| \right] , \qquad x \in \mathbb{R} \ . \tag{8.14.3}$$

Proof. The proof is classical and is based upon the fact that, if $g(x)$ is a continuous function, then one has the equality

$$\max_{p} \int_{\mathbb{R}} g(x) \, dP(x) = \max_{x} g(x) \tag{8.14.4}$$

which can be obtained as follows:

i)   Assume that $g(x)$ achieves its maximum value at $x = a$; it then follows that

$$\int g(x)\,dP(x) \leqslant g(a) \tag{8.14.5}$$

ii)   Let $I(x - a)$ denote the unit step function at $x = a$; one then has

$$g(a) = \int g(x)\,dI(x - a) \leqslant \sup_p \int g(x)\,dP(x) \tag{8.14.6}$$

iii) But according to (8.14.5), one also has

$$\sup_p \int g(x)\,dP(x) \leqslant g(a) \tag{8.14.7}$$

so that comparison of (8.14.6) with (8.14.7) directly yields the result.

Comment. This result is quite consistent with practical experiments regarding human vision. Indeed, it has been shown that when a human observer is identifying a human face for instance, his cortex selects the most salient features of this picture, which are mainly angles such as the nose. In doing so, the cortex is locally maximizing the term $\ln|f'(x)|$!

8.14.3 Entropy of a Mapping Defined on a Finite Interval

Taking into account the size of the interval over which the function is defined gives rise to two questions.

i)   How does one define the entropy of a deterministic mapping which itself is defined on a finite $L = [a, b] \subset \mathbb{R}$, that is to say which is equal to zero outside L?
ii)   Given a mapping $f(\cdot)$ defined on $\mathbb{R}$, what is the amount of uncertainty involved in the graph of $f(\cdot)$ over the range $[a, b]$?

Despite their superficial similarity, these two problems are different for the genuine reason that in the second case, we do not have a function which is equal to zero outside the range $[a, b]$. More explicitly, in the first case, the observer is fully aware that the mapping is defined only on $[a, b]$, so that the probability density $p(x)$ is also defined only on $[a, b]$. In contrast, in the second problem, $p(x)$ is defined on the whole of $\mathbb{R}$. As a consequence one can straightforwardly state the following

Result. Assume that $f: [a, b] \to \mathbb{R}$ is defined on a finite range only, then its entropy with respect to the family $\boldsymbol{P}$ of cumulative distributions defined on $[a, b]$ is given by the expression

$$H[f(\cdot)/\boldsymbol{P}] = \max_p \int_a^b \ln|f'(x)|\,dP(x)\ , \qquad P(x) \in \boldsymbol{P}\ . \tag{8.14.8}$$

8.14.4 Entropy of a Mapping with an Incomplete Probability Distribution

This heading refers to the second question posed in Sect. 8.14.3. In order to gain further insight, we consider the corresponding problem for the case of random variables.

Let X be defined by the probability density $p(x)$. How does one measure the amount of uncertainty $H(X; a, b)$ involved in X over the finite range $[a, b]$?

At first glance, it would seem that one could measure this uncertainty by the integral $-\int_a^b p(x) \ln p(x)\, dx$, but in fact this would be wrong, and for the well known reason that the amount of entropy associated with the value "a" is $-\ln p(a)$, in other words, we necessarily have the additional condition

$$H(X; a, a) = -\ln p(a) \; . \tag{8.14.9}$$

As a consequence, one defines $H(X; a, b)$ by the expression

$$H(X; a, b) := -\frac{\int\limits_a^b p(x) \ln p(x)\, dx}{\int\limits_a^b p(x)\, dx} \; . \tag{8.14.10}$$

Using the same rationale, we shall introduce the following measurement of uncertainty for deterministic mappings.

Definition 8.15.2. Assume that the domain of $f(\cdot)$ is $\mathbb{R}$ as the whole, and let $p^*(x)$ denote the probability density which defines $H(f/P)$; then the entropy $H(f/P, a, b)$ of $f(\cdot)$ contributed by the interval $[a, b]$ is defined as

$$H[f(x)/P; a, b] = \frac{\int\limits_a^b p^*(x) \ln |f'(x)|\, dx}{\int\limits_a^b p^*(x)\, dx} \; . \tag{8.14.11}$$

8.15 Entropy of Degree d of Differential Mappings

In Sect. 8.14 we defined the entropy of $f(\cdot)$ relative to a family of probability distributions, and the next question of interest is whether one can derive a class of such entropies which depend upon the definition of the function $f(\cdot)$ only, that is to say, which no longer involve $p(x)$. This is addressed in the following.

8.15.1 Trajectory Entropy of Degree d

Definition 8.15.1. Let $f(\cdot): [a, b] \to \mathbb{R}$ denote a continuously differentiable mapping; its entropy $H_d[f(\cdot)]$ of degree d, derived as a special case of the entropy $H(f/P)$ is defined by the expression

$$H_d[f(\cdot)] := \frac{\int\limits_a^b |f'(x)|^d \ln |f'(x)|\, dx}{\int\limits_a^b |f'(x)|^d\, dx} \; , \qquad d \in \mathbb{R} \tag{8.15.1}$$

where d is a real-valued scalar parameter.

Derivation. (i) We assume that P is the set of all probability densities whose Shannon entropy has a given fixed value, i.e. densities $p(x)$ satisfying

$$-\int_a^b p(x)\ln p(x)\,dx = C$$

where C is a given constant, with the obvious additional condition

$$\int_a^b p(x)\,dx = 1 \ .$$

ii) In order to maximize the expression (8.14.2) which defines the corresponding entropy $H(f/P)$, we consider the Lagrangian

$$\int_a^b p(x)[\ln|f'(x)| - \lambda_1 \ln p(x) + \lambda_2]\,dx$$

and a simple calculation yields

$$p(x) = \frac{|f'(x)|^d}{\int_a^b |f'(x)|^d\,dx} \tag{8.15.2}$$

and thence the result.

8.15.2 Some Properties of Trajectory Entropy of Degree d

Relation to $H(X)$. Assume that $f(x)$ is the cumulative probability distribution $P(x)$ of a random variable X with the probability density $p(x)$. One can then write the relation

$$H_1[P(\cdot)] + H(X) = 0 \tag{8.15.3}$$

where $H_1(P)$ is the entropy of degree 1. This equation may appear somewhat surprising at first glance, but on looking more closely, it is quite correct, as can be illustrated by the following remark. Assume that all we know about X is its range of values $[a, b]$. Then, according to the maximum entropy principle, we shall suppose that $p(x)$ is the density that maximizes $H(X)$, in other words, all we can do is to set $p(x) = 1/(b - a)$; but this mapping is exactly the one that involves the minimum amount of uncertainty concerning its definition.

In other words, the maximum of $H(X)$ coincides with the minimum of $H_1[P(\cdot)]$.

Relation to $H[f(\cdot)/X]$. We have the relation

$$H_0[f(\cdot)] = \frac{1}{b-a} \int_a^b \ln|f'(x)|\,dx \tag{8.15.4}$$

i.e., the entire situation may be reproduced by setting $p(x) = 1/(b - a)$ in the expression (8.13.3) for $H[f(\cdot)/X]$.

Limiting Value of $H_d[f(\cdot)]$. We have the following result.

Proposition 8.15.1. Let $|f'_M|$ denote the maximum value of $|f'(x)|$ over the interval $[a, b]$; it then holds that

$$\lim H_d[f(\cdot)] = \ln|f'_M| \quad \text{as} \quad d \uparrow \infty . \tag{8.15.5}$$

Proof. (i) *Lemma.* Let $g(x)$ denote a positive continuous function on the interval $[a, b]$, and let $h(x)$ be continuous on $[a, b]$. Let $M_g = \max g(x)$ and $M_h = \max h(x)$ on $[a, b]$. The following relation is then satisfied:

$$\int_a^b g^n(x)h(x)\,dx \cong (b-a)M_g^n M_h \quad \text{as} \quad n \uparrow \infty . \tag{8.15.6}$$

Proof of the Lemma. (a) Let ε denote a small positive number and define $m := M - \varepsilon$. Let c and e, $a < c < e < b$, denote the roots of the equation $m = g(x)$, and define the function $\hat{g}(x)$ as

$$\hat{g}(x) = \begin{cases} g(x), & c \leqslant x \leqslant e \\ 0 & \text{elsewhere.} \end{cases}$$

b) One can then write the inequality

$$\hat{g}^n(x) \leqslant g^n(x) \leqslant M_g^n , \qquad a \leqslant x \leqslant b$$

and therefore

$$\hat{g}^n(x)m_h \leqslant g^n(x)h(x) \leqslant M_g^n M_h , \qquad a \leqslant x \leqslant b$$

where m_h is the minimum of $h(x)$ on the interval $[a, b]$.

c) We now integrate over $[a, b]$ and refer to the definition of $\hat{g}(x)$ to obtain

$$(e - c)m^n m_h \leqslant \int_a^b g^n(x)h(x)\,dx \leqslant (b-a)M_g^n M_h .$$

d) By letting ε tends to zero, we have the lemma.

ii) We now return to the proof of the main proposition and apply the lemma to write successively

$$\int_a^b |f'(x)|^d \ln|f'(x)|\,dx \cong (b-a)|f'_M|^d \ln|f'_M|$$

$$\int_a^b |f'(x)|^d\,dx \cong (b-a)|f'_M|^d$$

thence the result.

8.15.3 Practical Meaning of Trajectory Entropy of Degree d

The trajectory entropy $H_d[f(\cdot)]$ increases as d increases and for large values of d, according to (8.15.5), it exactly describes the human vision scanning process whereby the cortex selects the angles of the pattern under consideration as characteristic features.

A smooth observation, that is to say, one in which the different points of the pattern are uniformly weighted by the scanning process, is defined by low values of d. In fact, if we denote by $|f'_m|$ the minimum of $|f'(x)|$ on the considered interval, one has

$$\lim H_d[f(\cdot)] = \lim |f'_m| \quad \text{as} \quad d \downarrow -\infty \ . \tag{8.15.7}$$

If we decompose the pattern into several adjacent portions and then determine the value of $H_d(f)$ on each of these parts, then for large d, we characterize the pattern by a finite number of salient points, i.e. those with maximum $|f'(x)|$, on each considered portion. This is quite consistent with the process of human vision.

The probability density $p^*(x)$ in (8.14.11), and consequently the parameter d, define the scanning frequencies in human vision. The value $d = 0$ characterizes the uniform scanning density.

8.16 Transinformation Between Differentiable Mappings

8.16.1 The Trajectory Entropy of Compositions of Functions

Problem. Let f and g, $\mathbb{R} \to \mathbb{R}$ denote two continuously differentiable mappings. How can we relate $H[f(g(\cdot))]$ to $H[f(\cdot)]$ and $H[g(\cdot)]$?

Solution. (i) We come back to (18.13.3) to write the equation

$$H[f(\cdot)/Y] = \int_{\mathbb{R}} q(y) \ln |f'(y)| \, dy \ . \tag{8.16.1}$$

We now make the transformation $y = g(x)$ and noting that the probability density $p(x)$ of X is $p(x) = q[g(x)]|g'(x)|$, we obtain

$$H[f(\cdot)/Y] = \int_{\mathbb{R}} p(x) \ln |f'_g g'_x| \, dx$$

$$=: H[f(g(\cdot))/X] \ . \tag{8.16.2}$$

ii) On writing (8.16.2) explicitly, we obtain

$$H[f(g)/X] = H[g(\cdot)/X] + \int_{\mathbb{R}} p(x) \ln |f'[g(x)]| \, dx \tag{8.16.3}$$

which is the sought relation.

On comparing this with the identity $H(X, Y) = H(X) + H(Y/X)$, we are led to introduce the following definition.

Definition 8.16.1. Let $p^*(x)$ denote the optimal probability density function defining $H[g(\cdot)/P]$ with respect to the class P of admissible probability density functions.

The conditional entropy $H[f(\cdot)/g(\cdot)]$ of the mapping $f(\cdot)$ given the mapping $g(\cdot)$ is then defined by the expression

$$H(f(\cdot)/g(\cdot)] := \int_{\mathbb{R}} p^*(x) \ln|f'[g(x)]| \, dx \ . \tag{8.16.4}$$

Definition 8.16.2. As a special case of (8.16.4), the conditional entropy of degree d of $f(\cdot)$ given $g(\cdot)$ is

$$H_d[f(\cdot)/g(\cdot)] := \frac{\int_a^b |f'(x)|^d \ln|f_g'[g(x)]| \, dx}{\int_a^b |f'(x)|^d \, dx} \ . \tag{8.16.5}$$

8.16.2 Application to Transinformation Between Mappings

In analogy to the expression $I(Y/X) = H(Y) - H(Y/X)$, we shall introduce the following definition.

Definition 8.16.3. Let $p^*(x)$ denote the optimal probability density function defining $H[g(\cdot)/P]$; then the amount of information contained in $f[g(\cdot)]$ about $f(\cdot)$ is defined as the transinformation

$$I[f(\cdot)/g(\cdot)] := H[f(\cdot)] - H[f(\cdot)/g(\cdot)] \tag{8.16.6}$$

$$= \int_{\mathbb{R}} p^*(x) \ln \left| \frac{f'(x)}{f_g'[g(x)]} \right| dx \ . \tag{8.16.7}$$

Definition 8.16.4. As a special case of (8.16.7), the transinformation of degree d is

$$I_d[f(\cdot)/g(\cdot)] = \frac{\int_a^b |f'(x)|^d \ln \left| \frac{f'(x)}{f_g'[g(x)]} \right| dx}{\int_a^b |f'(x)|^d \, dx} \ . \tag{8.16.8}$$

8.17 Trajectory Entropy of Degree d in Intrinsic Coordinates

Assume that the plane curve is defined by its intrinsic coordinates (s, θ) where s is the arc length and α is the angle from the x-axis to the tangent of the curve at the point considered.

Assume further that we randomize with respect to θ. We shall then represent the mapping by the equation $s = f(\theta)$ and its entropy of degree d will be

$$H_d[f(\cdot);a,b] = \frac{\int_a^b |f'(\theta)|^d \ln|f'(\theta)|\,d\theta}{\int_a^b |f'(\theta)|^d\,d\theta} \tag{8.17.1}$$

$$= \frac{\int_a^b R^d(\theta) \ln R(\theta)\,d\theta}{\int_a^b R^d(\theta)\,d\theta} \tag{8.17.2}$$

where $R(\theta)$ is the radius of curvature.

As a special case, consider the circle whose intrinsic equation is $s = R\theta$; one then has

$$H_d[f(\cdot);a,b] = \ln R \ .$$

From a practical standpoint, this model corresponds to the case in which the observer follows the trajectory path without referring to any external coordinate frame, and in this sense it could be considered as the counterpart to the global Markovian observation of stochastic processes.

8.18 Trajectory Entropy of an $\mathbb{R}^n \to \mathbb{R}^n$ Mapping

For the sake of simplicity, we considered $\mathbb{R} \to \mathbb{R}$ differentiable mappings only, but the results obtained can easily be extended to $\mathbb{R}^n \to \mathbb{R}^n$ differentiable mappings. In this case $|f'(x)|$ is the Jacobian determinant of the transformation.

8.19 Trajectory Entropy of Degree d of a Discrete Mapping

In order to measure the uncertainty involved in a discrete deterministic mapping defined on the finite set $x_1, x_2, x_3, \cdots x_m$, we shall refer to the equation (6.8.6) and shall obtain *the total trajectory entropy of degree d in the form*

$$H_d^e[f(\cdot)] = \frac{\sum_{i=1}^m \left|\frac{\Delta f(\xi_i)}{h_i}\right|^d \ln\left|\frac{\Delta f(\xi_i)}{h_i}\right|}{\sum_{i=1}^m \left|\frac{\Delta f(\xi_i)}{h_i}\right|^d} \tag{8.19.1}$$

$$= \frac{\sum_{i=1}^m |f'(x_i + \varepsilon_i)|^d \ln|f'(x_i + \varepsilon_i)|}{\sum_{i=1}^m |f'(x_i + \varepsilon_i)|^d} \ , \tag{8.19.2}$$

where the ε_i can be considered as error terms.

The entropy of degree zero is

$$H_0^e[f(\cdot)] = \frac{1}{m} \sum_{i=1}^{m} \ln|f'(x_i + \varepsilon_i)| \ . \tag{8.19.3}$$

Referring now to Sect. 6.2.1, we assume that the sequence $\xi_1, \xi_2, \ldots, \xi_i, \ldots$ is redefined in such a manner that

$$\Delta f(\xi_i) = h_i f'(x_i) \ ;$$

then, according to (8.19.3), $H_0^e[f(\cdot)]$ is exactly the Liapunov exponent of $f(\cdot)$.

8.20 Trajectory Entropy and Liapunov Exponent

Consider the dynamic equation

$$\dot{x}(t) = -V_x(x) \ , \qquad x(0) = x_0 \ , \qquad x \in \mathbb{R} \tag{8.20.1}$$

where $V(x)$ is the potential function of the system, and $V_x(x)$ holds for the derivative $dV(x)/dx$. According to (8.15.1) and (8.20.1) the entropy of order one of the trajectory $x(t)$ over the time range (t_0, t_1) is

$$H_1[x(\cdot)] = \frac{\int_a^b \sigma(x)\ln|V_x(x)|\,dx}{\int_a^b \sigma(x)\,dx} \tag{8.20.2}$$

with the notation

$$\sigma(x) := -\operatorname{sgn} V_x(x) \ ; \qquad a := x(t_0) \ ; \qquad b := x(t_1) \ . \tag{8.20.3}$$

Assume that $\sigma(x) \geq 0$ for $a \leq x \leq b$; one then has

$$H_1[x(\cdot); t_0, t_1] = H_0[V(\cdot); a, b] \ . \tag{8.20.4}$$

If we consider that $H_1[f(\cdot)]$ is equivalent to a thermodynamic entropy, we then conclude that the thermodynamic entropy of $x(\cdot)$ is equal to the Liapunov exponent of $V(\cdot)$.

As a final remark to conclude this chapter, we shall point out that it could be interesting to study the trajectory entropy of degree d (8.15.1) of stochastic processes, and to compare the result with their trajectory entropies as defined in Sect. 8.8.

9. A Theory of Relative Statistical Decision

Any observation process can be considered as a decoding problem in the broad sense of this term, insofar as we are identifying an object of our real universe, which is encoded by a formal representation. In most cases, this observation involves subjectivity, the latter being considered the result of interactions between prior internal definition and posterior measurement. Our purpose in the present chapter is to derive a quantitative model for this subjectivity in the form of various weighting coefficients.

To this end, we shall first consider the main underlying axioms and the equations of the observation process with informational invariance, and shall then apply this model to the practical situation in which one directly observes the amount of information contained in the state of the system under consideration. We shall then derive a new concept of *relative probability* which can be thought of, on the one hand, as an extension of probability, and on the other hand, as being related to the theory of *possibility*. By using this relative probability, we then straightforwardly obtain a *generalized maximum likelihood criterion* and a *generalized Bayesian criterion* which apply in statistical decision theory. As illustrative examples of the kind of results to be expected, we consider a problem of technical communication and a problem of pattern recognition.

9.1 Introduction

In order to summarize the question and to introduce our purpose, we first consider the main concepts of statistical decision. For this we shall refer to the encoding-decoding problem of communication, which is probably one of the best illustrative examples.

A communication channel involves a source of information and a destination. We shall denote by $\{x_1, x_2, \ldots, x_m\}$ the input alphabet; $\{y_1, y_2, \ldots, y_m\}$ the output alphabet; $p(y_j/x_i)$ the probability of receiving y_j when x_i is sent; X_K and Y_K the sets of all the sequences x and y of K symbols at the input and output respectively. The decoding process is a decision rule which associates with each $y \in Y_K$ one $x \in X_K$. Several criteria have been proposed (see for instance [9.1]) and below we mention some of them.

i) *Minimum Error Probability.* This rule minimizes the probability of decoding error for a given ensemble of messages, set of code words and channel. The corresponding decision is as follows: decode the received sequence y into $x_j \in X_K$ such that

$$p(x_j/y) \geqslant p(x_i/y) , \qquad i \neq j . \tag{9.1.1}$$

This scheme, which selects that x whose conditional probability is the greatest, is also referred to as the "ideal observer".

ii) *Maximum Likelihood Decoding*. The rule here is as follows: given the observed y, select that (or those) x_{i*} for which

$$p(y/x_{i*}) \geqslant p(y/x_i) , \qquad i \neq i^* . \tag{9.1.2}$$

When the messages have equal a priori probabilities, then the minimum-error-probability decision and the maximum-likelihood-decoding decision are equivalent [9.2].

iii) *Minimum Cost Decoding*. In this approach, we assume that there are different costs associated with the different types of possible errors; and given an observed y, we select that x_{m*} which minimizes the average cost [9.3].

iv) *List Decoding*. In this scheme, the decoding is not an application in the mathematical sense of this term, but rather a multi-valued mapping which maps the received symbol into a set of possible symbols. List decoding was first considered by *Elias* [9.4] for binary symmetric channels. *Shannon* et al. [9.5], *Ebert* [9.6] and *Forney* [9.7] derived bounds on the probability of error and of erasure.

v) *Weighted Decoding*. In this technique, one takes account of the actual data which have been received instead of the decision regarding the symbols themselves, in order to improve the efficiency of the decoding process. In general, this improvement is obtained at the expense of the complexity of the decoding. *Wolf* [9.8] considered this problem by using the Viterbi algorithm, and recently *Battail* [9.9–11] showed that it is possible to carry out a weighted decoding process of a given code in linear blocks, which is optimal in the maximum likelihood sense, but with lower complexity than in *Wolf*'s approach [9.8].

All these approaches are basically focused on two main problems; first, the selection of a suitable decision rule; and second, the determination of the corresponding error probability p^e.

Our main purpose here is to suggest a model of decision that allows one to tackle these problems when the decoder, be it a physical device or a human being, works with subjectivity. By the term subjectivity, we mean some prior knowledge of the meanings of the observable. This need not necessarily be expressed by means of prior probability, but can be given by more general weighting coefficients.

To this end, we shall first introduce a new concept of observed probability, which is derived from the model of Minkowskian observation, and shall then apply it to statistical decision.

9.2 Background on Observation with Information Invariance

9.2.1 Euclidean or Minkowskian Invariance?

We have shown (Chap. 4) that if we measure the amount of information contained in a source by its Shannon entropy, then when we observe a pair (X, Y) of random variables, there are necessarily coupling effects between X and Y, in such a manner that the observation results in linear combinations x_r and y_r of the actual values x and y. When we use the assumption of informational invariance only, we obtain two possible types of observation: the Euclidean one, which is defined by the rotation matrix, and the Minkowskian one described by means of the Lorentz equations. Thus we need additional hypotheses in order to select the appropriate transformation for a given problem.

We have seen that, loosely speaking, the Euclidean transformation is associated with dislearning processes while the Minkowskian matrix characterizes learning processes. But this remark is a general principle only, and sometimes further considerations may be required to refine this framework.

As an illustrative example, assume that we are observing two variables X and Y which satisfy the equation

$$x^2 + y^2 = \text{constant} , \tag{9.2.1}$$

with the additional condition that a given function $F(x, y)$ is symmetrical with respect to x and y, namely

$$F(x, y) = F(y, x) \tag{9.2.2}$$

At first glance, (9.2.1) suggests the use of the Euclidean matrix, but this may contradict the condition (9.2.2); and conversely (9.2.2) suggests the Minkowskian matrix, but then (9.2.1) is no longer satisfied. In order to cope with this difficulty, we have the following alternative.

i) First, one may assume that only one of these constraints is satisfied by the observation process. For instance, we may require that

$$F(x_r, y_r) = F(y_r, x_r) \tag{9.2.3}$$

while one may have $x_r^2 + y_r^2 \neq x^2 + y^2$. This point of view is quite reasonable since x_r and y_r are observed values which do not necessarily satisfy the *physical condition* (9.2.1).

ii) Second, one may assume that the Minkowskian observation does not apply to the variables X and Y themselves, but rather to the pair $(f(X), f(Y))$ where $f(\cdot)$ denotes a given function: clearly the observer does not perceive (x, y) but rather $(f(x), f(y))$. The level (accuracy) of observation is thus displaced from (x, y) to $(f(x), f(y))$.

It is exactly this second viewpoint that we shall adopt in order to derive a model of observation of probability distributions.

9.2.2 On the Practical Meaning of the Model

The parameter ω in (4.5.2) [or u in (4.5.5)] characterizes the subjectivity of the observer R, and evidently depends upon R's prior knowledge or misknowledge of the actual values of the observables. One can estimate u either priorly or posteriorly and apply a discrete scheme in the form

$$x_r(n + 1) = \varrho(u_n)[x(n + 1) + u_n y(n + 1)] \tag{9.2.4}$$

$$y_r(n + 1) = \varrho(u_n)[u_n x(n + 1) + y(n + 1)] \ . \tag{9.2.5}$$

In analogy with mechanics, one may define u by the equation

$$u := dx/dy$$

and therefore consider it as a degree of learning or dislearning depending upon its sign and the practical meanings of x and y. For instance, if x and y are two discrete informational entropies $H(\alpha)$ and $H(a)$, then the condition $u < 0$ corresponds to a learning process while $u > 0$ represents dislearning.

A comment of paramount importance is that this observation model applies to any pair of observables (provided they are directly observed!) so that all that is required is a careful analysis of the physical framework in order to determine the level of the observation.

9.2.3 Syntax and Semantics

In information theoretic applications, one of the main source of Minskowskian coupling effects is the duality *syntax-semantics* of natural languages. In such a case, x is a symbol, say the syntactic variable, while y represents the meaning that x may have, and is referred to as the semantic variable.

9.3 Relative Probability

9.3.1 Definition of Relative Probability

Let us consider a random experiment α which provides the outcomes $A_1, A_2, \ldots,$ A_m, with the respective probabilities $p(1), p(2), \ldots, p(m)$. According to Shannon, the total uncertainty about α, prior to any experiment, is defined by the entropy

$$H(\alpha) := -\sum_{i=1}^{m} p(i) \ln p(i) \tag{9.3.1}$$

where the natural logarithm is chosen for convenience only and is not mandatory at all.

Assume now that the observer R is observing the ith outcome (or event) A_i which involves the uncertainty $-\ln p(i)$. When R examines A_i from an informational viewpoint, then he is not interested in the symbol A_i itself, but rather in the amount of information it contains. In other words, he is not observing A_i but the variable $-\ln p(i)$.

Comments. Here we have exactly the case outlined at the end of the Sect. 9.2.1. Indeed, for the distribution (p, q), $p + q = 1$, for instance, one has on the one hand the invariance

$$p_r + q_r = p + q = 1 \tag{9.3.2}$$

and, on the other hand, and the property that the entropy $H(p, q)$ is symmetrical with respect to p and q,

$$H(p, q) = H(q, p) .$$ (9.3.3)

The Minkowskian observation applied to the pair (p, q) satisfies condition (9.3.3) but violates (9.3.2), while the Euclidean observation of $(\sqrt{p}, \sqrt{q})$ contradicts (9.3.3).

This being so, our claim is that, from a practical standpoint, the observer R is sensitive to the amount of information contained in the event A_i rather than to the probability $p(A_i)$ itself. Indeed, in most cases, R is not interested in the value of $p(A_i)$ but rather he uses A_i to reach decisions about a given concern. In this way, we can say that R observes the amount of information represented by A_i relative to a given topic of interest.

We have the following definition.

Definition 9.3.1. Assume that the outcome A_i has several possible meanings A'_{i1}, A'_{i2}, ..., A'_{ij_i}; and let $\tilde{H}_i$ denote their corresponding Shannon entropy. Assume further that the two local entropies $-\ln p(i)$ and $\tilde{H}_i$ are observed via a Minkowskian observation process to yield the equations

$$[-\ln p(i)]_r = \varrho(u_i)[-\ln p(i) + u_i \tilde{H}_i]$$ (9.3.4)

$$(\tilde{H}_i)_r = \varrho(u_i)[-u_i \ln p(i) + \tilde{H}_i] .$$ (9.3.5)

On defining $p_r(i)$ by the equation

$$[\ln p(i)]_r =: \ln p_r(i)$$ (9.3.6)

we directly obtain

$$p_r(i) = e^{-\varrho_i u_i \tilde{H}_i} p(i)^{\varrho_i} .$$ (9.3.7)

The distribution $\{p_r(i)\}$ so defined is referred to as the *relative probability distribution of a given the observer R*.   □

A Special Case of Interest. Assume that $\tilde{H}_i = 0$ for every i; then (9.3.7) yields the equation

$$p_r(i) = p(i)^{\varrho_i} ,$$ (9.3.8)

which, for instance, applies to the following two situations.

i) In the framework of discrete variables, the observer R believes that the outcome A_i has several meanings while it actually only has one. We then have $\tilde{H}_i = 0$ but $0 < u < 1$.

ii) According to the identification procedure which we used in Sects. 5.8 and 5.9 when we applied subjective entropy to encoding problems, we can identify $\tilde{H}_i$ with the entropy of the error term on $p(i)$.

This being so, in the absence of any prior information on the probabilities $p(i)$, all we can do is to assume that these errors are uniformly distributed on the interval $[0,1]$ so that we have

$$\tilde{H}_i = \ln(1-0) , \qquad i = 1, 2, \ldots, m .$$

Note that ϱ_i in (9.3.8) is quite similar to the exponent c which appears in the expression (2.9.1) for the Renyi entropy $H_c(X)$.

9.3.2 On the Practical Meaning of Relative Probability

It is clear that $p_r(i)$ is not a probability since one has

$$\sum_{i=1}^{m} p_r(i) \neq 1 .$$

As a matter of fact, this distribution should rather be thought of as related to the recent concept of *possibility*, first introduced by *Zadeh* [9.14] in the framework of fuzzy mathematics. As a brief illustration, the possibility that Michael eats five eggs at the breakfeast, and the probability that he eats five eggs are not the same.

If we are dealing with a discrete random variable X, an expression such as

$$E_r(X) := \sum_{i=1}^{m} x_i p_r(i) \tag{9.3.9}$$

is quite meaningful from a practical standpoint since we can consider it as the observed or subjective mathematical expectation measured by the observer.

In addition, we point out that $p_r(i)$ is not a subjective or prior probability in the usual sense of this term, but in contrast, it is the result of observation.

9.3.3 Semantic Entropy of a Real-Valued Variable

In terms of practical identification, a question of importance can be formulated as follows: on assuming that p_i is the occurrence probability of the ith value x_i of a random variable X, how can we define the corresponding semantic entropy $\tilde{H}_i$? The following answer is quite meaningful.

Making use once again of the pair (syntax, semantics) or likewise (symbol, meaning), we shall assume that the subscript i of x_i refers to the symbol, while the different meanings of x_i are defined by the actual values $x_i^1, x_i^2, \ldots, x_i^{m_i}$ which x_i can take, so that we have

$$\tilde{H}_i := - \sum_{j=1}^{m_i} p(x_i^j) \ln p(x_i^j) . \tag{9.3.10}$$

In this way, the entropy $\tilde{H}_i$ can be considered as characterizing a defect in the definition of the ith state itself. In the framework of fuzzy set theory, for instance, $\tilde{H}_i$ would measure the fuzziness of the state x_i.

It is now clear that the assumption $\tilde{H}_i = 0$ is quite a meaningful one. But even in this case, the Minkowskian observation process may work. This merely reflects the fact that the observer believes that this ith state may have several possible values, whereas it actually does not.

9.3.4 Relative Probability of Deterministic Events

Assume that $p(i) = 1$. Equation (9.3.4) then yields

$$p_r(i) = \exp(-\varrho_i u_i \tilde{H}_i) \ . \tag{9.3.11}$$

This result can be understood as follows: even though the event A_i is deterministic, the fact that one takes account of its possible practical meanings, creates some doubt to the observer and thus the term $p_r(i)$ can be thought of as a probability or a possibility which depends upon the situation. If $\tilde{H}_i$ refers to a discrete entropy, and if A_i has no meaning, we then have $p_r(i) = 1$, as expected since there is then no interference between symbols and meanings.

9.3.5 Relative Probability of the Impossible Event

As is evident, both the probability and the relative probability of the impossible event are zero.

9.4 Composition Laws for Relative Probability

9.4.1 Relative Probability of the Complement of an Event

Problem 9.1. Let A denote a random event with the probability $p(A)$, which is observed with the subjective coefficient u_A and with the semantic entropy $\tilde{H}_A$ to yield the relative probability

$$p_r(A) = \exp[-\varrho(u_A)u_A\tilde{H}_A][\varrho(A)]^{\varrho(u_A)} \ . \tag{9.4.1}$$

Let us now consider the parameters $\tilde{H}_{\bar{A}}$ and $u_{\bar{A}}$ of the complementary event which occurs when A itself is not achieved. Can we express them in terms of $\tilde{H}_A$ and u_A? $\qquad\qquad\square$

At first glance it seems that we cannot, except when dealing with certain special cases. Indeed, the semantic entropy $\tilde{H}_{\bar{A}}$ is defined irrespective of any reference to $\tilde{H}_A$; for instance, the observer may have some doubt about the meaning of A, while the meaning of $\bar{A}$ is clear to him. Furthermore, it is not obvious that the subjectivities u_A and $u_{\bar{A}}$ should be related. All we can write is the relation

$$p_r(\bar{A}) = \exp[-\varrho(u_{\bar{A}})u_{\bar{A}}\tilde{H}_{\bar{A}}][1 - p(A)]^{\varrho(u_{\bar{A}})} \ . \tag{9.4.2}$$

The following remarks may help to clarify some features.

   i) Assume that

$$u_A = u_{\bar{A}} = u \ . \tag{9.4.3}$$

Equation (9.3.2) then yields

$$-\ln p_r(A) = \varrho(u)[-\ln p(A) + u\tilde{H}_A] \ , \tag{9.4.4}$$

$$-\ln p_r(\bar{A}) = \varrho(u)[-\ln p(\bar{A}) + u\tilde{H}_{\bar{A}}] \ . \tag{9.4.5}$$

If we now define the observed entropy $H_r(\alpha)$, $\alpha := (A_1, A_2)$, as the mathematical expectation

$$H_r(\alpha) := E\{-\ln p_r(A)\} \ , \tag{9.4.6}$$

we then obtain the expression

$$H_r(\alpha) = \varrho(u)[H(\alpha) + u\tilde{H}_\alpha] \ , \tag{9.4.7}$$

where $\tilde{H}_\alpha$ is defined as

$$\tilde{H}_\alpha := \tilde{H}_A + \tilde{H}_{\bar{A}} \ . \tag{9.4.8}$$

Everything occurs as if the observer were observing the entropy $H(\alpha)$ itself instead of the respective entropies $-\ln p(A)$ and $-\ln p(\bar{A})$ of each event.

This assumption "u equal to a constant" is a valuable first approach in practical problems.

ii) Assume that A is a deterministic event. One then has

$$p_r(A) = \exp[-\varrho(u_A)u_A\tilde{H}_A] \ , \tag{9.4.9}$$

$$p_r(\bar{A}) = 0 \ , \tag{9.4.10}$$

that is to say

$$p_r(A) + p_r(\bar{A}) \neq 1 \ . \tag{9.4.11}$$

There is no doubt about $\bar{A}$ while A presents some ambiguity to the observer.

iii) In some practical cases one may have $\tilde{H}_A \neq 0$ and $\tilde{H}_{\bar{A}} = 0$.

9.4.2 Relative Probability of a Deterministic Event

If we assume that the space of objects under consideration is well defined to the observer, then we can usefully assume that a deterministic event does not, and cannot, involve any subjectivity. For instance, if we are aware that we are observing a message written in English, there is no doubt about the corresponding deterministic event and our subjectivity enters only when we try to guess which letter is effectively sent.

Thus, if Ω denotes the deterministic event, we shall set

$$u(\Omega) = 0 \tag{9.4.12}$$

$$p_r(\Omega) = 1 \ . \tag{9.4.13}$$

9.4.3 Relative Probability of Intersection of Events

Problem 9.2. Let A and B denote two random events, and consider the probability law

$$p(A \cap B) = p(A)p(B/A) \ . \tag{9.4.14}$$

Assume that $(u_A, \tilde{H}_A)$ and $(u_{B/A}, \tilde{H}_{B/A})$ are the parameters of A and (B/A), respectively. How does one define the counterpart of (9.4.14) in terms of relative probabilities?

□

Preliminary Remarks. On the surface, there are two possible ways to make this generalization. First, we can do so in such a manner that the new equation obtained gives (9.4.14) as a special case; second, we can suppose that this new equation is directly equivalent to (9.4.14) when we express the relative probabilities in terms of the usual ones.

Assume that we exploit the first idea and that we set, for instance, (this is the most straightforward hypothesis)

$$p_r(A \cap B) = p_r(A)p_r(B/A) \ . \tag{9.4.15}$$

Let $u_{A \cap B}$ and $\tilde{H}_{A \cap B}$ denote the parameters associated with $(A \cap B)$. One then has the relation

$$p_r(A \cap B) = e^{-(\varrho u \tilde{H})_{A \cap B}}[p(A \cap B)]^{\varrho_{A \cap B}} \ . \tag{9.4.16}$$

This being so, $p_r(A)$ is defined by (9.4.1). In addition one has

$$p_r(B/A) = e^{-(\varrho u \tilde{H})_{B/A}}[p(B/A)]^{\varrho_{B/A}} \ , \tag{9.4.17}$$

so that on substituting into (9.4.16), we would obtain the relation

$$e^{-(\varrho u \tilde{H})_{A \cap B}}p(A \cap B)^{\varrho_{A \cap B}} = e^{-(\varrho u \tilde{H})_A}e^{-(\varrho u \tilde{H})_{B/A}}p(A)^{\varrho_A}p(B/A)^{\varrho_{B/A}} \tag{9.4.18}$$

and at this stage, two situations may occur.

i)   The first possibility is that we do not know how $u_{A \cap B}$ depends upon u_A and $u_{B/A}$. In such a case, (9.4.18) could be quite an acceptable assumption and it would define $u_{A \cap B}$ in terms of u_A and $u_{B/A}$.
ii) Alternatively, we have at hand the function $u_{A \cap B} = f(u_A, u_{B/A})$. In this case, (9.4.18) is simply inconsistent.

As a matter of fact, we are interested in the latter case, and so we are forced to discard the approach via (9.4.15). Indeed, the equations of the Minkowskian observation define the law of the subjectivity u, so that the function $f(\cdot)$ above is a given feature of the model.

Derivation of the Law. We now take $p(A \cap B)$, $p(B)$ and $p(B/A)$ from (9.4.16), (9.4.1) and (9.4.17) respectively, and we substitute into (9.4.14) to obtain the equation

$$p_r(A \cap B)^{1/\varrho_{A \cap B}}\exp[(u\tilde{H})_{A \cap B}] = p_r(A)^{1/\varrho_A}p_r(B/A)^{1/\varrho_{B/A}}\exp[(u\tilde{H})_A + (u\tilde{H})_{B/A}] \ . \tag{9.4.19}$$

One therefore has the law

$$p_r(A \cap B) = p_r(A)^{\varrho_{A \cap B}/\varrho_A} p_r(B/A)^{\varrho_{A \cap B}/\varrho_{B/A}}$$

$$\times \exp\{\varrho_{A \cap B}[(u\tilde{H})_A + (u\tilde{H})_{B/A} - (u\tilde{H})_{A \cap B}]\} \; . \tag{9.4.20}$$

The task now is to calculate $u_{A/B}$. To this end, we shall use the Lorentz equations which define the observed entropy, and we may state straightforwardly the following:

Law of Relative Probability for the Intersection of Random Events. Let A and (B/A) denote the relative random events defined in problem 9.2, which implicitly assumes that one observes A first and then (B/A); and let $\tilde{H}_{A \cap B}$ denote the semantic entropy of the event $A \cap B$. The subjectivity parameter $u_{A \cap B}$ is then given by the equation

$$u_{A \cap B} = \frac{u_A + u_{B/A}}{1 + u_A u_{B/A}} \; , \tag{9.4.21}$$

and the relative probability $p_r(A \cap B)$ is expressed by the equation (9.4.20) together with (9.4.21). □

A Few Comments. (i) The process in which B is observed first and then A, provides $u_{B \cap A}$ in the form

$$u_{B \cap A} = \frac{u_B + u_{A/B}}{1 + u_B u_{A/B}} \tag{9.4.22}$$

and it is clear that, in general,

$$u_{A \cap B} \neq u_{B \cap A} \; . \tag{9.4.23}$$

Therefore

$$p_r(A \cap B) \neq p_r(B \cap A) \; .$$

Nevertheless, when A and B are independent from the subjectivistic viewpoint, that is to say when the subjectivity of the observer R regarding B is not affected by the previous observation of A, one has

$$u_{B/A} = u_B \qquad \text{so that} \tag{9.4.24}$$

$$u_{A \cap B} = u_{B \cap A} \qquad \text{and} \tag{9.4.25}$$

$$p_r(A \cap B) = p_r(B \cap A) \; . \tag{9.4.26}$$

ii) Can we relate $\tilde{H}_{A \cap B}$ to $\tilde{H}_A$ and $\tilde{H}_B$? At first glance, it is tempting to write

$$\tilde{H}_{A \cap B} = \tilde{H}_A + \tilde{H}_{B/A} \tag{9.4.27}$$

but unfortunately we cannot claim that this relation holds in every case. Indeed, a relation like (9.4.27) pictures the semantic space of the universe of discourse, and as such, it is a special case only. For instance, one could equally well have $\tilde{H}_{A \cap B} = \tilde{H}_A = \tilde{H}_{B/A}$, given that everything depends upon how the semantic space is described. So, in a practical problem, we have to analyze the different semantic spaces involved, and then define $\tilde{H}_A$, $\tilde{H}_B$ and $\tilde{H}_{A \cap B}$.

iii) Assume that

$$\tilde{H}_A = \tilde{H}_B = \tilde{H}_{A \cap B} = 0 \; ;$$

Equation (9.4.20) then yields

$$p_r(A \cap B) = p_r(A)^{\varrho_{A \cap B}/\varrho_A} p_r(B)^{\varrho_{A \cap B}/\varrho_{B/A}} \; . \tag{9.4.28}$$

This relation is useful when it is known that the observer possesses some subjectivity, but the semantic entropies are not given. In such a case, it is quite a valuable model.

If in addition we assume that

$$u_{B/A} = u_B$$

then (9.4.28) yields the form

$$p_r(A \cap B) = p_r(A)^{\varrho_{A \cap B}/\varrho_A} p_r(B)^{\varrho_{A \cap B}/\varrho_B} \tag{9.4.29}$$

which can easily be generalized to more than two events.

iv) Assume that A involves subjectivity while B/A does not. We then have

$$u_{B/A} = 0 \quad \text{and} \quad \varrho_{A \cap B} = \rho_A \; , \tag{9.4.30}$$

so that (9.4.20) yields

$$p_r(A \cap B) = p_r(A) p_r(B/A)^{\varrho_A} \exp[\varrho_A u_A(\tilde{H}_A - \tilde{H}_{A \cap B})] \; . \tag{9.4.31}$$

v) Assume that B is the deterministic event Ω. According to (9.4.12) one has

$$u_{A \cap \Omega} = u_A \tag{9.4.32}$$

and therefore the equality

$$\varrho_{A \cap \Omega} = \varrho_A \; . \tag{9.4.33}$$

In addition, one necessarily has

$$\tilde{H}_{A \cap \Omega} = \tilde{H}_A \; , \tag{9.4.34}$$

so that (9.4.19) yields the relation

$$p_r(A \cap \Omega) = p_r(A) \tag{9.4.35}$$

which is quite meaningful.

vi) Note that the condition $p(A \cap B) = 0$ implies that $p_r(A \cap B) = 0$.

9.4.4 Relative Probability of the Union of Events

Problem 9.3. Consider the framework of problem 9.2 and assume that we have at hand the coefficient u_B associated with the observation of the event B alone, together with the semantic entropy $\tilde{H}_{A\cup B}$ of the union $A \cup B$. How, under these conditions, can one generalize the law

$$p(A \cup B) = p(A) + p(B) - p(A \cap B) \qquad (9.4.36)$$

in terms of relative probability? □

i) First, with the usual rule of parsimony of assumptions (and in order to derive as general a model as possible) we shall postulate that

$$u_{A\cup B} = u_{A\cap B} , \qquad (9.4.37)$$

in other words, the subjectivities related to the events $A \cup B$ and $A \cap B$ are the same. This is the simplest hypothesis that we can make, and it can be justified by noting that the observations of a given random event C with respect to $A \cup B$ or $A \cap B$ involve the same operations: the comparison of C with A on the one hand, and of C with B on the other.

ii) Next, by using an approach similar to that of Sect. 9.4.3, we shall write

$$p_r(A \cup B) = [p(A \cup B)]^{\varrho_{A\cup B}} \exp\{-[\rho(u)u\tilde{H}]_{A\cup B}\} \qquad (9.4.38)$$

and writing $p(A)$, $p(B)$ and $p(A \cap B)$ in (9.4.36) explicitly by means of the corresponding relative probabilities, we directly obtain the law

$$p_r(A \cup B)^{1/\varrho_{A\cup B}} e^{(u\tilde{H})_{A\cup B}} = p_r(A)^{1/\varrho_A} e^{(u\tilde{H})_A} + p_r(B)^{1/\varrho_B} e^{(u\tilde{H})_B}$$

$$- p_r(A \cap B)^{1/\varrho_{A\cap B}} e^{(u\tilde{H})_{A\cap B}} . \qquad (9.4.39)$$

We can then state:

Law of Relative Probability for the Union of Random Events. Assume that $p_r(A \cap B)$ is defined by (9.4.20), and let $\tilde{H}_{A\cup B}$ denote the semantic entropy of the union $A \cup B$. Assume further that (9.4.37) is satisfied. Then the relative probability $p_r(A \cup B)$ is defined by (9.4.39). □

A Few Comments. (i) Assume that A and B are independent; then, according to the remark (vi) in Sect. 9.4.3, one has $p_r(A \cap B) = 0$, and (9.4.39) yields

$$p_r(A \cup B)^{1/\varrho_{A\cup B}} e^{(u\tilde{H})_{A\cup B}} = p_r(A)^{1/\varrho_A} e^{(u\tilde{H})_A} + p_r(B)^{1/\varrho_B} e^{(u\tilde{H})_B} . \qquad (9.4.40)$$

Furthermore, when

$$\tilde{H}_{A\cup B} = \tilde{H}_A = \tilde{H}_B = 0 ,$$

then we have the compact form

$$p_r(A \cup B)^{1/\varrho_{A\cup B}} = p_r(A)^{1/\varrho_A} + p_r(B)^{1/\varrho_B} \qquad (9.4.41)$$

which can easily be generalized to more than two events.

ii) Assume that B is the deterministic event Ω. Then by virtue of the relations (9.4.12), (9.4.13), (9.4.32) to (9.4.35) and (9.4.37), Eq. (9.4.39) provides

$$p_r(A \cup \Omega) = 1$$

which is quite meaningful from a practical viewpoint.

9.5 Generalized Maximum Likelihood Criterion

9.5.1 The Problem

The maximum likelihood criterion expressed by (9.1.2) is one of the most useful in statistical decision, and this is probably due to the fact that it is straightforward to apply since the conditional probabilities involved are generally given as characteristics of the system under consideration.

The results that have been obtained in practical applications (filtering, artificial vision, games, economics, etc.) were both amazing and powerful, so that in the opinion of many statisticians, the theory has achieved its final form. But this is only partially true. Indeed, in many instances, this approach is thoroughly inconclusive, so that the decision maker, be it a human being or a physical device, has to take account of its own parameters, i.e. its subjectivity, in order to reach a definitive verdict.

Our purpose in the present section is to suggest a new decision criterion which could be of help in such a situation.

9.5.2 Generalized Maximum Likelihood Criterion

Assume that, when the observer R examines or estimates the amount of information $-\ln p(y/x_i)$, then a Minkowskian observation process occurs, in such a manner that the observer no longer uses the probability $p(y/x_i)$ but refers rather to the relative or observed probability $p_r(y/x_i)$ defined by (9.3.5) and applies this as if it were the usual probability. We then obtain the following decision rule.

Generalized Maximum Likelihood Criterion. In the framework of observation processes involving coupling effects between syntax and semantics, given an observed y, from among all the possible observables x_i, select that one $x_{\bar{i}}$ which maximizes the relative probability $p_r(y/x_i)$, that is to say such that

$$p_r(y/x_{\bar{i}}) \geqslant p_r(y/x_i) , \qquad i \neq \bar{i} \tag{9.5.1}$$

or else, in the explicit form

$$e^{-(\varrho u \hat{H})_{\bar{i}}}[p(y/x_{\bar{i}})]^{\rho_{\bar{i}}} \geqslant e^{-(\varrho u \hat{H})_i}[p(y/x_i)]^{\varrho_i} , \qquad i \neq \bar{i} . \tag{9.5.2} \quad \square$$

9.5.3 Practical Meaning of the Generalized Maximum Likelihood Criterion

The best way to exhibit the practical significance of condition (9.5.2) is to examine some special cases.

i) Assume that $\tilde{H}_i = 0$ and $0 < u_i < 1$ for every i. This corresponds to the case where R erroneously believes that the variables (y/x_i) have several possible meanings. The criterion is then

$$[p(y/x_{\bar{i}})]^{\varrho_{\bar{i}}} \geqslant [p(y/x_i)]^{\varrho_i} \tag{9.5.3}$$

and it clear that one may have $x_{i*} \neq x_{\bar{i}}$. In this case it is sufficient that $\varrho_{\bar{i}}$ be large enough, i.e. that $u_{\bar{i}}$ be large enough, for the confusing effect to be important.

ii) Now assume that $|u_i| \ll 1$ for every i, so that one has $\varrho \cong 1$ for every i. The criterion (9.5.2) then takes the form

$$e^{-(u\tilde{H})_{\bar{i}}} p(y/x_{\bar{i}}) \geqslant e^{-(u\tilde{H})_i} p(y/x_i) \tag{9.5.4}$$

and two situations may occur depending upon the sign of u.

Case 1. $u_i > 0$ for every i. In the framework of discrete entropies one has $\tilde{H}_i > 0$ for every i, and therefore the inequalities

$$0 < e^{-(u\tilde{H})_{\bar{i}}} \quad \text{and} \quad e^{-(u\tilde{H})_i} < 1 \ . \tag{9.5.5}$$

Condition (9.5.4) is then quite similar to the inequality

$$p(E_{\bar{i}})p(y/x_{\bar{i}}) \geqslant p(E_i)p(y/x_i) \tag{9.5.6}$$

where $\{E_i\}$ is a family of events. It is well known that one derives exactly the same condition in certain problems of Bayesian statistical decisions.

Case 2. $u_i \leqslant 0$ for every i. Here it follows that

$$1 \leqslant e^{-(u\tilde{H})_{\bar{i}}} \quad \text{and} \quad 1 \leqslant e^{-(u\tilde{H})_i}$$

and the conditional probabilities are then weighted by coefficients related to the observer's prior knowledge about the system of events. For instance, if one has $u_i = 0, i \neq \bar{i}$, one obtains the condition

$$e^{-(u\tilde{H})_{\bar{i}}} p(y/x_{\bar{i}}) \geqslant p(y/x_i) \ , \qquad i \neq \bar{i} \tag{9.5.7}$$

which may hold even when $p(y/x_{\bar{i}}) < p(y/x_i)$, $i \neq \bar{i}$.

iii) In the more general case, when $u_i > 0$ for every i, criterion (9.5.4) can be rewritten in the form

$$p(E_{\bar{i}})[p(y/x_{\bar{i}})]^{\varrho_{\bar{i}}} \geqslant p(E_i)[p(y/x_i)]^{\varrho_i} \tag{9.5.8}$$

where $p(E_i)$ and $p(E_{\bar{i}})$, which are smaller than one, are weighting coefficients. Criterion (9.5.8) is then a straightforward generalization of (9.5.6).

9.5.4 A Simplified Criterion

From the theoretical standpoint, the coefficient $u_i = u_i(R)$ will depend both upon the observer R and the event i. Thus the criterion expressed by (9.5.2) is actually the more general one. Nevertheless, in some applications it may be difficult to use it, in the sense that it may not provide results in a compact form: thus it can be valuable to have simplified criteria that are more tractable in practical problems. This is the reason why we suggest the following decision rule:

A Variant of the Generalized Maximum Likelihood Criterion. Select x_i if

$$\exp[-(u\tilde{H})_i]p^a(y/x_i) \geqslant \exp[-(u\tilde{H})_{i'}]p^b(y/x_{i'}) , \qquad i \neq i' \qquad (9.5.9)$$

where a and b are two positive constants such that

$$a \geqslant 1 ; \qquad b \geqslant 1; \qquad a \geqslant b . \qquad\qquad (9.5.10) \quad \square$$

The criterion is simplified mainly because of the presence of the constants a and b in place of the variable $\varrho(u_i)$. The additional requirement $a > b$, that is to say $p^a < p^b$, is merely an insurance against making the wrong decision; and this somewhat pessimistic viewpoint is rectified by the presence of the coefficients $\exp[-(u\tilde{H})_i]$.

The simplest way to define a and b is to put

$$a := \max_i \varrho(u_i) \qquad\qquad (9.5.11)$$

$$b := \min_i \varrho(u_i) . \qquad\qquad (9.5.12)$$

9.5.5 Another Simplified Decision Criterion

Assume that all the coefficients $(u\tilde{H})_i$ are equal, that is to say, criterion (9.5.9) reduces to the form

$$p^a(y/x_i) \geqslant p^b(y/x_{i'}) , \qquad\qquad (9.5.13)$$

and let x_{i_0} denote the corresponding optimum solution. When one takes into account the coefficients $\exp[-(u\tilde{H})_i]$, one has the following alternatives: either this optimum solution remains the same, or it is replaced by a different one.

i) In the first case, if one has $\exp[-(u\tilde{H})_{i_0}] \geqslant \exp[-(u\tilde{H})_{i'}]$ for every i', then it is likely that the accuracy of the decision-making process will be improved by using the criterion (9.5.9). But one may have $\exp[-(u\tilde{H})_{i_0}] < \exp[-(u\tilde{H})_{i'}]$ for one or more i' in which case (9.5.9) is useless and it is better to take (9.5.13).

ii) In the second case, there is at least one coefficient $\exp[-(u\tilde{H})_{i'}]$ which is larger than $\exp[-(u\tilde{H})_{i_0}]$ and we are then in a position to apply the criterion (9.4.9).

This comment suggests another decision rule:

Alternative Decision Rule. Select x_i if

$$\exp[-(u\tilde{H})_i]p^a(y/x_i) \geqslant \exp[-(u\tilde{H})_{i'}]p^b(y/x_{i'}) , \qquad i \neq i' \qquad (9.5.14)$$

with

$$\exp[-(u\tilde{H})_i] \geqslant \exp[-(u\tilde{H})_{i'}] , \qquad\qquad (9.5.15)$$

otherwise follow the decision rule

$$p(y/x_i) \geqslant p(y/x_{i'}) \ . \tag{9.5.16} \quad \square$$

This alternative is justified as follows. The definition of the constants a and b is rather pessimistic, and is of interest only if the coefficients $\exp[-(u\tilde{H})_i]$ are meaningful. If they are useless, then the classical criterion $p(y/x_{\bar{i}}) \geqslant p(y/x_i)$ is just as good.

9.5.6 Comparison with Another Criterion

Recently, *N. L. Sharma* and *B. D. Sharma* [9.16] suggested a generalized criterion in the form

$$p^{\eta}(y/x_{\bar{i}}) \geqslant p^{\gamma}(y/x_i) \ , \qquad \eta > \gamma \ , \qquad \bar{i} \neq i \tag{9.5.17}$$

when η and γ are real-valued parameters which, according to these authors, allow the observer to make a decision with sufficient evidence is available to support the favoured choice.

As defined, this criterion looks like a formal generalization. Its main problem is that the practical meaning of the coefficients η and γ is not at all clear. Why are they constant? What is the rationale behind the requirement $\eta > \gamma$? Why can't we have $\gamma > \eta$? As so stated, this condition is rather pessimistic in the sense that it could contradict the criterion $p(y/x_j) \geqslant p(y/x_i)$ and, as a result, it is not at all clear how η and γ can completely characterize the subjectivity of the decision maker. Indeed, in some instances, this subjectivity could lead us to conclude that it is x which we have at hand even when $p(y/x_{\bar{i}}) \leqslant p(y/x_i)$. So we believe that, in order to rectify this drawback, it could be interesting to modify the criterion (9.5.17) by introducing linear gains F and G so that the new decision rule is

$$Gp^{\eta}(y/x_{\bar{i}}) \geqslant Fp^{\gamma}(y/x_i) \tag{9.5.18}$$

which bears a strong resemblance to our model.

9.6 Generalized Bayesian Criterion

In order to define the model in a general framework and to simultaneously illustrate it with a practical example, we shall consider the problem of statistical pattern recognition, which is also related to the problem of decoding a message in the presence of semantics.

9.6.1 Pattern Recognition

We assume that there are m possible pattern classes $x_1, x_2, \ldots, x_m$ to be identified and n features $c_1, c_2, \ldots, c_n$ to be extracted for classification; one uses these features to determine the class of the object under observation. Let the (noisy) measurement of the n features be denoted by $y_i = c_i + \text{noise}$, $i = 1, 2, \ldots, m$. Each set of n feature measurements can be represented as an n-dimensional vector $y \in \mathbb{R}^n$ or as a point in the n-dimensional feature space Ω_y. Let the a priori probability of each pattern class be $P(x_i)$, $i = 1, \ldots, m$, and the conditional probability density function of y for each class x_i be $p(y/x_i)$, $i = 1, 2, \ldots, m$. On the basis of the a priori information $p(y/x_j)$ and $P(x_j)$, $j = 1, 2, \ldots, m$, the function of a statistical classifier is to perform the classification task for minimizing the probability of misrecognition.

9.6.2 Formulation of the Statistical Decision Problem

i) In the framework of statistical decision theory, we define a decision function $d(y)$ by the rule

$$d(y) = d_i. \tag{9.6.1}$$

This is equivalent to the statement y is from the class c_i.

ii) Let $L(x_i, d_j)$ be the loss incurred by the classifier if the decision d_j is made when the input pattern is actually from c_i.

iii) The conditional loss (or conditional risk) for $d = d(y)$ is written in the form

$$r(x_i, d) = \int_{\Omega_y} L(x_i, d) p_r(y/x_i) \, dy \tag{9.6.2}$$

where $p_r(y/x_i)$ denotes the relative probability as defined in Sect. 9.3. Clearly one has

$$\ln p_r(y/x_i) = -\varrho(x_i) u(x_i) \tilde{H}(x_i) + \varrho(x_i) \ln p(y/x_i) \tag{9.6.3}$$

$$=: -(\varrho u \tilde{H})_i + \varrho_i \ln p(y/x_i) \ . \tag{9.6.4}$$

As pointed out above, $r(x_i, d)$ as defined, can be thought as an observed mathematical expectation.

iv) For a given set of a priori probabilities $P = \{P(x_1), P(x_2), \ldots, P(x_m)\}$ the average loss (or average risk) is

$$R(P, d) := \sum_{i=1}^{m} P(x_i) r(x_i, d) \ . \tag{9.6.5}$$

If we define the a posteriori conditional average loss $r_y(P, d)$ of the decision d for a given feature measurement y by the expression

$$r_y(P, d) := \frac{\sum_{i=1}^{m} L(x_i, d) P(x_i) p_r(y/x_i)}{p(y)} \tag{9.6.6}$$

then (9.6.5) becomes

$$R(P, d) = \int_{\Omega_y} p(y) r_y(P, d) \, dy \ . \tag{9.6.7}$$

v) The problem is then to choose the decision d_j, $j = 1, 2, \ldots, m$, so as to minimize $R(P, d)$. Let d^* denote this optimal decision, one then has

$$r_y(P, d^*) \leqslant r_y(P, d) \ , \tag{9.6.8}$$

or equivalently

$$\sum_{i=1}^{m} L(x_i, d^*) P(x_i) p_r(y/x_i) \leqslant \sum_{i=1}^{m} L(x_i, d) P(x_i) p_r(y/x_i) \ . \tag{9.6.9}$$

9.6.3 Sharp Decision Rule

Assume that the loss function takes the values 0 and 1 only, clearly

$$L(x_i, d_j) = 1 - \delta_{ij} \tag{9.6.10}$$

where δ_{ij} is the Kroneker delta symbol. Assume that the optimal solution is $d_{\hat{i}}$; then condition (9.6.9) yields for $k \neq \hat{i}$

$$\sum_{i=1; i \neq \hat{i}}^{m} P(x_i) p_r(y/x_i) \leqslant \sum_{i=1; i \neq k}^{m} P(x_i) p_r(y/x_i) \tag{9.6.11}$$

and thence the rule:

Sharp Decision Rule. Select $x_{\hat{i}}$ if

$$P(x_{\hat{i}}) p_r(y/x_{\hat{i}}) \geqslant P(x_i) p_r(y/x_i) \tag{9.6.12}$$

or in explicit form

$$e^{-(\varrho u \hbar)_{\hat{i}}} P(x_{\hat{i}}) p(y/x_{\hat{i}})^{\varrho_{\hat{i}}} \geqslant e^{-(\varrho u \hbar)_i} P(x_i) p(y/x_i)^{\varrho_i} \ . \tag{9.6.13}$$

9.6.4 Soft Decision Rule

Once more we consider the example above, but we now assume that the loss function $L(x_i, d_j)$ is defined as

$$L(x_i, d_j) = \begin{cases} 0, & i = j \\ \mu_i, & i \neq j \end{cases} \tag{9.6.14}$$

where μ_i is such that $0 < \mu_i \leqslant 1, i = 1, \ldots, m$.

This parameter μ_i represents a certain grade of fuzziness in the definition of the class x_i itself. Indeed, using the vocabulary of set theory, if x_i is defined as a crisp set, then the loss function expressed by (9.6.10) is quite suitable. On the other hand, if x_i is defined by a fuzzy set for every i, then we cannot be sure that the loss function will achieve its maximum value 1, therefore the equation (9.6.14). □

This being so, let $d_{\bar{i}}$ denote the corresponding optimal decision; it satisfies condition (9.5.9), that is

$$\sum_{i=1; i \neq \bar{i}}^{m} \mu_i P(x_i) p_r(y/x_i) \leqslant \sum_{i=1; i \neq k}^{m} \mu_i P(x_i) p_r(y/x_i) \tag{9.6.15}$$

which leads to the following rule:

Soft Decision Rule. Select $x_{\bar{i}}$ if

$$\mu_{\bar{i}}P(x_{\bar{i}})p_r(y/x_{\bar{i}}) \geqslant \mu_i P(x_i)p_r(y/x_i) \ , \qquad i \neq \bar{i} \tag{9.6.16}$$

or in explicit form

$$\mu_{\bar{i}}\mathrm{e}^{-(\varrho u \bar{H})_{\bar{i}}} P(x_{\bar{i}})p(y/x_{\bar{i}})^{\varrho_{\bar{i}}} \geqslant \mu_i \mathrm{e}^{-(\varrho u \bar{H})_i} P(x_i)p(y/x_i)^{\varrho_i} \ . \tag{9.6.17}$$

Definition 9.6.1. We shall refer to the criterion expressed by the inequality (9.6.13) as the *generalized Bayesian rule*, which may be compared to the customary Bayesian decision rule

$$P(x_{\bar{i}})p(y/x_{\bar{i}}) \geqslant P(x_i)p(y/x_i) \tag{9.6.18}$$

obtained when we choose the loss function

$$r(x_i, d) := \int_{\Omega_y} L(x_i, d)p(y/x_i)\,dy \ . \tag{9.6.19} \quad \square$$

9.7 Generalized Bayesian Decision and Path Integrals

9.7.1 Formulation of the Problem

In some decision-making processes we may have to select not a vector, but a trajectory, and it is then reasonable that the corresponding formulation should arrive at the concept of path integrals or something similar. The following is a preliminary approach to this question.

We consider a sequence of times $t_0, t_1, \ldots, t_N$, at which the system is observed, with measured $y_i \in \mathbb{R}$ at time t_i, $i \geqslant 1$, while the actual value is x_i. We shall assume that the observation process at each instant t_i is Minkowskian.

Let $\tilde{Y}^N$ denote the trajectory as measured from the time t_0 to the time t_N, and let $\{\tilde{X}_I^N\}$, $I \in N^N$, denote the family of the actual trajectories of the system. The problem is to decide which one of the trajectories $\tilde{X}_I^N$ is realized in view of the observed one $\tilde{Y}^N$.

According to the generalized Bayesian rule (9.6.13), we shall select the trajectory $\tilde{X}_{\hat{I}}^N$ such that

$$\mathrm{e}^{-(\varrho u \bar{H})_{\hat{I}}} P(\tilde{X}_{\hat{I}}^N)p(\tilde{Y}^N/\tilde{X}_{\hat{I}}^N)^{\varrho_{\hat{I}}} \geqslant \mathrm{e}^{-(\varrho u \bar{H})_I} P(\tilde{X}_I^N)p(\tilde{Y}^N/\tilde{X}_I^N)^{\varrho_I} \ , \qquad \hat{I} \neq I \tag{9.7.1}$$

where the coefficients u_I and $\bar{H}_I$ refer to the trajectory to be determined.

9.7.2 The Main Assumptions and Solution

Assumption A1. The dynamical process $\{x(t)\}$ is Markovian. $\qquad \square$

This is generally the price to be paid in this type of problem, but from a practical standpoint, it is well known that it is quite realistic. Indeed, either the physical process under consideration is actually Markovian or, by increasing the dimension of its state vector, we can describe it by a Markovian model.

Assumption A2. The following relation holds

$$p(y_{i+1}, t_{i+1}/y_i, t_i, \tilde{X}_I) = p(y_{i+1}, t_{i+1}/y_i, t_i, x(t_{i+1}))$$

which emphasizes that the dependence of the observation upon the actual trajectory is summarized in the dependence upon the last state $x(t_{i+1})$ only.   □

Under these conditions, one can write

$$p(\tilde{Y}^N/\tilde{X}_I^N) = \prod_{t=t_0}^{N-1} p(y_{i+1}, t_{i+1}/y_i, t_i, x(t_{i+1})) \tag{9.7.2}$$

and the problem is then to calculate the corresponding relative probability. To this end, we shall recursively apply the equation (9.4.21).

Let $\tilde{u}_{i+1}$ denote the subjectivity associated with the trajectory from the time t_0 to the time t_{i+1}, and let u_i denote the subjectivity related to the pair (y_i, x_i) at time t_i. One then has the recursive relation

$$\tilde{u}_{i+1} = \frac{\tilde{u}_i + u_i}{1 + \tilde{u}_i u_i} \tag{9.7.3}$$

whence we can derive $\tilde{u}_I$ and $\varrho(\tilde{u}_I)$.

It now remains to calculate the semantic entropy $\tilde{\tilde{H}}_I$ of the trajectory, and, to this end, we shall make the following hypothesis.

Assumption A3. We shall identify the semantic entropy $\tilde{H}_i$ of the ith state with the entropy of an error term on the definition of this state itself, and we shall assume the error terms for different states are independent.   □

With this assumption, we can straightforwardly write the equation

$$\tilde{\tilde{H}}_I = \sum_{i=1}^{I} \tilde{H}_i , \tag{9.7.4}$$

and the relative probability of the trajectory from the time t_0 to the time t_N is

$$p_r(\tilde{Y}_I/\tilde{X}_I) = \exp[-(\tilde{\varrho}\tilde{u}\tilde{\tilde{H}})_I]p(\tilde{Y}_I/\tilde{X}_I)^{\tilde{\varrho}_I} \tag{9.7.5}$$

where $\tilde{u}_I$ and $\tilde{\tilde{H}}_I$ are defined by (9.7.3) and (9.7.4) respectively.

9.8 Error Probability and Generalized Maximum Likelihood

9.8.1 Definition of the Problem

In this section, using a technique similar to *Gallager*'s [9.1], we shall derive a new expression for the upper bound of the probability of decoding error in the case where one applies the simplified version of the generalized criterion (9.5.2).

So we consider a memoryless channel with input alphabet $X = \{x_1, x_2, \ldots, x_m\}$, and output alphabet $Y = \{y_1, y_2, \ldots y_n\}$ and the transition probabilities $p(j/i) := p(y_j/x_i), i = 1, \ldots, m, j = 1, \ldots, n$. $\{\pi_i\} := \{\pi(x_i)\}$ is the probability distribution of the x_i which are assumed to be stochastically independent; finally X_K and Y_K denote respectively the set of input words of length K and the set of output words of length K.

The decision rule is the simplified one (9.5.9) which we rewrite in the form

$$G_i p^a(y/x_i) \geqslant G_{i'} p^b(y/x_{i'}) , \qquad i' \neq i , \qquad 1 \leqslant i' \leqslant M \tag{9.8.1}$$

where G_i is defined by the expression

$$G_i := e^{-(u\tilde{H})_i} \tag{9.8.2}$$

and M is the number of encoded words of length K.

9.8.2 Application of the Generalized Maximum Likelihood Criterion

Let P_i^e denote the error probability when $x_i \in X_K$ is transmitted. One has the following result:

Proposition 9.8.1. Consider the channel described in Sect. 9.8.1. Then for the family of words with length K, there exists a code for which the mean probability $\overline{P_i^e}$ of error, when one uses the criterion (9.8.1), is bounded by

$$\overline{P_i^e} \leqslant \left[\sum_{i' \neq i} \left(\frac{G_{i'}^b}{G_i^a} \right)^{1/(a+b\gamma)} \right]^{b\gamma/a} \exp[-K E_{a,b}(\gamma, \Pi)] \tag{9.8.3}$$

with

$$E_{a,b}(\gamma, \Pi) := -\ln \sum_{j=1}^{n} \left\{ \sum_{i=1}^{m} \pi_i [p(j/i)]^{a/(b+b\gamma)} \right\}^{1+(b\gamma/a)} \tag{9.8.4}$$

where γ is a real-valued parameter in the range $0 \leqslant \gamma \leqslant 1$.   □

Proof of This Result. (i) We write the probability P_i^e in the form

$$P_i^e = \sum_{y \in Y_K} p(y/x_i) \Psi_i(y) \tag{9.8.5}$$

where $\Psi_i(y)$ is defined as

$$\Psi_i(y) := \begin{cases} 1 & \text{if } G_i p(y/x_i)^a < G_{i'} p(y/x_{i'})^b \\ 0 & \text{otherwise .} \end{cases} \tag{9.8.6}$$

A bound on $\Psi_i(y)$ can be written in the form

$$\Psi_i(y) \leqslant \left(\frac{\sum_{i' \neq i} [G_{i'} p(y/x_{i'})]^{b/(a+b\gamma)}}{[G_i p(y/x_i)]^{a/(a+b\gamma)}} \right)^{b\gamma/a} \tag{9.8.7}$$

and on substituting into (9.8.5) we obtain

$$P_i^e \leqslant \sum_{y \in Y_K} p(y/x_i)^{b/(a+by)} \left[\sum_{i' \neq i} \left(\frac{G_{i'}^b}{G_i^a} \right)^{1/(a+by)} p(y/x_{i'})^{b/(a+by)} \right]^{by/a} . \tag{9.8.8}$$

ii) Expression (9.8.8) is an upper bound on P_i^e for a given special set of encoded words. One can simplify it by taking its average over the ensemble of codes. To this end, we define a probability distribution $p(x)$ over the set of all possible inputs, and we generate an encoding by randomly choosing the x's, independently of each other, according to this probability. As a result, a code defined by the words $x_1, x_2, \ldots,$ x_M will have the occurrence probability $\prod_{i=1}^{M} p(x_i)$. Furthermore, there exists at least one code for which the error probability is as small as the ensemble average of the error probabilities. On using the notation $\overline{(\cdot)}$ to represent the ensemble average over all possible codes, and on noting that when $\gamma < 1$, as will be assumed henceforth, the following relation is satisfied:

$$\overline{Z^\gamma} \leqslant (\bar{Z})^\gamma , \qquad \gamma < 1 , \tag{9.8.9}$$

one has

$$\overline{P_i^e} \leqslant \sum_{y \in Y_K} \overline{p(y/x_i)^{b/(a+by)}} \left[\sum_{i' \neq 1} \left(\frac{G_{i'}^b}{G_i^a} \right)^{1/(a+by)} \overline{p(y/x_{i'})^{b/(a+by)}} \right]^{by/a} . \tag{9.8.10}$$

iii) This being so, the definition of $p(x)$ yields

$$\overline{p(y/x_i)^{b/(a+by)}} = \sum_{x \in X_K} p(x)[p(y/x)]^{b/(a+by)} \tag{9.8.11}$$

so that one has

$$\overline{P_i^e} \leqslant Q_i(a,b,\gamma) \sum_{y \in Y_K} \left\{ \sum_{x \in X_K} p(x)[p(y/x)^{b/(a+by)} \right\}^{1+(by/a)} \tag{9.8.12}$$

with the additional conditions

$$0 \leqslant \gamma \leqslant 1 , \qquad b < a ,$$

and where $Q_i(a,b,\gamma)$ is defined by the expression

$$Q_i(a,b,\gamma) := \left[\sum_{i' \neq 1} \left(\frac{G_{i'}^b}{G_i^a} \right)^{1/(a+by)} \right]^{by/a} . \tag{9.8.13}$$

iv) We now assume that the channel is memoryless and that each letter of the coding word is chosen independently of the others with the probability distribution $\pi(x)$, $x \in X$. If we set $x^t := (x_1, x_2, \ldots, x_K)$ and $y^t := (y_1, y_2, \ldots, y_K)$ where the superscript denotes the transpose, one has

$$p(y/x) = \prod_{j=1}^{K} p(y_j/x_j) \qquad \text{and} \tag{9.8.14}$$

$$p(x) = \prod_{i=1}^{K} \pi(x_i) ; \tag{9.8.15}$$

so that we can rewrite (9.7.12) in the form

$$\overline{P_i^e} \leqslant Q_i(a,b,\gamma) \prod_{i=1}^{K} \sum_{y_i \in Y} \left\{ \sum_{x_i \in X} \pi(x_i)[p(y_i/x_i)]^{b/(a+b\gamma)} \right\}^{1+(b\gamma/a)} . \tag{9.8.16}$$

We now note that all the terms in the right-hand-side product are equal, to finally obtain

$$\overline{P_i^e} \leqslant Q_i(a,b,\gamma) \left\{ \sum_{j=1}^{m} \left[\sum_{i=1}^{m} \pi_i[p(j/i)]^{b/(a+b\gamma)} \right]^{1+(b\gamma/a)} \right\}^{K} \tag{9.8.17}$$

and thus we have proved proposition 9.8.1.

Analysis of This Result. (i) Assume that $G_i > G_{i'}$ for every $i' \neq i$, and define

$$1 - \bar{\varepsilon}_i := \max_{i'} (G_{i'}/G_i) . \tag{9.8.18}$$

The inequality (9.8.3) then yields

$$\overline{P_i^e} \leqslant (1 - \bar{\varepsilon}_i)^{[b/(a+b\gamma)]b\gamma/a} \left(\frac{G_i^b}{G_i^a} \right)^{[1/(a+b\gamma)]b\gamma/a} (M-1)^{b\gamma/a} \exp[-KE_{a,b}(\gamma, \Pi)] \tag{9.8.19}$$

or similarly

$$\overline{P_i^e} \leqslant (1 - \bar{\varepsilon}_i)^{b\gamma/(a+b\gamma)} \left(\frac{G_i^b}{G_i^a} \right)^{\gamma/(a+b\gamma)} M^\gamma \exp[-KE_{a,b}(\gamma, \Pi)] . \tag{9.8.20}$$

Let R denote the rate of transmission; it is known that one has $M = \exp(KR)$, so that one can rewrite inequality (9.8.20) in the form

$$\overline{P_i^e} \leqslant (1 - \bar{\varepsilon}_i)^{b\gamma/(a+b\gamma)} G_i^{(b-a)\gamma/(a+b\gamma)} \exp\{-K[-\gamma R + E_{a,b}(\gamma, \Pi)]\} . \tag{9.8.21}$$

When $a = b$, $E_{a,b}(\gamma, \Pi)$ is identical to the term $E_0(\gamma, \Pi)$ defined by *Gallager* [9.1], and one has

$$\overline{P_i^e} \leqslant (1 - \bar{\varepsilon}_i)^{\gamma/(\gamma+1)} \exp\{-K[-\gamma R + E_0(\gamma, \Pi)]\} \tag{9.8.22}$$

whereas when $\bar{\varepsilon}_i = 0$, one has exactly the bound obtained by *Gallager*.

ii) It may be of interest to compare $E_{a,b}$ with $E_{a,a}$ to gain more insight into the accuracy of the result. As a matter of fact, this problem is equivalent to studying the variation of the function

$$g(\xi) = \ln \sum_j \left[\sum_i \pi_i a_{ij}^{1/\xi} \right]^\xi$$

where ξ is defined by the expression

$$\xi := 1 + \frac{b}{a}\gamma$$

and at first glance it seems far from trivial. However, given that γ is an arbitrary parameter, we see that the condition

$$\frac{b}{a}\gamma = \gamma_0$$

provides

$$E_{a,b}(\gamma) = E_{a,a}(\gamma_0) \ .$$

Thus we are sure to get at least the same value of E in both cases. Clearly, the improvement of the accuracy that may be obtained with the coefficients a and b is mainly due to the presence of the gains G_i as shown by the expression (9.8.22).

iii) Assume that $G_i < G_{i'}$ for every $i' \neq i$ and define

$$1 + \hat{\varepsilon}_i := \max_{i'} (G_{i'}/G_i) \tag{9.8.23}$$

then, in a similar manner, one has

$$\overline{P_i^e} \leqslant (1 + \hat{\varepsilon}_i)^{b\gamma/(a+b\gamma)} G_i^{(b-a)\gamma/(a+b\gamma)} \exp\{-K[\gamma R + E_{a,b}(\gamma, \Pi)]\} \ . \tag{9.8.24}$$

iv) These two results, (9.8.22) and (9.8.24), express the variation of the accuracy with respect to the reference rule

$$p^a(y/x_i) \geqslant p^b(y/x_{i'}) \ , \tag{9.8.25}$$

which we obtain by putting $G_i = G = $ constant for every i. In the first case, we improve the accuracy of the criterion (9.8.25) while in the second case, we destroy it. The first situation corresponds to a good prior knowledge, whereas in the second case, we are dealing with prior misknowledge.

9.8.3 Application of the Generalized Bayesian Rule

With the notation of Sects. 9.6 and 9.8, and for the same technical reasons as above, we shall use the following simplified criterion:

Simplified Decision Rule. Select x_i if

$$P(x_i)G_i p^a(y/x_i) \geqslant P(x_{i'})G_{i'} p^b(y/x_{i'}) \tag{9.8.26}$$

with $i \neq i'$; $1 \leqslant i' \leqslant M$; and where G_i is defined by the expression (9.8.2).   □

The meaning of this criterion is obvious. One may have $p^a(y/x_i) \leqslant p^b(y/x_{i'})$, but if $G_i P(x_i)$ is large enough, one will nonetheless select x_i. The term $P(x_i)$ can be thought of as the prior probability of x_i, while u and $\tilde{H}$ picture the related fuzziness or subjectivity. With this notation, the results of Sect. 9.8 apply straightforwardly. For instance, assume that

$$G_i P(x_i) > G_{i'} P(x_{i'}) \ , \qquad i \neq i' \tag{9.8.27}$$

then on defining

$$1 - \bar{\varepsilon}_i := \max_{i'} \frac{G_{i'} P(x_{i'})}{G_i P(x_i)} \tag{9.8.28}$$

one will have the bound

$$\overline{P_i^e} \leqslant (1 - \bar{\varepsilon}_i)^{b\gamma/(a+b\gamma)} [G_i P(x_i)]^{(b-a)\gamma/(a+b\gamma)} \exp\{-K[\gamma R + E_{a,b}(\gamma, \Pi)]\} . \tag{9.8.29}$$

9.9 A Pattern Recognition Problem

9.9.1 An Illustrative Example

In order to illustrate the kind of results one may expect when using the preceding criteria, we consider the following simple example:

Problem 9.4. Assume that we are identifying hand-printed B's and hand-printed 8's only, in other words one has that

$$P(B) + P(8) = 1 . \tag{9.9.1}$$

These symbols are characterized by two parameters which are respectively

X_1: the straightness ratio, that is to say the ratio between the endpoints of the arc to the arc length itself, and

X_2: the ratio of the maximum width of the top half of the symbol to the maximum width of the bottom half.

Let X denote the vector (X_1, X_2) or more explicitly define $X_B := (X_1^B, X_2^B)$; and let m_B and m_8 denote the statistical expectations

$$m_B := E\{X_B\} ; \qquad m_8 := E\{X_8\} . \tag{9.9.2}$$

Let σ_1^2 and σ_2^2 denote the variances of X_1 and X_2 respectively.

Lastly, we shall assume that the conditional probability densities of X are

$$p(x/B) = K \exp[-\tfrac{1}{2}(x - m_B)^t \Sigma^{-1}(x - m_B)] \tag{9.9.3}$$

$$p(x/8) = K \exp[-\tfrac{1}{2}(x - m_8)^t \Sigma^{-1}(x - m_8)] \tag{9.9.4}$$

with

$$K := \frac{1}{2\pi |\Sigma|^{1/2}} , \tag{9.9.5}$$

$$\Sigma := \begin{pmatrix} \sigma_1^2 & 0 \\ 0 & \sigma_2^2 \end{pmatrix} . \tag{9.9.6}$$

The superscript t indicates the transpose and $|\Sigma|$ is the determinant of Σ.

9.9.2 Application of the Sharp Decision Rule

For the sake of simplicity, we make the following assumptions.

(A1) The a priori probabilites $P(B)$ and $P(8)$ are equal

(A2) The semantic entropies $\tilde{H}_B$ and $\tilde{H}_8$ are both zero.

Under these conditions, according to the criterion (9.6.12) we shall select B if one has

$$\varrho(u_B)\ln p(x/B) \geqslant \varrho(u_8)\ln p(x/8) , \tag{9.9.7}$$

that is to say, on taking account of the expressions (9.9.3) and (9.9.4), when

$$\varrho(u_B)(x - m_B)^t \Sigma^{-1}(x - m_B) - 2\varrho(u_B)\ln K$$

$$\leqslant \rho(u_8)(x - m_8)^t \Sigma^{-1}(x - m_8) - 2\varrho(u_8)\ln K . \tag{9.9.8}$$

The decision boundary is given by the condition

$$\varrho(u_B)[(x - m_B)^t \Sigma^{-1}(x - m_B) - 2\ln K]$$

$$= \varrho(u_8)[(x - m_8)^t \Sigma^{-1}(x - m_8) - 2\ln K] \tag{9.9.9}$$

which we expand in the form

$$[\varrho(u_B) - \varrho(u_8)](x^t \Sigma^{-1} x) - x^t(u_B \Sigma^{-1} m_B - u_8 \Sigma^{-1} m_8)$$

$$- [\varrho(u_B)m_B^t - \varrho(u_8)m_8^t]\Sigma^{-1}x + [\varrho(u_B)m_B^t \Sigma^{-1} m_B - \varrho(u_8)m_8^t \Sigma^{-1} m_8]$$

$$- 2[\varrho(u_B) - \varrho(u_8)]\ln K = 0 . \tag{9.9.10}$$

We can now concludes as follows. When $u_B = u_8$, that is to say for the standard Bayesian decision rule, the decision boundary is defined by the equation

$$(x - m_B)^t \Sigma^{-1}(x - m_B) = (x - m_8)^t \Sigma^{-1}(x - m_8) \tag{9.9.11}$$

which is equivalent to

$$x^t \Sigma^{-1}(m_B - m_8) - \tfrac{1}{2}(m_B + m_8)^t \Sigma^{-1}(m_B + m_8) = 0 \tag{9.9.12}$$

This equation (9.9.12) defines a straight line D. In contrast, the equation (9.9.10) of the generalized Bayesian rule defines an ellipse E, and the corresponding result is pictured in Fig. 9.1. The interesting feature is that, in the vicinity of the straight line D of the standard Bayesian rule, the generalized approach can improve the decision.

9.9.3 Application of the Soft Decision Rule

In our example, according to condition (9.6.17), the soft decision rule is to select B if

$$\varrho(u_B)\ln p(x/B) - r_B \geqslant \rho(u_8)\ln p(x/8) - r_8 \tag{9.9.13}$$

where r_B is defined by the expression

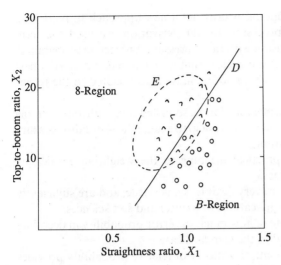

Fig. 9.1. Decision boundary based on generalized Bayesian decision rule

$$r_B := \varrho(u_B)u_B\tilde{H}_B - \ln \mu_B P(B) \tag{9.9.14}$$

and likewise for r_8.

The equation of the corresponding decision boundary is

$$[\varrho(u_B) - \varrho(u_8)]x^t\Sigma^{-1}x - x^t[\varrho(u_B)\Sigma^{-1}m_B - \varrho(u_8)\Sigma^{-1}m_8]$$

$$- [\varrho(u_B)m_B^t - \varrho(u_8)m_8^t]\Sigma^{-1}x + [\varrho(u_B)m_B^t\Sigma^{-1}m_B - \varrho(u_8)m_8^t\Sigma^{-1}m_8]$$

$$-2[\varrho(u_B) - \varrho(u_8)]\ln K + 2(r_B - r_8) = 0 \tag{9.9.15}$$

with

$$r_B - r_8 = \varrho(u_B)u_B\tilde{H}_B - \varrho(u_8)u_8\tilde{H}_8 - \ln\frac{\mu_B P(B)}{\mu_8 P(8)} . \tag{9.9.16}$$

When the difference $r_B - r_8$ is small, then (9.9.15) merely pictures a translation of the boundary E in Fig. 9.1, to the left or to the right depending upon the sign of $r_B - r_8$.

9.10 Concluding Remarks

In the development above, by using very simple and straightforward axioms, and on assuming that it is the information involved by each individual event which is observed rather than the information contained by the experiment as the whole, we derived a new concept of relative probability which allowed us to generalize the maximum likelihood criterion and the Bayesian statistical decision rule. The main contributions of this model can be summarized as follows.

i) First, from a general standpoint, it provides a new approach to modelling subjectivity in decision-making processes. In our derivation, we used the term relative probability to avoid confusion with the expression "subjective probability" which refers to prior probability. But it is clear that we have in fact derived a new model of subjective probability which, in addition, is closely related to the recent so-called possibility theory.

ii) We have derived a practical meaning for the so-called Renyi entropy in terms of the subjectivity of the observer, and this may help to extend the use of this measure of uncertainty in practical applications.

iii) The model gives a new practical meaning to the weighting coefficients sometimes used in decoding schemes.

iv) These new decision rules are very flexible, i.e. versatile, and are sufficiently general to cover a broad class of applications in natural and soft sciences.

v) We have an explicit estimate of how much the error probability in decoding problems is improved as compared to the standard case.

vi) From a theoretical standpoint, this theory of relative probability provides a link between probability and possibility, or alternatively can be considered as a uniform approach to these questions.

vii) The coefficient u in the model can be considered as an adaptive parameter which provides a direct way to implement a computerized decision scheme with feedback.

10. Concluding Remarks and Outlook

In this brief concluding chapter, we would like to summarize the main features of the book and discuss their possible implications for future research.

What we have achieved can be summarized as follows. We have obtained:

(i) a unified approach to discrete entropy and continuous entropy, (ii) a theory of subjective information based on a slight modification of Shannon's framework, (iii) a theory of relative information derived from a model of observation with informational invariance, (iv) a uniform approach to various definitions of informational entropies which have been suggested in the literature, (v) some models of informational entropies for stochastic processes, (vi) an introduction to a general theory of information without probability for deterministic functions, (vii) and a basis for a generalization of the Bayesian statistical decision theory, which involves subjective parameters.

All these topics are dealt with in the same unified approach which originates from the following two tenets. First, a theory of information should explicitly refer to an observer, who considers the information in his own semantic frame; and second, the Shannon theory is a self-referencing theory in the sense that it contains within itself the seeds of an appropriate generalization.

We believe that the relative information theory thus obtained could be an Ariane's thread allowing us to re-evaluate the maze of general systems theory, and its various components such as thermodynamics, dynamical systems, synergetics, subjectivity, fuzziness, and complexity. Let us mention some suggestions for future investigation.

i) It still remains to expand the information theory of deterministic functions initiated in Chap. 8 (some results have already been obtained in this way [10.1]) for the purpose of applications. For instance, one could conceive of new approaches to pattern recognition, and of a possible thermodynamics of forms. Indeed, notice that, if we define the thermodynamic entropy of a line $(C) := \{x, y; y = f(x)\}$ as the minimum of $H(f(\cdot); \Omega)$ for all possible co-ordinate frames, then we then find that the thermodynamic entropy of a straight line is minus infinity, a result which is quite consistent with the Nernst principle!

ii) Recently, *Haken* [10.2] has extensively applied the maximum entropy principle to the study of self-organization, and it might be interesting to examine the types of result that one could obtain by using the same approach, but in the framework of relative information. There are two possible methods. First, one can straightforwardly apply the maximum entropy principle to the relative entropy as defined in Chap. 4; second, one can consider the new entropic function of a random variable X, defined by the expression

$$H_c(X, p) := -\frac{\int_{\mathbb{R}} p^c(x) \ln p(x)\, dx}{\int_{\mathbb{R}} p^c(x)\, dx}\ . \tag{10.1}$$

iii) A valuable hypothesis is to assume that complexity originates from constraints, that is to say, increase of complexity is associated with the self-creation of constraints. The question which then arises is: can we identify these constraints with semantics of information?

iv) One has $H_c(X, p) < H(X)$ when $c < 1$ and $H_c(X) > H(X)$ for $c > 1$, and as a result, one could use c as a coefficient of information transfer in neural networks. The problem would then be to determine the dynamics of c, which would depend upon whether the system is learning or dislearning.

v) The relative entropy $H_r(X)$ has an interpretation in terms of the entropy of open systems, and it would be interesting to pursue this idea in order to deepen the possible relationships between relative information and the thermodynamics of open systems.

vi) One might ask whether the information theory without probability presented herein could not provide a new approach to a mathematical theory of evidence different from that of *Shafer* [10.3].

vii) The fractional derivative of order δ of the function $y = f(x)$, $x \in \mathbb{R}$, $y \in \mathbb{R}$ is

$$D^\delta f(x) := \frac{1}{\Gamma(-\delta)} \int_0^x (x - t)^{-\delta-1} f(t)\, dt, \qquad \delta < 0 \tag{10.2}$$

$$:= \frac{d^n}{dx^n}[D^{-n+\delta} f(x)], \qquad n - 1 < \delta < n\ . \tag{10.3}$$

In an attempt to generalize the entropy of deterministic functions, can we consider the quantity $\ln |D^\delta f(x)|$ as a density of uncertainty?

viii) It appears that a parameter of interest is the entropic variance defined by the expression

$$v_H(x) := \int_{\mathbb{R}} p(x) \ln^2 p(x)\, dx - H^2(X)\ , \tag{10.4}$$

which could be a valuable measure of the organizational properties of a system [10.4]. So the idea is to introduce the entropic variance of order c of a random variable, by using (10.1), and to examine its possible utilization in the study of self-organization.

References

Chapter 1

1.1 Nyquist, H.: Bell Syst. Techn. J. **4**, 324 (1924)
1.2 Nyquist, H.: AIEE Trans. **47**, 617 (1928)
1.3 Hartley, R. V.: Bell Syst. Techn. J. **7**, 535 (1928)
1.4 Shannon, C. E.: Bell Syst. Techn. J. **27**, 379 (1948)
1.5 Shannon, C. E.: Bell Syst. Techn. J. **27**, 623 (1948)
1.6 Brillouin, L.: *Science and Information Theory* (Academic, New York 1956)
1.7 Jumarie, G.: J. Inform. and Optimization Sci. **1**, 166 (1980)
1.8 Glansdorff, P., Prigogine, I.: *Thermodynamic Theory of Structure, Stability and Fluctuations* (Wiley, New York 1971)
1.9 Jumarie, G.: *Subjectivity, Information, Systems. Introduction to a Theory of Relativistic Cybernetics* (Gordon and Breach, New York 1986)
1.10 Jumarie, G.: Intern. J. Syst. Sci. **6**, 249 (1975)

Chapter 2

2.1 Hartley, R. V.: Bell Syst. Techn. J. **7**, 535 (1928)
2.2 Shannon, C. E.: Bell Syst. Techn. J. **27**, 379 (1948)
2.3 Weaver, W., Shannon, C. E.: *The Mathematical Theory of Communication* (Univ. of Illinois Press, Urbana 1949)
2.4 McMillan, B.: Ann. Math. Stat. **24**, 196 (1953)
2.5 Feinstein, A.: *Foundations of Information Theory* (McGraw-Hill, New York 1958)
2.6 Khintchin, A.: Uspekhi Matem. NAUKA **11**, 17 (1956)
2.7 Renyi, A.: Magyar Tud. Akad. Mat. Fiz. Oszt. Kozl. **10**, 251 (1960)
2.8 Campbell, L. L.: Inform. and Control **8**, 423 (1965)
2.9 Jumarie, G.: Annales des Télécommunications **34**, 521 (1979)
2.10 Kullback, S.: *Information Theory and Statistics* (Wiley, New York 1959)
2.11 Renyi, A.: *Probability Theory* (North-Holland, Amsterdam 1970)
2.12 Aczel, J., Daroczi, Z.: *On Measures of Information and Their Characterizations* (Academic, New York 1975)
2.13 Daroczi, Z.: Inform. and Control **16**, 36 (1970)
2.14 Cover, T. M., Hart, P. E.: IEEE Trans. Inform. Theory IT **13**, 21 (1967)
2.15 Vajda, I.: Information Transmission Problems **4**, 9 (1968)
2.16 Ito, T.: "Approximate Error Bounds in Pattern Recognition" in *Machine Intelligence* (Edinburgh Univ. Press 1972) **7**, 369–376
2.17 Devijver, P. A.: IEEE Trans. Comput. C **23**, 70 (1973)
2.18 Boekee, D. E., Van der Lubbe, A. J. C.: Inform. and Control **45**, 136 (1980)
2.19 Jumarie, G.: Intern. J. Syst. Sc. **6**, 249 (1975)
2.20 Aczel, J., Daroczy, A.: RAIRO Theoretical Comput. Sc. **12**, 149 (1978)
2.21 Hatori, H.: Kodai Math. Sem. Rep. **10**, 172 (1958)
2.22 Ashby, W. R.: Cybernetica **8**, 5 (1965)
2.23 Kampé de Fériet, J., Forté B.: Comptes Rendus Academie des Sciences de Paris, **265**A, 110; 142; 350 (1967)

2.24 Haken, H.: "Towards a Dynamic Information Theory" in *Thermodynamics and Regulation of Biological Processes*, ed. by Lamprecht, I. and Zotin, A. I. (Walter de Gruyter, Berlin 1984) pp. 93–104
2.25 Zadeh, L. A.: Fuzzy Sets and Systems **1**, 3 (1978)
2.26 Sugeno, M.: "Fuzzy Measures and Fuzzy Integrals: a Survey", in *Fuzzy Automata and Decision Processes*, ed. by Gupta M. M. (North-Holland, Amsterdam 1977) pp. 89–102
2.27 Higashi, M., Klir, G. J.: Intern. J. General Syst. **9**, 43 (1982)

Chapter 3

3.1   Thom, R.: *Structural Stability and Morphogenesis* (Benjamin, New York 1975)
3.2   Jumarie. G.: *Subjectivity, Information, Systems. Introduction to a Theory of Relativistic Cybernetics* (Gordon and Breach, New York 1986)
3.3   Faddeev, D. K.: Uspehi Mat. NAUKA **11**, 227 (1956)
3.4   Feinstein, A.: *Foundation of Information Theory* (McGraw-Hill, New York 1958)
3.5   Kullback, S.: *Information Theory and Statistics* (Wiley, New York 1959)
3.6   Brillouin, L.: *Science and Information Theory* (Academic, New York 1956)
3.7   Lindeberg, J. W.: Math. Zeit. **15**, 211 (1922)
3.8   Linnik, Yu. V.: Theory of Prob. and Applications **4**, 288 (1959)
3.9   Feller, W.: *An Introduction to Probability Theory and its Application* (Wiley, New York 1950)
3.10 Jaynes, E.T.: Phys. Rev. **106**, 620; **108**, 171 (1957)
3.11 Jumarie, G.: J. of Math. Phys. **26**, 1173 (1985)
3.12 Shore, J. E., Johnson, R. W.: IEEE Trans. Inform. Theory IT **26**, 26 (1980)
3.13 Weaver, W., Shannon, C. E.: *The Mathematical Theory of Communication* (Univ. of Illinois Press, Urbana 1949)
3.14 Bar Hillel, Y.: *Language and Information* (Addison Wesley, Reading 1964)
3.15 Ryan, J. P.: J. Theoretical Biology **84**, 31 (1980)
3.16 Haken, H. "Towards a Dynamic Information Theory" in *Thermodynamics and Regulation of Biological Processes*, ed. by I. Lamprecht and A. I. Zotin (Walter de Gruyter, Berlin 1984) pp. 93–104

Chapter 4

4.1   Weaver, W., Shannon, C. E.: *The Mathematical Theory of Communication* (Univ. of Illinois Press, Urbana 1949)
4.2   Brillouin, L.: *Science and Information Theory* (Academic, New York 1956)
4.3   Ashby, W. R.: *An Introduction to Cybernetics* (Chapman and Hall, London 1956)
4.4   Bongard, N. M.: "On the Notion of Useful Information" in *Problems of Cybernetics* (Fizmatgiz, Moscow 1963) **9**, pp. 71–102 (in Russian)
4.5   Stratonovitch, R. L.: *Information Theory* (Sovetskoye Radio, Moscow 1975) (in Russian)
4.6   Stratonovitch, R. L.: "On the Problem of the Valuability of Information" in *Thermodynamics and Regulation of Biological Processes*, ed. by Lamprecht, I. and Zotin, A. I. (Walter de Gruyter, Berlin 1984) pp. 105–120
4.7   Haken, H.: "Towards a Dynamic Information Theory" in *Thermodynamics and Regulation of Biological Processes*, ed. by Lamprecht, I. and Zotin, A. I. (Walter de Gruyter, Berlin 1984) pp. 93–104
4.8   Jumarie, G.: Intern. J. Syst. Sc. **6**, 249 (1975)
4.9   Jumarie, G.: Annales des Télécommunications **39**, 523 (1984)
4.10 Jumarie, G.: *Subjectivity, Information, Systems. Introduction to a Theory of Relativistic Cybernetics* (Gordon and Breach, New York 1986)
4.11 Jumarie, G.: Intern. J. General Systems **5**, 99 (1979)

Chapter 5

5.1 Brillouin, L.: *Science and Information Theory* (Academic, New York 1956)
5.2 Jumarie, G.: Annales des Télécommunications **33**, 13 (1978)
5.3 Jumarie, G.: Annales des Télécommunications **34**, 491 (1979)
5.4 Jumarie, G.: Annales des Télécommunications **34**, 521 (1979)
5.5 Jumarie, G.: J. Inform. and Optimization Sci. **1**, 166 (1980)
5.6 Jumarie, G.: Annales des Télécommunications **35**, 281 (1980)
5.7 Jumarie, G.: J. Inform. and Optimization Sci. **2**, 273 (1981)
5.8 Jumarie, G.: Annales des Télécommunications **39**, 523 (1985)
5.9 Hirota, K.: "Ambiguity Based on the Concept of Subjective Entropy" in *Fuzzy Information and Decision Process*, ed. by Gupta, M., Sanchez, E (North-Holland, Amsterdam 1982) pp. 29–40
5.10 Jumarie, G.: Annales des Télécommunications **37**, 201 (1982)
5.11 Jumarie, G.: J. Inform. and Optimization Sci. **5**, 105 (1984)
5.12 Zadeh, L. A.: J. Math. Analysis and Applications **23**, 421 (1968)
5.13 de Luca, A., Termini, S.: Inform. and Control **20**, 301 (1972)
5.14 Jumarie, G.: "A New Approach to the Transinformation of Random Experiments Involving Fuzzy Observations" in *Cybernetics and Systems Research* ed. by Trappl, R. (North-Holland, Amsterdam 1984) pp. 567–572

Chapter 6

6.1 Aczel, J., Daroczy, Z.: *On Measures of Information and Their Characterization* (Academic, New York 1975)
6.2 Faddeev, D. K.: Uspehi Mat. NAUKA **11**, 227 (1956)
6.3 Shannon, C. E.: Bell Syst. Techn. J. **27**, 379 (1948)
6.4 Shannon, C. E.: Bell Syst. Techn. J. **27**, 623 (1948)
6.5 Hatori, H.: Kodai Math. Sem. Rep. **10**, 172 (1958)
6.6 Thom, R.: *Structural Stability and Morphogenesis* (Benjamin, New York 1975)
6.7 Linnik, Yu. V.: Theory of Prob. and Applications **4**, 288 (1959)
6.8 Jaynes, E. T.: Phys. Rev. **106**, 620 (1957)
6.9 Jaynes, E. T.: Phys. Rev. **108**, 171 (1957)
6.10 Shore, J. E., Johnson, R. W.: IEEE Trans. Inform. Theory IT **26**, 26 (1980)
6.11 Hartley, R. V.: Bell Syst. Techn. J. **7**, 535 (1928)
6.12 Renyi, A.: "On Measures of Entropy and Information" in *Proc. 4th Berkeley Symp. on Math. Statistics and Probability* (Univ. of California Press, Berkeley 1960) pp. 547–561
6.13 Renyi, A.: *Probability Theory* (North-Holland, Amsterdam 1970)
6.14 Brillouin, L.: *Science and Information Theory* (Academic, New York 1956)
6.15 Jumarie, G.: J. Syst. Sc. **6**, 249 (1975)
6.16 Aczel, J., Daroczy, Z.: RAIRO Theoretical Comput. Sc. **12**, 149 (1978)

Chapter 7

7.1 Hartley, R. V.: Bell Syst. Techn. J. **7**, 535 (1928)
7.2 Shannon, C. E.: Bell Syst. Techn. J. **27**, 379; **27**, 623 (1948)
7.3 Renyi, A.: Magyar Tud. Akad. Mat. Fiz. Oszt. Kozl. **10**, 251 (1960)
7.4 Renyi, A.: *Probability Theory* (North-Holland, Amsterdam 1980)
7.5 Jumarie, G.: "Total Entropy. A Unified Approach to Continuous Entropy and Discrete Entropy" in *Cybernetics and Systems*, ed. by Trappl, R. (Reidel, Dordrecht 1986) pp. 131–138
7.6 Jumarie, G.: Intern. J. Syst. Sc. **6**, 249 (1975)
7.7 Zadeh, L. A.: J. Math. Analysis and Applications **23**, 421 (1968)
7.8 Belis, M., Guiasu, S.: IEEE Trans. Inform. Theory IT **14**, 593 (1968)
7.9 Kullback S.: *Information Theory and Statistics* (Wiley, New York 1959)
7.10 Kannapan, P.: Metrika **27**, 91 (1980)

Chapter 8

8.1   Kolmogorov, A. N.: Dokl. Akad. Nauk. USSR **98**, 527 (1959)
8.2   Mandelbrot, B. B.: *The Fractal Geometry of Nature* (Freeman, New York 1977)
8.3   Dupain, Y., Kamae, T., Mendeš France, M.: Arch. for Rat. Mech. **94**, 155 (1986)
8.4   Oswald, J.: *Theorie de L'Information ou Analyse Diacritique des Systèmes* (Masson, Paris 1986)
8.5   Jumarie, G.: Systems Analysis, Modelling, Simulation **6**, 323–363 (1989)

Chapter 9

9.1   Gallager R. G.: *Information Theory and Reliable Communication* (Wiley, New York 1968)
9.2   Ash, R. B.: *Information Theory* (Interscience, New York 1965)
9.3   Berger, T.: *Rate Distortion Theory: A Mathematical Basis for Data Compression* (Prentice Hall, Englewood Cliffs 1971)
9.4   Elias, P.: *List Decoding for Noisy Channels* (M.I.T. Research Lab. of Electronics, Tech. Report 335, 1957)
9.5   Shannon, C. E., Gallager, R. G., Berlekemp, E. R.: Inform. and Control **10**, 65; **10**, 522 (1967)
9.6   Ebert, P. M.: *Error Bounds for Parallel Communication Channels.* (M.I.T. Research Lab. of Electronics, Tech. Report 448, 1966)
9.7   Forney, G. D.: IEEE Trans. Inform. Theory IT **4**, 206 (1968)
9.8   Wolf, J. K.: IEEE Trans. Inform. Theory IT **24**, 76 (1978)
9.9   Battail, G.: Annales des Télécommunications **38**, 3 (1983)
9.10   Battail, G.: Annales des Télécommunications **38**, 443 (1983)
9.11   Battail, G.: Annales des Télécommunications **39**, 99 (1984)
9.12   Jumarie, G.: Annales des Télécommunications **35**, 281 (1980)
9.13   Jumarie, G.: Annales des Télécommunications **39**, 524 (1985)
9.14   Zadeh L. A.: Fuzzy Sets and Systems **1**, 3 (1978)
9.15   Sharma, N., Sharma, B. D.: Indian J. Pure Appl. Math. **9**, 1091 (1978)

Chapter 10

10.1   Jumarie, G.: Annales des Télécommunications **44**, 1 (1989)
10.2   Haken, H.: *Information and Self-Organization*, Springer Ser. Synergetics, Vol. 40 (Springer, Berlin, Heidelberg 1988)
10.3   Shafer, G.: *A Mathematical Theory of Evidence* (Princeton University Press, Princeton 1976)
10.4   Jumarie, G.: Cybernetics and Systems **20**, 265 (1989)

Subject Index